NATIONAL AND SUB-NATIONAL ECONOMIC DEVELOPMENT

POST-ECONOMIC REFORMS

NATIONAL AND SUB-NATIONAL ECONOMIC DEVELOPMENT

POST-ECONOMIC REFORMS

Edited by

P. JEGADISH GANDHI
Director
Vellore Institute of Development Studies, Vellore

and

P. GANESAN
Assistant Professor
College of Management Sciences
Vellore Institute of Technology
Deemed University, Vellore

Foreword by

DR. P. RADHAKRISHNAN
Vice-Chancellor
Vellore Institute of Technology
Deemed University, Vellore

DEEP & DEEP PUBLICATIONS PVT. LTD.
F-159, Rajouri Garden, New Delhi-110027

ISBN 81-7629-442-X

Typeset by ASHISH TECHNOGRAPHICS,
3190, Mohindra Park, Shakur Basti, Delhi-110034.

Printed in India at MAYUR ENTERPRISES,
WZ Plot No. 3, Gujjar Market, Tihar Village, New Delhi-110018.

Published by DEEP & DEEP PUBLICATIONS PVT. LTD.
F-159, Rajouri Garden, New Delhi-110027.
Phones: 25435369, 25440916
E-mails: ddpbooks@yahoo.co.in • deep98@del3.vsnl.net.in
Showroom:
2/13, Ansari Road, Daryaganj, New Delhi-110002 • Telefax: 23245122

Contents

Foreword ix

Preface xi

List of Contributors xiii

PART A

NATIONAL MACRO ECONOMIC DYNAMICS: INDIA

1. *P.R. Brahmananda*
A Decade of Reforms: Where to Now? 3

2. *C. Rangarajan*
Regulation of Tariffs in the Power Sector 11

3. *R. Parthasarathy*
Future of Banking and Insurance 17

4. *P. Ganesan*
Price Transmission between Global and Indian Prices in Agricultural Commodities Market 23

5. *K. Venkatasubramanian*
A Plan with a Difference 49

6. *P. Jegadish Gandhi*
"India Vision 2020"—Is it Utopian or Cornucopian? 54

PART B

SUB-NATIONAL ECONOMIC DIALECTS: TAMIL NADU

SECTION I

Overview Dimensions

7. *G. Viswanathan*
Political Economy of Tamil Nadu 63

8. *K.V. Palanidurai*
Tamil Nadu Economy:
Progress during Nineties and Challenges Ahead 72

9. *Biman Chandra De*
Growth Performance of Tamil Nadu:
Interfacing with Andhra Pradesh 79

10. *Ram Naresh Thakur*
The Economy of Tamil Nadu: Marching Ahead 89

11. *R. Arunachalam and K. Nandha Kumar*
Growth and Development:
A Comparative Study of Tamil Nadu and India 119

12. *Gautam Naresh and J.V.M. Sarma*
Performance of Public Sector Undertakings in
Tamil Nadu 134

SECTION II

Primary Sector Prism

13. *D. Rudrappan*
Utilisation of Irrigation for Sustainable
Agricultural Development in Tamil Nadu 167

14. *T. Govindaraj and R. Rajendran*
Increasing Population and Decreasing Agricultural
Land in Tamil Nadu 184

15. *J. Govindadass*
Effect of Education in the Adoption of Agricultural Technologies in Tamil Nadu: A Micro-Level Analysis 188

16. *K. Pazhani*
Development Prospects of Fisheries Sector in Tamil Nadu 197

SECTION III

Services Sector Signals

17. *K.T. Rengamani and P. Ganesan*
Reforms in Power Sector: An Analysis 215

18. *P. Jegadish Gandhi*
Pricing of Bus Transport Services: A Case Study of Tamil Nadu Transport Corporations 224

19. *P. Ganesan and P.N. Ravi*
Asymmetrical Performance of Scheduled Commercial Banks in Tamil Nadu 235

20. *B. Murali Manohar and S. Ganesh*
Dynamics of IT Industry in Tamil Nadu 243

SECTION IV

Financial Facets

21. *R. Balaji*
Tamil Nadu State Finances: Some Crucial Issues 259

22. *Gautam Naresh and J.V.M. Sarma*
A Recursive Macro Fiscal Adjustment Model for Tamil Nadu 277

SECTION V

Gender Dynamics

23. *A. Muthuraja*
Gender and Employment in Tamil Nadu: Some Observations 305

24. *S. Lakshmi*
A Study on Women Empowerment in Tamil Nadu 318

SECTION VI

Social Sector Skewness

25. *M. Naganathan and K. Jothi Sivagnanam*
Economic Reforms and Social Sector Development in Tamil Nadu 333

26. *Rekha Jaganathan*
Public Expenditure and Social Sector Development in Tamil Nadu 346

27. *A. Barathan*
Economic Growth and Decline of Poverty in the Post-Reform period of Tamil Nadu 355

SECTION VII

Economic Externalities

28. *P. Mohammed Yousuf*
Role of Leather Industry in the Economy of Tamil Nadu 365

29. *N. Rajalakshmi, D. Janagam, J. Sacratees and R. Annadurai*
Environmental Assessment of Industrial Effluent in River Cauvery 375

30. *P.S. Subrahmanian*
Tannery Pollution: Its Impact on Tamil Nadu Economy 388

Index 396

Foreword

Many small countries in Asia like, South Korea, Taiwan have per capita GNP much higher than India. The recent survey conducted and reviewed the per capita GNP of India is only US $ 0.5 as against US $ 38 in USA. Considering the fact that our population is large, there is need for an enhancing economic activity of the country.

Though the country has gained independence more than five decades ago, the overall economic progress of the country is still sluggish. A large percentage of our population is still below poverty line. Unless there is all around economic progress, the situation is not likely to improve. If only there is economic progress, our Human Resource Development Index will improve.

Vellore Institute of Technology had the privilege of hosting the 84th Annual Conference of the Indian Economic Association with the active support and encouragement from Shri G. Viswanathan, Chancellor, Vellore Institute of Technology in December 2001. This volume, *National and Sub-National Economic Development* is a collection of papers presented at the special session on Tamil Nadu economy in the Conference. Besides, eminent economists in the country have focused on macro-economic changes and perspectives.

The Editors Dr. P. Jegadish Gandhi and Dr. P. Ganesan have done an excellent job of compiling this very interesting volume which will be extremely useful to the students of economics, research scholars, administrators and planners.

I commend the excellent effort of the Editors in making this significant contribution in the field of applied economics.

P. RADHAKRISHNAN
Vice-Chancellor
Vellore Institute of Technology
Deemed University, Vellore

Preface

In the post-reform period, Indian economy shows welcome changes in industrial and services sectors and worrisome problems in social sectoral development shifts. Part A of the book contains analytical papers on the Indian Economic dynamics. A distinguished panel of experts—Professor. P.R. Brahmananda, His Excellency Dr. C. Rangarajan, Mr. R. Parthasarathy, Dr. K. Venkatasubramanian and the Editors—reviewed the decadal reforms and the performance of power sector, the futuristic trends of banking and insurance sectors, price transmission in global and domestic agricultural commodity markets, the perspectives of the Tenth Five Year Plan (2002-07) and a focus on "India Vision 2020" of the President of India, Dr. A.P.J. Abdul Kalam.

The development experience of each state in India tells its own tale of performance and problems. Economic development is associated with shifts in the sectoral allocation of the workforce which, in turn, is related to shifts in the production structure. Tamil Nadu is considered a trend-setter in many of the socio-economic regeneration programmes since Independence and is a worthy object of study on this account. It is generally observed that development is accompanied by a progressive diversification in the employment structure, reflected in a fall in the share of the primary sector and a rise in that of secondary and tertiary activities. The sectoral shifts in the composition of national income and state income over a period are a measure of the structural transformation taking place in the economy.

Part B of the book presents an analytical study of the Tamil Nadu economic development in the post-reform period. To have a clear picture, the contents are divided into seven sections—macro-economic spectrum, primary sector prism, services sector signals, financial facets, gender dynamics, social sector skewness and economic externalities of tanning industries. The papers are selected from the presentation of the technical session on "Tamil Nadu Economy" conducted as part of the 84th Annual Conference of Indian Economic Association in Vellore.

We record our sincere thanks to His Excellency Dr. C. Rangarajan, Governor, Government of Andhra Pradesh and Professor P.R. Brahmananda for the ready permission to reproduce their published papers. Our special thanks are due to Dr. P. Radhakrishnan, Vice-Chancellor, Vellore Institute of Technology, Deemed University, Vellore for his Foreword to this book. Equally, we are thankful to each and every contributor to the Tamil Nadu section not only from different parts of Tamil Nadu but also from other states. Special thanks are due to Dr. Biman Chandra De (West Bengal), Prof. Ram Naresh Thakur (Bihar), Dr. Gautam Naresh (New Delhi) and J.V.M. Sarma (Hyderabad) for their incisive comparative analysis of Tamil Nadu development with that of other states in India.

This publication would not have been possible without the timely help of Prof. Debendra Kumar Das, Vice-President of the Indian Economic Association. We are thankful to Mr. R. Srinivasan, Faculty, Department of Languages, Vellore Institute of Technology, for his help in the process of manuscript. Many thanks are due to Mr. G.S. Bhatia, Deep and Deep Publications Pvt. Limited, New Delhi for his friendly co-operation to bring out the book within a short time-frame.

Vellore P. JEGADISH GANDHI
P. GANESAN

List of Contributors

PART A

1. **P.R. Brahmananda**, Managing Editor, *The Indian Economic Journal* and Honorary President, International Economic Association.
2. His Excellency **C. Rangarajan**, Governor, Government of Andhra Pradesh.
3. **R. Parthasarathy**, Management and Financial Consultant, New Delhi.
4. **P. Ganesan**, Assistant Professor, College of Management Sciences, Vellore Institute of Technology, (Deemed University), Vellore.
5. **K. Venkatasubramanian**, Member, Planning Commission, Government of India, New Delhi.
6. **P. Jegadish Gandhi**, Director, Vellore Institute of Development Studies, Vellore.

PART B

7. **G. Viswanathan**, Chancellor, Vellore Institute of Technology, (Deemed University), Vellore.
8. **K.V. Palanidurai**, Full-Time Member, State Planning Commission, Government of Tamil Nadu, Chennai.
9. **Biman Chandra De**, Reader in Economics, B.N. Mahavidyalaya, Itachuna, Hooghly, West Bengal.
10. **Ram Naresh Thakur**, P.G. Centre of Economic Studies, Samastipur College, Samastipur, Bihar.

11. **R. Arunachalam**, Professor, Department of Economics, University of Madras, Chennai.

12. **K. Nandha Kumar**, Ph.D. Research Scholar, Department of Economics, University of Madras, Chennai.

13. **Gautam Naresh**, National Institute of Public Finance & Policy, New Delhi.

14. **J.V.M. Sarma**, Professor of Public Finance, Central University of Hyderabad, Andhra Pradesh.

15. **D. Rudrappan**, Department of Economics, Presidency College, Chennai.

16. **T. Govindaraj**, Department of Economics, AVVM Sri Pushpam College (Autonomous), Poondi, Tamil Nadu.

17. **R. Rajendran**, Department of Economics, AVVM Sri Pushpam College (Autonomous), Poondi, Tamil Nadu.

18. **J. Govindadass**, Lecturer in Economics, Government College, Kumbakonam, Tamil Nadu.

19. **K. Pazhani**, Reader in Economics, T.D.M.N.S. College, T. Kallikulam, Tamil Nadu.

20. **K.T. Rengamani**, College of Management Sciences, Vellore Institute of Technology, (Deemed University), Vellore.

21. **B. Murali Manohar**, Assistant Professor, College of Management Sciences, Vellore Institute of Technology, (Deemed University), Vellore.

22. **S. Ganesh**, Lecturer, College of Management Sciences, Vellore Institute of Technology, (Deemed University), Vellore.

23. **R. Balaji**, Reader in Economics, A.M. Jain College, Chennai.

24. **A. Muthuraja**, P.G. Department of Economics, The American College, Madurai.

25. **S. Lakshmi**, Professor, Department of Economics, Bharathidasan University, Tiruchirappalli, Tamil Nadu.

26. **M. Naganathan**, Professor and Head, Department of Economics, University of Madras, Chennai.
27. **K. Jothi Sivagnanam**, Reader, Planning Commission's Chair and Unit, Department of Economics, University of Madras, Chennai.
28. **Rekha Jaganathan**, Faculty of Economics, Christ College, Bangalore.
29. **A. Barathan**, Reader in Economics, Aditanar College of Arts and Science, Virapandianpatnam, Tamil Nadu.
30. **P. Mohammed Yousuf**, Managing Director, Vaniyambadi Tanners Enviro-Control Systems Limited, Vaniyambadi, Tamil Nadu.
31. **Rajalakshmi**, Professor, Department of Economics, University of Madras, Chennai.
32. **D. Janagam**, Research Scholar, Department of Economics, University of Madras, Chennai.
33. **J. Sacratees**, Research Scholar, Department of Economics, University of Madras, Chennai.
34. **R. Annadurai**, Research Scholar, Department of Economics, University of Madras, Chennai.
35. **P.S. Subramanian**, Advocate and Honorary Secretary, Vellore Citizens' Welfare Forum, Vellore.

PART A

NATIONAL MACRO ECONOMIC DYNAMICS: INDIA

1 CHAPTER

A Decade of Reforms: Where to Now?

P.R. Brahmananda

The last week of July, 2001 marks a decade of reforms in the Indian economy. Ordinarily, this should have been an occasion for the nation to contemplate what has happened to the economy in the last ten years. Unfortunately, except for some analyses in a few financial newspapers, the issue has not been discussed. *Has the economy moved forward in terms of improving the rate of growth of the well-being of the people in this period? Has the economy's future prospects in the above sphere improved?*

I

WELL-BEING OF THE PEOPLE

Since the rate of growth of real national income seems as low as 6 per cent in the past year and probably slightly higher this year, which are lower than the rates reached sometime after the reforms were initiated, the answer to the first question cannot be a definite affirmative. But, are there other indicators related to the growth of well-being which indicates an improvement? Insofar as the employment growth rate is concerned, the Planning Commission feels this has received a setback. National Sample Survey data indicate that poverty has declined on a comparable basis. But, there are many States where progress in this respect is not satisfactory. In terms of the growth rate of real wages of ordinary agricultural labour and other unskilled labour, the progress has been negative in some States. Meanwhile, literacy has increased.

The progress in the reduction of birth rates has not been satisfactory in a number of areas. On the price stability front, the inflation rate, which showed a downward tendency, has started moving up this year. An inflation rate of 6 per cent over the year and probably more seems to be on the cards. There is no official concern about the high inflation rate and its upward drift. That high issue prices of foodgrains have led to the increase in public stocks, but whether the proposed reduction will improve the lot of the lower-income classes is not certain. Also, whether lower issue prices to the above-poverty-line groups can improve their economic status is a moot question. It may not. Instead of pushing forward work schemes, the authorities seem to have thought otherwise. This year, there are fears of drought in some States. How to link the excess grains with the PDS to alleviate the misery in drought-hit areas without additional burdens on State finances is a question that has not yet been addressed.

I wish there could be an index each year of the rate of increase in crime, the rate of increase in accidents, the rate of growth of disruption in normal activities due to public discontent, the rate of growth of mortality in hospitals, etc. Several years ago, I pleaded with V.M. Dandekar, the then NSS Chairman, that an annual sample survey on indicators of well-being should be brought out and the assistance of the State governments should be sought for this purpose. But, nothing happened. The NSS organization can help conduct a quick survey each year and the results would help check the policies of Central and State Governments and change policies and their implementation.

Bloating Fiscal Deficit

Meanwhile, the gross fiscal deficit for the entire economy was about 10 per cent of GDP in 1990-91. It came down to 6.4 per cent in 1996-97. However, at present, it should be about 11.5 per cent or slightly higher on a comparable basis. The GFD ratio seems to have increased by at least 1.5 percentage points compared to 1990-91. And this is the sad part of the story. This increase is not due to any increase in the ratio of capital expenditure to GDP. The State's involvement in investment for the economy has been falling. In 1990-91, this ratio was about 2.1 per cent so far as the Centre was concerned. Now, it should be about one per cent. It is well-known that almost all the States have been reducing the ratios of capital expenditure to state domestic products. The increase in the economy's GFD ratio is due to reasons other than an increase in the ratio of capital expenditures by the governments. The overall public expenditure ratio to GDP was 28-29 per cent in 1990-91. The current ratio would be more than 30 per cent.

Declining Ratio of Tax

What is worrisome is the decline of the ratio of tax to GDP. In 1990-91, it was about 15 per cent and, at that time, the political leaders were thinking of raising it to 17 per cent. The tax reforms have led to a reduction in the ratio of tax to GDP. The current ratio would be close to 13.5-14 per cent. Naturally, other sources of financing government expenditures have gone up and the most prominent among these is the fiscal deficit component. Clearly, the growth rate of the M3 compared to that in 1995-96 and even in 1990-91 has risen. In 1990-91, this rate was about 15.1 per cent. In 1995-96, it came down to 13.7 per cent. In 2000-01, the growth rate of the M3 would have been about 16.3 per cent. Equally worrisome is that the overall corporate investment in 2000-01 at current prices was placed at Rs. 61,901 crore compared to Rs. 65,874 crore in 1995-96 and Rs. 72,230 crore in 1996-97 at the then prices. Note that even at current prices corporate investment in 2000-01 would have been lower by about 15 per cent compared to 1996-97. In real terms, the absolute decline would have been by more than 35 per cent. Also, corporate sector has never had it so good in terms of official patronage in the new economic regime.

Slowing Down in Real Capacity

These are the estimates of RBI researchers on the basis of financial support from public and related financial institutions. If the growth rate of real capacity is slowing down, would it not be reflected in the growth rates of the economy? This is a question the Finance Ministry must ask itself. The decline in the growth rate is not due to any recessionary factors from the demand side, but due to the declining rates of the growth of capacity. The interest rates are being lowered with the idea the problem arises because of a deficiency of demand. It is not. It is due to a decline in the growth of real capital in the economy. The policy measures are compounding the nation's difficulties. There is a big difference in what the economists think is the cause of the malaise and the points of view of the authorities. The latter think the problem is one of deficiency in aggregate real purchasing power in terms of nominal incomes. The former think the problem is due to decelerating real capital formations and this is due to the decline in the rate of growth of aggregate real savings. If this process continues we may risk achieving 'Hindu' growth rates, a term coined by Prof. Rajkrishna.

Pyramiding Financial Transactions

Let me now turn to the financial sector's performances. The financial sector has to redeem itself in the performance of the real sectors. The RBI data indicates that the financial interrelations ratio has been rising. This means that for a given measure of ultimate issues the financial superstructure measure is increasing. There is a sort of pyramiding. The measure of transactions among a number of financial institutions is going up though even in nominal terms the issues are the same. In real terms we are increasing the measure of gross financial activity for any given real investment. Why is this? The financial liberalisation process is trying to reduce the imperfections in the system. However, the scope for free arbitraging increases and this enables the measure of financial sector in the overall economy increases, though for all purposes the measure of change in the real sector has not increased proportionately. Such arbitraging opportunities lead to insider trading when there is no effective monitoring of public institutions. The owners, namely, the Government, of such institutions should ensure effective monitoring, though it is deemed to be kept in check by Parliament.

Theoretically, if we keep one rate of return in a public financial sector higher than elsewhere and keep open opportunities for the corporate sector to trade in and out the liabilities of that sector, alert entities could profit. The problem is not to allow a higher rate of return in any public financial sector for comparable risks, and neither will it disappear only by taking action against executives in such a sector. However, the problem is deeper. Financial pyramiding on slender real growth is not desirable. If one sector's return is kept higher than that in other sectors, then clearly exit and entry options have to be restricted as is the case with provident funds. The real problem in the reform period, as in earlier years, is that the economy's response to the growth of real investment and real savings in the financial pyramiding process has been declining. The response to the changes in real investment in the corporate sector to changes in stock market indicators are also at a low ebb.

So far as the reform process is concerned, it may have landed itself in the desert as far a real sector achievements are concerned. This issue has to be addressed seriously by the Government and the Reserve Bank of India. That is the only way the reforms process can vindicate themselves.

II

DECLINING LONG-TERM FIXED INVESTMENT

The crucial long-term fixed investment ratio to GDP started falling from the mid-1990s. This coincides with the fiscal crisis and the insistence of the World Bank on commercial viability. Probably, these interests wanted the private corporate sector to grow at a higher rate. But this has had an unfortunate fallout on various crucial ratios.

No developing economy can do without a relatively high and steady proportion of long-term investments to GDP. The long-term investment process is primarily in fixed capital formations. These require long gestation/construction periods and the projects are durable over a long period. Such investments, when completed, expand the horizon of short-term profitabilities to investments by the private sector. Since long-term investments involve several years of waiting for full recoupment of historical capital costs, the private sector generally all over the world is reluctant to undertake such investments. When the authorities shifted their focus from social profitability to private profitability as a result of fiscal difficulties, they reduced their own investments in the public sector. Consequently, the economy has tended to depend primarily on the private sector for additions to capital formations concerning the long period.

By nature, such investments are outside the periphery of the private sector's vision. This is the central reason why the economy's growth prospects are shrinking year by year. We must also note that commercial profitability is not necessarily the goal of public sector investments. Further, unless the political process has a measure of continuity in its vision over the long-term, the public sector will not undertake long-term investments whose benefits belong to the future. The Planning Commission was designed to fill the gap in this vision, which will not emanate from the private sector and also from the financial authorities of the governments. Further, the bulk of such investments fall in the realm of the State governments, and these governments have been in very severe fiscal distress which is continuing. Thus, short-term populist visions have crowded out long-term perspectives and efforts for the same.

Comparison between 1980s and 1990s

In 1980-81, the aggregate net fixed capital formation for the long-term capital development were nearly 93 per cent of total such capital formation per year. This proportion came down to 75 per cent in 1992-93 and is now around 80 per cent. In other words, there has been a decline by about 12 percentage points in long-term fixed investment proportion of the public sector to total such investment. The overall proportion of net long-term fixed capital formation to NDP at 1993-94 factor cost was 3.6 per cent in 1980-81. The bulk of this was undertaken by the public sector. The overall long-term fixed capital formation is currently at about 2 per cent of GDP. The population growth rate is around 1.8 per cent. If we assume that the net capital-output ratio would be around 3.5 to 4 in long-term investments, the normative investment in fixed capital should formation should have been between 6 to 9 per cent of GDP in 1999-2000. But, unfortunately this is just 2.1 per cent. Note the huge and growing gap between desired long-term fixed investment and the actual such investments.

The net fixed capital investment ratio to NDP started steeply declining from 1995-96 onwards. But the net long-term fixed capital formation ratio, the crucial long-term fixed investment ratio to GDP started declining recently from around the middle of the 1990s. This ratio was relatively best during the early 1980s. Throughout the 1980s, by and large, this ratio was higher than it has been during the 1990s. The long-term vision of the economy has shifted downwards from about the latter period. This coincides with the fiscal crisis and the insistence of the World Bank, etc., on commercial viability. Probably, these interests wanted the private corporate sector to grow at a higher rate. But, unfortunately, this sector is not interested in the long-term investment process. The ratio of net fixed capital formation in the public sector to NDP has started declining from late 1980s when the crisis in the public sector's budgetary operations started showing up. The declining drift has been almost continuous. We compared the trends in long-term fixed capital formation in the public sector during the 1980s and during the 1990s. Whereas during the 1980s, the trend was positive at 0.03 per cent. During the 1990s, the trend was negative and at (-) 0.02 per cent per year. This matter has to be examined very seriously by the economists of the country, independent of ideological predilections.

Pursuing Proper Pricing Policies

Historically, the investments in railways, power and irrigation by the public authorities have been the powerful motivators for expanding the orbit of short-term and medium-term investment by the private sector. If proper pricing policies could be followed, such long-term investments yield a return of above 5 per cent. In fact, during the British period, such investments yielded higher returns than the above. With long-term real interest rates of 3-4 per cent, such investments were profitable. But, often, the government promoted such investments in the private sector by offering minimum guarantees in terms of rates of return. Had this not been done, there would have been very little of such investments in India from a historical angle.

Even now, if correct pricing policies are followed, long-term investments in irrigation, power, flood control, canals, etc., can be profitable. The problem is not with the investments but the difficulty of levying charges. In such cases, other methods of collection of charges should be devised. Even otherwise, so long as the net producers and consumers' surpluses can promise net social benefits above social costs, such investments are productive from the society's angle. In order to encourage the private sector, we have to provide guaranteed rates of returns from the Budget. We have a lot to learn from the British practice. If we ideologically oppose such guarantees and we do not also invest over the long-run in such capital, posterity will be huge loser. During the British period, the objection was that it was the foreign investor who was getting the benefit of guarantees. Why don't the chambers of commerce work out a programme of long-term investments and ask for some guarantees of, say, a minimum of 5 per cent returns?

The RBI's Annual Report 2001-02 indicates that the nominal rates of return of both short-term and long-term borrowings have almost converged. This means that society is indifferent between the short-term and the long-term insofar as returns are concerned. The long-term returns are concerned. The long-term return, in real terms, works out to less than 4-3 per cent, whereas the short-term real return is higher. *Thus, we have inverted the philosophy of development without being aware of the consequences.* It is time we start paying some attention to the future.

2

CHAPTER

*Regulation of Tariffs in the Power Sector**

C. RANGARAJAN

Power is one of the key inputs required for sustained economic growth. In fact, the demand for power grows at a much faster rate than the rate of growth of the national product. The elasticity of demand is now close to 1.2. Over the years, India has done well in creating new generation capacities, extending the transmission and distributing network and making electricity available to a large section of the society. Electricity generation in the country which was only 4.1 billion units in 1947 increased to about 350 billion units by 1995, registering a compounded annual growth rate of 7.5 per cent. It has, since then, increased to 500 billion units in 2000-01. Despite this, the power sector has been afflicted by serious shortage of supply in relation to demand particularly in some States. Electricity cannot be easily imported (though not completely ruled out) or stored and hence creation of generation capacity domestically is critical for meeting the

* Extracted from the Address delivered at the Conference of Power Regulators held at Hyderabad on August 30, 2002.

country's demand for power. State Electricity Boards or their distribution network, low quality of service, tariffs not covering costs, rampant theft, high subsidy and cross-subsidy and poor revenue recovery from consumers. From a recent study of the Planning Commission, it is found that the estimated commercial losses of State Electricity Boards without subsidy during 2001-02 were Rs. 33,177 crore as compared to Rs. 11,305 crore during 1996-97. The commercial losses with subsidy payable by State Government for the above years are Rs. 24,837 crore and Rs. 4,674 crore respectively. Those States that are compensating the Electricity Boards for their commercial losses through subventions are facing a huge dent in the State finances. Their revenue deficits are rising. On the other hand, States that are not financially supporting the power sector are facing restriction in supply from central generators, as the defaults to these suppliers are mounting. It is unfortunate fact that the current operations of State Electricity Boards remain unviable. Revenue realization per unit of power produced is much less than the average cost of production and supply, with the result the State Electricity Boards are running deficits. There is a large transmission and distribution loss ranging from 20 to 50 per cent of the supplied energy. No lasting solution to the problems of the power sector is possible without making the current operations of the State Electricity Boards or their successors financially viable. The prevailing conditions in the power sector would not only cause serious damage to the electricity industry but also cripple the finances of the State Governments.

ELEMENTS IN THE POWER REFORM PROCESS

Because of its monopolistic nature, the electricity industry has always been subject to regulation. The first legislation of electricity in India was enacted as early as 1910. In the wake of economic reforms introduced in 1991, reforms in the power sector assumed importance. The objective of the reform process is to make the industry viable and efficient. To achieve this objective, the State Governments have enacted legislations to enable setting up of regulatory authorities, restructuring of the electricity industry along functional lines and creating opportunities for private participation in the electricity industry both in the spheres of generation and distribution. It is significant to note that these are common themes in the power reform process in almost all countries. Obviously, there are several issues in restructuring and regulation unique to each country. However, there is a commonality of approach.

In 1991, the first policy statement with regard to reform of the electricity sector was announced involving private sector participation in the generation of electricity. The setting up of a regulatory framework was an integral part of the restructuring of the industry. Orissa initiated the process in 1995 and many other States have followed suit by enacting suitable legislations and set-up independent regulatory bodies to govern the industry. In 1998, the Central Electricity Regulatory Commission Act was passed and the Central Regulatory body was formed to generally regulate the functioning of the Central sector players and inter-state supply.

ROLE OF REGULATORY COMMISSIONS

The mandate to the regulatory commissions is usually wide. It goes very much beyond the determination of tariffs. For example, Section 11 of the Andhra Pradesh Electricity Reform Act specifies a wide gamut of functions aimed at the development of the electricity industry. In effect the Act wants the Commission to take measures conducive to the development and management of the electricity industry in an efficient, economic and competitive manner. Nevertheless, tariff fixation remains the chief tool for achieving the results. It is in this context that the enunciation of long-term tariff principles assumes importance. Obviously, tariff levels cannot be set for many years to come as many elements that form part of the cost such as fuel prices keep changing from year to year. However, by laying down the tariff fixation methodology and the principles on specific aspects such as loss reduction, and incentives and disincentives, efficiency can be promoted.

TARIFF FIXATION

Fixation of tariffs in the electricity industry is a complicated exercise. The literature on the subject is large. However, for a regulator, one important question to ask is: if pricing is to be based on a cost plus formula, how should costs be determined? Costs, as stated, by the licensees cannot simply be accepted. There must necessarily be a certain normative element. Without such a normative element, it can only end up in a high cost situation. One perplexing question before all the regulators has been the determination of T & D loss i.e., transmission and distribution loss. In some States these losses have been creeping up instead of coming down. Of course, one common reason cited for not being able to determine precisely these losses is that the flow of power to agriculture is not metered. It is high time that the regulators as well as electricity boards initiated appropriate steps to determine technical losses and commercial losses. If metering is essential for this purpose, the regulators must insist on this. Technological answers are available for reducing technical losses. Commercial losses are only an euphemistic expression for theft. Quite clearly, a reduction in T & D losses even by a few percentage points can bring about considerable improvement in the financial position of electricity boards. Inter-state comparisons in this regard can also provide the basis for action. In this context, it may be desirable to fix certain targets of efficiency in respect of T & D losses which could be achieved over a multi-year period. This is not uncommon in the case of price fixation for other commodities such as fertilizer or chemicals.

PRICE DISCRIMINATION

In the supply of power, price discrimination is inevitable. Even in a normal situation when a monopoly supplier faces different markets, prices differ from one market to another. Monopoly power and price discrimination have been described as Siamese Twins. However, in the Indian context, it is not only the different demand curves in the different markets but also socio-economic considerations that lead to different prices. Subsidies are once again inevitable in such a situation. However, the issue to be addressed is how subsidies can be fashioned to meet well-defined target groups and how they can coexist with efficiency and prevention of waste. There must be a recognition that there are limits to cross-subsidisation.

TARIFFS AND COMPETITION

Needless to say, many of the regulatory measures including tariff fixation that are currently followed are within the traditional mould of regulating monopolies. The cost-based regulation may need a relook as regulatory commissions move towards creating conditions for more competition. Many States are following the single buyer model. In this model generation is first unbundled, followed by transmission, distribution and much later of retail supply. Under the prevailing model, the single buyer which is the Transmission Company purchases all power and sells it to the distribution companies. At present, Power Purchase Agreements are screened by the regulators to ensure that bulk supply cost does not go up disproportionately. It is also a fact that in a single buyer model, investment in generation will be forthcoming only under 'take or pay' contract. Distribution companies even when they are privatised remain smaller private monopolies. Under a competitive regime which may prevail at the generating and distribution levels, the role of the regulator will completely change. His role as a tariff fixer may wither away. However, that future is nowhere in sight. Nevertheless, regulators must explore how competition can be enhanced at each stage. How can the industry transit from 'competing for the market' to 'competing in the market'? Some have argued that competition in generation can be introduced, if generators are allowed to sell directly to large consumers. This can accentuate the problems of SEBs. However, this issue needs to be examined in all its implications.

OTHER ISSUES

There are other matters which are partly of

administrative nature which are of concern to regulators. In some States, Governments have either stayed the orders of the Commission or instructed the utilities not to comply with the orders of the Commission. This defeats the very purpose of creation of Independent Regulatory Commissions. In some cases, tariffs are asked to be reduced by the Government without providing required subsidy. The jurisdiction of courts over the orders passed by Regulatory Commissions is also a contentious area. Should the jurisdiction extend to all aspects of the orders or should it be restricted only to some? In the meanwhile it will be in the interest of regulators to provide detailed reasoning for their orders so that the public can have a better appreciation of their task.

CONCLUSION

The appropriate fixation of tariff is a difficult exercise. Several considerations come into play. The regulators have a three-fold task of ensuring (a) efficiency in operations, (b) affordable price to the consumers, and (c) adequate flow of capital to the sector. While in the long-run, all these objectives may be congruent, in the short-run, they may not. Regulators may have to balance the interest of consumers on the one hand with that of the share holders on the other. They face the daunting task of making the sector financially viable while safeguarding the interest of the consumer.

3

CHAPTER

Future of Banking and Insurance

R. PARTHASARATHY

Reforming the financial sector is central to second-generation reforms. This covers three important segments—banking, insurance and the capital market. Some reform has already taken place in the capital market, though strengthening the institutional mechanism to prevent unethical practices is receiving the Government's attention. The latest to be opened up for private investment, including foreign direct investment, is the insurance sector. On a rough reckoning, commercial bank deposits account for 25 per cent of GDP and credit extended by banks may be 15 per cent of GDP. This leaves out transactions by industrial financial institutions, non-banking financial companies, cooperative banks, deposits in public provident funds treasury payments some of which may be agency functions of the banks. Thus, regular bank credit transactions alone account for a substantial percentage of GDP by way of servicing economic activities.

CONVERGENCE OF BANKING AND INSURANCE SECTORS

A gradual convergence is taking place in the banking and insurance sectors. Several major banks are floating subsidiaries to enter both life and non-life insurance businesses. Some of them are looking at niche markets such as corporate insurance. There are reports that Tata-AIG will be launching "Mobile Claims Service" in four metros and Bangalore and Hyderabad for quick settlement of customer claims. SBI, in collaboration with Cardiff of France, is planning to enter life insurance. Features common to both sectors are financial discipline, regulatory framework and prudential norms in investment management. Given the kind of convergence taking place, there is need for closer institutionalized cooperation among the RBI, Insurance Regulatory and Development Authority of India (IRDA) and the Securities Exchange Board of India. A single regulatory authority is unfeasible. This has also been the experience of Canada, the US, the UK and Germany.

The banking sector has been undergoing reforms for over a decade now based largely on the report of the Narasimham Committee on Bank Reforms. Considerable progress has been made in the gradual reduction of non-performing assets of banks which stood at alarming 12-15 per cent six or seven years ago. It is now around 7 per cent on net basis. Reform of the insurance sector began with the decision to open up this sector for private participation with foreign insurance companies being allowed entry with a maximum of 26 per cent capital investment. The major step, however, was the passing of the Insurance Regulatory Authority Act, 1999 on April 20, 2000. With this, 14 companies in life insurance and nine in non-life insurance have been given permission by the IRDA so far, and within the next one year this figure may go up to 30.

INNOVATIVE PRODUCTS AND ETHICS IN MARKETING

The future will offer a wider choice for policy-holders, with innovative products to suit particular needs. But as often is said, insurance policies are sold and not bought. This means ethical marketing practices must be strictly observed and enforced. Deceptive packaging of policies or misleading advertisements should attract stern penalties. This is one area of focus for corporate governance and insurers must self-regulate this activity by evolving a code of ethics in marketing.

Some of the major areas where IRDA has made regulations or issued guidelines are analysed below:

1. Actuarial Report, Abstract and Role of Appointed Actuary

This is a key reporting document which, if truthfully executed, will bring out the true state of affairs of the business. In the life insurance business, a key person in the system of supervision is the appointed actuary for which a separate provision exists in IRDA regulations. The actuary has a wide range of responsibilities, especially to determine reserves, and to ensure the continuing viability of the insurance products and projecting a true and fair picture of the company's financial affairs. This will, thus, constitute a major area of corporate governance.

2. Obligations of Insurers to Rural and Social Sectors

A minimum percentage starting from 5 per cent and going up to 12 per cent, of total insurance must be set apart for rural and social sectors, with stipulation on the number of lives to be insured in order to increase penetration. This should motivate insurers to innovate products best suited for weaker sections of society and the rural segment of the population. Under Indian conditions, the innovative capability of the insurer will be fully tested in coming up with suitable products to suit different socio-economic strata. Currently, bench mark statistics on claims settlement or cost/benefit analysis may not be readily available. But considering the gradual rise in rural incomes and existence of insurable risks, the rural sector will provide greater opportunities.

3. Insurance Advertisements and Disclosurers

This is an important area for sharing information, not only with the insurance regulatory authority but also policy-holders and share-holders. This will be a key area of corporate governance. The IRDA has guidelines to help insurance companies adhere to norms.

4. Licensing of Insurance Agents

In the insurance business, most selling takes place through tied agents, and companies tend to launch lavish and aggressive campaigns that raise commissions and selling costs. There could be a multiplicity of distribution channels—bank assurance, corporate bodies and independent brokers. The agent's role in life insurance is particularly important. Currently, in India with LIC and the erstwhile subsidiaries of General Insurance Corporation (GIC) having near monopoly position, there can only be tied agencies. But what about the future? With the emergence of several new players, should there be tied agents and brokers with multiple affiliations? These issues need to be considered.

5. General Insurance-Reinsurance

General insurance in India is more focused on industry and commercial enterprises with emphasis on fire, theft risks and property damage. While the four subsidiaries of GIC will focus on general insurance, GIC itself will function as a reinsurer under the new dispensation. Despite the vast untapped market potential, health insurance has not attracted as much attention as other forms of business. Perhaps, some life insurance companies may have plans of part coverage of health under their scheme. Vehicle insurance is another major area of general insurance activity. Marine insurance will increasingly become important, but at present, there are established international players in this field, such as Lloyds, UK.

Technology brings its own demands. For instance, with the emergence of information technology, new areas of risk coverage will come to the fore. Also, product liability and professional risk coverage schemes which are relatively new in the Indian context may emerge as insurable risks. Proper risk analysis and internal guidelines within companies in regard to these new forms of business will be important and necessary functions of corporate governance.

6. Assets, Liabilities and Solvency Margin of Insurers

Valuation of assets and provision for liabilities should be done realistically. International practices in this matter differ widely. Unrealised investment gains may not be reflected in the profit-and-loss account and, thus, cannot form the basis of determining distributable profits. This is a prudent and one conservative accounting practice. On the contrary, in the UK, companies have the freedom to choose market value, historical cost or a value between the two. The conservative approach might seem better suited to the Indian conditions, given the volatility of investment markets and the nascent state of the insurance industry under competitive conditions. The IRDA, according to press reports, recently relaxed the norms for investments for new entrants in rated securities. The Regulator has also permitted '+A' rated instruments instead of the earlier 'AA'.

The problems of availability of instruments with higher rating must be recognized at a time when the capital market is witnessing listless conditions. The question that needs to be addressed is to what extent investment in offshore debt instruments may be allowed, and what should be the criteria for such investments? Already, mutual funds are allowed to invest in offshore instruments. Regarding solvency margins, there are two approaches. One is fixing of premiums at levels that may be adequate to pay for future claims and avoid insolvencies. The other approach is solvency monitoring. Normally, one would prefer the second method as it leaves flexibility in the hands of insurers to fix premia for specific policies, particularly in the context of emerging competition and product differentiation.

7. Condition of Service of Officers and other Employees

Manpower planning and training will be crucial to successful operation of business, particularly in the competitive environment. Of the population of more than one billion, those covered by some form of insurance or the other may be around 40 million. According to one estimate, the potential market is about 200-250 million, with an annual growth rate of 15 per cent.

8. Insurance Surveyors and Loss Assessors

Insurance surveyors and loss assessors are an important link in the insurance business, particularly in general insurance, where assessing the insurable risk and premium of the property to be insured and, subsequently, in the event of a claim settlement arising, assessing the mount of settlement may determine the loss or gain to the insurer from such a transaction.

WHAT ABOUT THE FUTURE?

What will the future of Indian banking and insurance look like? Will the reform in banking and insurance sectors face the same fate as in power and telecom? It is increasingly evident that the economy offers opportunities but no security! Therefore, the future will belong to those who develop good internal controls, checks and balances and a sound market strategy.

4
CHAPTER

Price Transmission between Global and Indian Prices in Agricultural Commodities Market

P. GANESAN

India's signing of General Agreement on Trade and Tariff (GATT) agreements in 1994 and her joining of World Trade Organisation (WTO) as a founder member has put Indian agriculture into framework of global competition and the rule of global market. Under various WTO agreements, developing economies like India are subject to less stringent rules and disciplines in their trade policies. They have also pledged less significant tariff reductions than developed economies and are given longer time periods for implementing their commitments in the Uruguay Round. Obviously, under the auspices of the WTO, the member countries signed many trade-related agreements, for the first time, an Agreement on Agriculture (AOA) was reached to reform and dismantle trade barriers in the agricultural sector.

By the end of 1999, WTO will complete its 5 years of experience. At that time, re-negotiations on AOA will also begin. These re-negotiations will take stock of the experience of the last five years and potential for further commitments to the reform process. The main objective of these re-negotiations is to reform world trade in general and agricultural sector in particular. The massive direct and indirect subsidies given by developed countries to their agricultural sector over the years have distorted international trade in agriculture. WTO's agreement on agriculture is an attempt to correct this distortion. The agreement establishes a basis for initiating a process of reform of trade in agriculture with the long-term objective of establishing a fair and market-oriented agricultural trading system.

Many economists felt that reduced support level and rationalisation of trade barriers would increase production and export of various commodities in developing countries like India which have comparative advantage in the production agricultural commodities.

REVIEW OF EARLIER STUDIES

Studies conducted by Tyer and Falvey (1989), Mundlak and Larson (1992), Jacques Morisset (1998) have regressed domestic prices with world prices, exchange rate, trade policies, wage rate, etc. and concluded that variations in domestic prices were contributed by variations in world prices.

It is observed from the studies of Anderson and Tyres (1993), Deepak Nayyar and Abhijit Sen (1994), Pomeranz, Kenneth (1994), Chan Ling Yap (1996), Servass Storm (1997), Krueger, Anne (1999) that because of GATT Agreement on Agriculture the changes in world prices would benefit to developing countries compared to developed countries. On the other hand, Subramanian (1993), Parikh *et al.*, (1995), Barrett and Dorosh (1996), Warr, P.G. (1997), Anderson, J.E. (1998), Gill and Brar (1998), Ramesh Chand (1998 and 1999), Deodhar (1999) arugued that most of the developing countries have had adverse effect on welfare, terms of trade, consumer and producer surplus due to GATT/WTO Agreement on Agriculture.

It could be seen from the above studies that the results of the studies are contradictory to each other. Most of the above studies focussed on commodity markets are disaggregated at the commodities level but typically aggregated countries into board group namely developing countries and developed countries. No study has focussed on disaggregated commodity and country level, hence this study attempted to analyse the spread between world prices and domestic prices on the one hand and how the world prices are transmitted to domestic prices for the commodity RICE.

One group of economists, policy-makers and alike strongly believed that the country as a whole would be the loser even a rise in world price because asymmetrical transmission to the domestic price. The other group has argued that there would be a gain to the country as a whole and agriculturists in particular irrespective of small, marginal and large farmers. Therefore, this study seeks to answer to the following questions:

1. Whether there any significant percentage variation in world prices, domestic prices, nominal exchange rate, export and production of rice?
2. What is the type of trend in spread between world price and domestic prices?
3. What proportion of the variations in world price is transmitted to domestic price? and
4. Is the world prices major contributor to variations in domestic prices?

COMMODITY SELECTION AND DATA SOURCE

The analysis is based on the price of Non-Basmati variety Akkulu has taken for the data analysis purpose. The Akkulu variety from Andhra Pradesh is selected because (a) Andhra Pradesh is not only the largest rice producing state but also it normally concentrates on export of rice (till the end of October 1998) the state had exported about 10 lakh tonnes of rice. Moreover, during recent years, the export of Non-Basmati varieties have increased substantially compared to Basmati. Hence the Non-Basmati variety Akkulu has taken for the purpose of analysis, and (b) the data consistency between consumer prices and wholesale prices.

The study is based on secondary data, which is collected

from various sources. The study period was between 1969 and 1995. The data on domestic consumer (the retail price for Akkulu is a proxy for consumer price) and wholesale prices for rice were compiled on an annual basis from the Agricultural Prices in India, Directorate of Economics and Statistics, Ministry of Agriculture and Co-operation, Government of India. International commodity price for rice was obtained from the International Financial Statistics Year Book, International Monetary Fund (the price of Thailand rice variety white milled is used as a proxy for international rice price). The nominal exchange rate (NER) for Rupee *versus* Dollar was compiled from Global Financial Data, Los Angels (the monthly exchange rates have averaged). The per capita wage rate was collected from the Indian Labour Journal, Labour Bureau, Ministry of Labour, Government of India.

B. Measuring the Variations in Spreads between World and Dc ıestic (Commodity) Prices

$$\Delta \quad = \Delta pc_i - \Delta \text{ (NER x } p_i^*) \qquad (1)$$

where,

ı is the log of the spread (or mark up) associated with product i,

pc is the log domestic consumer price of project j,

NEk is the Nominal Exchange rate (dollar/Rupee), and

p_i^* is the log of world price of the commodity i.

The above equation capture the changes in the spread between world and domestic consumer price. To account for the influence of changes in the inflation rate on the measurement of the spread over time, all variables are expressed in logs so that their sample variations represent relative changes.

$$\Delta\mu_i = [\Delta pc_i - \Delta pw_i] + [\Delta pw_i - (\text{NER x } p_i^*)] \qquad (2)$$

where,

pw_i is the domestic wholesale price.

In equation (2) the domestic wholesale price is introduced because of two reasons: (i) it captures the impact of the spread on the final demand for the commodities, and (ii) how prices are transmitted through the stages of processing.

For presentation purposes, the results are reported in index values rather than in percentage variation. The base year is 1990 for all variables (1990 = 100), and the index values are derived from the yearly percentage variations in the spreads. To account for the annual volatility produced by seasonal and climatic factors, five-year moving average of the spread index is calculated.

C. To Answer the Second and Third Questions the Model Developed by Mundlak and Larson (1992) and Jacques Morisset (1998) is used

$$\Delta \ln CP = \alpha j + \beta \Delta \ln p^* + \theta NER + \gamma \Delta \ln CPt\text{-}1 + \lambda \Delta \ln w + \lambda t + e \quad (1)$$
$$\Delta \ln WP = \alpha j + \beta \Delta \ln p^* + \theta NER + \gamma \Delta \ln WPt\text{-}1 + \lambda \Delta \ln w + \lambda t + e \quad (2)$$
$$\Delta \ln CP = \alpha j + \beta \Delta \ln WP + \gamma \Delta \ln WPt\text{-}1 + \lambda \Delta \ln w + \alpha t + e \quad (3)$$

Equation (1) captures the relationships between world and domestic consumer prices, while equations (2) and (3) capture those between world and domestic wholesale prices and between domestic wholesale and consumer prices, respectively. The exchange rate as an explanatory variable from the equation (3) because it only involved domestic prices. All variables have been described in the text are expressed in logs.

The aj coefficients reflect time-invariant changes in trade and tax policies. The b coefficients explains the elasticity of the change in domestic prices with respect to the change in world prices (or equivalently in wholesale prices in equation 3), referred to as the elasticity of transmission. Domestic inputs principally reflect processing costs that are concentrated in consumer markets, which can be captured by changes in their nominal wages (Δw_i).

Other costs such as marketing, transport and storage are difficult to observe. Knetter (1992) showed that they can be incorporated into the model using fixed-time effect (α_t) when their changes are common to all the destination market.

Finally, as emphasized by Mundlak and Larson (1992), it is certainly a too-strong assumption to believe that tax and trade policies are uniform across countries, leading to a possible bias in the estimated transmission elasticities. This assumption can be weakened by considering the differences in these policies are captured by country time-invariant variable (α_j) in the empirical tests.

In order to test specifically for asymmetries in the responsive of domestic prices to changes in world prices, the full period is divided into upward and downward changes in world prices and in domestic wholesale prices. Rather than divide the full period between the years with upward and downward movements, which obviously would limit the number of observations and reduce the quality of the empirical results, equations of world prices 1, 2 and wholesale price equation 3 multiplied by two zero—one dummy variables. The first variable takes the value 1 for the upward movements in world prices and zero elsewhere; the second takes the value 1 for the downward movements in world prices and zero elsewhere. The three above equations can be rewritten as follows:

$$\Delta lnCP = \alpha j + \beta 11\Delta lnp^* + \beta 12\Delta lnp^* + \theta NER + \gamma\Delta lnCPt\text{-}1 + \lambda\Delta lnw + \alpha t + e \quad (1a)$$
$$\Delta lnWP = \alpha j + \beta 11\Delta lnp^* + \beta 12\Delta lnp^* + \theta NER + \gamma\Delta lnWPt\text{-}1 + \lambda\Delta lnw + \alpha t + e \quad (2a)$$
$$\Delta lnCP = \alpha j + \beta 11\Delta lnwp + \beta 12\Delta lnwp + \gamma\Delta ln\ CPt\text{-}1 + \lambda\Delta lnw + \alpha t + e \quad (3a)$$

If upward movements in world rice prices (Δp_i^*) have been transmitted to domestic prices more systematically than have downward movements ($\Delta p2_i^*$) then it should be expected that $b_{11}>b_{12}$ and $b_{21}>b_{22}$ in equations (1a) and (1b). Indentically, in equation (3a), the asymmetric transmission from changes in wholesale to consumer prices should result in $b_{31}>b_{32}$.

DATA ANALYSIS AND INFERENCES

The collected data were analysed and inferences drawn at appropriate places with statistical tools like simple percentage variations compound annual growth rates and regression models. The present chapter divided into three sections:' Section one analyses the present trend of output, export (in terms of quantity and value), domestic prices of Indian rice, world prices of rice, and share of Indian's rice export to world trade. Section two examines the trend of spread between domestic consumer prices and world prices, domestic consumer and wholesales prices, and domestic wholesale and world prices. Section three presents the regression results of what proportion of the variations in world prices is transmitted to domestic prices? And what proportion of the variations in domestic prices can be attributed to variations in world prices?

Table 1 presents the percentage variations of world prices of rice, nominal exchange rate, and consumer and wholesales prices of Indian rice during the period between 1969 and 1995. The world price of rice has increased from US $ 186.88 per metric ton to $ 320.80 per metric ton during 1969 and 1995 respectively with annual average growth rate of 1.72 per cent. The annual percentage variation of world price shows high volatility and particularly it was depressed during 1982-86. In 1988 drastic changes occurred in the world supply and demand situation for rice. Reflecting the large production shortfalls in 1987, international rice prices in 1988 were sharply higher. In a similar way, rice trade and prices soared in 1994 due to larger purchase of Japan, China and Indonesia.

In 1995, Nominal Exchange Rate (Dollar/Rupee) has raised by 4 times than the initial year 1969. In other words, NER was Rs. 7.50 per dollar in 1969, due to various policy measures in particular depreciation of rupee by Reserve Bank of India; it has increased to Rs. 32.43 against dollar in 1995 registering an average annual growth rate of 6.18 per cent per annum. The domestic consumer price of rice in 1969 was Rs. 1048.30 per metric ton and has raised to Rs. 8150 per metric ton in 1995 with an annual compound rate of growth of 7.25 per cent. The domestic wholesale price for rice has raised by 7 times in 1995 than the initial period 1969. In other words, domestic world price has increased to Rs. 7350 per metric tonne from Rs. 1010.80 per metric ton during 1995 and 1969 respectively with an increase of 7.25 per cent per annum.

During eighties and early 1990s, the rate of increase in domestic prices of rice has moved faster than seventies. This trend is clearly because of lifting some of the restrictions and

TABLE 1

Percentage Variations of World Prices for Rice, Nominal Exchange Rate, Domestic Consumer Price and Wholesale Price for Rice Between 1969-95

Year	*WP**	*AGR (%)*	*NER***	*AGR (%)*	*DRP****	*AGR (%)*	*DWP@*	*AGR (%)*
1969	186.88		7.5		1048.3		1010.8	
1970	144	-22.95	7.5	0	1090	3.98	930	-7.99
1971	128.96	-10.44	7.49	-0.13	1200	10.09	1040	11.83
1972	147.12	14.08	7.59	1.34	1324.5	10.38	1150	10.58
1973	349.99	137.89	7.42	-2.24	1320	-0.34	1274.2	10.8
1974	542.02	54.87	8.1	9.16	1866.7	41.42	1863.3	46.23
1975	363.17	-33	8.42	3.95	1887.5	1.11	1837.5	-1.38
1976	254.08	-30.04	8.96	6.41	1733.3	-8.17	1588.3	-13.56
1977	272.42	7.22	8.74	-2.46	1858.3	7.21	1829.2	15.17
1978	368.5	35.27	8.19	-6.29	1699.1	-8.57	1612.5	-11.85
1979	334.33	-9.27	8.13	-0.73	1666.7	-1.91	1625	0.78
1980	433.67	29.71	7.86	-3.32	1929.2	15.75	1850	13.85
1981	482.83	11.34	8.66	10.18	2254.2	16.85	2191.7	18.47
1982	293.38	-39.24	9.46	9.24	2541.7	12.75	2750	25.47
1983	276.83	-5.64	10.1	6.77	2677.3	5.34	2821.1	2.59
1984	252.25	-8.88	11.36	12.48	2945.8	10.03	3583.3	27.02
1985	217.42	-13.81	12.37	8.89	2727.3	-7.42	2679.2	-25.23
1986	195.67	-10	12.61	1.94	3358.3	23.14	3100	15.71
1987	214.42	9.58	12.96	2.78	3533.3	5.21	3170	2.26
1988	277.25	29.3	13.92	7.41	4570.8	29.36	3880	22.4
1989	299.75	8.12	16.33	17.31	4495.5	-1.65	3810	-1.8
1990	270.67	-9.7	17.05	4.41	4220.8	-6.11	3650	-4.2
1991	293.67	8.5	22.74	33.37	5570	31.97	4310	18.08
1992	267.67	-8.85	25.92	13.98	5980	7.36	4810	11.6
1993	237.25	-11.36	30.49	17.63	6050	1.17	5720	18.92
1994	269.46	13.58	31.37	2.89	7400	22.31	6820	19.23
1995	320.8	19.05	32.43	3.38	8150	10.14	7350	7.77
CAGR	1.72		6.18		7.25		7.25	

CAGR: Compound Annual Growth Rates.

* World Price (US $/metric ton); ** Nominal Exchange Rate (US $/Rupee).

*** Domestic Consumer price (Rupees/metric tonne).

@ Domestic Wholesale price (Rupees/metric tonne).

Source: Agricultural Prices in India for Domestic Price; International Financial Statistics for World Price for Rice; Global Financial Data for NER.

reduction in trade protection in agriculture sector in Indian economy. Due to oil shocks during 1973-74, 1979-80 and Gulf crisis in 1990-91, both internal prices and domestic prices have increased. Output and Export (in terms of quantity and value) of Indian Rice is given in Table 2. It is observed that the output of Indian rice in 1995 was 81.81 million tonnes against the initial year output of 39.76 million tonnes thus regarding an annual average rate of growth of 2.93 per cent.

At present Indian exports rice to some 80 countries in the world. India's exports of rice was 1.42 lakh tonnes in 1978 and has increased to 49.14 lakh tonnes in 1995 thus registering an average annual growth rate of 9.35 per cent per annum. The export of non-basmati rice was occupied higher proportion of rice exports after 1991. The percentage variations shows an unstable growth in the export of rice, that is, 451.76 per cent in 1995 as against (-)64.93 per cent in 1983. As a result of growth in the export, the value of exports of rice has registered a significant growth of 19.28 per cent per annum. That is, the total value of export of rice has raised to US $ 1361 from US $ 12 during 1995 and 1973 respectively.

India's share in world trade in rice is exhibited in Table 3. It is noticed that the world trade of rice significantly increased by 7 times compated to initial year from the value of $ 925 million to $ 6136 million during 1970 and 1995 respectively. The export of Indian's rice performed better than world trade, that is, export of Indian rice has raised by 36 times to $ 327 million in 1995 from $ 9 million in 1970. As a result of the high value of trade of Indian rice, the share of Indian rice in world has continuous increase from 0.1 per cent to 6.4 per cnt in 1970 and 1995 respectively with sudden fall of 5.3 per cent in 1995.

SPREAD BETWEEN DOMESTIC CONSUMER PRICE AND WORLD PRICE

Table 4 explains the spread between domestic consumer price and world price for rice. The index of percentage variation of the spread was at peak of 2359.22 per cent in 1991 as compared to lowest level of 31.16 per cent in 1971. Out of 26 years, the spread was negative during 1973, 1984, 1988 and

TABLE 2

Production and Export of Rice Between 1969-95

Year	Production (in lakh tonnes)	AGR	Export			
			Quantity ('000 tonnes)	AGR (%)	Value	AGR (%)
1970	40.43	1.69				
1971	42.23	4.45				
1972	43.07	1.99				
1973	39.25	-8.87			12	
1974	44.05	12.23			26.2	118.33
1975	40.25	-8.63			12	-54.2
1976	48.74	21.09			13.9	15.83
1977	41.92	-13.99	142895		6	-56.83
1978	52.67	25.64	343825	140.61	51.4	756.67
1979	53.77	2.09	142895	-58.44	112	117.9
1980	42.19	-21.54	343825	140.61	160	42.86
1981	53.63	27.12	425845	23.86	379.79	137.37
1982	53.25	-0.71	919171	115.85	267.9	-29.46
1983	47.12	-11.51	500841	-45.51	109.97	-58.95
1984	60.09	27.53	175661	-64.93	142.05	29.17
1985	58.34	-2.91	247685	41	161.97	14.02
1986	63.83	9.41	245013	-1.08	154.98	-4.32
1987	60.56	-5.12	295241	20.5	261.14	68.5
1988	56.86	-6.11	388796	31.69	227.26	-12.97
1989	70.49	23.97	349561	-10.09	288	26.73
1990	74.05	5.05	421221	20.5	254	-11.81
1991	74.29	0.32	505029	19.9	307	20.87
1992	74.68	0.52	678241	34.3	376	22.48
1993	72.87	-2.42	580409	-14.42	410	9.04
1994	80.3	10.2	767687	32.27	384	-6.34
1995	81.81	1.88	890613	16.01	327	-14.85
CAGR	2.93		9.35		15.45	

CAGR : Compound Annual Growth Rate.

Sources: (1) Economic Survey (Various Issues), Table 1.15, State-wise estimates of Production of Food Grains for Col. 2.

(2) International Trade Statistics Year Book, United Nations for Cols. 3 and 4.

TABLE 3

India's Share of World Trade in Rice Market, 1970-95

Year	*World*	*India*	*India's Share (%)*
1970	925	9	0.1
1975	1984	12	0.6
1980	4355	160	3.7
1985	2916	162	5.6
1990	3995	254	6.4
1995	6136	327	5.3

Source: Economic Survey, Government of India Publication.

TABLE 4

Spread Index for Rice, 1971-95

(Annual Average, 1990=100)

Year	*Consumer Price/ World Price*	*Consumer Price/ Wholesale Price*	*Wholesale Price/ World Price*
1971-75	-241.869	-76.9583	-198.248
1976-80	380.0155	8.25633	166.8364
1981-85	280.7225	-8.95072	228.1638
1986-90	450.3691	21.8751	59.58251
1991-95	644.867	8.801908	426.6212

Source: Author's Calculations.

1989. The trend values based on 5 year moving average of spread index explained that the spread is increased by 1.7 times from a value of 380 to 645 between 1976-80 and 1991-95 respectively. The negative trend during 1971-75 was mainly due to high variability in world prices. This result is confirmed with the find of Hazell *et al.* (1990) study on high variability with 10 year moving coefficient of variation of rice price. The declining trend in 1981-85 was due to continuous depressed levels of world prices. The spread index of 5 year moving average of percentage variation followed a positive trend after the initial period fluctuations.

SPREAD BETWEEN DOMESTIC CONSUMER AND WHOLESALE PRICES

The spread index of percentage variations between domestic consumer and wholesale price for rice during 1969-95 is presented in second column of Table 4. The index of percentage variation Of 27 years, the negative spread index was witnessed during 1973, 1976, 1982, 1984 and 1993. It is noted that after liberalisation the spread index started declining with moderate recovery during last two years 1994 and 1995. The trend of 5 year moving average spread index shows high fluctuations. That is, it has risen from 8.25 to 21.87 during 1976-80 and 1986-90, but there was sudden decline in index by 13 during 1991-95. Figure 4.2 explains the fluctuations in 5 year moving average spread index between consumer price and wholesale prices.

SPREAD BETWEEN WHOLESALE PRICE AND WORLD PRICE

The third column of Table 4 reveals that the spread between domestic wholesale price and world price for rice during 1969-95. It is noted that spread index of percentage variation has raised from (-) 22.46 in 1971 to 714.90 in 1995 with high fluctuations. Further, it is noticed that the percentage variation shows a negative trend during 1971, 1973, 1984, and 1993 during the period under study. Liberalisation policies have brought about significant change in spread between domestic wholesale prices and world prices for rice during the study period. It is clear that spread has increase near by 2.5 times, that is, from 166 in 1976-80 to 427 in 1991-95. It is noticed from 5 year moving average that the spread index increased by 2.5 times, from 166 in 1976-80 to 427 in 19971-95 with a sluggish index of 59 during 1986-90

The spread index shows that an increasing trend of spread between domestic consumer price and world price attributed by rise in domestic wholesale prices compared with world prices and rise in consumer price than wholesale prices as evidenced from Table 4. Therefore, it is concluded that the increase in world price and India's domestic wholesale price are effectively pass-through the domestic consumer prices over the period under study.

Table 5 indicates the regression results of price transmission with respect to world price to domestic consumer price. The second column regression results are without time-effect and third column regression results with time-effects. The regression results explain two aspects: firstly, the proportion of the variations in world prices is transmitted to domestic consumer prices and secondly the proportion of the variations in domestic consumer prices could attribute to variations in world prices.

TABLE 5

Results and Discussion on Transmission of Domestic Consumer Price with World Price

$$\Delta \ln CP = j + \ln p^* + \theta NER + \gamma \Delta \ln CP_{t-1} + \lambda \Delta \ln w + \alpha t + e \quad (1)$$

Indicators	*Co-efficient*	*'t' value*
Time invariant (α_j)	0.0971	1.5583
Time-effect (α_t)	0.0009	0.2864
Change in world price ($b\Delta \ln p^*$)	0.0786	0.8789
Nominal Exchange Rate (θNER)	0.0596	1.2552
Lag of Change in Consumer Price ($\gamma \Delta \ln CP_{t-1}$)	-0.3681	1.711
Changes in Wages ($\lambda \Delta \ln w$)	-0.4344	1.3842
R^2	0.2678	
F	1.3897	
DW	2.105	

* Significance at 1 per cent level.
** Significance at 5 per cent level.
*** Significance at 10 per cent level.
Source: Author's Calculation.

Since, we are interested mainly in the transmission elasticity, it is desirable to eliminate the effect of the exchange rate. We considered the first option suggested by Mundlak and Larson (1992), namely, we computed within-year regression (that is, regression with year dummies based on annual growth rate of nominal exchange rate: if percentage variation is greater than 5 the dummy is 1 and elsewhere 0).

The estimated transmission elasticity of change in world price is 0.0753 reveals that elasticity of domestic consumer prices with respect to world prices is relatively very low and it is also statistically insignificant. This low value can be expected with regression in variation rather than values (Morrisset, 1999).

The coefficients of other explanatory variables: time invariant, time-effect, nominal exchange rate, changes in wage and lagged dependent variable are not statistically significant in explaining the variations in domestic consumer prices.

The answer to the second aspect is related to the value of R^2 indicates that 26 per cent of variation in domestic consumer price is attributed to variations in world prices. The low value of F-statistic did not accept the restriction on the time invariant and time-effect. The Durbin-Watson statistic nearer to value 2 indicates there is no first order serial correlation, either positive or negative.

TABLE 6

Results and Discussion on Transmission of Domestic Wholesale Price with World Price

$$\Delta \ln WP = \alpha j + \beta \Delta \ln p^* + \theta NER + \gamma \Delta \ln WP_{t-1} + \lambda \Delta \ln w + \alpha t + e \quad (2)$$

Indicators	*Co-efficient*	*'t' value*
Time invariant (αj)	0.1038	1.4261
Time-effect (αt)	-0.0005	0.1123
Change in world price ($\beta \Delta \ln p^*$)	0.1186	1.101
Nominal Exchange Rate (θNER)	0.0778	1.3028
Lag of Change in Wholesale Price ($\gamma \Delta \ln WP_{t-1}$)	-0.3185	1.5568
Changes in Wages ($\lambda \Delta \ln w$)	-0.4456	1.2113
R^2	0.2378	
F	1.1858	
DW	2.051	

* Significance at 1 per cent level.
Source: Author's Calculation.

The elasticity transmission between world prices to domestic prices and contribution of variations in world prices to variations in domestic wholesale prices is exhibited in Table

6. The estimated 0.12 elasticity value of change in world prices indicated that price transmission in the variations in world prices to domestic wholesale prices is indeed very small. In other words, the low elasticity value indicated that the variations in world prices are not fully transmitted to domestic wholesale prices. Thought the expected signs are noticed with other explanatory variables, the estimated 't' values of coefficients of the explanatory variables are not statistically significant. The value of R^2 indicated that a 24 per cent of variations in domestic wholesale prices are accounted for by the variations in world prices. The low value of F-statistic explains the imperfections of the explanatory variables in the model. However, the Durbin-Watson statistic about 2.05 indicates no auto-correlation during the study period.

TABLE 7

Results and Discussion on Transmission of Domestic Consumer Price with Domestic Wholesale Price

$$\Delta \ln CP = \alpha j + \beta \Delta \ln WP + \gamma \Delta \ln WP_{t-1} + \lambda \Delta \ln w + \alpha t + e \quad (3)$$

Indicators	*Co-efficient*	*'t' value*
Time invariant (αj)	0.028	0.7148
Time-effect (αt)	0.0015	0.7454
Change in wholesale price ($\beta \Delta \ln WP$)	0.6403	5.9112*
Lag of Change in Consumer Price ($\gamma \Delta \ln CP_{t-1}$)	-0.1448	1.0829
Changes in Wages ($\lambda \Delta \ln w$)	-0.1131	0.5838
R^2	0.7049	
F	11.9456*	
DW	2.4	

* Significance at 1 per cent level.
Source: Author's Calculation.

The proportion of the variations in domestic wholesale prices is transmitted to domestic consumer prices and secondly the proportion of the variations in domestic consumer prices can be attributed to variations in wholesale prices are presented in Table 7. The estimated elasticity of domestic wholesale prices indicated that elasticity of price transmission from domestic wholesale prices to domestic consumer prices is relatively high with value of 0.64 which is statistically significant. Thus, it is evident that there is a significant price transmission from domestic wholesale prices to domestic consumer prices. The other independent variables: time invariant (j), time-effect (t), lagged dependent variable (CP_{t-1}), and changes in wages are statistically insignificant in explaining the proportion of variation in domestic consumer prices.

It is noticed from the R^2 value that 70 per cent of variations in domestic consumer price is explained by variations in domestic wholesale prices because all other explanatory variables are statistically insignificant. The value of F-stastic explains the high degree of model fitness between independent variables and domestic consumer price.

For the measurements of asymmetry of price transmission, we have multiplied the world rice price in equations (1) and (2) and the domestic whole price in equation (3) by two zero-one dummy variables. The first variables takes the value 1 for the upward movements in world rice prices and zero elsewhere; the second takes the value 1 for the downward movement in world prices and zero elsewhere. The asymmetry of price transmission with upward movement and downward movement of world prices to domestic consumer prices is given in Table 8.

The empirical results of the price transmission is not supported the hypothesis, namely, the estimated elasticities of upward movement is higher than the downward movement of world prices to the domestic consumer prices. In contrast to hypothesis (11>12), the elasticities of consumer prices with respect to change in world prices exceeds only 0.06 when the world prices were raising and reaches by 0.11 when the world prices were decreasing. However, the estimated 't' values of estimated elasticities of upward movements (11) and downward movements are statistically insignificant. The estimated elasticities of other explanatory variables are statistically insignificant in explaining the variations in domestic consumer prices. The R^2 value explains 27 per cent of variations in domestic consumer price is explained by the explanatory variations and this was categorically supported with low value of F-statistic. The Durbin-Watson statistic value

TABLE 8

Results and Discussion on Transmission of Domestic Consumer Price with World Price, Upward and Downward Price Movement

$$\Delta \ln CP = \alpha j + \beta 11 \Delta \ln p^* + \beta 12 \Delta \ln p^* + \theta NER + \gamma \Delta \ln CP_{t-1} + \lambda \Delta \ln w + \alpha t + e \quad (1a)$$

Indicators	*Co-efficient*	*'t' value*
Time invariant (αj)	0.1037	1.3188
Time-effect (αt)	0.0007	0.1765
Upward changes in World Prices ($\beta 11 \Delta \ln p^*$)	0.0616	0.4131
Downward changes in World Prices ($\beta 12 \Delta \ln p^*$)	0.1077	0.4868
Nominal Exchange Rate (θNER)	0.0604	1.2309
Lag of change in consumer price ($\gamma \Delta \ln CP_{t-1}$)	-0.3586	1.5558
Changes in Wages ($\lambda \Delta \ln w$)	-0.4306	1.332
R^2	0.2686	
F	1.1019	
DW	2.083	

Source: Author's Calculation.

2.083 reveals that no serial correlation.

Table 9 present estimated elasticities on asymmetric transmission of world price into domestic wholesale prices. It is observed that asymmetric transmission was taken between world price to domestic wholesale price with the hypothesis that the estimated elasticities of upward price movement (11:0.1925) appeared higher than the estimated elasticity value of downward price movement (12:0.0001). That is, the asymmetric values explains that the elasticities of domestic wholesale price with respect to change in world price exceeds of 0.20 where world prices increasing that is 100 per cent change in world prices lead to 120 per cent change in domestic wholesale prices, where the reaches zero unit when world prices declines in international market.

Though the estimated elasticity values of other explanatory variables are with expected signs, they are statistically insignificant in explaining variations in domestic wholesale prices of rice. The R^2 value of the model reveals that the included independent variables explaining variations in

TABLE 9

Results and Discussion on Transmission of Domestic Consumer Price with World Price, Upward and Downward Price Movement

$$\Delta \ln WP = \alpha j + \beta 21 \Delta \ln p^* + \beta 22 \Delta \ln p^* + \theta NER + \gamma \Delta \ln WP_{t-1} + \lambda \Delta \ln w + \alpha t + e \quad (2a)$$

Indicators	*Co-efficient*	*'t' value*
Time invariant (αj)	0.0743	0.7783
Time-effect (αt)	0.0007	0.1387
Upward changes in World Prices ($\beta 21 \Delta \ln p^*$)	0.1925	1.0265
Downward changes in World Prices ($\beta 22 \Delta \ln p^*$)	0.0001	0.0003
Nominal Exchange Rate (θNER)	0.0757	1.2388
Lag of change in Wholesale price ($\gamma \Delta \ln WP_{t-1}$)	0.3526	1.6009
Changes in Wages ($\lambda \Delta \ln w$)	-0.452	1.2029
R^2	0.2477	
F	0.988	
DW	2.094	

Source: Author's Calculation

domestic wholesale prices in only 25 per cent and remaining 75 per cent variations explained by other variables.

The results related to asymmetric transmission of domestic wholesale prices to domestic a consumer price is given in Table 10. The theoretical expectation of asymmetric transmission is statistically proved that upward price movements in domestic wholesale prices to domestic consumer prices is significantly higher than the downward price movement (11>12). The estimated coefficients of upward changes in wholesale prices reveals that elasticities of consumer prices in relation to domestic wholesale prices increase by 0.81 when wholesale prices were raising and reaches only 0.36 when those prices were falls. That is, when domestic wholesale prices increased by 100 per cent as a result, the domestic consumer prices would increase by 181 per cent. On the other hand, when domestic wholesale prices declines by 100 per cent leads to 36 per cent reduction in domestic consumer prices. Both estimated elasticities values are statistically significant at 1 per cent and 10 per cent respectively.

Though the estimated elasticity values of other explanatory variables are with expected signs, they are statistically insignificant in explaining variations in domestic wholesale prices of rice. It is noticed from the R^2 value that 73 per cent of variations in domestic consumer price is explained by variations in domestic wholesale prices because all other explanatory variables are statistically insignificant. The value of F-statistic explains the high degree of model fitness between independent variables and domestic consumer price. However, the Durbin-Watson statistic shows a positive serial correlation in the study period.

TABLE 10

Results and Discussion on Transmission of Domestic Consumer Price with Wholesale Price, Upward and Downward Price Movement

$\Delta lnCP = \alpha j + \beta 31\Delta lnwp + \beta 32\Delta lnwp + \gamma\Delta ln\ CPt\text{-}1 + \lambda\Delta lnw + t + e$ (3a)

Indicators	*Co-efficient*	*'t' value*
Time invariant (αj)	-0.0015	0.0335
Time-effect (αt)	0.0015	0.7985
Upward changes in Wholesale Prices ($\beta 31\Delta lnwp$)	0.8152	4.8244*
Downward changes in Wholesale Prices ($\beta 32\Delta lnwp$)	0.3576	1.5064***
Lag of change in consumer price ($\gamma\Delta lnCP_{t-1}$)	-0.1049	0.7796
Changes in Wages ($\lambda\Delta lnw$)	-0.1236	0.6498
R^2	0.7301	
F	10.2806	
DW	2.335	

Source: Author's Calculation.

There are several reasons for asymmetric transmison of price or why country would not benefit by export pointed out by various authors especially Morrisset (1992), Gill and Brar (1996) and Ramesh Chand (1999). The reasons are: first, the presence of trade restrictions in the main consumer commodities. For instance, import of about 2700 item in India is covered under some sort of the quantitative restrictions out of which about 500 are agricultural commodities. In addition, Non-Technical Barriers imposed by European Communities on

Indian Rice. In internal side, adaptation of dual pricing system for rice to safeguard the consumer as well as producer. Second, continuous increase in processing and other costs particularly transport cost of agricultural commodities that act as bottleneck in the trade of commodities. For instance, Gill and Brar (1996) estimated this costs and the annual average rate of growth is 10.80 per cent per annum between 1980-81 and 1994-95. Third, differentiated changes in productivity across the stages of processing over time. Last and least, the oligopoly and oligopsony world rice market and influence of multinational companies in the trading activities of rice in international market.

FINDINGS AND POLICY IMPLICATIONS

1. The world price for rice recorded an annual growth rate of 1.72 per cent. Due to various policy measures, the exchange rate of Indian rupee has raise by 4 times against US $ in 1995 than initial year 1969.
2. Compared to international price for rice, Indian rice price domestically raised at the rate of 7.5 per cent per annum. Due to oil shocks (1973-74 and 1979-80) and Guld crisis (1990-91) both international and domestic prices for rice have increased.
3. Production of rice in India over a period between 1969-95 registered an annual average rate of growth of 2.93 per cent per annum. Export quantity and value of export of rice recorded an annual average growth rate of 9.35 per cent and 15.45 per cent respectively during 1969-95.
4. Compared to world trade of rice (7 times), India's export of rice has increased significantly by 36 times. As a result, the relative share of India's share of world trade is above 5 per cent during 1980s and 1990s.
5. Spread index for rice for the period 1971-95 is measured by three ways: first, consumer price and world price; second, consumer price and wholesale

price and wholesale price and world price.

5.1 The trend value based on 5 year moving average of spread index between domestic consumer price and world price increased by 1.7 times from a value of 380 in 1976-80 to 645 in 1991-95.

5.2 The spread index between domestic consumer and wholesale price has raised from 8.25 to 21.87 during 1976-80 and 1986-90, but there was sudden decline in index by 13 during 1991-95. The spread index between domestic wholesale price and world price increased by 2.5 times, from 166 in 1976-80 to 247 in 1991-95 with a sluggish index of 59 in 1986-90.

5.3 The spread index shows that an increasing trend of spread between domestic consumer price and world price attributed by rise in domestic wholesale prices compared with world price and rise in consumer price than wholesale prices. This finding is consistent with the empirical analysis of Morisset (1998) with respect to rice.

5.4 The estimated transmission elasticity of change in world price is 0.0753 revealed that elasticity of domestic consumer price with respect ot world prices is relatively vcry low and the value of R^2 indicated that 26 per cent of variation in domestic consumer price is attributed to variations in world prices.

5.5 The estimated 0.12 elasticity value of change in domestic wholesale prices to change in world prices is indeed very small. The value of R^2 indicated that a 24 per cent of variations in domestic wholesale prices are accounted for by the variatons in world prices.

5.6 The estimated elasticity of domestic wholesale prices indicated that elasticity of price transmission from domestic wholesale prices to domestic consumer price is relatively high with value of 0.64 which is statistically significant.

The value of R^2 explains that 70 per cent of variations in domestic consumer price is explained by variation in domestic wholesale prices.

5.7 The elasticities of asymmetry of price transmission with upward and downward move of world price to domestic consumer prices indicated that the elasticities of domestic consumer prices with respect to change in world prices exceed only 0.06 when the world prices were raising and reaches by 0.11 when the world prices were decreasing. The R^2 value explains 27 per cent of variations in domestic consumer prices is explained by world prices.

5.8 The hypothesis related to upward price movement (b11) exceeds downward price movement (b12) is not proved. The asymmetric transmission was taken between world price to domestic wholesale prices with the estimted elasticities of upward price movement b11=0.01925 appeared higher than the estimated elasticity value of downward price movement b12=0.00001.

5.9 The elasticities of asymmetric transmission of domestic wholesale prices to domestic consumer price is that elasticities of consumer prices in relation to domestic wholesale price increased (b11=) 0.81 when wholesale prices were raising and reaches only (b12=) 0.36 when those prices were falls. Hence the hypothesis is proved that b11 > b12.

5.10 The estimated results of our study related to price transmission without upward and downward trend and asymmetric transmission of rice are very much consistent with the emprical findings of Morisset with respect to Rice.

6. The other explanatory variables other cost, tax and trade policies, change in wage rates have no effect on the change in domestic prices.

From the empirical analysis, it can concluded that the increase in world price and India's domestic wholesale price are effectively pass-through the domestic consumer prices over the period under study. The estimation of asymmetric transmission reflects when there is upward change in world price or domestic wholesale price, which is perfectly transmitted into the domestic consumer prices, where as downward change in world price for the rice is transmitted at relatively low rate and even zero rate of transmission. As a result, the spread between domestic consumer price and world prices and the spread between domestic consumer and wholesale price continuously increased. The rise in spread due to asymmetric transmission of world and domestic wholesale price to domestic consumer price have had negative impact on farmers by giving less benefit from rise in world prices, welfare loss to the consumer, and in terms of trade as a country whole.

Therefore, at domestic there is a need for further liberalisation and structural reforms to take advantage of increasing opportunities in the international market for agricultural commodities in general and rice in particular. Constant and continuous effort shall be made with respect to increase in productivity of rice through a wide variety of measures and programmes is relevant. Instead of providing various forms of subsidies, investment in agricultural and rural development programmes, better technology and technical assistance, investment in infrastructure are required to increase the competitive strength of the India's agricultral trade.

At international level, there should be strict monitoring on the reduction in tariff and non-tariff by developed countries. Similarly, control over the Multinational corportations which are dominated in agricultural commodities trade should brought under control.

This study empirically tested the spread between domestic prices and world price on the one hand and transmission of world price to domestic prices on the other hand for the commodity rice only, therefore, there is scope for further research to include other important agricultural commodities whose share in world trade is higher like Wheat,

Sugar, Coffee, Tead, Bananas, Cotton, and Jute. Similarly, the effect of multinational firms (3-6 firms) who enjoy monopolistic power in agricultural commodities whose share in rise alone is 85-90 per cent of world export did not capture in this study due to non-availability of data. So this is an another area for further research.

References

Anderson, K. and Tyres, R (1993): "More on Welfare Gain to Developing Countries from Liberalising World Food Trade", *Jl. of Agr. Econ.*, Vol. 44, No. 2, May, pp. 189-204.

Anderson, J.E. (1998): "The Uruguay Round and Welfare in Some Distorted Agriclutral Economies", *Jl. of Development Economics*, Vol. 56, No. 2, August, pp. 393-410.

Barrett and Dorosh (1996): "Farmers' Welfare and Changing Food Prices: Non-Parameteric Evidence from Rice in Madagascar", *Amer. Jl. Agr. Econ.*, Vol. 78, No. 3, August, pp. 656-69.

BM (1997): "India and WTO: Falling in line, Smartly", *Economic and Political Weekly*, Vol. XXXII, No. 23, June 7-13, pp. 1304-04.

Chan Ling Yap (1996): "Implications of the Uruguay Round on the World Rice Economy", *Food Policy*, Vol. 21, Nos. 4/5, pp. 371-91.

Deepak Nayyar and Abhijit Sen (1994): "International Trade and the Agricultural Sector in India", *Economic and Political Weekly*, Vol. 29, No. 20, May 14, pp. 1187-1203.

Hazell, P.B.R., Jarmillo, M. and Williamson, A. (1990): "The Relationship between World Price Instability and the Prices Farmers Receive in Developing Economies", *Jl. of Agril. Eco.*, Vol. 41, No. 2, May, pp. 227-41.

Deodhar, S.Y. (1999): "WTO Agreement and Indian Agriculture: Restrospection and Prospects", in Samar, K. Datta and Satish, Y. Deodhar (1999), Impact of WTP Agreement on Indian Agriculture, Report Submitted to the Ministry of Agriculture, Government of India, Ch. 2, Vol. I, June, pp. 2.1-2.11.

Donald O. Mitchell and Ronald C. Duncan (1987): "Market Behaviour of Grains Exporters", *World Bank Research Observer*, Vol. 2, No. 1, January, pp. 3-21.

FAO (1984), *Commodity Review and Outlook, 1983-84*, FAO Economic and Social Development Series, No. 29, FAO of the United Nations, Rome.

FAO (1989), *Commodity Review and Outlook, 1988-89*, FAO Economic and Social Development Series, No. 29, FAO of the United Nations, Rome.

FAO (1994), *Commodity Review and Outlook, 1994-95*, FAO Economic and Social Development Series, No. 29, FAO of the United Nations, Rome.

Food and Agriculture Organisation (1994): "A Preliminary Assessment of the Uruguay Round Agreement on Agriculture", *Indian Dairyman*, Vol. 46, No. 9, September, pp. 523-32.

Gill, S.S, and Brar, J.S. (1998): "Global Market and Competitiveness of Indian Agriculture: Some Issues, *Economic and Political Weekly,* August 19, p. 2175.

Ingersent, K.A. and Rayer and Hine, R.C. (1995): "Ex-post Evaluation of the Uruguay Round Agriculture Agreement", *The World Economy,* Vol. 18, No. 5, September, pp. 707-28.

Jacques, Morisset (1998): "Unfair Trade? The Increasing Gap Between World and Domestic Prices in Commodity Markets during the Past 25 Years", *World Bank Economic Review,* Vol. 12, No. 3, pp. 503-26.

Jason, G. Hartell and Johan, F.M. Swinnen (1998): "Trend in Agricultural Price and Trade Policy Instruments since 1990 in Central European Countries", *The World Economy,* Vol. 21, No. 2, March, pp. 261-80.

Kirit, S. Parikh, Narayana, N.S.S., Manoj Panda, Ganesh Kumar A (1995): "Strategies for Agricultural Liberalisation: Consequences for Growth, Welfare and Distribution", *Economic and Political Weekly,* Vol. 30, No. 39, September 30, pp. A90-A92.

Krueger, Anne (1999): "The Developing Countries and the Next Round of Multilateral Trade Negotiations", *World Economy,* Vol. 22, No. 7, September, pp. 909-32.

Nlandu, Mamingi (1996): *"How Prices and Macro Economic Policies Affect Agricultural Supply and Environment"*, Policy Research Working Paper, No. 1645, The World Bank Policy Research Department, World Bank, Washington, D.C.

Merlinda, D. Ingco (1997): *"Has Agricultural Trade Liberalisation Improved Welfare in the Least Developed Countries? Yes"*, Policy Research Working Paper, No. 1748, The World Bank Policy Research Department, World Bank, Washington, D.C.

Misra, J.P. (1997): "Export Competitiveness for Export Performance of Agricultural Commodities", *SBI Monthly Review,* Vol. 36, No. 2, pp. 90-101.

Mundlak, Yair and Donald, F. Larson (1992): "On the Transmission of World Agricultural Prices", *The World Bank Economic Review,* Vol. 6, No. 3, September, pp. 423-38.

Pomeranz, Kenneth (1994): "Growing Global", *World Trade,* Vol. 7, No. 4, May, pp. 120 and 128.

Ramesh Chand (1998): "Removal of Import Restrictions and India's Agriculture", *Economic and Political Weekly,* April 11, pp. 850-54.

Ramesh Chand (1998): "Liberalisation of Agricultural Trade and Net Social Welfare: A Study of Selected Crops", *Economic and Political Weekly,* Vol. 35, No. 52, December 25, pp. A153-A159.

Richard Blackhurst (1997): "The WTO and the Global Economy", *The World Economy,* Vol. 20, No. 5, August, pp. 527-44.

Rod, Tyers and Rod, Falvey (1989): "Border Price Changes and Domestic Welfare in the Presence of Subsidised Exports", *Oxford Economic Review,* Vol. 41, No. 2, April, pp. 434-51.

Servaas Storm (1997): "Agriculture Under Trade Policy Reform: A Quantitative Assessment for India", *World Development,* Vol. 25, No. 3, pp. 425-36.

Suman Sahai (1998): "Protecting Basmati", *Economic and Political Weekly*, Vol. XXXIII, No. 9, February 28-March 6, pp. 442-43.

Subramanian, S. (1993): Agricultural Trade Liberalisation and India, Paris: OECD.

Suman Sahai (1998): "Of Basmati and Champagne: Protection under TRIPS", *Economic and Political Weekly*, Vol. XXXIII, No. 9, March 2, pp. 513 -14.

Tangermann, S. (1996): "Implementation of the Uruguay Round Agreement on Agriculture: Issues and Prospects", *Jl. of Agril. Eco.*, Vol. 47, No. 3, September, pp. 315-37.

Warr, P.G. (1997): "The Uruguay Round and the Developing Countries: Thailand and the Philippines", *The Developing Economies*, Vol. 55, No. 2, June, pp. 142-65.

Yongheng Yang (1996): "China's WTO Membership: What's at Stake?", *The World Economy*, Vol. 19, No. 6, November, pp. 661-82.

5

CHAPTER

A Plan with a Difference

K. VENKATASUBRAMANIAN

PM ANNOUNCES 8-POINT AGENDA FOR 8% GROWTH

The Prime Minister, Mr. Atal Bihari Vajpayee, has outlines an eight-point economic agenda to achieve "an ambitious GDP growth target of eight per cent during the Tenth Five Year Plan". In his opening remarks at the meeting of his Economic Advisory Council, Mr. Vajpayee noted that enhanced implementation of policies, speedier economic reforms, employment-oriented growth and re-targeting of subsidies, among others, would help in accelerating the GDP growth to eight per cent and beyond. "The first and foremost challenge, is that of implementation. Policies and programmes are only as good as their implementation. The priority should therefore be to improve implementation capabilities across the board in the Government". In this context, Mr. Vajpayee noted that a comprehensive review of the current regulatory procedures, which impose significant transaction costs and delays on implementation of projects, is under way. Often these are traceable to poor project preparation, appraisal and absence of a system of evaluation of the experience of completed projects to draw lessons for the future. These issues are common to both physical and social infrastructure.

The second challenge is to further speed up economic reforms so that the country becomes a clear-cut market economy, with the Government withdrawing from production barring a few clearly specified strategic sectors. "However, the Government must retain and further strengthen its role in policy-making regulation and facilitation. We need to ensure that regulation of markets is by competent and independent regulatory agencies. These should follow transparent procedures, guided by the Government's clearly articulated policy-objectives".

Thirdly, the Government would have to continue to shoulder dominant, though not exclusive responsibility for physical and social infrastructure. However, the goals of a welfare state will now have to be pursued within a new framework of broadening public-private partnership. The fourth item on the agenda was that even as we try to speed up growth, it will have to be employment-oriented. In this context, the Government would endeavour to target 10 million employment opportunities per year.

Mr. Vajpayee also noted that higher growth demands higher rate of savings and channeling the savings into productive investments. The fifth agenda would therefore be to remove the imperfections that are plaguing our financial markets. It should be a special endeavour to ensure that the poor and the unorganized sector have access to savings, credit and insurance services.

Another essential element of the poverty alleviation strategy will have to be reduction and re-targeting of subsidies so that the essential consumption of the poor, including social services is protected, but the overall fiscal deficit is reduced. Barring those who deserve subsidy, a culture should be developed of making all others pay for what they use. The Prime Minister stated that in the last four years, much attention has been paid to expanding and modernizing various aspects of connectivity both physical and digital. To further widen its commitment to connectivity, the Government will soon launch an initiative for accelerated completion of Railway projects that are both critical and remunerative. If necessary, non-budgetary resources for this purpose will be raised.

Lastly, Mr. Vajpayee said that the long-term growth strategy should be closely aligned to the strategy on population. The encouraging demographic transition, which has been revealed in the 2001 census, needs to be further accelerated.

Courtesy: *Business Line*, July 14, 2002.

On October 5, 2002 the full Planning Commission met under the chairmanship of the Prime Minister and approved the draft Tenth Plan. In his opening remarks, the Prime Minister dealt at length on the biggest challenge to achieve speedier and more balanced development. Usually the Plan projections talk of development about recognized sectors, but here is a plan that has imaginatively forged ahead towards new goals. The Prime Minister emphasized clearly the issues when he stressed on speed and balance and added that the development should be a people's movement and requested the cooperation of all including voluntary agencies.

The draft three volume Plan covers strategies of development, governance and implementation methodologies. It has now been accepted that governance is the most important one among all things. One more important parameter about which all are worried is the performance of the States. First time perhaps the Prime Minister clearly pinpointed that "it is obvious that the State governments would have to extended their fullest and most enthusiastic cooperation to the Centre if all the daunting tasks are to be accomplished".

The Tenth Plan contains again for the first time a serious mention on the role of the States. The State-wise growth targets, worked out in consultation with the states, are a clear pointer. National targets are framed, of course, but unless the State targets are there, the States cannot move in the national direction. We have called for doubling the per capita income in ten years and achieving a growth rate of 8 per cent of GDP per annum. Is this possible? Yes, it can be achieved if these are real governance.

The Prime Minister emphasized that not only economic growth should be our object, but improvement in the quality of life and he described this as Human Well Being (HWB). The Plan is projecting a reduction in poverty ratio from 26 per cent to 21 per cent by 2007, reduction in population from 21.3 per cent to 16.2 per cent before 2011. We are to bring by next year all children to schools and also see that they complete five years of schooling by 2007. Gender gaps in literacy and wage rates will be specially attended to. We hope to increase the literacy rates from 65 per cent to 75 per cent by 2007. Infant mortality rate will have to be reduced from 72 to 45 by 2007. We visualize a big jump in savings and investment. These are desirable goals. But will we achieve this is the question?

In the Full Planning Commission meeting we were very happy to see "firm political will" of the Prime Minister. He clearly underlined and emphasized stimulative investment and plan for disinvestments and increasing annual FDI flows to at least $ 7.5 billion. October 5 would be a turning point in India's economic development because unusually everyone who spoke including the Finance and External Affairs ministers touched about the efficient fiscal management.

Agriculture is recognized as the prime concern and the Tenth Plan is for eliminating inter-State barriers to trade and commerce here and also for replacement of various acts dealing with food by one comprehensive Food Act. The labour law reform is to be given priority. Again for the first time the Tenth Plan has special monitorable target that should be attained along with the growth target. So far there has not been an in-depth measurement of these. We have often emphasized general targets but these should be translated into balanced regional development as State targets. For the first time the Planning Commission is to monitor progress of the various ministries. A steering committee will be set-up after the approval of the Plan by the National Development Council (NDC) to monitor implementation with special reference to economic reforms. Each sector has been given a separate programme for economic reforms on monitorable targets.

The year 2002-03 marks the beginning of the Tenth Plan though it has started a bit late for causes beyond control. The Prime Minister called the Tenth Plan a formidable document and every economist and thinker who spoke about the Plan wanted greater determination, discipline and political will for all round development with definite governance to go ahead. These sharp goals could be achieved through two important performance objectives: (a) governance, and (b) performance of States. Therefore, perhaps for the first time in 50 years the Yojana Bhavan is recognizing the governance aspect for development. Again for the first time, the Tenth Plan has a Chapter especially on governance. This will emphasise governance as the thing for development today.

It is unfortunate that governance in many States is simply not there and perhaps this is a clear danger signal to the economy. States are worried about politics than economics and hence governance is a rare commodity in quite a few states. Here the implementation of the Midday meals scheme in schools in the States can be cited as historic example. The Government gives free rice and wheat to the States for distribution to schools and unfortunately only 50 per cent of this free gift is utilized by States and except a few States most of them cannot implement this free laudable scheme which will bring in children to schools and retain them there including the girl children. It is surprising to find that many States are not even ready to lift free grains in spite of the Central Government giving them transport charges also.

The draft Tenth Plan has been approved by the Full Planning Commission and will now be placed before the Cabinet and thereafter before the NDC for final approval. The Tenth Plan has eminent goals. It is a carefully prepared document. But it will succeed only if the *mantra* of governance is implemented and the States realize their responsibilities. Economic reforms should be speeded up to achieve the laudable goals. If these reforms are not rushed then the entire Plan may be a mere fantasy.

6

CHAPTER

"India Vision 2020"— Is it Utopian or Cornucopian?

P. JEGADISH GANDHI

The ascendancy of Dr. A.P.J. Abdul Kalam from the pilgrim center of Rameswaram to the citadel of power as the 12th President of Indian at the Rashtrapati Bhavan in New Delhi is a historical event with unparalleled precedents—a self-made man, a satellite scientist, an indigenous missile innovator, an innervator of young minds, a non-political leader, an inter-faith symbolizer, a social thinker and above all, a nationalist. Unlike his predecessors, Abdul Kalam has got an ignited vision of development for the country. In his maiden Presidential Address, Kalam has mandated that there must be vision to transform India into a "developed nation". In, *India 2020: A Vision for the New Millennium*, he has outlined a blueprint for improving our core competencies and competitiveness, optimizing technology-based development, utilizing internal strategic strengths and enlarging the social and economic opportunities for our people.

WHAT IS DEVELOPMENT?

In economic lexicon, "development" denotes two-dimensional growth-quantitative and qualitative. Developed stage is the obverse of low per capita income, primary producing occupational pattern, heavy population and density pressure, prevalence of chronic unemployment and underemployment, low rate of capital formation, maldistribution of wealth/assets, poor quality of human capital, prevalence of low level of technology, low level of social infrastructural facilities, low living standards of people, low per capita consumption of all essential social goods and services and poor economic organizational structures related to saving potential, investible destination, financial institutions and lendable resources. In short, it is a low-cum-poor syndrome. How to break this vicious circle?

CORE STRENGTHS

The envisaged vision includes developing self-reliance in national security, capitalizing on the core strengths of agriculture and the value addition of agro-food sector, capitalizing on the vast mineral wealth, bio-diversity and marine resources, transforming chemical industry, resurging of engineering industry, emerging services sector as a global leader, mastering the strategic technologies, generating employment potential, in building poverty-reduction programmes, emerging an excellent health service sector cover and the enabling infrastructural facilities with rural-urban connectivity.

Can the country be geared up for action to realize the new vision for India 2020? While some become pessimistic and aver that India can't improve because of the pervasive corruption, mindless bureaucracy and greedy politicians, there are also others who want to try and make things better because the post-liberalization economy gives them an opportunity. The explosive growth in television, thanks primarily to satellite communications, exposes people to the realities existing elsewhere, the world over. Everywhere there is a genuine interest to act, to break the vicious cycle of pessimism and inaction. However, a major but unstated problem is how to initiate such action. We need to initiate action with an overall vision of developed India. If each of us attempts to do so in our spheres or work the status of developed India will arrive sooner than we expect, because our country has many natural core strengths and competitive advantages. The five mega-mission—Agriculture and food processing, Electric power, Education and health, Information sectors and strategic sectors with strong linkages when integrated and implemented with a national focus, will result in actions which will shape the second vision of the nation.

MEGA MISSIONS

In order that India marches towards the cherished goal of a developed nation, there is an urgent need to change the present methods of working and the mindset that has developed because of centralized power. Many existing governmental structures would need to be drastically reduced. There should be reduction of monopolies and a greater competition in the implementation of many packages of these mega missions. Therefore, private sector participation would be required along with more liberal and simplified procedures. Healthy competition leads to greater efficiency and innovation.

CONSTITUTE A NATIONAL SOCIO-ECONOMIC ADVISORY COUNCIL

India is a nation of a billion-plus people. A nation's progress depends upon how its people think. It is thoughts which are transformed into actions. The President could constitute a National Socio-Economic Advisory Council to realize his mission of "developed India". Moreover, the vision could be realized within a definite directional framework of implementation with the help of proactive partnership of parliamentarians and planners. The constitution of the council would facilitate the flow of suggestions for the creation of a 'resurgent India'. The suggestions could, in turn, be presented to Parliament with recommendations. Further, the Planning Commission could be advised to include a chapter on 'India 2020' in the Tenth Plan document for discussion among policy pundits and plan strategists. The NGOs sector could be advised to discuss and disseminate the tracts of "developed

India" all over the country. The book should be prescribed for detailed study at all levels of education in the country. Seminars, symposia, workshops and consultations should be conducted at the school, college and university to ignite the young minds.

The Planning Commission in its latest National Human Report indicates four basic amenities of development appropriate to the Indian Context—provisioning of *pucca* houses, proper and timely medical care at child birth and high school attendance and connectivity to a large market. It should be noted that Kalam was the important person to emphasise the importance of connectivity in developmental programmes. That *mantra* will integrate the Planning Commission's measures of development with the Prime Minister's desire for the 8 per cent rapid growth and Dr. Kalam dream for a truly developed India. (P.V. Indiresan, *Business Line*, July 29, 2002). The ultimate goal of any type of development programme in the 21st century is to make men and women better-off in their own environment without any discrimination and deprivation.

In conclusion, Dr. Kalam's dream is that "both our houses of Parliament would adopt a resolution for the second vision of a great nation: "India will transform into a developed nation before the year 2020. A billion people are our resource for this national transformation". Providentially, he has been given an electoral opportunity and constitutional responsibility as the President of India, to realize the long cherished vision of developed India.

PART B

SUB-NATIONAL ECONOMIC DIALECTS: TAMIL NADU

SECTION I

Overview Dimensions

7

CHAPTER

Political Economy of Tamil Nadu

G. VISWANATHAN

For the first time I am participating in the deliberations of the Indian Economic Association (IEA). Let me tell you first that I am not an economist. I am a student of economics. I continued to be a student of economics. But fortunately we had the benefit of witnessing and participating in 10 Union budgets in Lok Sabha and another 10 budgets in Tamil Nadu assembly. I had a number of tall leaders in Lok Sabha when I entered in 1967. I was 27 years old at that time. Almost all the party leaders were present and about 6 former ICS were also member of Lok Sabha. About 30-35 former maharajas and maharanis were present in the Lok Sabha. But the one person I always remember speaking on the budget whom I can never forget was Mr. Minoo Masani, who was the leader of the then Swatantra Party. He will criticise the government, he will attack the government on various policies but he will also present a viable alternative to the government. In every budget when he was there in Lok Sabha his speech on budget was like an alternative budget presented to the government or to the country. I think we would expect such eminent people to enter Lok Sabha, Rajya Sabha and assemblies.

It was Dr. Raja Chelliah at the Conference held at Mysore in 1994, who pointed out that unless the State governments adopt the reforms, it would be very difficult for them in the future. It was 7 years ago, when Dr. Raja Chelliah gave his advice to the State government and still many of them are not following his advice. Except for a few States, where they have started the reforms, for example, Andhra Pradesh, Karnataka, Gujarat and one or two other states. He pointed out that in the tax system immediate reformation should take place and especially there should be uniformity in the sales tax but it has not come about. On deficits, continuous deficits is seen in almost all the states, he pointed out that we should try to balance the budget, which remains even now a far cry. He wanted the State governments to cut down their expenditure especially on its staff strength and non-plan expenditure, but that is not being followed. The most important thing he pointed out is that about the Power sector reforms, which probably only Andhra Pradesh, Karnataka, Gujarat and Orissa are trying to reform. Other states want to follow but still they are unable to do it. As far as, Tamil Nadu is concerned, you know pretty well that we have one of the best administrations available in the country. When the Britishers entered India, it was 3 cities—Kolkata, Mumbai and Chennai where they established their rule. And we had the benefit of the system of British administration and even now, if at all we have some good administration, it is due to the heritage left behind by the British and of course, we have very good officials also. But in spite of all these facts and amount of resources available in the State except for water, where we are in shortage and of course, we are always hungry for power, I mean electric power. The growth rate is going down at the national level and it is around 5.5 per cent and as also in the State. I understand the agricultural growth rate is 1.89 per cent and in the manufacturing sector it is just 3 per cent. I think Mr. Palanidurai must be able to correct these because he is the person who is sitting in the government now as Member of the State Planning Commission. Therefore, what we have planned for 8th Plan it was about 7 per cent and during the 9th Plan it came down to 6.5 per cent and now it is further going down. It means that we are slipping back. At one point of time, the state was number three in the whole country when the major states were compared in the growth rate, per capita income etc. We were number three, I think now the position of Tamil Nadu is some where in fifth position or sixth among the Indian states. But I should congratulate the successive government of Tamil Nadu as far as population growth rate is concerned whereas all India average is 21.30 per cent, growth rate of Tamil Nadu has been brought down to 11.19 per cent. But compare it to Kerala, where it is 9.4 per cent growth rate in population. Unless we curb our population growth, our planning are going to fail and our growth rate cannot be achieved to the extent, which we would like it to grow. But due to political compulsion we are unable to take any decisions on populations. China is able to contain its population, it is just negligible and almost they are brining it to 0 per cent. There, one child family norm is adopted and those who defy it are being punished.

It is time now that we should take a decision regarding eradication of poverty. In Tamil Nadu, poverty alleviation programme is being implemented well and the percentage of people living below the poverty line is 21.12% whereas the national average around 44%. But in spite of it, in per capita income, it is much behind Punjab, Haryana, Maharashtra and Gujarat and in energy requirements and energy generation also Maharashtra, U.P., Gujarat, A.P., M.P. are ahead of Tamil Nadu. I would very much like the Tamil Nadu Government to concentrate on the infrastructure development. In fact, Mr. Palanidurai was telling me how we are going to do away with this deficits of 4400 crores. According to Tamil Nadu budget, we are loosing around 2000 crores in food subsidy, about 1500 crores on electricity and another about 400-500 crores on state transport undertakings and may be 100-200 crores in various public sector undertakings. When I was in-charge of food and civil supplies, I was appointed as a chairman of a committee by Government of India to revamp the public distribution system (PDS). We went around the country to ascertain the views of Government. We looked at the operations in various segments of society and which the Centre and the State Governments are implementing. Then, we suggested a number of ways and means to cut down the subsidy on rice, wheat and some other products.

Because when you issue the ration cards, everybody

come and stands in the same queue and Government is not in a position, whether it is State or Union Government to subsidise food for everybody. For those who are living below poverty line, it is possible but that also in a phased manner, it has to be given up. But I don't understand why we should loose on electricity and transport. For example, transport in Tamil Nadu, we have around 22,000 bus routes and about 17,000 are in the public sector and with various transport undertakings owned by the government and about 5,000 are in the private hand.

The states which are ruled by the leftists till recently, like Bengal and Kerala, they have taken only about 10-15% in the government hands and rest are in the private hands, so they are not loosing much on the state transport undertakings. But in Tamil Nadu, it was a political decision about 30 years ago and now they do not want to go back because there are very many vested interests. I don't want to go into details but I would like you to know what is happening in the transport undertakings and in the road transport corporations. Almost to run a bus by the government we have to subsidise 2 lakh of rupees per annum. I belong to a family of bus operators and even now we have some bus routes. Even a worst manager can get 1 lakh profit in a normal bus route and the government is loosing 2 lakh per annum per bus and about 500 crores are going as subsidy to run these buses by the government. In passenger bus service, the government fixes the timing, the government fixes the passenger transport fare, the government fixes bus tax and the route permits are issued by the government. So, nobody can run as they like, they cannot charge as they like, it is not possible because there are regional transport officers who can take penal actions against bus operators. But what happens now is that, on this account we are loosing 500 crores and we are unable to spend on many important sectors like education particularly *higher education*, what we spend for this very very meager. Thus it is high time that Tamil Nadu government should concentrate on this. Here I would like the economists present here if the state economic association is formed, already there are 2 associations, I hope soon it will become one association, so that they can advise the government irrespective of who is there in Fort St. George.

They can advice the government on various issues, especially where due to political compulsions they are unable to change their decisions, to take certain progressive actions, etc. Suppose if the government takes a decision on the advice of the economists and others, the 17,000 bus routes are privatised the government can easily mobilise 25,000 to 30,000 crores, even if it is a phased manner. The only problem will be the labourers and the employees. In fact I would suggest if the trade unions are very serious they could be given bus routes and they can run them if it is possible. Once we had co-operative transport corporations run by the ex-service men, they were running very well. This is one of the major causes for the inefficiency of the public sector undertakings. I would very much request the government to go into the details and see whether this can be done by doing away with the government investment and they can get enough money on the hands, which can be spent on the various sectors where it is necessary. The other sector is power. Tamil Nadu is one among the premier states where power is utilised but like the other states in India our TND loss is around 17-18 per cent. I think the national average is 27 per cent. We are efficient in that way. It is not so in the advanced countries. TND loss is only to the tune of 7 per cent. So we are loosing lot of electricity on theft and transmission loss, very often the theft is also calculated and added to transmission loss and already there is power shortage in the state. Our requirement is very high and we are able to generate only three fourth of our requirement. Even though it is suggested by the Centre, after the New Economic Policy, that they should take up reforms in the power sector, Tamil Nadu government has not done so. I hope they will be doing so soon. Already Andhra Pradesh has done it, Karnataka and Gujarat have done it. In fact, Gujarat has, as I have been told, has cut down their expenditure on their staff by 10 per cent, which is a very good step and I would like the other States to emulate it. In order to get more power we have to generate more power and more investments has to go in, which is not possible under such circumstances in Tamil Nadu. Therefore, we are already in deficit of Rs. 4400 crores and you know the problems in Tamil Nadu. There are two states in India—Tamil Nadu and Punjab where a decision were taken very long back to give free supply of power to farmers. In Tamil Nadu not only free supply to farmers, there are huts and various others, where free supplies of power are given. In fact, we do not know how much power they are consuming. There is proverb in Tamil, 'Aathil Pottalum Azhandhu Podu". Even if you throw something into the river measure it and throw it out. But we are not doing it and we do not know how much power is being wasted. As far as my knowledge goes no farmer in Tamil Nadu is asking for free power, they were asking for concession. I hope you remember, there was a big agitation when the power rate was increased from 10 paise to 12 paise. There was an agitation by late Mr. Narayanasamy Naidu. Even Narayanasamy Naidu did not ask for free power in Tamil Nadu. It is therefore because of the political rivalry between the 2 giants, 2 political parties, it was given free to the farmers. I remember an incident when I went to Trivanandhapuram to meet one of my friends who was with me in Lok Sabha and who became a Minister in Kerala. He was asking me what is happening in Tamil Nadu government. It was long back about 10 years ago. I asked what is it? He told me that he has land in Tamil Nadu in Tirunelveli district. He owns four pump sets in Tamil Nadu. He was regularly paying his electric bills and one day his tenants came and told him Sir, you need not pay your bills hereafter as Tamil Nadu government has given us free supply. He said as a landlord he was very happy but as a minister in-charge of electricity in Kerala he said it is a foolish decision by the government, but I cannot say so, as I was a part of the government. Well again, I would like to quote a proverb, 'Nair Pudicha Puli Vaal'. It was proverb in Tamil. It was like catching the tail of a lion, you cannot go on catching it or you cannot leave it. That is how we are suffering in Tamil Nadu. I would like the Tamil Nadu Association, IEA to come to the rescue of the state government. You have to suggest the ways and means and how to do it. Therefore, it is a political decision to give free supply to the farmers and now it has to be done away with it. There is no possibility in continuing with this. If they continue the Tamil Nadu Electricity Board will have to be closed down. You cannot give Rs. 1500 crores every year to Tamil Nadu board when power reforms are already been undertaken in our neighbouring states. I know they are aggressively doing it. Andhra Pradesh government under Telugu Desam and Karnataka government under the Congress government are competing with each other in reforms, even though they may not be the same at the Centre. But the States are very keen to have reforms in both the States and we have to compete with them, like India competing with China. Tamil Nadu has to compete with Andhra Pradesh and Karnataka. In fact, once Andhra Pradesh was rated as number 25 as far as their investments are concerned. I think *Business India* took a survey and put it as number 25 about 5 years ago and now the same paper says that according to the investors, it is in the 3rd rank next only to Maharashtra and Gujarat. Tamil Nadu is far behind at 5th or 6th position. It is high time that the reforms introduced in 1991 by the then government of Narasimha Rao and Manmohan Singh has to be adopted in full in Tamil Nadu. They should not lag behind in introducing the reforms and especially in the power sector where they have to introduce and have to create the various organisations as suggested like the State Regulatory Electricity Commission, which is already been done in Orissa, Haryana and Andhra Pradesh. I think Tamil Nadu government is in the process. I hope it will be able to do it quickly so that the problems of the budget could be solved and there will not be any deficit or that the deficit will be cut down.

When recently there was a steep like in the administered prices in Tamil Nadu in rise in bus fare, etc., there was a loud protest from opposition of course from the public also. The Tamil Nadu government also justified it saying that we are in precarious position and we have Rs. 4400 crore deficit and we have to make it up. I went through the history of deficit of the State, it was around Rs. 5000 crores in 1990-91. In 1999-2000 the revenue receipts grew from Rs. 5880 crores to Rs. 16328 crores. In the same period, the revenue expenditure increase from Rs. 5638 crores and Rs. 20728 crores, that is why there is a deficit and the revenue deficit swelled from a mere Rs.550 crore in 1990-91. Now it is Rs. 4400 crore in 1999-2000. Thus there has been a phenomenal growth in the expenditure of the government and in the deficit and that is how this has happened. I understand from the report of the

Auditor and Comptroller General that there has been a grave deterioration in the tax collection performance of Tamil Nadu. In 1991, the arrears which was not collected was Rs. 519 crores representing 15 per cent of the revenue raised. By 1994-95, the arrears went upto Rs.1700 crore forming 26 per cent of the revenue. It swelled to 39 per cent in 1997-98 and to 59 per cent in 1998-99 to about 71 per cent in 1999-2000. The arrears due are to the tune of 71 per cent in Tamil Nadu now. In fact, Mr. Era Sezhiyan, says collection of taxes, which is a prime duty of Tamil Nadu government, has miserably failed. Some of the arrears have been kept pending for more than 5 years and is not as if they are one or two years old. Sales tax is the major taxation measures which almost two-third of the revenue of the State. In the collection of Sales Tax of the year 1999-2000, the total sales tax is Rs. 7024 crores and in the same year the arrears is Rs.7244 crores. The deficit is only Rs. 4400 crores. The State government collects even a 50 per cent of the arrears, there will be a relief to the State government. They need not go from pillar to post even for the payment of their officers every month. Somehow the administration was not serious in collecting this tax, arrears and that is why we are in a precarious position and it is high time now that the Tamil Nadu government has to do something. I am very happy that the government has appointed a Committee under Mr. A.M. Swaminathan to see how the expenditure can be cut down by the State government. I hope Swaminathan gives a report very soon, he is a very good officer and the government after giving the report, and they have to implement it irrespective of the political problems. In fact, I would very much like that there is a consensus in some of the issues facing the state. At least there is some discussion between the government and the opposition in the Union level, but it is not so at the State level. I do not know about the other states but in Tamil Nadu they do not even meet each other, they do not wish each other, even on important days. Democracy cannot function like this. After all we are working in the interest of the people and welfare of the people should be the utmost importance. The political leaders and political parties in such economic matters and financial matters where the whole future of the state is involved, I would very much like the political parties to put their heads together and see how it could be resolved with the least disturbance and least hurt to the poor people. As I pointed out on the inaugural day many of the political parties have not studied the budget.

As economist we are above caste, creed, religion, etc. We will be guided by economic consideration of the welfare of the people. And it is upto the political parties and the governments, to take it or leave it but I think it is high time that the Tamil Nadu State Economic Association should be strengthened and they must be able to give same advise to Tamil Nadu Government, which would be very helpful to the government of the day.

8

CHAPTER

Tamil Nadu Economy: Progress during Nineties and Challenges Ahead

K.V. Palanidurai

The last decade of the 20th Century is an important milestone in the history of economic development in India. The crisis in the early 90s provided an opportunity to review the economic policy and development strategy pursued in the post-independence period and to re-define the role of Government in economic development. Thus, started an era of economic reforms with wide ranging implications for the National and State economy. The impact of economic reform measures on growth, equity, employment, poverty reduction and on several aspects has been extensively reviewed by numerous researchers and scholars. Undoubtedly the mid-90s witnessed acceleration in growth of Gross Domestic Product. Investment levels, especially private investment witnessed an increasing trend. But during the last two years deceleration is noticeable and attention is focused on revival of economy. Despite, the slow down—a phenomena observed at the global level, India is one of the eight fastest growing economies in the world. The reform process opened up new avenues and opportunities for the States to play a much larger role in infrastructure building and industrialization by attracting private investment. Tamilnadu is ranked among the developed States in India and is one of the six fastest growing States judged by per capita Income and several other social and economic indicators such as literacy rate, enrolment rate of students in schools, Life Expectancy at Birth, Infant Mortality Rate, containing population growth, poverty reduction and infrastructure facility, Tamilnadu occupies a place among the top five or six states. Tamilnadu is a pioneer in implementation of several social welfare schemes, such as Noon Meals to school children and old age pension to the aged, which were later adopted as national schemes. While highlighting the significant progress made by Tamilnadu in several fronts it is equally important to point out the areas of concern which need to be addressed. Employment growth in the public sector and in the organized private sector has not been significant enough to absorb the growing labour force and the educated. A sizeable section of the labour force continues to depend on the agricultural sector, even though the agricultural sector's contribution to the Gross Domestic Product is declining. Traditional industries in the State such as Handlooms, Textiles, Leather and Engineering goods are facing severe problems. The out-moded technology and low efficiency levels are the main reasons. In the Agricultural sector, net sown area is declining or remaining stable and the extent of fallow land is very high. Any incremental production is expected from more intensive use of land for which water availability is crucial. Here again, the State has already fully harnessed the surface water potential and ground water exploitation reached alarming proportion leading to environmental and ecological problems. The quality of services provided by the Government in the health and education sectors leave much to be desired. The cost of delivering these services is mounting. The State is not in a position to mobilize adequate resources to step up plan outlays and public investment, as the Tax-GDP ratio for Tamilnadu is already high. The financing of Eighth and Ninth Plan was mostly through borrowings and interest payment has emerged as a major item of expenditure. The State Government finances are not in a healthy status. An attempt is made in this paper to present some salient features of Tamilnadu Economy and the areas of concern and challenges ahead.

GROWTH OF STATE DOMESTIC PRODUCT

Tamilnadu registered an impressive growth in Gross State Domestic Product of 7% p.a. during the Eighth Plan. The growth momentum was maintained in the early years of the Ninth Plan but does not seem to have sustained in the later half. The State is witnessing a deceleration in the growth rate. The Ninth Plan targeted growth of 7% p.a. is unlikely to be achieved. The annual growth rate in the first four years of the Ninth Plan is 6.52%. The performance of agricultural sector is not on the expected line and its growth is fluctuating, showing a negative growth of -7.8% in 1999-2000 and an insignificant growth of 1.89% in 2000-2001. The secondary sector, especially manufacturing sector is also not doing well with a growth of less than 3% p.a. The performance of tertiary sector is promising and has contributed substantially for maintaining the overall growth performance.

The sectoral composition of Gross Domestic Product is undergoing significant changes. The share of primary sector is declining and that of the tertiary sector is increasing. The secondary sector's share remains constant. The following table shows the trends in sector-wise contribution to the GSDP.

Sector	*Percentage Distribution*							
	1993-94	*94-95*	*95-96*	*96-97*	*97-98*	*98-99*	*1999-00*	*2000-01*
Primary	24.82	24.49	20.66	19.51	19.62	20.04	17.71	17.21
Secondary	33.72	34.55	36.56	35.61	33.82	32.48	33.58	33.04
Tertiary	41.46	30.96	42.78	44.88	46.56	47.48	48.71	49.75
GSDP	100.00	100.00	100.00	100.00	100.00	100.00	100.00	100.00

Per capita income (at 1993-94 prices) of Tamilnadu has increased from Rs. 8952 in 1993-94 to Rs. 12954 in 2000-2001. The State's per capita income is well above the all India per capita income of Rs. 10664 in 2000-2001.

DEMOGRAPHIC CHANGES

According to 2001 census the population of Tamilnadu is 6.21 crores. During the decade 1991-2001, the State recorded a growth of 11.19% in the population against all India growth of 21.30%. Tamilnadu's decadal growth rate is one of the lowest among the States. Kerala recorded the lowest growth rate of 9.4%. Tamilnadu has taken sustained efforts to contain growth of population and has largely succeeded in it. The sex ratio is improving. As against 974 females per 1000 males in 1991 there were 986 female in 2001.

Poverty Levels

A total of 13 million people accounting for 21.12% State's population is estimated to be living below poverty line in 2000. Incidence of poverty is pronounced in the urban areas where 21.11% of the population is living in poverty as compared to 20.55% in rural areas. Tamilnadu witnessed a reduction of 14 percentage points in poverty ratio between 1993-94 and 2000. In 1993-94, 35.03 of States population was living below poverty line.

Unemployment

As per the recent NSS (1999-2000), the percentage of unemployment to the labour force on usual principal status has been estimated at 2.0% in the rural areas and 4.0% in urban areas corresponding to 3.44 lakh persons and 3.67 lakh persons, respectively. The unemployment rate for males is higher than that for females in the rural areas. However, in the urban areas female unemployment rate is higher than that of males. The total unemployment rate for the State as a whole has been estimated at 2.4% corresponding to 7.10 lakh persons. These estimates do not reflect true unemployment situation in the state. It does not capture the existence of disguised unemployment and underemployment. The Employment Exchanges data show about 43 lakh applicants in the live registers of which one-third are women applicants and 70% is educated with matriculation and above qualifications.

STATE FINANCES

The State finances is undergoing severe stress with expenditure increasing at a faster rate than the rate of growth of revenue receipts. From 1987-88 Tamilnadu's budget is continuously showing Revenue deficit. A combination of factors has led to the worsening of the fiscal situation. The State has not periodically revised upwards the fare structure of state owned transport corporation, tariffs in the State Electricity Board and the issue price of foodgrains in the public distribution system during the last decade. These factors continued to be a drag on the state finances. The revision of pay scale of the Government servants according to the Fifth Pay Commission recommendations and the mounting interest burden as well as pension payments have added to the problems of the State finances The financing pattern of the Ninth Plan shows the increasing levels borrowings to implement the plan. The State Government has come out with a White Paper on Tamilnadu Government finances explaining the reasons for the worsening of the fiscal situation and called for "a comprehensive fiscal course correction exercises for arresting fiscal deterioration trends and bringing economy back on the rails".

CHALLENGES AHEAD

Tamilnadu is preparing the Tenth Five Year Plan (2002-2007) at a time when the State is faced with serious financial problems and Indian economy experiencing a deceleration phase. The Planning Commission (Government of India) in its approach paper to the Tenth Plan has set a target of 8% GDP growth for the Plan. In the past Tamilnadu has always set a target growth equal to the national target or slightly higher. Going by the experience Tamilnadu would also aim at a growth rate around the national target. This would necessitate stepping up of investment, especially the private sector investment substantially. Tamilnadu has attracted higher levels of Foreign Direct Investment and also domestic private sector investment during the last decade. The State has to vigorously pursue an investor friendly policy and take concerted effort to improve the infrastructure to attract private investment. In this context Tamilnadu may have to initiate reforms in several areas to take full advantage of the liberalization policy of the Government of India. Dr. Rajah Chelliah in his presidential address to the 77th Annual Conference of the Indian Economic Association held in 1994 has emphasized the urgency of the State level reforms to achieve high growth rate and listed six items which are relevant even today. I would only like to recall his following observations:

> "Achievement of a high growth rate requires that the State governments must also undertake reform and raise the capability of the Indian economy. In the medium and longer-term context, it is clear that they must take the following steps:
>
> (a) Reform of the tax system, in particular indirect taxes such that there will be no taxation of inputs or escalation of costs, and no barrier to trade between States. This requires adoption of the value added tax and zero rating of Inter-State exports. There should be greater uniformity in sales tax rates and abolition of what is called 'rate war' among the States. There should also be no attempt to attract investment by offering undue concessions. There should be general agreement as to the kind and extent of concessions which could be justifiably given to compensate for backwardness of particular areas.
>
> (b) Budget balance should be restored, with the revenue deficit being phased out during the next five years or so. This would require bold steps to stop the rapid growth of the government in terms of staff strength and the size of non-development expenditure. Simultaneously, government should get out of many areas and open those areas to the private sector.
>
> (c) Infrastructure development: Among the infrastructure industries, the power sector is the most important at the State level. State governments should accept and implement the

Pawar Committee's recommendations on Electricity Boards. Similarly, it would be necessary to disinvest government capital in road transport corporations. The private sector should be allowed and encouraged to build roads, bridges and ports. Policies must be implemented quickly.

Closing down of the loss-making PSUs and disinvesting in PSUs which do not have any promotional aim.

9

CHAPTER

Growth Performance for Tamil Nadu: Interfacing with Andhra Pradesh

BIMAN CHANDRA DE

This paper attempts to highlight the growth performance of Tamil Nadu over the period 1980-97. At the same time, a comparison of the growth performance of this state with that of Andhra Pradesh, a neighbouring state is also presented.

The economic growth of any state is the outcome of a logical process. It is normally believed that industrialization is a driving force in the growth process. So the growth economists put more stress not only on more rapid industrialization but also on raising productivity. Thus they believe in shift in demand as well as shift in resources from agriculture to industry.[1]

Of course, there is an alternative view. It is also believed that the shifts in demand and the movement of resources from one sector to the other are relatively unimportant provided labour and capital produce equal marginal returns in all uses.[2] Therefore, economic growth can be estimated by the relative contributions of the growth of capital and labour (corrected by quality changes) on the one hand and the total factor productivity growth on the other. But studies relating to such type of analysis to estimate the growth performance of a state are lacking. Because of this limitation we are to rely on the time series analysis to estimate the growth performance of a state.

The period of our study, 1980-81 to 1996-97, consists of 17 years. To analyze the growth performance we have considered the trends in some of the important variables, which give us relating to the nature of economic growth of these two states. To obtain a measure of growth we postulated a hypothetical function for the trends of the output series. We estimated semi-logarithmic time trends of the important variables. Thus the trend equation, Y = ABt is put in logarithmic form,

$$\log Y = \log A + t \log B + Ut$$

where, Ut is the disturbance and this utilizing data for a specific period, the regression equation coefficient in each case yields an estimate of an annual compound growth rate.[3]

The findings are presented in the following way. First the case of Tamil Nadu is represented and then that of India and finally the results are compared with those of another state, the state of Andhra Pradesh.

I

TRENDS IN GROSS STATE DOMESTIC PRODUCT: TAMIL NADU

The trend in Gross State Domestic Product (GSDP) of Tamil Nadu is presented for the entire period 1980-81 to 1996-97. The data are given in Table 1. The exponential curve in semi-logarithmic form gives,

$$\log Y = \log A + t \log B + Ut$$

where log Y = GSDP of Tainil Nadu for the period 1980-81 to 1996-97. The estimated trend equation,

$$\log GSDP\ 5.87622 + 0.023868\ t \qquad (1)$$

$$[874.931] \quad [36.411]$$

$$r^2 = 0.98 \quad DF = 15 \quad DW = 1.85$$

TABLE I

Data Sheet for the State, Tamil Nadu
Economic Activity by Industry of Origin

AT 1980-81 PRICES

(Rupees lakh)

Year	*Agri-culture*	*Manu-facturing*	*Transport and Communica-tion*	*Electricity, gas and water supply*	*Hotel, Trade and Restaurants*	*SGDP*
1980-81	189432	220109	58404	15476	124745	808051
1981-82	237896	227352	62726	16890	138265	893130
1982-83	183852	242073	64558	18580	133348	855543
1983-84	221374	244933	66080	18767	137056	906893
1984-85	260810	283389	74100	20781	145420	1017765
1985-86	243205	283249	93891	27189	168731	1065572
1986-87	245175	275228	99653	23791	162390	1058834
1987-88	249078	279692	97223	30440	188563	1126496
1988-89	243143	331956	88405	39292	200425	1216419
1989-90	275830	20442	103277	40861	197652	1300657
1990-91	286913	48793	101208	43706	211188	1394836
1991-92	319690	322840	113048	38249	218498	1436326
1992-93	327157	346117	123942	45295	225086	1509313
1993-94	357833	378777	132176	48086	261739	1645887
1994-95	391892	412780	145678	51858	291464	1799571
1995-96	331379	423413	164111	55610	286671	1809732
1996-97	342389	448384	180167	59851	2990231	1919556

Source: National Accounts Statistics of India, 1950-51 to 1996-97, *Economic and Political Weekly*, Research Foundation, Mumbai, India, October 1998.

The coefficients are highly significant. The compound growth rate is 5.65% per annum. In order to ascertain whether there was any deceleration in the rate of growth we have fitted the equation,

$$\log Y = \log A + t \log B + t\ 2 \log C$$

to the same data. The estimated relationship is given below in Table 2.

TABLE 2

Data Sheet for All India
Economic Activity by Industry of Origin

AT 1980-81 PRICES

(Rupees lakh)

Year	*Agri-culture*	*Manu-facturing*	*Transport and Communica-tion*	*Electricity, gas and water supply*	*Hotel, Trade and Restaurants*	*SGDP*
1980-81	42466	21664	5724	2070	14713	122427
1981-82	45145	23382	6013	2264	15671	129889
1982-83	44570	24908	6280	2415	16546	133915
1983-84	49753	27277	6692	2588	17417	144865
1984-85	49702	29153	7302	2863	18173	150433
1985-86	49855	30320	7951	3099	19649	156566
1986-87	48995	32445	8483	3422	20852	163271
1987-88	49528	34818	9227	3692	21801	170322
1988-89	57940	37865	9804	4080	23385	188461
1989-90	58568	42285	10663	-4505	25231	201453
1990-91	60991	44863	11164	4797	26580	212253
1991-92	59398	43200	11785	5258	26827	213983
1992-93	63327	45005	12367	5700	28653	225240
1993-94	56762	48770	13065	6060	30923	239145
1994-95	69206	54570	14091	6632	34647	257700
1995-96	66863	62207	15264	7113	39968	276132
1996-97	72362	66785	16664	7466	43313	296845

Source: National Accounts Statistics of India, 1950-51 to 1996-97, *Economic and Political Weekly*, Research Fundation, Mumbai, India, October 1998.

$$\log GSDP_{tn} = 5.8796 + 0.0234673\, t + 0.0003334\, t \qquad (2)$$
$$[838.18] \quad [23.531] \qquad [0.54]$$
$$R^2 = 0.98 \quad DF = 14 \quad DW = 1.92$$

Here it is found that the estimated value of the coefficient C is positive indicating no deceleration in the rate of growth. And since the t-ratio is not at all statistically significant we refrain ourselves in making any comment regarding the nature of the rate of growth of the GSDP of

Tamil Nadu.

The rate of growth of GSDP of Tamil Nadu is now compared with that of another southern state, Andhra Pradesh for the same period. The data for the state are given in Table 3. The estimated relationships are given below:

$$\log GSDP_{an} = 5.90211 + 0.0195872\ t \qquad (3)$$
$$[610.981] \quad [20.771]$$
$$r^2 = 0.96 \ DF = 15 \ DW = 1.5$$

$$\log GSDP = 5.90173 + 0.019793\ t - 0.0000171\ t \qquad (4)$$
$$[579.881] \quad [13.671] \qquad [-0.191]$$
$$R^2 = 0.96 \ DF = 14 \ DW = 1.17$$

From the estimated equation (3) it is observed that the rate of growth of GSDP of Andhra Pradesh for the same period is less than that of Tamil Nadu. It is 4.61%. The coefficients are highly significant at 1% level of significance. Another interesting point which is revealed from this investigation is that there was the evidence of deceleration in the rate of growth of the GSDP of Andhra Pradesh, although the t-value of the coefficient of C in equation (4) is not statistically significant.

II

TRENDS IN GROSS DOMESTIC PRODUCT OF INDIA, 1980-81 TO 1996-97

In order to compare the growth rate of Tamil Nadu with that of India we adopted the same exercise to estimate the trend in Gross Domestic Product of India for the same period. The data are given in Table 2.

The estimated trend equation for the above period is—

$$\log GDP = 5.05931 + 0.0234639\ t \qquad (5)$$
$$[1057.961] \ [50.271]$$
$$r^2 = 0.99 \ DF = 15 \ DW = 1.05$$

TABLE 3

Data Sheet for the State, Andhra Pradesh
Economic Activity by Industry of Origin

AT 1980-81 PRICES

(Rupees lakh)

Year	*Agri-culture*	*Manu-facturing*	*Transport and Communica-tion*	*Electricity, gas and water supply*	*Hotel, Trade, and Restaurants*	*SGDP*
1980-81	331486	100376	49208	13853	110708	819149
1981-82	403577	109684	52366	16053	131155	935475
1982-83	400348	115075	54980	6284	130926	950184
1983-84	419640	119349	57388	19412	136684	993528
1984-85	383269	126467	61039	22387	128445	972385
1985-86	384377	137562	65156	21993	157997	1023239
1986-87	343009	140477	68416	23390	155370	994204
1987-88	389236	144994	71916	25957	165367	1085812
1988-89	465182	156017	74617	26085	188570	1240820
1989-90	476946	160521	78601	8502	193718	1285470
1990-91	463007	170544	80169	38588	193907	1316362
1991-92	472292	173060	88187	1634	198772	1357514
1992-93	467253	167745	93620	41334	198206	1359390
1993-94	519298	181298	98034	45230	244028	1485615
1994-95	499456	182168	103664	8648	313746	1596554
1995-96	541236	192047	111330	59083	335588	1692752
1996-97	572030	199701	119789	60483	352655	1779422

Source: National Accounts Statistics of India, 1950-51 to 1996-97, *Economic and Political Weekly*, Research Foundation, Mumbai India, October 1998.

The coefficients are highly significant at 1% level. The compound growth rate is 5.55% per annum. The value of Adjusted R^2 is highly satisfactory.

But the rate of growth of GSDP of Tamil Nadu is above that of the growth rate of All India. What is more significant is that the estimated second degree equation is—

$$\log GDP = 5.05807 + 0.0241274\, t - 0.0005379t2 \qquad (6)$$
$$[1060.921 \quad [35.361] \qquad [-1.30]$$

Adjusted R^2 = 0.98 DF = 14 DW = 1.18

shows the evidence of deceleration in the rate of growth and the t-value of the coefficient C is significant at 100% level of significance.

Thus the observations reveal two important facts: (i) The rate of growth of the state gross domestic product of Tamil Nadu exceeds the rate of growth of GDP of All India, and (ii) it does not show any evidence of deceleration in its rate of growth over the period under consideration.

III

The trends of some important variables, which comprise the GSDP of Tamil Nadu are discussed below. Indeed, the components give us the anatomy of the growth process. This we will do for the same period.

The following linear functional relationship is assumed:

$$Y_t = b_0 + b_1 \log Agr_t + b_2 \log Manu_t + b_3 \log Trans_t + b_4 \log Elec_t + b_5 \log Hotel_t + U_t \quad (7)$$

Here the b_i are the coefficients and U_t is the error term. Again here,

Y_t = log value of GSDP of Tamil Nadu at constant prices 1980-81 for the period 1980-81 to 1996-97;
Agr_t = log value of agricultural output at constant prices;
$Manu_t$ = log value of manufactures at constant prices;
$Trans_t$ = log value of transport, storage and communications at constant prices;
$Elec_t$ = log value of electricity, gas and water supply at constant prices; and
$Hotel_t$ = log value of trade, hotels and restaurants.

The data are given in Table 1. We expect that the estimated values of the coefficient b_i would be positive and statistically significant.

The result of the log-linear regression equation is reported below:

$$\log Y_t = \underset{[0.911]}{0.503897} + \underset{[1.831]}{0.157133} \log Agr_t + \underset{[1.351}{0.253161} \log Manu_t +$$
$$\underset{[0.861]}{0.0815056} \log Trans_t + \underset{[0.331]}{0.030159} \log Elec_t + \underset{[2.941]}{0.53009} \log Hotel_t \quad ...(8)$$

Adjusted $R^2 = 0.98$ DF = 11 DW = 1.58

The result shows that all the variables have not influenced the composition of the GSDP of Tamil Nadu significantly. This is evidenced from the t-value of the coefficients of the variables. Of the variables that we have taken up for consideration only the coefficient of the variable, $Hotel_t$, is significant at 1% level and it has the expected sign. This shows that tourism is taking an important role in the composition of the GSDP of Tamil Nadu. The coefficient of the variable namely Agr_t is significant at 5% level. It means that agriculture is still an important source in the composition of the GSDP. The contribution of manufacturing has not still become important in relation to agriculture. The coefficient of the variable is not significant at 5% level. It is significant only at 10% level. The contributions of electricity, gas and water supply and the contributions of transport and communication are not significant at all although the coefficients of these variables have the expected positive signs. Furthermore, the value of the adjusted R^2 of the equation is highly satisfactory. The only unsatisfactory feature is, however, the low D.W. Statistic.[4]

In Table 4 we have given in detail the results of the log-linear equations taking all the explanatory variables of GSDP of Tamil Nadu one after another. We regressed each variable with respect to the regressor time, t. The estimated value of the coefficient of the 1st degree equation gives us the growth rate of the dependent variable and the estimated value of the coefficient C in the 2nd degree equation gives us a measure of deceleration in the rate of growth of the dependent variable. By going through Table 4 a curious reader can easily estimate the long-term effect of these variables on the GSDP of Tamil Nadu.

TABLE 4

Log-linear Regression Equations : Dependent Variable Y_t
Name of the State: Tamil Nadu

Name of the variable	*Constant term*	*Value of the coefficient b*	*Value of the coefficient c*	*t-ratio of b*	*t-ratio of c*	*Adjusted R^2*	*DW Statistic*
log Agr_t	5.2817	0.01704		9.28		0.85	1.11
Do	5.2857	0.01489	0.00017	5.44	1.06	0.84	1.32
log $Manu_t$	5.32737	0.01825		18.15		0.95	1.99
Do	5.32598	0.019	-0.0006	12.39	-0.65	0.95	2.07
log $Trans_t$	4.73681	0.02853		17.2		0.95	1.03
Do	4.73318	0.03047	-0.0016	12.33	-1.05	0.94	1.17
log $Elec_t$	4.16226	0.03795		18.23		0.95	1.44
Do	4.16315	0.03747	0.00039	11.64	0.19	0.95	1.45
log $Hotel_t$	5.06112	0.02461		24.28		0.97	1.83
Do	5.06242	0.02391	0.00057	15.43	0.6	0.97	1.88

1st degree equation: $\log Y_t = a + b_t$.
2nd degree equation: $\log Y_t = a + b_t + c_t^2$.

CONCLUDING OBSERVATIONS

The preceding sections have presented and discussed the various regression equations which have been estimated in the present study to explain the nature of the different industrial activities, namely, agriculture, manufacturing, transport, electricity, restaurants, trade and hotels. The regression equation which is given in equation (8) is satisfactory although the coefficients of the variables, $Trans_t$ and $Elec_t$, have not been turned out to be statistically significant. The regression equation has a high value of R^2 and the estimated values of the three regressors are statistically significant at various levels of significance. Thus over period under study the growth performance of Tamil Nadu could be satisfactorily explained in terms of the three variables, namely, agriculture, manufacturing and trade hotels and restaurants. This pattern of development quite suits with the development pattern of the Union of India where the share of agricultural sector is still high and the share of the service sector is overpowering the contributions of the agriculture and that of the manufacturing sectors. This study also highlights the ample scope of development of the sectors like electricity, gas and water supply and the transport and communication, which comprise the building of a healthy infrastructure of any state.

Notes and References

1. H.B. Chenery (1986), Growth and Transformation Log Issues in Economic Development, p. 95.
2. *Op. cit.*, p. 95.
3. Let $Y= AB_t$, where $[B = (1 + r/100)]$ and $r = (B-1).100$. Then r is the compound growth rate of Y.
4. The DW statistic for $K'= 5$, the number of explanatory variables, $d_L = 0.67$ and 2.10.

References

Bhambhiri C.P., *The Indian States after Independence.*

Chakraborty Sukhomoy (1993), *Selected Economic Writings.*

Chakraborty Sukhomoy (1998), *Writings on Economic Development.*

Chenery, H.B. (1986), Growth and Transformation, Reprinted in Mier's *Leading Issues in Economic Development.*

De Biman Chandra (1998), *Import Substituting Industrialisation: Iron and Steel Industry in India*, an unpublished thesis, the University of Burdwan, Burdwan, West Bengal.

Koutsoyannis, A. (1977), *Theory of Econometrics*, Macmillan.

Maddala, G.S. (1989), *Introduction to Econometrics*, Macmillan.

Nath, Pradip (1986), India's Imports during the Last Three Decades: An Econometric Study, Sankhya, *The Indian Journal of Statistics*, Calcutta.

Sinha, B.K., *The Indian Economy, 21st Century.*

National Accounts Statistics of India, 1950-51 to 1996-97, *Economic and Political Weekly*, Research Foundation, Mumbai (India), October 1998.

10

CHAPTER

The Economy of Tamil Nadu: Marching Ahead

RAM NARESH THAKUR

Tamil Nadu is one of the Southern States of India. The others are Andhra Pradesh, Karnataka and Kerala. This State is in the extreme sourth-east in part of India. It is situate in 1,30,058 Square Kilometers Land. Its population is 62,110,839, consisting of 3,12,68,654 males and 3,08,42,185 females according to the 2001 census. The percentage increase of its population remained 15.39 in 1981-91 and 11.19 in 1991-2001. The density of population is 478 persons per square kilometers in 2001, increasing from 429 in 1991. The male-female ration is 986 (in 2001 census) increasing from 974 in 1991, 933 (in 2001) and 927 (in 1991) of all India figure. The literacy level is 73.47 p.c., consisting of 82.33 per cent males and 64.55 per cent females (out of 65.38 per cent) consisting of 75.85 per cent males and 54.16 per cent females at all India level.

TAMIL NADU AND INTER-STATES INEQUALITY

The economic and social inequality among the State has remained the grestest challenge in India. But it goes in favour of Tamil Nadu. Tamil Nadu is one of those 15 states in India where the total population is 96 per cent of the country. The remaining 10 small states and 7 union territories cover 4 per cent of population. Within 15 such states there are two groups of States—(a) advanced group (marching ahead)—and (b) backward group. The economy of Tamil Nadu leads the advanced group of states alongwith other 7 states, i.e., Andhra Pradesh, Kerala, Maharashtra, Punjab, Gujarat, Haryana and Karnataka. Whereas the backward group of states covers the Uttar Pradesh and West Bengal (7 states before reorganisation of Chhatisgarh, Uttranchal and Jharkhand). The 42 per cent population of India resides in the advanced group of states (including Tamil Nadu), whereas 54 per cent population resides in the backward group of states. The backward states are facing different demographic and economic crisis. The condition of the advanced group of states (including Tamil Nadu) is better than that of the backward group of states and other states in respect of mines, assets, water resources, quality of soils, industries and trade, etc.

According to the demographic expectation the rate of growth of population during 2006 to 2016 will be 2.3 per cent annual in U.P. 18 per cent annual in Rajasthan, 1.75 per cent in Bihar and 1.73 per cent in Madhya Pradesh. On the other hand, this annual rate of growth will be less than 1 per cent in Tamil Nadu along with Kerala, Andhra Pradesh and Maharastra during that period. The position of total population strength is sixth in India, whereas the position of male population is seventh and that of female population is sixth. But it is a favourable symptom that the position of percentage growth of population in the last decade (1991-2001) has remained 33rd (i.e., 2nd from below and only more than Kerala). This rate is 11.19 of Tamil Nadu and 9.42 of Kerala, whereas it is 64.41 of Nagaland, 59.20 of Dadar and Nagar Haveli and 55.59 of Daman and Deo. In the enumeration of male-female ratio the position of Tamil Nadu is 4th in the country (986) which is the symbol of women's empowerment in the state. The position of total, male and female literacy is 13th in the country (including Union territories). The position of density of population (persons per square kilometer) is 11th in the country (478).

When we observe the literacy rate data, the position of

TABLE I

Position of Male-Female Ratio and Literacy Rate

States/UT	*Male-Female ratio*	*Male literacy*	*Female literacy*	*Total literacy*
Andhra Pradesh	978	70.85	51.17	61.11
Arunachal Pradesh	901	64.07	44.24	54.74
Assam	932	71.93	56.03	64.28
Bihar	921	60.32	33.57	47.53
Chhatisgarh	990	77.86	52.40	65.18
Goa	960	88.88	75.51	82.32
Gujarat	921	80.50	58.60	69.97
Haryana	861	79.25	56.31	68.59
Himachal Pradesh	970	86.02	68.08	77.13
Jammu & Kashmir	900	65.75	41.82	54.46
Jharkhand	941	67.94	39.38	54.13
Karnataka	964	76.29	57.45	67.04
Kerala	1058	94.20	87.86	90.92
Madhya Pradesh	920	76.80	50.28	64.11
Maharashtra	922	86.27	67.51	77.27
Manipur	978	77.87	59.70	68.87
Meghalaya	975	66.14	60.41	63.31
Mizoram	938	90.69	86.13	88.49
Nagaland	909	71.77	61.92	67.11
Orissa	972	75.95	50.97	63.61
Punjab	874	75.63	63.55	69.95
Rajasthan	922	76.40	44.34	61.03
Sikkim	875	76.73	61.46	69.68
Tamil Nadu	986 (IV)	82.33 (XIII)	64.55 (XIII)	73.47 (XIII)
Tripura	950	81.47	64.51	73.66
Uttar Pradesh	898	70.23	42.98	56.36
Uttranchal	964	84.01	60.26	72.28
West Bengal	934	77.58	60.22	69.22
Andman Nicobar Island Group	846	86.07	75.29	81.18
Chandigarh	773	85.65	76.65	81.76
Daman, Deo	709	88.40	70.37	81.09
Dadar and Nagar Haveli	811	73.32	42.99	60.03
Delhi	821	87.37	75.00	81.82
Lakshdwip	947	93.15	81.56	87.52
Pondicherry	1001	88.89	74.13	81.49
All India	933	75.85	54.16	65.38

Tamil Nadu is good. Although its position is 13th in the country, if we exclude the data of Union Territories (7 small regions), Tamil Nadu stands at the 7th position in total, male and female literacy rates among all the states in the country. This is a very good indicator of human development index as well as of women's empowerment index. The male-female ratio also stand at the 4th position in the country (other three states are Kerala, Pondicherry and Chhatisgarh) which reflects the women's empowerment status of the State.

ENROLMENT OF CHILDREN AND DROPOUT

If we take the enrolment of children in the Class-I as a base year we may estimate the 'position of enrolments' in other classes as well as 'dropout' properly. In Tamil Nadu 88.53 per cent children are enrolled in Class-II in respect of Class-I. In this way only 67.79 per cent children are enrolled in Class-V and only 40.79 per cent. Children are enrolled in Class-VIII according to the estimate of the current previous year. Thus the figure of dropout in the enrolment of Class-VIII is 59.31 per cent in respect of being enrolled in Class-I basically, which is alarming for the academic health and economic base of the State.

In 1997-98, the States of Assam, Gujarat, Karnataka, M.P., Maharashtra and Tamil Nadu have crossed 100 per cent enrolment. In Tamil Nadu the enrolment ratio was as high as 94.13 per cent in 1970-71, which touched the rate of 108.5 per cent in 1998-99. This is a great achievement for Tamil Nadu. Tamil Nadu should have by now reached almost cent per cent literacy particularly in the targeted age group of 15-35 years. But in Tamil Nadu alone as many as 89.71 lakh illiterate persons are there in this age group.

If we see and compare the gross enrolment ratio (per cent) in Classes I-V students in 1997-98, it become evident that the gross enrolment rate is higher in Tamil Nadu. Tamil Nadu stands at 3rd position in respect of girls' as well as total enroment and at 4th position of boys' enrolment. It proves the implementation of scheme in the field of 'Education to All' under the spirit of the Directive Principle of State Policy of the Constitution of India.

TABLE 2(A)

Enrolment of Children in Classes II, V and VIII as Percentage of Enrolment in Class-I

States/UT	*Class I*	*Class II*	*Class V*	*Class VIII*
All India	100	73.41	49.28	31.11
Andhra Pradesh	100	64.03	38.02	15.88
Bihar	100	59.50	34.47	19.82
Gujarat	100	73.04	50.61	30.03
Haryana	100	91.74	68.52	53.12
Karnataka	100	77.99	47.50	28.74
Kerala	100	106.10	98.84	81.31
M.P.	100	89.97	64.14	36.70
Maharashtra	100	77.32	54.67	34.67
Orissa	100	80.15	47.10	27.92
Punjab	100	102.31	65.15	48.82
Rajasthan	100	47.61	27.55	18.50
Tamil Nadu	100	88.53	67.79	40.79
U.P.	100	90.44	58.57	47.31
W. Bengal	100	56.34	38.15	21.90

Source: 5th All India Education Survey, National Education Council, New Delhi.
Kurushetra (Hindi), September, 2001.

Although Tamil Nadu is not considered among a academically backward states of India., i.e., Assam, Andhra Pradesh, Bihar, Jammu and Kashmir, M.P., Orissa, U.P., Rajasthan and West Bengal (having slum areas and scheduled tribes population—before reorganization of States), the position of children enrolment is poor and the position of dropout is severe.

In Tamil Nadu the number of schools is enough as opposed to other states. The number of Primary Schools is 30,098 and that of middle schools is 5,608.

ACTUAL ENROLMENT IN SCHOOLS

In 1992-93, the position of enrolment in primary schools was 79,36,000, whereas in middle schools it was 34,09,000 and the rate of dropout upto colleges was 45.42 per cent. On the whole, after analysing the percentage of literacy rates,

TABLE 2(B)

Gross Enrolment Ratio in Classes I-V, 1997-98

States/UT	*Boys*	*Girls*	*Total*
Andhra Pradesh	92.3	86.7	89.5
Bihar	90.9	59.4	75.9
Gujarat	117.4	113.5	115.7
Karnataka	107.2	101.9	104.6
Kerala	91.3	88.7	90.0
M.P.	114.5	89.4	102.3
Tamil Nadu	109.6 IV	107.3 III	108.5 III
Maharashtra	115.7	109.9	112.9
U.P.	74.1	48.9	62.3
W. Bengal	98.5	85.6	92.2
All India	97.7	81.2	89.7

Source: *Economic Survey*, 1998-99, Government of India, *Yojana* (Eng.) (2001), November, p. 15.

combined enrolment and educational attainment index, the rank of Tamil Nadu is 2nd (only after Kerala). It is visible by the Table 4.

DEVELOPMENT OF TAMIL NADU

South-West *versus* North-West: the mirror of paradigm of south-west *versus* north-east. The position of south-west stages (i.e, Andhra Pradesh, Karnataka, Tamil Nadu, Maharashtra, Gujarat, etc.) is comparatively far better than that of north-east states (i.e., West Bengal, Delhi, Bihar, Assam, Haryana, Punjab, Rajasthan, U.P.) in the context of increase of investment, industrialisation and development as well as the decrease of crime and corruption etc. on the whole. A business survey was made in January, 2000 consisting of opinions of 107 companies. In the report it was revealed that in the near future (5 years) all these big companies would make investment only in five states of south-east on the basis of priority. Out of all, 32 per cent of the companies decided to invest in Tamil Nadu, and 10 per cent companies desired to invest in U.P. and only 4 per cent were in favour of investing in Bihar. 32 to 54 per cent

TABLE 3

Number of Schools in Important States

States	Primary Schools	Middle Schools
Bihar (Joint)	53,292	13,495
Andhra Pradesh	50,201	6,330
Assam	28,876	5,703
Gujarat	14,448	17,781
Kerala	6,776	2,931
Punjab	12,464	1,436
Tamil Nadu	30,098	5,608
U.P. (Joint)	78,804	15,463
West Bengal	50,827	4,179

TABLE 4

States	Literacy %age		Combined enrolment percent	Educational Attainment Index	Rank
	1991	2001			
Kerala	89.8	90.92	38.8	0.728	1
Tamil Nadu	92.7	73.47	47.6	0.576	2
Punjab	58.5	69.95	34.6	0.505	5
U.P.	41.6	56.36	26.1	0.364	14
Bihar	38.5	47.53	27.9	0.350	15

companies expressed their willingness to invest in the western and southern states only (including Tamil Nadu).

If we see the graph of total investment in the Stage of India, Tamil Nadu stands ahead along with four other south-west states. In the year 1998-99, more than 50 per cent share (actual 51.63 per cent) of the total investment remained concentrated in the only 5 states situated at the south-west (including Tamil Nadu). The position of only one state of Hindi belt (or north-east states) Madhya Pradesh remained better than the southern states (Andhra Pradesh, Karnataka, and Tamil Nadu). The share of the above six states in the investment was 60.90 per cent. The worst situation remained with the seven north-eastern states whose gross investment remained less than even that of Himachal Pradesh. The figure

TABLE 5

Sl. No.	States	Companies' decision in favour of investment (%age)
1.	Maharashtra	54
2.	Andhra Pradesh	47
3.	Gujarat	44
4.	Karnataka	36
5.	Tamil Nadu	32
6.	West Bengal	15
7.	M.P.	14
8.	Delhi	10
9.	U.P.	10
10.	Haryana	09
11.	Rajasthan	9
12.	Goa	8
13.	Orissa	8
14.	Punjab	8
15.	Pondicherry	8
16.	Himachal Pradesh	6
17.	Kerala	6
18.	Bihar	4
19.	Arunachal Pradesh	2
20.	Assam	2

Source: *Business Today*.

depicts the higher position of Tamil Nadu in investment. In Tamil Nadu 7.48 per cent (sixth position in Tamil Nadu) investment took place (Table 6).

The study made recently on the financial and development situation of the states of India reveals the fact that the position of the south-western states (including Tamil Nadu) is prosperous, where the position of north-eastern states is worse comparatively. Overall the economic condition of Tamil Nadu alongwith Maharashtra, Gujarat, Karnataka and Andhra Pradesh is better. The north-eastern states are in more backward position and inferior to them in all respects. The northern states are in the worst condition.

TABLE 6

Capital-Investment Concentrated in only 5 States (South-West States) in 1998-99

Sl. No.	*States*	*%age of Capital Investment*
1.	Maharashtra	16.77
2.	Gujarat	11.15
3.	M.P.	09.27
4.	Andhra Pradesh	8.37
5.	Karnataka	7.86
6.	Tamil Nadu	7.48
7.	U.P.	6.64
8.	Orissa	4.46
9.	West Bengal	4.27
10	Rajasthan	3.18
11.	Bihar	2.73
12.	Himachal Pradesh	2.38
13.	Assam	1.66
14.	Punjab	1.59
15.	Kerala	1.44
16.	J & K	1.29
17.	Haryana	1.15
18.	Delhi	1.06
19.	Arunachal Pradesh	0.31
20.	Mizoram	0.27

Due to such conditions, there may be emergence of great inequality between the south-west and north-eastern states. The result of such inequality may be very dangerous. As the foreign capital and consumer culture had divided the nation into two parts, this inequality may divide the nation in the same way. This analysis was made by the study of 'National Council of Applied Research' in the guidelines of CII. When we see and compare, the growth rate of the economy of Tamil Nadu alongwith other south-western states it is more than that of north-eastern states. In Tamil Nadu (alongwith south-western states) proper attention was paid to industrialisation alongwith agriculture and the services sector.

Industries

The major industries in Tamil Nadu are cotton, woolen and silk textiles, chemical, chemical fertilizers, paper, printing and allied enterprise, leather works, diesel engines, automobile, cycle, cement, sugar, iron and steel industries, electric equipment, rubber tyres and tubes, bricks and tiles, etc.

Industrial Cities

The main industrial cities (belt) consist of Chennai, Coimbatore, Madurai and Kanchipuram, etc. In Tamil Nadu, the range of tax structure is also widened and development takes place through the channels of 'Panchayat Raj'. In Tamil Nadu Panchayati Raj is very strong and running smoothly. So the rate of economic development is also fast and the effect crimes, corruption and mafias are minimized. The other states of strong Panchayati Raj roots are West Bengal, Kerala, Gujarat and Andhra Pradesh, etc.

PER CAPITA GROSS DOMESTIC PRODUCT

In the comparative figures of the percentage increase of per capita gross domestic product (GDP in the decades 80 and 90 respectively), the picture of Tamil Nadu is bright. It is 3.9 per cent in the decade 1980 and 4.5 per cent in the decade 1990 (4th position). To the contrary, the picture of north-eastern states including Bihar and U.P. etc. is gloomy, very poor and pitiable. It remained at 2.5 per cent and 1.1 per cent in Bihar and 2.6 per cent and 1.2 per cent in U.P during the same period. The tendency is that the rate of GDP is decreasing in north-eastern states in the stipulated period, whereas that is increasing in Tamil Nadu and other south-western states. The maximum increases was recorded by Gujarat (7.6 per cent) and Maharashtra (6.1 per cent). If this tendency of fall and rise continues in the next 5 year the per capita GDP of Bihar and U.P. will be zero, whereas Tamil Nadu alongwith its allied states (south-west) will established higher record (Table 7).

In 1990-91 the net domestic product of Tamil Nadu was Rs. 7,646 crores which increased to Rs. 77,302 crores in 1997-98 and its per capita income was Rs. 4,978 in 1990-91 which increased to Rs. 12,989.

TABLE 7

Average Increase in the Per Capita Gross Domestic Product (GDP)

(in percentage)

Zone	*Sl. No.*	*States*	*In the decade 1980*	*In the decade 1990*
West	1.	Gujarat	3.1	7.6
West	2.	Maharashtra	3.6	6.1
South	3.	Andhra Pradesh	3.3	3.7
South	4.	Tamil Nadu	3.9	4.5
South	5.	Kerala	2.2	4.5
South	6.	Karnataka	3.3	3.5
East	7.	Bihar	2.5	1.1
East	8.	Orissa	2.4	1.6
East	9.	W. Bengal	2.4	5.0
North	10.	Punjab	3.3	2.8
North	11.	Haryana	3.9	2.7
North	12.	U.P.	2.6	1.2
North	13.	Rajasthan	4.0	3.5
North	14.	Himachal Pradesh	3.1	3.0
North	15.	Delhi	3.1	4.0

Capital-Investment

In the comparision of capital investment the position of Tamil Nadu alongwith south-west allied states is far ahead of north-eastern states. In 1998-99, in Tamil Nadu there was a total investment of Rs. 1,38,814 crore. The distribution of this investment is such as government investment 55.1 per cent, foreign investment 14.9 per cent, domestic/private investment 29.9 per cent. The percentage of investment in different sectors is divided as follows: irrigation 0.2 per cent, electricity 49.3 per cent, construction 28.1 per cent, mines 8 per cent and service 14.4 per cent. The highest total investments are covered by Maharashtra and Gujarat. The position of Tamil Nadu is only third from above (Table 8).

TABLE 8

Capital Investment in the States (1998-99)

States	Gross Investment (Rs. in Crore)	% of Investment			% of Investment in different services				
		Govt.	Foreign	Domestic	Irrigation	Electricity	Construction	Mines	Services
Maharashtra	146809	54.9	23.1	21.9	19.7	26.1	22.4	1.4	30.5
Gujarat	144373	47.3	3.6	49.0	10.4	27.0	32.8	1.9	28.0
Tamil Nadu	138814	55.1	14.9	29.9	0.2	49.3	28.1	8.0	14.4
Orissa	98796	35.2	38.7	26.1	3.7	39.4	22.4	25.5	9.0
Andhra Pradesh	96492	48.7	21.2	30.1	17.4	35.2	13.8	4.8	28.8
Karnataka	95646	30.3	27.0	42.7	11.9	44.3	26.1	1.5	16.2
U.P.	72943	49.3	9.9	40.8	8.0	45.0	33.9	0.5	12.5
M.P.	65247	42.2	13.1	44.7	16.6	51.8	16.4	9.2	6.0
W. Bengal	60868	39.4	21.7	38.9	00	41.6	27.4	4.4	24.9
Kerala	47508	62.8	10.5	26.7	2.6	51.8	27.1	00	18.5
Bihar	42574	92.7	00	7.3	8.5	68.8	9.1	4.2	9.4
Rajasthan	37601	46.2	01	52.8	12.8	70.0	10.9	00	6.3
H.P.	29795	72.9	6.6	20.5	0.4	96.8	2.6	00	0.1
Punjab	25071	37	6.1	56.9	3.6	37.2	52.2	00	7.0
Haryana	17934	80.5	8.2	15.3	0.9	36.1	57.1	00	5.8
Delhi	14164	55.1	18.6	26.3	00	42.5	0.2	00	57.4
J&K	11767	98.9	00	1.1	1.8	70.6	0.3	00	27.3
Assam	11440	59.3	00	40.7	5.8	14.0	56.6	00	23.6
Goa	9108	76.7	2.9	20.5	2.6	0.1	14.6	00	82.7
Arunachal Pradesh	4376	94.7	00	5.3	0.8	97.7	00	00	1.1

INDUSTRIAL-INVESTMENT PROPOSALS IN THE PERIOD OF ECONOMIC AND LIBERALISATION

The worst factor of the pattern of industrial development in the last 10 years has remained constant that it has widened the different (inequality) between developed and backward states. Although there may be many caused responsible for it. The cases may be of either domestic direct investment (DDI), or foreign direct investment (FDI), the former industrially developed states had become success in obtaining the greater shares of domestic as well as foreign investment (Tables 9 and 10).

Domestic Investment

Out of total 41,158 memorandum-proposals offered by industrial entrepreneurs in total investment of Rs. 3,54,708 crores 6.38 per cent investment (Rs. 54,564 crore) went to Tamil Nadu, which is the VIth position among all states, although the number of proposals was IVth in the rank. 23.16 per cent investment (Rs. 1,97,909 crore) went in the share of the most industrially developed states. Maharastra, remaining on the first position. In Tamil Nadu, out of the aforesaid investment the number of employment creation took place of 5,75,391 which becomes 8.26 per cent of employment opportunities provided throughout the country in the stipulated period (1990-2000), that is the fourth position among all states. In respect of investment and employment creating Maharashtra remained in the first position, Gujarat in the second, U.P. (having maximum population) in the third position, M.P. in the fourth and Andhra Pradesh in the fifth position. Besides providing all facilities, the memorandum-investment of the seven states of north-eastern region remained less than one per cent of total memorandum-investment. In Bihar the proposed investment remained only 1.56 per cent, Orissa 2.36 per cent and in Jammu and Kashmir it remained 0.07 per cent (Table 9).

Foreign Investment

As far the question of foreign direct investment (F.D.I.) is concerned, in the previous ten years of the era of globalisation, liberalisation and economic reform, the total foreign direct investment (F.D.I.) took place of Rs. 2,46,768.56 crores. Out of this amount Rs. 18,940.90 crores went in the share of Tamil Nadu, which is 7.68 percent of the total amount. Due to this, Tamil Nadu stands at the fourth position among all the states of nation in obtaining foreign direct investment (F.D.I.). The most industrially developed state Maharashtra stands at the first position by obtaining Rs. 41,750.14 crore (16.92 percent), Delhi stands at the second place by obtaining Rs. 32,234.57 crores (13.07 percent) and always remaining ahead in the race of development. Karnataka got the third rank by obtaining Rs. 19,921.37 crores (8.08 percent). In this way Andhra Pradesh achieved fifth position and Gujarat got sixth postion in obtaining foreign direct investment (F.D.I.). The industrially backward states U.P. and Bihar could get the shares of 1.63 percent and 0.29 percent (almost zero percent) respectively of foreign direct investment (F.D.I.). At the same time the richest state, in context of underground mineral resources, Jharkhand could get only 0.06 percent of F.D.I. The condition of the north-eastern states is worse. In those states not even Rs.100 crores F.D.I. could be approved during the previous ten years of liberalisation period (Table 10).

The main causes of higher percentage of D.D.I. and F.D.I. in Tamil Nadu are strong infrastructural facilities, satisfactory supply of electricity, proper rail facilities, better condition of roads, strong banking system, lack of red tapism and nepotism, minimized crimes and corruption, elastic labour laws, strong and proper law and order, etc.

Financial Assistance

The total assistance by the all-India financial institutions to Tamil Nadu in the different years of the decade 90 is thus— in 1995-96 Rs. 6,628 crores, in 1996-97 Rs. 4,760 crores, in 1997-98 Rs. 7,371 crores. The cumulative amount upto end-march, 1998, was Rs. 38,538 crores (Data relates to L.I.C. & U.T.I. only). Tamil Nadu obtained assistance from state financial corporations in this form, e.g., Rs. 388.9 crores loans was sanctioned during 1994-95, Rs. 632.7 crores during 1997-98. The total amount of loans sanctioned upto 1997-98 was Rs. 3,526.5 crores.

TABLE 9

Sl. No.	States/U.T.	Proposals Number	Proposals % of Total	Proposed Investment	Proposed % of Total	Employment Creation Number	Employment Creation % of Total	
1.	Maharashtra	8338	20.26	197909	23.16	1471949	21.13	I
2.	Gujarat	5464	13.28	146458	17.14	889627	12.77	II
3.	U.P.	3966	9.64	68740	8.04	632586	9.08	III
4.	Tamilnadu	3632	8.82	54564	6.38	575351	8.26	IV
5.	Andhra Pradesh	2644	5.42	59045	6.91	432225	6.21	
6.	Haryana	2511	6.01	27681	3.24	375756	5.39	
7.	M.P.	2286	5.55	63849	7.47	473144	6.79	
8.	Rajasthan	2113	5.13	35173	4.12	395393	5.68	
9.	Punjab	1969	4.78	39679	4.32	465700	6.69	
10.	W. Bengal	1816	4.41	30094	3.52	299029	4.29	
11.	Karnataka	1515	3.68	39679	4.64	248836	3.57	
12.	Dadar & Nagar Haveli	1256	3.05	17436	2.04	141253	2.03	
13.	Daman and Deu	586	1.42	3726	0.44	45221	0.65	
14.	Bihar	442	1.07	13350	1.56	70628	1.01	
15.	Kerala	426	1.04	7462	0.87	67475	0.97	
16.	Delhi	460	1.12	6450	0.75	46711	0.67	
17.	Pondicherry	424	1.03	5905	0.69	40326	0.58	
18.	Himachal Pradesh	380	0.93	8460	0.99	86366	1.24	

Expenditure Pattern

The composition of the state government's is marked by the gradual increase in capital expenditures to the total expenditures, although in many north-eastern states capital-expenditure marked its sharp decline to total expenditure. During the period from 1991 to 1997 capital is increasing. It was Rs. 1,50,000.00 crores during the stipulated period, although it was Rs. 1,40,000 crores for Maharashtra, Rs. 1,20,000 crores for Gujarat and Rs. 1,05,000 crores for Andhra Pradesh and it remained only less than Rs. 100 crores in the share of Bihar (Table 11). Tables 8, 9 and 10 are also visible in this context.

In the same way the performance of Tamil Nadu in mobilizing resources of matching contribution for "centrally sponsored schemes" has been quite encouraging. For example, during 1992-93 to 1995-96 capital investment for agricultural

TABLE 10

Foreign Co-operation and Foreign Direct Investment (F.D.I.) (Approved Proposals from August, 1991 to December, 2000)

Sl. No.	States/U.T.	Number of approved proposals		Approved Investment	
		Total	% of Total	Rs. in Crore	% of Total
1.	Maharashtra	3,043	16.36	41.750.14	16.92 I
2.	Tamil Nadu	1,724	09.27	18,940.90	7.68 IV
3.	Karnataka	1,485	07.99	19,921.37	8.08 III
4.	Delhi	1,376	07.40	32,234.57	13.07 II
5.	Gujarat	932	05.01	11,179.43	4.53 IV
6.	Andhra Pradesh	826	04.44	12,101.09	4.91 V
7.	Haryana	697	3.75	29,91.45	1.21
8.	U.P.	662	3.56	4,016.20	1.63
9.	W. Bengal	523	2.81	8,389.00	3.40
10.	Rajasthan	298	1.60	2,591.09	1.05
11.	M.P.	210	1.13	9,140.10	3.71
12.	Kerala	203	1.09	1,292.26	0.52
13.	Punjab	171	0.92	1,951.92	0.79
14.	Goa	143	0.77	530.46	0.22
15.	Orissa	131	0.70	7,986.79	3.24
16.	Pondicherry	94	0.51	394.85	0.16
17.	Himachal Pradesh	90	0.48	361.66	0.15
18.	Jharkhand	70	0.38	143.82	0.06
19.	Dadar and Nagar Haveli	69	0.37	123.95	0.05
20.	Uttranchal	46	0.25	125.65	0.05
21.	Bihar	44	0.24	707.86	0.29
22.	Chandigarh	42	0.23	616.69	0.25
23.	Daman & Deu	38	0.20	45.59	0.02
24.	Chandigarh	34	0.18	143.08	0.06
25.	Assam	17	0.09	1.50	0.00
26.	Andaman & Nicobar	01	0.04	13.79	0.01
27.	J. & K.	05	0.03	8.41	0.00
28.	Meghalaya	04	0.02	52.96	0.02
29.	Arunachal Pradesh	02	0.02	11.06	0.00
30.	Nagaland	02	0.02	3.68	0.00
31.	Others	5609	30.37	68931.24	27.96
	Grand Total	18598	100.00	246768.56	100.00

growth sector under the Centrally Sponsored Schemes was at Rs. 19,653.47 crores (7.62 percent). It is a very good figure at all-India record (Table 12).

During 2000-2001, the Finance Department of the Government of India sactioned loans from the amount collected under net small savings. The share of Tamil Nadu was Rs. 1,287 crores. To W. Bengal it was Rs. 4,949 crores, to Maharashtra it was Rs. 4,660 crores, to Punjab Rs. 2,330 crores, to Rajasthan Rs. 2,204 crores, to Andhra Pradesh it was Rs. 1,787 crores, to Bihar Rs. 1,605 crores, to Karnataka it was Rs. 1,180 crores, to M.P. it was Rs. 992 crores and in other states it was Rs. 3,442 crores.

TABLE 11

Capital-Investment for Industrial Development

Sl. No.	*States*	*Capital-Investment for Industrial growth (during 1991-97) (Rs. in Crores)*	*Rank*
1.	Tamil Nadu	1,50,000	I
2.	Maharashtra	1,40,000	II
3.	Gujarat	1,20,000	III
4.	Andhra Pradesh	1,05,000	IV
5.	Bihar	100 (Not upto the range of Rs. 100 crores even)	

FINANCIAL ALLOCATION FOR GUARANTEED EMPLOYMENT SCHEMES IN 2001-2002

Out of total Rs. 1,29,850.00 lakh over all-India expenditure (Central assistance) for 28 districts of Tamil Nadu a total of Rs. 6,101.26 lakh was allotted. Out of this amount as an incentive to the Panchayati Raj institutions twenty percent central allocation was made i.e., Rs. 1,220.25 lakh and rest issued under general procedure was Rs. 4,881.01 lakh. In addition to this the financial assistance allotted by the state was Rs. 2,033.75 lakh. Altogether the grand total of

TABLE 12

Capital-Investment for Agriculture Development

Sl. No.	States	Capital-Investment for agricultural growth (Expenditure from 1992-93 to 1995-96) (In Rs. Crores)	Percentage	Rank
1.	Andhra Pradesh	22,032.36	8.54	
2.	Assam	1,910.08	0.74	
3.	Bihar	3,331.93	1.29	
4.	Gujarat	12,099.37	4.69	
5.	Haryana	9,110.97	3.53	
6.	Karnataka	22,063	8.55	
7.	Kerala	12,873.55	4.99	
8.	M.P.	23,163.61	8.98	
9.	Maharashtra	39,486.00	11.82	
10.	Orissa	13,340.10	5.17	
11.	Punjab	10,557.94	4.11	
12.	Rajasthan	25,115.69	9.73	
13.	Tamil Nadu	19,653.47	7.62	VII
14.	U.P.	31,294.85	12.13	
15.	W. Bengal	5,720.89	2.22	
16.	Others	15,206.82	5.89	
	Total	2,58,000.00	100.00	

State-wise Expenditure on Central/Centrally Sponsored Schemes of The Deptt. of Agriculture and Co-operation, Govt. of India.

Small Saving Loans sactioned to the State during 2000-2001.

Rs. 8,135.01 lakh was allotted to the state for this purpose. Total Rs. 8,135.01 lakh remained in the share of Tamil Nadu out of Rs. 1,73,092.15 lakh over all-India basis (total spread over 570 districts).

The various "institutional sources of resource transfer" in terms of loans, assistance, aids, etc. to Tamil Nadu had also been adequate.

Banking System and Facilities

The banking system and facilities of the state are very

strong and enough in comparison with other states. The per capita bank deposit was Rs. 6,468 in March, 1998 (increasing from Rs. 4,326 in March, 1995 and Rs. 5,420 in March, 1997 respectively) in the share of Tamil Nadu. The per capita credit was Rs. 6,215 in March, 1998 (increasing from Rs. 3,944 in March, 1995 and Rs. 5,420 in March, 1997 respectively). The per capita credit-deposit ratio (C.D. Ratio) was 96.1 percent in March, 1998 (increasing from 91.2 percent in March, 1995). The C.D. ratio recorded a minor fall in March, 1998 from March, 1997, because in March, 1997 it was at its peak point 100.4 percent. After all, C.D. ratio of Tamil Nadu is at the peak of all-India record (in March, 1998 too). It is a sign of the gradual and continuous progress of the economy of Tamil Nadu in the near future (or incoming 10 years) certainly. The economy of Tamil Nadu will be developed by leaps and bounds and one day it may lead the nation's growth if this tendency persists further (Table 13).

Although Maharashtra has been on the top position in the comparison of per capita deposit as well as per capita credit in different years, but in the C.D. ratio Tamil Nadu stands on the top in different years. It reveals the fact that the economy is marching ahead of the path of development continuously.

Poverty

The population of Tamil Nadu is 6,21,10,839 (2001 census), in 1991 its population was 5.88 crore, but the number of poor persons in the country was 5.88 crore (35.03 percent) in 1993-94 (15th position), and it became 130.48 lakh (21.12 percent) in 1999-2000 (15th position). In the last decade a survey was made by the government of India at all India basis in which the 100 poorest districts were deducted, but fortunately enough in that report not one district was selected from Tamil Nadu. The poverty alleviation programmes also are in progress in this state. The position of poverty in comparison to other states is depicted in the Table 14.

Unemployment

Though the graph of industrialization and development increased in the state swiftly, the graph of unemployment also

TABLE 13

State-wise per capita Bank Deposit, Bank Credit and C.D. Ratio* (Comparative increase-decrease during the periods March 1995, March 1997 and March 1998

Sl. No.	States	Per capita Depost (Rs.)			Per capita Credit (Rs.)			Per capita C.D. Ratio		
		1995	1997	1998	1995	1997	1998	1995	1997	1998
1.	Tamil Nadu	4326	5401	6468	3944	5420	6215	91.2	100.4	96.1
2.	Maharashtra	9372	11588	13200	6591	7956	9542	70.3	68.7	72.3
3.	Andhra Pradesh	2794	3538	4286	2116	2746	3092	75.7	77.6	72.1
4.	Karnataka	4109	5259	6281	2784	3759	4286	67.8	71.5	68.2
5.	M.P.	1856	2396	3028	989	1254	1558	53.3	52.3	51.5
6.	Gujarat	5283	6282	7430	2462	3124	3583	46.6	49.7	48.2
7.	Rajasthan	2165	2767	3258	994	1223	1545	45.9	44.4	47.4
8.	West Bengal	3844	4805	5774	2089	2404	2662	54.3	50.0	46.1
9.	Orissa	1528	2052	2506	826	1005	1132	54.1	49.0	45.2
10.	Kerala	5532	7330	8586	2487	3437	3802	45.0	46.9	44.3
11.	Haryana	4048	5468	6335	1890	2335	2717	46.7	42.7	42.9
12.	Punjab	8184	10138	11962	3391	3966	4620	41.4	39.1	38.6
13.	J & K	4127	5130	6144	1766	1990	2295	42.8	38.8	37.4
14	Assam	1605	2019	2359	611	710	775	38.1	35.2	32.9
.15.	U.P.	2356	3021	3608	824	955	1032	35.0	31.6	28.6
16.	Bihar	1599	3657	2664	531	682	733	33.2	18.6	27.5
17.	H.P.	4797	5943	6873	1264	1392	1485	26.3	23.4	21.6
	All India	4121	5175	6132	2440	2967	3403	59.2	57.3	55.5

* related to Scheduled Commercial Banks.

increased at par with the development and it aided in the inequality between rich and poor. In India the number of unemployed persons was 58.3 percent in 1988, when it became 69.3 percent in 1988. In 1998 it became 1 crore 58 lakh (educated unemployed). In this figure the industrially developed states (including Tamil Nadu) aided abundantly in number. In Tamil Nadu the number of unemployed persons was 43.7 lakh, only in Maharashtra it was 41.8 lakh, in Kerala 38.8 lakh, in West Bengal 56 lakh etc. It is alarming that if the

TABLE 14

Number of Persons Below Poverty Line (B.P.L.) in the States

Sl. No.	*States*	*Percentage of Persons (B.P.L.) (1993-94)*	*Percentage of persons (B.P.L) (1999-2000)*
1.	Bihar	54.96	42.60
2.	Orissa	48.56	47.15
3.	M.P.	42.52	37.43
4.	U.P.	40.85	31.15
5.	Maharashtra	36.86	25.02
6.	West Bengal	35.66	27.02
7.	Tamil Nadu	35.03	21.12
8.	Karnataka	33.16	20.4
9.	Rajasthan	27.41	15.28
10.	Kerala	25.43	12.72
11.	Haryana	25.5	8.74
12.	Gujarat	24.21	14.07
	All	35.97	26.10

The states with less poverty were Punjab and Chandigarh having only 11.77 and 11.35 percent persons respectively below poverty line (B.P.L.).

number of unemployed persons increases in the same ratio in the next ten years (the further phase of liberalisation), the state itself will be divided into two parts of rich and poor.

Industrial Development

Tamil Nadu is far ahead in the race of industrial development. In 1996-97 the number of factories in Tamil

Nadu was 19,203 (out of 1,34,556 in the country), i.e., 14.3 percent of the country. The total 'Capital Invested' in those factories was Rs. 49,935 crores (out of Rs. 5,30,662 crores at all-India level), i.e., 9.4 percent of the country, and 'gross output' and 'Value-added' produced were equivalent to Rs. 74,163 crores (10.8 percent) and Rs. 14,593 crores (10.2 percent) respectively (Table 15).

In this way in 1993-94, Tamil Nadu made industrial investment with the help of non-governmental financial institutions in this ratio (Table 16).

During 1993-94 different states attracted investment from their former citizens residing in Foreign Countries (non-resident Indians—N.R.I's) Tamil Nadu also became successful in attracting Rs. 558 crores for industrial development from N.R.I's (Table 17).

VOLUME OF EMPLOYMENT OPPORTUNITIES

The volume of employment opportunities created within the stipulated period was 12,39,000 manpower (out of 97,07,000 at all-India level), 12.8 percent of the country. The total strength of the employment opportunities in the state was 6,43,000 in the year 1980, 8,59,000 in 1990, 9,91,000 in 1993, 12,37,000 in 1996 and 12,39,000 in 1997. This proves the smooth path of development and creation of employment opportunities too in Tamil Nadu, which is reflected in Table 18.

Infrastructure

There are many facets of infrastructure. But production and consumption of the energy is one of the real parameters of development. The total production capacity of electricity of India was 70,976 megawatt in previous decade. Tamil Nadu's capacity was 4,311 megawatt. It forecasts the development outcome of the state (Table 19).

In the same way the position of Tamil Nadu is in the fore-runners states in context of real electric production and per-capita electric consumption also (Table 21). The per capita electric consumption of Tamil Nadu was 430.7 kilowatt having 5th position among the states.

TABLE 15

(Rs. in Crore)

Sl. No.	States	Factories (No.)	Invested Capital	Gross Output	Value Added
1.	Andhra Pradesh	18377	35500	44443	8324
		(13.7)	(6.7)	(6.4)	(5.8)
2.	Gujarat	13405	64296	81763	17554
		(10.0)	(12.1)	(11.8)	(12.3)
3.	Maharashtra	20186	103311	143531	30342
		(15.0)	(19.5)	(20.7)	(21.2)
4.	Karnataka	7277	25854	37268	8772
		(5.4)	(4.9)	(5.4)	(6.1)
5.	Tamil Nadu	19203	49935	74163	14593
		(14.3)	(9.4)	(10.8)	(10.2)
6.	M.P.	4431	32918	39926	7943
		(3.3)	(6.2)	(5.8)	(5.6)
7.	Punjab	7178	20321	28682	5102
		(5.3)	(3.8)	(4.1)	(3.6)
8.	U.P.	10176	53447	60526	13786
		(7.5)	(10.1)	(8.7)	(9.6)
9.	West Bengal	6727	34040	34563	7845
		(5.0)	(6.4)	(5.0)	(5.5)
10	Bihar	3363	23335	25054	7004
		(2.5)	(4.4)	(3.6)	(4.9)
11.	Others	24233	87705	122601	21811
		(18.8)	(16.5)	(17.7)	(15.2)
	All India	134556	530622	992520	143076
		(100.0)	(100.0)	(100.0)	(100.0)

Note: Date relates to 196-97.

15,587 villages of Tamil Nadu were electrified till April, 1981 and now all the villages (15,822) are electrified (till November, 1996) and thus 100 percent electrification is complete in Tamil Nadu which focuses the future possibilities of industrial and agricultural development as well as maximum exploitation of natural resources and vast hope of using potentialities. The energy requirement figure of Tamil Nadu is given in Table 21.

TABLE 16

Capital Investment in 1993-94

Sl. No.	States	Capital Investment (Rs. Crores)
1.	Gujarat	10,784
2.	Maharashtra	6,297
3.	U.P.	4,167
4.	Andhra Pradesh	3,209
5.	M.P.	2,878
6.	Tamil Nadu	2,098
7.	Bihar	104

TABLE 17

Investment from N.R.I's

Sl. No.	States	Investment (Rs. in Crores)
1.	Maharashtra	1513
2.	Delhi	955
3.	Orissa	799
4.	M.P.	582
5.	Tamil Nadu	558
6.	Bihar	1.40

The main items of Tamil Nadu concerning economic importance and industrial development etc. are as follows:

Minerals

Main minerals in the Tamil Nadu are Magnesite, limestone, salt, coal, cromite, bozite, manganese, quartz, zymsum, felspar, abharakh, etc.

Forest Products

Main forest products are sandal, soft wooded timbers, honey, bamboo, kazoo, silcona tree-cover etc.

TABLE 18

Factory Employment*

(in 000)

Sl. No.	States	1980	1990	1993	1996	1997	%age
1.	Andhra Pradesh	522	613	654	1190	1018	10.5
2.	Bihar	375	483	N.A	336	327	3.4
3.	Gujarat	636	748	796	956	848	8.7
4.	Karnataka	492	752	765	512	579	6.0
5.	M.P.	388	516	556	525	483	5.0
6.	Maharashtra	1235	1220	1268	1518	1455	15.0
7.	Punjab	203	369	405	473	482	5.0
8.	Tamil Nadu	643	859	991	1237	1239	12.8
9.	U.P.	534	571	N.A	797	818	8.4
10.	W. Bengal	905	906	N.A	825	768	7.8
	Others	N A	N.A	N.A	N.A	1690	17.4
	All India	7017	8431	8935	10045	9707	100.0

* The figure denotes the average daily number of workers at work, and not the total number on pay-roll.

TABLE 19

Electricity-Production Capacity and Real Production (in megawatt)

Sl. No.	States	Production Capacity (in megawatt)	Real Electric Production (in million kw)
1.	Maharashtra	9099	38467
2.	U.P.	5075	17846
3.	Gujarat	4890	23055
4.	Tamil Nadu	4311 IV	16931 V
5.	Andhra Pradesh	4224	18619
6.	M.P.	3533	13617
7.	Punjab	3499	12718
8.	W. Bengal	3315	10066
9.	Karnataka	3072	11568
10.	Orissa	1742	5193
11.	Bihar	1550	2954

TABLE 20

Real Electric Production and Real Per Capita Consumption

Sl. No.	States	Real Electric Production (in million kw)	Electric Consumption (in kilowatt)
1.	Maharashtra	38467	312.4
2.	U.P.	17846	209.3
3.	Gujarat	23055	622.4
4.	Tamil Nadu	16931 V	430.7 V
5.	Andhra Pradesh	18619	365.1
6.	M.P.	13617	356.8
7.	Punjab	12718	863.1
8.	W. Bengal	10066	N.A
9.	Karnataka	11568	672.9
10.	Orissa	5193	524.3
11.	Bihar	2954	60.0
12.	Rajasthan	N.A.	320.0

TABLE 21

Sl. No.	Financial Years	Energy Requirement (in Bn. Kwh)
1.	1990-91	19.2
2.	1995-96	29.4
3.	1999-2000	36.5
4.	2001-2002	40.5
5.	2006-2007	52.2

Cereal Grains

Main cereal grains produced here are rice, maize, jowar, bajara, ragi and pulses, etc.

Commercial Crops

Main commercial crops grown are sugar-cane, oilseeds, kazoo, cotton, tobacco, coffee, tea, rubber and chilly, etc.

Main Rivers

Main rivers situated here are Kaveri, Palar, Ponnar, Cethugar, Meyar, Bhawani, Amarawati, Wegai, Chinnar, Tamr, Vellar, Noil, Waipar, Warshali, etc.

Main Towns and Cities

Main towns or cities are Chennai, Kanchipuram, Thanjavur, Tutikorin, Madurai, Vellore, Neyveli, Coimbatore, Tiruchirapalli, etc.

ATOMIC ENERGY POWER STATION: KALPAKKAM

Irrigation and Hydro-Electric Projects

The main irrigation and hydro-electric projects are Nichali Bhawani, Amaravati, Wagai, Parabaikulam, Aliar, Krishnagiri, Satnur, Pullambari and Katalai, etc.

Main Ports

Main ports are Chennai, Tutikorin, Kaddalur, Nagapattinam, Coimbatore, etc.

Main Tourism Attractions

The main tourism centers are Ooti, Kodaocanal, Hilly areas of Yarkod, Kanyakumari (Bharatmata Temple, Vivekanand rock, etc.), Kanchipuram, Rameshwaram, Suchindram, Tiruchendur, Chidambaram (Natraj temple), Thanjavur, Mamallapuram (Sea shore temple), Thirukalukkundram (Pakshitracham), Madurai (Minakshi temple), Chennai (St. Jeorge Fort, Museum, Marina Beach, Madras University) and Perumbadur, etc. Those places are centers of attraction which attract the domestic as well as foreign tourists in large number, which aids in income of the state.

Corruption

Though Tamil Nadu is full of resources, mines, industries as well as good development graph, corruption also grips the economy off and on as on the peak level many scams, e.g. Hotel 'Pleasant Stay' scam, Tansi land scam, colour T.V. purchase scam, unappropriate assests scam and purchase of coals scam, etc. took place, which broke the bones of the economy. It is now time to be aware from such scams and scandals prevailing the state.

Bright Future

The future of the Tamil Nadu's economy seems to be very bright in the mirror of different paradigms and standards. According to an economic expectation the future population growth trend of the state will be decreasing. The C.D. ratio is going on in increasing trend. Investment rates by different channels are increasing swiftly, thereby producing more 'gross output' and 'value-added' for the economy. Volume of employment opportunities had been increasing during the past decade. The people are industrious. Poverty ratio is reducing as well as crime and corruption are minimized. Literacy rate is increasing. Male-female ratio is increasing and so women's empowerment is also strengthening. The expenditure pattern of the state is also favourable for the industrial growth because it is more capital-investment-oriented rather than total expenditure. The infrastructure of the state economy is very strong including roads, electricity, communication, literacy, schooling, education, etc. Human development index and women's empowerment index both are improving. By virtue of all these qualities analysed on the basis of different figures and datas, it is evident that the state economy will grow smoothly in the near future certainly. Not only will it march ahead, but it is hoped that it may lead the race in the first half of the 21st century.

REFERENCES

Asthana, P. (1985), "Institutional Finance for Industry and Regional Disparities in India" in G.P. Mishra (ed.).

SLBC (1986, 1989, 1990), Proceedings of State Level Bankers' Committee, Banks of India, Patna.

Report (1993), N.N. Vohra Committee, Govt, of India, Ministry of Home Affairs, N. Delhi.

Lenin, V.I. (1970), Selected Works, Progress Publishers, Moscow.

Prasad, Pradhan, H. (1997), "Liberalisation in Theory and Practice", *Economic and Political Weekly*, March 29.

Prasad, K.N. (1999), Dimensions of Development Series, Vol. I, Agriculture (Bihar *v.* All India), Concept, New Delhi.

Narain, J.P. (1958), Towards a New Society.

Thakur, R.N. (2001), Crime and Corruption, Obstacles to Development, Crime, Corruption & Development (Ed. N. Narsimha Reddy), Deep & Deep Publications, New Delhi.

Thakur, R.N. (2001), Participation of Women in Works and Employment, Problems & Prospects, Women & Employment (Ed. S. Murty), R.B.S.A. Publishers, Jaipur.

Thakur, R.N. (1996), Role of Expansion of Banks in Economic Development—In Special Context of Rural Development, Inter-Disciplinary Dialogue (Ed. P.S. Pandey) A.S.C., Gorakhpur University.

Thakur, R.N. (2000), Economic Reforms and Employment in India—Economic Reforms and Employment (Ed. P. Hajela and M.P. Goswami), Deep & Deep Publishers, N. Delhi.

Thakur, R.N. (1997), Bihar's Development on the Cross-Roads, Bihar's Revival, Ed. A.K. Sinha.

Thakur, R.N. (1998), Education as Social Infrastructure of Bihar, *Bihar Economic Journal* (Ed. A.K. Thakur).

Thakur, R.N. (1999), Infrastructure in Bihar—A Comparative Study, *Bihar Economic Journal* (Ed. A.K. Thakur).

Thakur, R.N. (2000), A Study in the Perspective of Socio-Economic Development in Bihar, *Bihar Economic Journal* (Ed. J. Prasad), Vol. I, No. I.

Thakur, R.N. (2000), Education & Political Status of Indian Women—Key of Economic Development, Women and Economic Development (Ed. A. Banerjee & R.K. Sen), Deep & Deep Publications, New Delhi.

Kurukshetra (Hindi) (2001), September, pp. 21, 28.

Pratiyogita Darban (Hindi) (2001), May, pp. 1786, 1787.

Pratiyogita Darban (Hindi) (2001), July, pp. 2152, 2153.

Pratiyogita Darban (Hindi) (2001), August, pp. 166, 179.

Pratiyogita Darban (Hindi) (2001), September, pp. 293.

Pratiyogita Darban (Hindi) (2001), October, pp. 423, 459, 470.

Civil Services Chronicle (Hindi), July, p. 41.

Statistitical Outline of India (1999-2000), Tata Services Limited, Department of Economics & Statistics, Bombay House, Mumbai.

Thakur, R.N. (2001), Economy of J. & K.—Seeking Path of Development, Economy of J. & K. (Ed. Bhatt).

Thakur, R.N. (2001), Infrastructure and Social Sector Development: A Case Study of Primary Education in Bihar.

Thakur, R.N. (2001), Dualism of Fiscal Federalism with Backward States, Specially Bihar, *Conference Volume*, Vellore, I.E.A.

Primary Report (2000), National Council of Applied Economic Research (NCAER).

Business Today (2000), Janurary.

11

CHAPTER

Growth and Development: A Comparative Study of Tamil Nadu and India

R. ARUNACHALAM AND K. NANDHA KUMAR

The dynamics of growth in an economy causes transformation normally from primary to secondary and in turn to tertiary sector, thus shifting the intensity of economic activity from one sector to another. In the course of such a transformation, productivity of factors of production along with gainful employment of labour are expected to take place for the sustenance of higher level growth. In a context like India, considerable importance is given to equitable distribution of the gains of development, particularly, the benefits going to the bottom 40% of poor population. This paper attempts to review the performance of Tamil Nadu economy along with the national economy in terms of the structural changes, distributional aspects of income and the problem of poverty. While section I deals with the structural changes both at the state and national level, section II is concerned with certain aspects of dynamics of growth in Tamil Nadu. Attempt is also made to review the growth dynamics with a focus on the situation of post-reform period in India.

Mention must be made about earlier empirical works in this connection. For example, Fisher (1936), Clark (1940), Kuznets (1956-57, 1971), Chenry (1990), Chenry and Taylor (1960), Cehnry and Syrquin (1970), Hasim (1990), Krishna Mazumdar (1995) and Arunachalam (forthcoming) all bring out the happenings of economic transformation. Recent works of Hasim (1994), Deepak Lal *et. al.* (2001) and Narayana (2001) focus a reduction in poverty in India as well as at the regional levels. These studies bring about the contrast in the findings of certain surveys relating to the variations in poverty. This present work is eclective in nature to present a combined version of the earlier works in the light of the ongoing economic reform measures.

SECTION I

SECTORAL DYNAMICS

Analysis of sectoral contribution to National Domestic Product (NDP) decade-wise (Table 1) yields some useful insights into the development process. For example, during 1950-60, at the national level, the share of primary sector to NDP was between 49-51 percent; the contribution of secondary sector was of the order of 17-20 percent and that of the tertiary secotr's share was 34-37 percent. In the following decade of 1960-70, the sectoral shares were 51 to 43 percent, 20 to 24 percent and 29 to 32 percent showing a steep decline in the contribution of primary sector and service sector and increases in secondary sector in their share to NDP.

Between 1970-80, the share of primary sector further declined to 40 percent, the share of secondary sector remaining constant and services sector share increased. During the decade 1980-90, the contribution of primary sector further fell to 32.7 percent, that of secondary sector's share declined to 20 percent and the share of tertiary sector's contribution further increased to 39 percent. In the current decade (1990-2000), the contribution of primary sector further diminished to around 24-25 percent, that of industrial sector was 22 and services sector share enhanced to nearly 50 percent.

At Tamil Nadu level, as on 1960-70 (Table 2) the share of

TABLE 1

Sector-wise Distribution of NDP at Constant Prices

(Figures in %)

Base Year	*Time Period*	*Primary*	*Secondary*	*Tertiary*
1948-49	1950-51 to 1959-60	49-51	17-20	34-37
1960-61	1960-61 to 1969-70	43-51	20-24	29-32
1970-71	1970-71 to 1979-80	40-49	21-24	30-36
1980-81	1980-81 to 1989-90	33-40	20-24	36-39
1993-94	1990-91 to 1994-95	31-33	25-27	39-42
1993-94 (GDP)	1995-96 to 1999-2000	27.5-28	25-29	43-48
	2000-2001	26.27	24.7	49.03

Sources: 1. National Accounts Statistics: 1950-51, 1979-80, 1980-81, 1986-87, Central Statistical Organisation.
2. 1995-96 to 1999-2000, CSO as quoted in *EPW*, October, 2001.

primary sector to NSDP was 48.19 percent, that of secondary sector's share was 21.40 percent and the contribution of services the sectoral shares in the above order was 37.56, 27.37 and 35.07. As found at the national level, in Tamil Nadu too,

TABLE 2

Sector-wise Distribution of NSDP at Constant Prices

(Figures of %)

Base Year	*Time Period*	*Primary*	*Secondary*	*Tertiary*
1960-61	1960-61 to 1969-70	48.19	21.4	30.41
1970-71	1970-71 to 1979-80	37.56	27.37	35.07
1980-81	1980-81 to 1989-90	25.37	31.47	43.16
1993-94	1990-91 to 1994-95	21.79	30.97	46.68
1993-94 (GDP)	1995-96 to 1999-2000	19.51	34.41	46.08
	2000-2001	17.22	33.04	49.74

Source: Tamil Nadu, An Economic Appraisal—Various Issues and Unpublished data from 1995-96 to 1999-2000 from Directorate of Economics and Statistics, Government of Tamil Nadu.

there was a steep decline in the share of primary sector to NSDP. Passing through the 80s and 90s, it is found that primary sector's contribution to NSDP further fell to 25.37 percent; the share of secondary sector is 31.47 percent and the role of service sector is of the order of 43.16 percent. Between 1990-2000, the contribution of these sectors to NSDP were 19.5, 34 and 46 respectively. Thus the above situation at the national and state level of Tamil Nadu clearly indicates the emerging role of Tertiary sector as a dominant one. However, in Tamil Nadu, the share of Industrial sector to NSDP is sizeable unlike at national level.

Looked at in terms of decadal compound growth rates, (Table 3), it is found that the primary sector recorded a growth rate of 2.90 percent (50-51 to 60-61), 2.26 percent (60-61 to 70-71), 1.70 percent (70-71 to 80-81), 2.90 (80-81 to 90-91) and 2.80 (90-91 to 96-97). In terms of compound growth rate barring the 70s, one does not find significant variation in the growth of the primary sector. Obviously, the decade 1970 was the initial stage of the introduction of the new agricultural strategy coupled with higher rate of inflation and a situation of political uncertainty. Another aspect of the growth rate is that there is difference between the pre and post-reform compound growth rate of the primary sector showing a decline recently. On the other hand, the growth rate of the secondary sector ranges between 3.7 and 5.35. But the growth rate of the service sector ranges between 5 percent (first 3 decades) and more

TABLE 3

Decadal Compound Growth Rate of NDP

Period	*Compound Growth Rate*		
	Primary	*Secondary*	*Tertiary*
1950-51 to 1960-61	2.92	5.36	4.69
1960-61 to 1970-71	2.26	5.02	4.96
1970-71 to 1980-81	1.7	3.7	5.1
1980-81 to 1990-91	2.9	6.8	5.9
1990-91 to 1996-97	2.8	5.35	6.33
1997-98 to 2000-01 (GDP)	1.82	3.99	4.59

Source: Computed using data from Table 1.

than 6 percent in 1990s. Thus, the service sector shows a sustained uptrend over the five decades since 1950s. However, the compound growth rate of all sectors show a decline during second half of 1990s.

In Tamil Nadu, the growth rate of the primary sector was actually negative (Table 4) in 1960s, increased to 1.7 percent in 1970s, 4.3 percent in 1980s and declined to 1.14 percent in the recent times. The growth rate of secondary sector was 5 percent (60-70) declined to 4 percent (1980s) and then increased to 5.6 (1990s). The growth rate of service sector was hardly 3 percent in 1960s, surged to 4 percent in 1970s and further increased to 5.7 percent in 1980s. The same shot upto 8.3 percent in 1990s, particularly of the mid-1990s.

TABLE 4

Decadal Compound Growth Rate in Tamil Nadu

(At Constant Prices in %)

Period	*Compound Growth Rate*		
	Primary	*Secondary*	*Tertiary*
1960-61 to 1969-70	-0.53	5.24	3.17
1970-71 to 1979-80	1.7	5.14	4.19
1980-81 to 1992-93	4.28	4.06	5.74
1993-94 to 2000-01 (GSDP)	1.14	5.61	8.31

Source: Computed using data from Table 2.

A cursory glance at the constituents of these individual sectors (Table 5) clearly reveals that within the primary sector, agriculture alone accounts for nearly 90 percent of the share of the primary sector and the remaining is contributed by logging, fishery, mining and quarrying. However, towards the end of 1990s, agriculture's share has declined to 89 percent of primary sector. In the case of the secondary sector, manufacturing alone accounts for nearly 73 percent of the secondary sector of which registered manufacturing contributes to 40 percent and unregistered manufacturing accounts for 33 percent, as on 1980-81. Over the years, the share of registered manufacturing gradually increased and that

TABLE 5 (A, B AND C)

Sub-Sectors Contribution To NNP and Constant Prices

5A Primary Sector

Year	*Agriculture*	*Forestry and Logging*	*Fishing*	*Mining and Quarrying*	*Primary Sector*
1980-81	36.30 (87-89)	2.93	0.73	1.34	41.3
1990-91	30.37 (89.11)	1.59	0.7	1.42	34.08
1995-96	23.80 (89.14)	1.08	0.67	1.15	26.7
2000-01	24			2.26	26.26

5B Secondary Sector

Year	*Manufacturing*	*Registered*	*Unregis-tered*	*Electri-city*	*Construc-tion Sector*	*Secondary Sector*
1980-81	16.95 (73.66)	9.11	7.84	0.83	5.23	23.01
1990-91	20.71 (77.74)	12.43	8.29	1.12	4.52	26.64
1995-96	20.41 (78.38)	12.67	7.73	1.3	4.33	26.04
2000-01	17.14			0.24	0.51	17.89

5C Tertiary Sector

Year	*Trade Hotels*	*Transports*	*Finance*	*Community and Other Services*	*Tertiary Sector*
1980-81	12.98	3.38	8.4	10.95	35.71
1990-91	13.55	3.89	10.27	11.57	39.28
1995-96	15.85	4.05	12.27	11.16	43.33
2000-01	22.28		13.2	13.54	49.02

Notes: (i) Data for 2000-01 are percentage of GDP.
(ii) Figures in percentages are percentage of the respective sectors to indicate their dominance.

In the case of service sector, trade and hotels and finance and community services are major contributors.

Source: computed from Table 1.

of unregistered manufacturing declined. Following the manufacturing sector, construction accounted for about 22 percent of the secondary sector as of 1980s.

The same declined to 15 percent in 1996-97. At the same time, the sub-sector, electricity accounted for around 7.4 percent of the secondary sector.

As regards the services sector, at the national level trade and hotel contributed to nearly 33.6 percent as on 1980-81, but the same increased to 34.1 percent as on 1996-97. Finance and community services together contributed nearly 53.91 percent to Tertiary sector but the same slightly declined to 52.8 percent. Thus, within the services sector, finance and community services account for dominant share.

In Tamil Nadu too within the primary sector (Table 6). Agriculture itself contributed nearly 95 percent of the total of primary sector as on 1980-81 and the same slightly declined to 90 percent as 1994-95. Forestry and logging, fishing and mining and quarrying together account for only 7 to 10 percent of the total of primary sector. Similarly, as seen at the National level within the secondary sector, as of 1980-81, the manufacturing sector accounted for nearly 81 percent of secondary sector's contribution at constant prices. The same declined to 70 percent in 2000-2001, while the share of Registered manufacturing increased from 58 percent in 1980-81 to 71 percent of the total of manufacturing sector, that of unregistered manufacturing accounted for a reduced share from 45 percent in 1980-81 to 28.5 percent in 1994-95. Constructions contributed nearly 21% in 1980-81 and the same increased to 27.2 percent in 1994-95.

At the state level, again trade and hotel's share was as much as 41.5 percent as on 1980-81 and the same declined to 17 percent in 1994-95. However, the contribution of finance and community service together accounted for 39.13 percent of the Tertiary sector, but the same increased to 53.7 percent. Therefore, both at the National and State level, finance and community services are major contributors to the Tertiary sector and eventually to the NDP and NSDP respectively. The impact of financial sector reform and increased government expenditure on community services may account for such a contribution of these sub-sectors.

TABLE 6 (A, B AND C)

Sub-Sectors Contribution to NNP and Constant Prices

6A Primary Sector

Year	*Agriculture*	*Forestry and Logging*	*Fishing*	*Mining and Quarrying*	*Primary Sector*
1980-81	24.57 (94.79)	0.24	0.63	0.48	25.92
1990-91	22.03 (93.00)	0.74	0.33	0.6	23.7
1995-96	18.49 (89.50)	0.62	0.9	0.65	20.66
2000-01	15.52 (90.18)	0.53	0.71	0.45	17.21

6B Secondary Sector

Year	*Manufacturing*	*Registered*	*Unregis-tered*	*Electri-city*	*Construc-tion Sector*	*Secondary Sector*
1980-81	27.42 (81.85)	15.95	12.47	0.44	5.64	33.5
1990-91	23.71 (74.09)	16.39	7.32	1.47	6.82	32
1995-96	28.70 (78.50)	18.6	10.1	2.53	5.33	36.56
2000-01	23.32 (70.58	15.04	8.28	3.19	6.53	33.04

6C Tertiary Sector

Year	*Trade Hotels*	*Transports*	*Finance*	*Community and Other Services*	*Tertiary Sector*
1980-81	16.87 (41.60)	5.84	8.24	9.65	40.6
1990-91	16.69 (37.62)	6.06	10.45	11.17	44.37
1995-96	14.80 (34.60)	7.59	10.6	9.79	42.37
2000-01	13.51 (27.16)	8.63	14.82	12.79	49.75

Notes: 1. 1995-96 and 2000-01 Data are Percentage of Gsdp.
2. Figures in Parentheses Are Percentage of the Sectors (Primary, Secondary and Tertiary Sector) to Indicate their Dominance.

Source: Tamil Nadu—An Economic Apraisal, Various Issues.

INFLATION AND GROWTH

Table 7 throws light on the trend in the real as well as nominal growth rates along with the rate of inflation measured in terms of the GDP deflator and NSDP deflator for national and state level respectively. It is found that the nominal growth rate of NSDP increased from 7.5 percent during the period 60-61 to 69-70 to 17.73 percent in 1990-97. The real NSDP increased from 2.1 percent to 7.3 percent during the above period. However, the rate of inflation doubled during this period from 5 to 10 percent. Though, the growth rate in real terms more than trippled, in each time period the rate of inflation was greater than that of the real NSDP growth rate in Tamil Nadu.

TABLE 7

Growth Rate and Inflation Rate

Year	*Tamil Nadu*			*India*		
	At Current Price	*At Constant Price*	*Rate of Inflation*	*At Current Price*	*At Constant Price*	*Rate of Inflation*
1960-61 To 1969-70	7.5	2.1	5.28	10.12	3.47	6.42
1970-71 To 1979-80	11.12	5.16	10.52	11.52	5.01	8.48
1980-81 To 1989-90	14.37	5.42	8.5	13.87	5.71	7.86
1990-91 To 1994-95	17.73	7.33	10.44			
1990-91 To 1996-97				16.6	6.04	10.31

Source: Economic Survey, Government of India. Tamil Nadu—An Economic Appraisal, Government of Tamil Nadu, Various Issues.

At the All India level, the GDP in nominal terms increased by 50 percent from 10 to 16.6 percent (between 1960-61 and 1996-97) in real terms, the same is doubled from 3.5 to 6 percent. However, the rate of inflation, unlike in Tamil Nadu fell short of two times increase during the above period. In any case, the rate of inflation was more than the real GDP growth rate in each time period as obtained in Tamil Nadu. Evidently, when the rate of inflation outstrips the growth rate, living conditions of the people, particularly that of the poor are adversely affected. The growth rate both in Tamil Nadu and at the national level is appreciable and sustained during the 1980s and thereafter, when compared to the first three decades since 1950.

POVERTY TREND

The impact of growth on poverty and income distribution is viewed differently by differently studies (Table 8). The earlier work of Simon Kuznets brings out a negative relationship between the extent of inequality and the level of growth in the name of growth-inequality syndrome. Some of the recent empirical works in India point out reductions in poverty consequent on higher level growth and certain other studies point out increases in poverty particularly, after 1991 despite greater level of growth. For instance, the work of Mahendra Dev (2000) refers to reduction in rural poverty during the post-reform period. At the same time, he finds increasing interstate inequalities measured in terms of per capita consumption and per capita SDP. On the other hand, Raghbendra Jha (2000) using NSS data on consumption finds that the rank concordance index across states does not usually show convergence. A worrisome development according to him is that there is greater dispersion in rural poverty across the states, though he also finds convergence of inequality, poverty and mean consumption measures in selected states.

The table in the next page presents the trend in the magnitude of rural and urban poverty measured in terms of head-count ratio by different sources. It is found that at All India level, the percentage of poor below poverty line was nearly 53.07 percent as on 77-78 and declined to around 39 percent in 1990-91. However, the same quickly shot up to 45 percent in 1998. The studies of World Bank as well IGIDR bring out a falling and an urban context too. In Tamil Nadu (Table 9) unlike in the case of 38.04 percent in 1987-88 to 8 percent in 1997-98; than in rural fact, the planning commission has given a projected poverty reduction estimate at 8.96 percent by 2006-07 and at 3.59 percent at 2001-12.

The magnitude of inequality seems to have widened measured by gini-coefficient, particularly during the decade of

TABLE 8

Poverty Estimates in All India

(Head Count Ratio)

Year	*Rural*			*Urban*			*All India*
	PC	*WB*	*IGIDR*	*PC*	*WB*	*IGIDR*	
1977-78	53.07	50.6	50.64	45.24	40.5	40.5	51.32
1983-84	45.65	45.31	45.31	40.79	36.65	35.65	44.48
1987-88	39.09	39.23	39.52	38	36.2	35.6	39
1990-91	NA	36.43	36.43	NA	32.76	32.76	NA
1992-93	NA	43.47	43.47	NA	NA	NA	NA
1993-94	37.27	36..66	38.7	32.36	30.51	30.09	35.97
1997-98	38.5	35.78	34.22	NA	NA	NA	NA
1998	45.2	NA	NA	34.6	NA	NA	NA
1999-2000							26.1

Sources: PC = Planning Commission (1997) Estimated Based On Expert Committees Estimtes.
WB = World Banks Reported in Datt (1995).
IGIDR = Indira Gandhi Institute of Development Research, Estimates Reported in Jha (1999).
Estimated Quoted in Deepak Lal *et. al. EPW*, March 24, 2001 (p. 1019).

TABLE 9

Poverty Trend in Tamil Nadu

(Head-Count Ratio)

Year	*Urban*	*Rural*	*Total*
1987-88	38.04	45.6	43.98
1989-90	33.43	35.67	34.72
1993-94	21.66	26.3	24.63
1994-95	39.77	32.48	35.03
1997-98	8	13.54	11.54
1999-2000 Projected	22.1	20.55	21.12
2000-2007			8.96
2011-2012			3.59

Source: Planning Commission and MISH as quoted in Table 8.

reform measures. The gini-coefficient for rural India according to the study of Indira Gandhi Institute of Development Research was estimated at 33.74 as on 1957-58 and at 35.90 for urban India. The same declined to 27.71 for rural India and to 33.95 for urban India, as on 1990-91. During 1990s, the gini-coefficient increased to 30.11 and 36.12 for rural and urban India respectively, measured as on 1997-98. This finding was further supported by MISH as well as World Bank and Tendulkar estimates, though there are statistical variations in their estimates (*EPW*, March 24, 2001).

The gini-coefficient for rural Tamil Nadu as on 1958 was 32.12 and for urban Tamil Nadu, it was 41.16 and the same declined to 27.29 (Rural), 34.02 (Urban) and to 29.24 (Tamil Nadu) as 1991 from 34.38. However, as on 1997, these figures were 26.22, 26.49 and 26.30 for Rural, Urban and Tamil Nadu respectively.

It is found that going by the above estimates, unlike the situation in All India, inequalities have come down in Tamil Nadu, even during the time period of economic reform measures. In fact, these findings are further supported by the work of Mahendra Dev (*EPW*, March 4, 2000) that though at all India level, poverty has increased both in rural and urban India during the period of economic reform measures along with increase in gini-coefficients indicating increase in inequalities in Tamil Nadu, his work points out reduction in poverty between (1987-88 and 1993-94), 39.7 percent to 31.3 percent, measured by HCR. Having analysed the issues relating to growth, poverty and inequalities at the State level, we now turn to bring examination of district level indicators of growth in Tamil Nadu.

DISTRICT DEVELOPMENT INDICATORS

As of now there are 29 districts in Tamil Nadu which are divided into five groups based on their average per capita income. The first group comprises Chennai, Kancheepuram and Tiruvallur, whose per capita income exceeds Rs. 20,000. For convenience the category of districts is given in Table 10.

From the Table 10, it is seen that per capita income of Tamil Nadu as a whole as on 1996-97 is Rs. 11,215 as against

TABLE 10

Classification of Districts

Group	*Name of Districts*	*PCI Range (Rs.)*	*Classification*
G-I (3)	Chennai, Kancheepuram, Tiruvallur	Above 20000	Very High Income
G-Ii (5)	Salem, Coimbatore, Erode, Madurai, Tuticorin	15000-20000	High Income
G-Iii (7)	Vellore, Nagapattinam, Namakkal, Nilgris, Tiruchi, Viruthunagar, Tirunelveli	12000-15000	Medium Income
G-Iv (8)	Dharmapuri, Karur, Perambalur, Pudukottai, Theni, Dindukal, Ramanathapuram, Kanyakumari	10000-12000	Medium Low Income
G-V (6)	Tiruvannamalai, Cuddalore, Vilupuram, Thanjavur, Sivagangai, Tiruvarur	5000-10000	Low Income

PCI of All India [At Currenty Prices (1996-97], 10579, Tamil Nadu 11215.
Source: As given in Table 11.

All India average of Rs. 10,579 at current prices. It is also found that barring the Group-V six districts, the remaining 23 districts have an average per capita income exceeding the national average, going by certain crucial development indicators such as per capita income, literacy rate, enrolment rate, life expectancy rate, poverty, gini index and infant mortality rate as given in Table 11, certain interesting relationships are found. Firstly, there exists a positive relationship between per capita income on the one hand and literacy rate, enrolment rate and life expectancy rate.

Secondly, there seems to be a negative relationship between PCI and poverty and IMR, though there are a few exceptions to this. Thirdly, irrespective of PCI, barring Group-I, the extent of distributional inequality measured by Gini coefficient is more or less the same. As regards, Group-I, we have combination of a metropolitan city (Chennai) and two sub-urban town areas. This probably explains the relatively greater distributional inequality in Group-I districts. Based on the type of relationship between PCI and other indicators it may be concluded that higher the growth rate, relatively smaller is the percentage of people below poverty line, also

TABLE 11

District Development Indicators

(Figures In Percentage)

Districts	*PCI (1996-97)*	*LR*	*ER*	*LER*	*Poverty*	*Gini Index*	*IMR*
G-I (3)	20624.66 (30.91)	71.46	84	70.28	28.52	31.25	27.85
G-II (5)	170821.80 (29.32)	62.58	73.18	66.82	30.32	26.92	46.11
G-III (7)	13460.43 (16.85)	63.08	72.83	66.74	28.58	26.91	40.56
G-IV (8)	11008.75 (11.85)	61.6	70.39	65.33	31	25.14	46.79
G-V (6)	9038.83 (11.05)	58.98	70.16	66.42	36.92	26.21	39.59

Notes: PCI—Per Capita Income at Current Prices (average of the group).
LR—Literacy Rate.
ER—Enrolment Ratio.
LER—Life Expectancy Rate.
IMR—Infant Mortality Rate.
Figures in parentheses are percentage share of NDDP (based on average values for 1990-91 to 1996-97).

Source: Computed from Draft Chapter on Per Capita-Income—State and Districts, Government of Tamil Nadu, State Planning Commission.

implying that the gains of growth seem to have reached the poorer better in Tamil Nadu. Evaluated by alternative indicators, particularly, the components of physical quality life index the district groups seem to have achieved better living conditions, as there exists positive relationship between PCI and LR, ER and LER.

Going by the growth trend at the national and Tamil Nadu level, as agricultural sector and industrial sector are found to be significant in terms of their potential for employment of labour and the consequent reduction of poverty. So greater importance to be given to these sectors in future plans. Service Sector's Contribution to National and State product, though very high, it does not seem to provide greater employment opportunities, particularly for the unskilled rural labour and labour in Urban informal sectors.

References

Arunachalam, R., Dimensions of the Dynamics of Service Sector in India (Forthcoming).

Chenry, H.B. (1979), Structural Change and Development Policy, Oxford University Press, London.

Deepak Lal, Rakesh Mohan, Natarajan, I. (2001), Economic Reforms and Poverty Alleviation (TW), Vol. XXXVI, No. 12), March 24.

Fisher, A.G.R. (1989), Production, Primary, Secondary and Tertiary Sectors, *Economic Record*, Vol. 15, June.

Hasim, S.R. (1991), Forty Years of Indian Economy: Structure and Dimensions of Growth, *The Indian Economic Journal*, Vol. 38, No. 3, Janurary-March.

Krishna Mazumdar (1995), Disproportional Growth of Service Sector in India: 1960-1990, *The Indian Economic Journal*, Vol. 43, No. 2, October-December.

Kuznets, S. (1975), *Modern Economic Growth*, Oxford and IBH.

Mahendra Dev, S. (2000), Economic Reforms, Poverty Distribution and Employment, *EPW*, Vol. XXXIV, March 4.

Raghabendra Jha, Growth, Inequality and Poverty in India, Spatial and Temporal Characteristics, *EPW*, Vol. XXXV, March 11.

Rao, V.K.R.V. (1979), Changing Structure of Indian Economy, *Economic and Political Weekly*, December 15.

Streeton, Paul and Frances Stewart (1972), Conflict between Output and Employment Objectives in Developing Countries, The Frontiers of Development Studies, MacMillan, London.

12

CHAPTER

Performance of Public Sector Undertakings in Tamil Nadu

GAUTAM NARESH AND J.V.M. SARMA

India is forging ahead with the task of economic reform with firm commitment. The second-generation reforms focus at the State level fiscal management. The key ingredients in this regard are: restoration of fiscal sustainability, reforming Public Sector Undertakings (PSUs), encouraging private sector participation in infrastructure, and evolving suitable policy and institutional framework for promoting competition and efficiency. In the process, government participation in commercial activities is supposed to be minimized and its activity is confined to mere regulation and maintenance of law and order.

As a first step a medium-term fiscal framework needs to be developed first that can help restoring the much needed fiscal stability and sustainability. It is a fact that States are faced with deteriorating budgetary positions, with serious implications on their developmental efforts. Insufficient revenue sources and uncontrolled growth of current expenditures has been pushing the States to unsustainable levels of indebtedness. The constraints on States' borrowings makes the burden of adjustment to fall mainly on capital and maintenance leading to declining productivity of public sector investment and deceleration in long-term growth of the economy. Therefore, the framework for fiscal restoration should include: better expenditure management through control of current expenditure; prioritisation of capital expenditure through core investment plan; enhanced outlays on certain key sectors; and improved resource mobilization through appropriate tax and non-tax reforms. In addition, there is a need for speeding up the restructuring of PSUs for bringing about transparency and accountability through closure, sale or merger as needed keeping in view their role in the overall economic development.

These issues are common to all States although certain State-specific factors aggravate the problem. In this paper, we shall confine ourselves to the current state of PSUs, which will have direct bearing in affecting the budgetary health of the State. Here, we make an attempt to have an overview of the situation of PSUs in Tamil Nadu in section 1. Based on this overview, in section 2, a course of re-structuring is suggested. In section 3, directions of reform are put forward with a summary in section 4.

I. GENERAL OVERVIEW

As in the case of many States, the performance of State Public Sector Undertakings (PSUs) in Tamil Nadu has been a cause for concern. Except for the eight development finance corporations, the financial performance of the 67 PSUs has been in general poor with no significant contribution to the State. Not only the return on the investment by way of dividends and interest is nil or negative, they block over Rs. 5,000 crore (of which 38 percent owned by the Government of Tamil Nadu) from being put to more productive alternative uses. The Rs. 1,500 crore GSDP originating from the PSUs forms an insignificant proportion of the total. Thus, the PSUs in Tamil Nadu have not had a great impact on the economy of the State except for direct employment of 1.6 lakh persons.

As many as 20 out of 67 PSUs are in the transport sector. Other important areas of operation are development finance and manufacturing. The 20 passenger transport companies

TABLE 1

Tamil Nadu: Summary of Financial Performance of PSUs: 1991-97

	1991-92	1992-93	1993-94	1994-95	1995-96	1996-97
Number of PSUs (number)	60	62	64	67	67	68
Total capital (Rs. crore)	2,379	2,530	3,027	3,935	4,547	5,339
Government share in total (%)	38%	39%	41%	39%	39%	38%
Equity (%)	20%	20%	17%	14%	13%	16%
Loans (%)	19%	19%	24%	25%	26%	22%
Others share in total (%)	62%	61%	59%	61%	61%	62%
Gross income (Rs. crore)	4,043	4,390	4,943	5,908	6,933	8,301
Net surplus/profit (+/-) (Rs. crore)	35	22	54	23	-115	-257
Dividend (Rs. crore)	14	12	16	18	16	16
Number of employees (lakh)	1.5	1.6	1.6	1.6	1.6	1.6

Source: Government of Tamil Nadu, Review of State Public Sector Enterprises and Statutory Boards in Tamil Nadu, Various issues.

also account for the largest employment (1.15 lakh out of the total PSU employment of 1.61 lakh) while development finance companies account for the largest share in terms of size of capital (Table 2).

During the financial year 1996-97, of the 67 PSUs, only 27 showed a profit of Rs. 84 crore and the remaining 40 incurred a loss of Rs. 340 crore. The biggest loss-making group is the transport companies. Of the overall net loss of Rs. 257 crore, over 80 percent is accounted by the 20 transport undertakings. In contrast, development finance companies show a net overall profit of Rs. 34.5 crore. Among the 10 manufacturing PSUs, 5 companies showed profit.

2. NEED FOR RESTRUCTURING PSUS

The major cause of the poor performance of some of the PSUs is not difficult to understand. First, the PSUs are being managed more as State government departments than as business entities. The government influence is all pervading in the management of the PSUs. Thus, there is a clear need for divestment of the controlling equity and eliminating the need

Table 2

Tamil Nadu: Distribution of PSUs by Major Groups: 1996-97

	Number	*Total Capital (Rs. crore)*	*Government financing (Rs. crore)*	*Number of Employees ('000)*
Agriculture & allied	5	47	28	11
Construction	3	79	57	1
Development finance	11	2,780	1,036	3
Development non-financial	9	102	89	3
Goods transport	1	121	21	0.184
Manufacturing	10	841	357	12
Mining	2	33	31	4
Passenger transport	20	609	210	115
Trading	1	43	31	12
Miscellaneous	5	11	7	1
All PSUs	67	4,667	1,865	161

Source: as in Table 1.

Table 3

Tamil Nadu: Profitability of the PSUs by Major Groups: 1996-97

(Rs crore)

	No.	*Profit*	*No.*	*Loss*	*Total No.*	*Overall Profit/ loss*
Agriculture & allied	2	7.8	3	-2.9	5	5.0
Construction	1	0.2	2	-3.2	3	-3.0
Development finance	8	36.9	3	-2.3	11	34.5
Development non-financial	4	1.1	5	-2.2	9	-1.1
Goods transport	0	0.0	1	-4.2	1	-4.2
Manufacturing	5	32.0	5	-16.1	10	15.9
Mining	2	3.6	0	0.0	2	3.6
Passenger transport	0	0.0	20	-309.7	20	-309.7
Trading	0	0.0	1	0.0	1	0.0
Miscellaneous	5	2.5	0	0.0	5	2.5
All PSUs	27	84.1	40	-340.7	67	-256.6

for their accountability to the Legislative Assembly. Second, the decision-making at present is very much dominated by the government. At present even in some of the PSUs with less than 51 percent government equity, the government dominates the decision-making process.[1] Thus, there is also a need to induct professional management experts outside the government, to improve efficiency.

Directions for future reform of PSUs in the State thus rest on the role of this sector in its economy for which it was created and expanded. In view of the non-viable operations of the PSUs radical measures of restructuring does seem necessary. Depending upon the profit-making capability, we have grouped all the 67 PSUs into four categories as in Table 4. The list of PSUs in each group is as in Table A.4. The 16 PSUs under category A can be retained in the present form, and those 40 units categorised under B and C should be considered for partial disinvestment and for restructuring while remaining 11 PSUs under category D are obvious candidates for winding up.

TABLE 4

Tamil Nadu: Classification of PSUs based on their Profit/ Loss-making Behaviour: 1990-96

Profit category	*Number of PSUs*
A. Consistently making profits in recent years (that is, since 1990)	16
B. Showed profits most of the time but not every year	15
C. Showed losses most of the time but did make profits in some years	25
D. Habitually incurring losses	11

The question of restructuring of PSUs in Tamil Nadu was examined earlier by the Venkataraman Committee in 1977, Ramanathan Committee in 1988[2] and more recently by the Raghavan Committee. The Raghavan Committee has recommended: (a) retention of 14 enterprises in the present form, (b) restructuring and disinvestments of 34 enterprises (including the 19 transport undertakings), and (c) winding up of 18 enterprises. It also recommended setting up of a Tamil Nadu Public Sector Disinvestments Commission to work out the modalities and undertake the restructuring.

Among the PSUs, the two groups—road transport undertakings and development finance companies merit a more detailed attention.

A. Road Transport

The public transport sector comprising 21 State-owned Road Transport Corporations (SRTCs) in Tamil Nadu has the third strongest fleet in the country with 17,227 buses. Their operational efficiency and professional management is comparable to the better performing States such as Andhra Pradesh, Haryana, Kerala, Maharashtra and Rajasthan (Table 5). For example, vehicle productivity in Tamil Nadu is the highest in India, cost is next only to that in Orissa, number of passenger-kilometres operated per bus per day is the highest and fleet utilization is high. However, in some areas like breakdown and accident rate, optimum utilization and fuel consumption[3] there is room for improvement.

1. Financial Performance

Overall, financial performance however, has not been satisfactory. In Tamil Nadu, SRTCs depend on the government for about 16-17 percent of their financial resource availability (Table 6). The rest is financed through bank borrowings, internal resources and others such as the Tamil Nadu Transport Development Finance Corporation (TDFC). The total operating loss is projected to further deepen to Rs. 3,105 crore during the Ninth Plan period.

2. State Subsidies in lieu of Tariff Concessions

In 1991-92, the amount of State subsidies *in lieu* of tariff concessions was Rs. 11.47 crore, and in 1995-96 it grew to Rs. 41.16 crore. Out of the 19 SRTCs, only Thiruvalluvar Transport Corporation and Rajiv Gandhi Transport Corporation operating on inter-State and express bus service routes did not receive any subsidy. The highest taker has been Pallavan Transport Corporation, operating in Chennai Metropolitan Area (CMA), and it was the sole recipient of

TABLE 5

Tamil Nadu: Performance of Transport Undertakings in 1993-94

Parameters of performance	*Tamil Nadu*	*Best State*	*Value*	*All India*
Size				
Total number of buses in public sector in 1994	14,949	Maharashtra	16,422	102,143
Ratio of public sector buses to total (%)	46.79	Maharashtra	58.90	27.13
Buses/lakh population	57.22	Kerala	104.37	47.36
Capital Productivity				
Vehicle productivity (km/bus/day)	384	Tamil Nadu	384	266
Fleet utilization (of buses on road to the fleet)	92	Andhra Pradesh, Punjab	96	87
Over-aged buses (to total fleet)	26.1	Andhra Pradesh	0	16.8
Passenger kilometers operated per bus/day	18,819	Tamil Nadu	18,819	10,804
Load factor (actual traffic earnings/estimated traffic earnings with full capacity)	76	Haryana	85	72
Worker Productivity				
Staff productivity (km. covered in a day/worker)	47.0	Haryana	56.7	37.5
Bus-staff ratio on fleet operated	7.51	Punjab	5.5	7.95
Staff cost per worker/day (Rs.)	129.46	Orissa	62.81	117.34
Fuel Efficiency				
Fuel cost/revenue earning bus km. (Paise)	182.13	Rajasthan	150.02	172.12
Fuel efficiency (km/litre)	4.23	Andhra Pradesh, Gujarat	5.01	4.48
Total cost/bus/km (Paise)	711.44	Orissa	706.46	816.83

Source: Government of India (1995): A Study on the Performance of the State Road Transport Undertakings, Planning Commission, September.

TABLE 6

Tamil Nadu: Structure of Financing in the Road Transport Corporations during 1990-96

(Percent to total)

	1990 91	*1991- 92*	*1992- 93*	*1993- 94*	*1994- 95*	*1995- 96*
(a) Paid up capital (Government)	4.45	4.13	3.83	3.99	3.66	2.86
(b) Borrowings	33.94	33.97	35.92	34.33	37.48	46.61
Government	8.43	8.09	11.59	7.63	6.66	14.19
Commercial Banks	0.00	0.00	0.00	1.11	0.34	0.23
Others	25.50	25.88	24.32	25.59	30.48	32.19
(c) Internal resources	61.61	61.90	60.24	61.69	58.86	50.53
Free reserves	0.00	0.00	0.00	0.01	0.02	0.02
Other reserves	0.47	0.46	0.45	0.46	0.47	0.39
Depreciation	61.14	61.44	59.67	61.03	58.29	50.09
Deferred payments liability	0.01	0.00	0.12	0.19	0.08	0.03
Total resources	100.00	100.00	100.00	100.00	100.00	100.00

Source: Government of Tamil Nadu, Review of State Public Sector Enterprises in Tamil Nadu, State Bureau of Public Enterprises, Chennai.

subsidy in 1990-91. Nevertheless, the share of this corporation went down to 25 percent in 1995-96. Subsequently, Dr. Ambedkar Transport Corporation also joined Pallavan to serve CMA and the combined share of subsidy of these two corporations constituted roughly half in 1993-94.

3. *Fare Structure and Tariff Concessions*

The financial viability of SRTCs is seriously impaired in an environment of rising costs, uneconomic fares, concessional travel, operation of uneconomic routes and above all, a high level of taxation. Periodic increases in the prices of essential inputs have pushed up the production cost of vehicles, the burden of which has been passed on to the corporations. There is a need to have a mechanism for automatic increase in passenger fare linked with any increase in input costs particularly staff, fuel/diesel, tyres and tubes.

In Tamil Nadu, despite the last two revisions in the fare

TABLE 7

Tamil Nadu: Financial Status of the Road Transport Corporations

Period	*No. of years*	*Loss (Rs. crore)*
1972-73 to 1994-95	22	326
1995-96 to 1996-97	2	500
1997-98 to 1999-2000	3	2,279
Total accumulated losses		3,105

Source: Government of Tamil Nadu, Annual Plan, 1998-99, Contribution of Road Transport Corporations, Chennai.

structure in 1993, 1997, and 1998 the weighted average rate is just 18 paise per km, and is still one of the lowest in the country and not adequate to break-even financially. To have an idea of the required fare revision, it can be noted that the average tariff rate in Rajasthan where the transport undertakings are run profitably, is 38 paise per km.

Further, the intermittent fare revisions have provided only short respites from losses and have not been strong enough to sustain financial viability, particularly, with escalating costs of inputs. For example, after the fare revision in 1993, there was a turn around and indications of profit in 1994. However, this profit could not be sustained and there was a net loss in 1995-96. Hence, the need for tariff revisions at regular intervals should be recognized and backed up by suitable action.

B. Development Finance Corporations

The development finance corporations are created with a view to mobilize resources from extra-budgetary sources such as term-lending institutions and public deposits to finance the developmental activities. The other objectives of setting up these companies are to provide necessary technical and administrative guidance and facilities necessary to the companies in the areas of infrastructure and capital development. In Tamil Nadu eight of the eleven development finance companies have succeeded in fulfilling this objective. Perhaps, this is one of the reasons why the budget allocations for capital expenditure are lower than in other States.

Among these companies, the following five companies have the objective of developing the industry in general:

1. Tamil Nadu Industrial Development Corporation (TIDCO),
2. State Industries Promotion Corporation of Tamil Nadu (SIPCOT),
3. Tamil Nadu Small Industries Development Corporation (SIDCO),
4. Tamil Nadu Corporation for Industrial Infrastructure Development (TACID), and
5. Tamil Nadu Industrial Investment Corporation (TIIC).

The remaining three companies cater to specific industries—textiles and electronics. These are:

6. Tamil Nadu Handloom Development Corporation (TNHDC),
7. Tamil Nadu Textile Corporation (TNTC), and
8. Electronics Corporation of Tamil Nadu (ELCOT).

And the following three companies cater to the infrastructure development:

9. Tamil Nadu Transport Development Finance Corporation (TDFC),
10. Tamil Nadu Power Finance and Infrastructure Development Corporation (POWERFIN), and
11. Tamil Nadu Urban Finance and Infrastructure Development Corporation (TUFIDCO).

Except for the TNHDC and TNTC, the financial performance of PSUs in this group has been encouraging. The group accounts for a capital investment of Rs. 2,780 crore of which government funding is about 37 percent (Table 8). About 90 percent of the equity capital and a third of the

TABLE 8

Tamil Nadu: Financial Aggregates of the Development Finance Group of PSUs:1991-96

(Rs. crore)

	1991-92	*1992-93*	*1993-94*	*1994-95*	*1995-96*
Total capital	1330.35	1622.05	1999.65	2383.57	2779.85
Share capital	240.56	253.04	300.75	232.57	237.15
Term loans	1,089.79	1,369.01	1,698.90	2,151.00	2,542.70
Total Government investment		550.01	679.49	889.51	1036.13
Government equity		190.33	189.29	207.96	212.49
Government loans		359.68	490.20	681.55	823.64
Share of the Government in the funds		33.9%	34.0%	37.3%	37.3%
Equity		75.2%	62.9%	89.4%	89.6%
Loans		26.3%	28.9%	31.7%	32.4%
Net profits	8.68	8.01	29.30	12.12	20.87
Rate of return on equity	3.6%	3.2%	9.7%	5.2%	8.8%

Source: as in Table 1.

borrowings come from the Government. The notable feature of this group is that most of the companies in this group make positive profits with reasonable and growing rates of return on equity.

3. DIRECTIONS OF REFORM

Taking note of the facts, directions for future reforms of PSUs in the State basically thus rests on the role of this sector in its economy for which it was created and expanded and the future role of this sector should be assigned to this sector. The charge of inefficiency is due to, apart from public ownership, monopoly power, organizational structure, bureaucratic regulation, political interference and price control. Therefore, it is recommended that the undertakings be given freedom to function as a corporate and political and beaurucratic control be relaxed and the head of the undertakings be appointed with professional acumen and technical knowledge. Further, those manufacturing units running in red may be privatised with ample of disinvestments of its equity. Private participation in their management should be adequate to nullify non-commercial governmental approach.

Depending upon the profit-making capability, we have grouped all the PSUs into four categories as in Table 4.

- The PSUs under category A can be retained in the present form, and those under categories B and C should be considered for partial dis-investment and restructuring while PSUs under category D are obvious candidates for winding up.
- Those undertakings that are recommended for restructuring should be given freedom to function as corporate entities. Political and bureaucratic control should be relaxed and the head of the undertakings should be appointed with professional acumen and technical knowledge.

In the transport sector, there is a need to evolve a mechanism for automatic periodic revision of passenger fares to compensate for the increases in the input costs (as being attempted in the case of irrigation tariffs). In addition, with a view to making the public transport corporations compete with the private counterparts, it is necessary to compensate them for tariff concessions and losses due to plying on uneconomic routes, particularly in metro areas. At the same time, it is necessary to improve the operational efficiency by computerization, up-gradation of the fleet, and modernization of the fleet maintenance facilities as also bringing down the bus-staff ratio. Further, to improve administrative efficiency, merger of those transport corporations whose area of operations overlap should be considered. Similarly, financially weaker undertakings can be considered for merging with stronger ones to break-even.

The existence of as many as eleven Development Finance Companies with more or less similar objectives creates confusion and perhaps it will be useful to merge those companies with similar areas of operation. The six companies—TIDCO, SIPCOT, SIDCO, TACID, TIIC and ELCOT—can be merged into a single development finance company, e.g., Tamil Nadu Industrial Development Finance Company. Similarly, the TDFC, POWERFIN, and TUFIDCO can be consolidated into a single Tamil Nadu Infrastructure Development Finance Corporation.

The annual growth rate of subsidies be brought down to 1.3 percent from current 29 percent so that the expenditure on subsidies grows exactly in tandem with the size of population. This will be achieved by phasing out subsidies to PSUs, TNEB and the Road Transport Undertakings. Particularly the latter two will be allowed to revise their tariffs for breaking even and reduce their dependence on the government.

In addition to the direct borrowings, the State government also provides guarantees to the loans raised by various State public sector undertakings and cooperatives[4] although these do not involve budgetary outflows except in cases of defaults. The outstanding value of these borrowings currently is about Rs. 3,703 crore. Over a half of the outstanding guarantee amount—Rs. 1,882 crore—is in respect of borrowings raised by the TNEB. So far, the budgetary burden due to these guarantees has been zero as there are no defaults. In the unlikely event of defaults, the Government has set-up a fund by charging an annual guarantee commission equal to half a percent of the respective outstanding amount of guarantee from each of the PSUs.

4. SUMMARY

In the overall economic reform process in the country as in the case of many States, the performance of PSUs in Tamil Nadu has been a cause for concern. Except for the eleven development finance corporations, the financial performance of the rest of the 56 PSUs has been poor with no significant contribution to the State. Not only the return on the investment by way of dividends and interest is nil or negative, they block roughly over Rs. 5,000 crore (of which 38 percent or roughly Rs. 2,000 crore invested by the Government of Tamil Nadu) from being put to more productive alternative uses. The GSDP originating from the PSUs at Rs. 1,500 crore is an insignificant proportion of the total GSDP of the State. Thus, the PSUs in Tamil Nadu have not had a great impact on the economy of the State except for direct employment of 1.6 lakh persons.

In view of the non-viable operations of the PSUs radical measures of restructuring does seem necessary. The question of restructuring of PSUs in Tamil Nadu was examined earlier by several committees, the latest being the Raghavan Committee.

Among them, the twenty-one State Road Transport Corporations (SRTCs) in Tamil Nadu together owns the third strongest fleet in the country and their operational efficiency and professional management is comparable to the better performing States. Overall, financial performance however, is seriously impaired in an environment of rising costs, uneconomic fares, concessional travel, operation of uneconomic routes and above all, a high level of taxation. Periodic increases in the prices of essential inputs have pushed up the production cost of vehicles, the burden of which has been passed on to the corporations. Further, the fare revisions made so far, have provided only short respites from losses and have not been strong enough to sustain financial viability, particularly, with escalating costs of inputs. Thus, there is a need for tariff revisions at regular intervals.

On the contrary, eight of the eleven development finance companies have succeeded in fulfilling the objective of mobilizing extra-budgetary resources such as term lending institutions and public deposits to finance the developmental activities. Perhaps, this is one of the reasons why the budget allocations for capital expenditure are lower (in terms of GSDP) than in other States. Among these companies, the five companies have the objective of developing the industry in general, three companies cater to specific industries—textiles and electronics, and three companies cater to the infrastructure development. The financial performance of PSUs in this group has been encouraging and most of the companies in this group make positive profits with reasonable and growing rates of return on equity. However, the existence of as many as 11 companies with more or less similar objectives creates confusion and perhaps it will be useful to merge those companies with similar areas of operation.

Notes and References

1. Tamil Nadu Newsprint and Papers Ltd. is an example as to how a PSU should not be run.
2. The Ramanathan Committee (1977) reiterated that the role of government should confine to three types of activities: (i) where the activity is specifically reserved for the public sector under government policy and it will not be possible for the private sector to undertake the activity, (ii) where the private sector is unwilling to take up the activity because of large capital needs with no immediate return, and (iii) where the private sector is reluctant to involve in the development of backward areas.
3. The government of Tamil Nadu has entered the transport business as early as in 1947 and serviced the Madras City. In 1967, the government took over all routes from Madras and Kanyakumari districts. It was in 1971 major legislation for taking over the bus operators holding more than 50 buses, was passed. Originally, four regional transport companies were formed to have a closer management and efficient supervision. The nationalization did result in providing better access for the farmers to the markets in urban areas, easy access to the educational institutions and bringing long-distance travel within the reach of rural poor. Over the years, however, the financial performance has become dismal an offshoot of which has been the unhampered growth of two and three wheelers and illegal operations of truckers.
4. The guidelines for providing guarantees are well laid out in Tamil Nadu. The criteria for giving guarantees as suggested by the Public Accounts Committee for 1969-70 (*GO Ms No. 101, dated January 29, 1974*) are that the proposal should be: (a) justified by the public interest—for approved developmental purpose or for working capital needs; (b) in line with the credit worthiness of the borrower in relation to the risk involved; (c) in line with the Reserve Bank of India guidelines; and (d) follow the other conditions of the government regarding the period of levy, levy of a fee to cover the risk, representation for the government to be on the Board of management, mortgage or lien on the assets, submission of the accounts periodically to the government would be taken. Also, a guarantee commission of half a percent per annum on the outstanding guaranteed amounts is charged with some exceptions (*GO Ms No. 1227, dated December 18, 1976, GO Ms No. 580, dated July 14, 1995*). In 1998, the guidelines and procedures for issue of guarantees are revised. Earlier, guarantees were issued by the concerned administrative departments in consultation with the Finance department. However, under that practice, it was difficult to monitor or review the performance of the organizations on whether the loans are being repaid promptly and the guarantee commission paid on time. Consequently, the power of processing, issuing and administration of guarantees is vested in the Finance Department.

References

India, Government of (1999): *A Study on the Performance of State Road Transport Undertakings*, Planning Commission, New Delhi, September.

India, Government of (1997): *Annual Report on the Working of State Electricity Boards and Electricity Departments, Planning Commission, Power and Energy Division*, New Delhi. (February)

India, Government of (1993): *Report of the Committee on Norms for Maintenance of Roads*, Ministry of Surface Transport (Road Wing), New Delhi (March).

Raghavan, S.N. (1994): *Public Sector in India*, Asian Institute of Transport Development, New Delhi.

Sarma, J.V.M., G. Naresh and O.P. Bohra (1999): *State Fiscal Studies—Tamil Nadu*, Report Submitted to World Bank, Chennai.

Tamil Nadu, Government of (1997): *Note on Policy on Road Transport Services and Shipping*, Chennai.

Tamil Nadu, Government of: *Review of State Public Sector Enterprises in Tamil Nadu* (Various issues).

STATISTICAL STATEMENTS

TABLE A.1

Tamil Nadu: Sector-wise Capital Investment of PSUs, 1991-96

(Rs. crore)

	1991-92	*1992-93*	*1993-94*	*1994-95*	*1995-96*
Share Capital					
Agriculture and allied	13.81	14.11	14.33	14.47	15.06
Construction	27.83	31.87	40.48	45.66	51.41
Development finance	240.56	253.04	300.75	232.57	237.15
Development others	17.14	24.92	37.47	48.38	76.25
Goods transport	10.80	20.53	20.53	20.53	20.53
Manufacturing	154.25	156.25	159.75	183.66	171.22
Mining	14.27	19.27	24.52	24.52	24.52
Passenger transport	32.10	33.35	34.41	34.89	35.19
Trading	26.44	26.94	27.44	28.91	30.92
Miscellaneous	7.86	8.42	8.37	9.37	10.37
Total	545.06	588.70	668.05	642.96	672.62
Term Loans					
Agriculture and allied	21.68	20.33	22.72	30.86	32.10
Construction	5.36	7.89	14.98	22.62	27.77
Development finance	1,089.79	1,369.01	1,698.90	2,151.00	2,542.70
Development others	9.89	11.28	10.84	27.90	25.52
Goods transport	138.65	111.04	82.07	114.05	100.90
Manufacturing	127.13	99.97	177.79	589.98	669.95
Mining	10.99	5.76	5.09	12.53	8.74
Passenger transport	263.84	312.60	340.22	358.00	573.32
Trading	2.80	1.07	1.04	5.76	12.29
Miscellaneous	3.18	2.58	1.09	0.47	0.89
Total	1,673.31	1,941.53	2,354.74	3,313.17	3,994.18
Total Investment					
Agriculture and allied	35.49	34.44	37.05	45.33	47.16
Construction	33.19	39.76	55.46	68.28	79.18
Development finance	1330.35	1622.05	1999.65	2383.57	2779.85
Development others	27.03	36.20	48.31	76.28	101.77
Goods transport	149.45	131.57	102.60	134.58	121.43
Manufacturing	281.38	256.22	337.54	773.64	841.17
Mining	25.26	25.03	29.61	37.05	33.26
Passenger transport	295.94	345.95	374.63	392.89	608.51
Trading	29.24	28.01	28.48	34.67	43.21
Miscellaneous	11.04	11.00	9.46	9.84	11.26
Total	2218.37	2530.23	3022.79	3956.13	4666.80

Source: Government of Tamil Nadu, *Review of State Public Sector Enterprises in Tamil Nadu*, various years, State Bureau of Public Enterprises (Finance Department), Chennai.

TABLE A.2

Tamil Nadu: Sector-wise Government Funding of PSUs during 1991-96

(Rs crore)

	1992-93	*1993-94*	*1994-95*	*1995-96*
Government Equity				
Agriculture and allied	14.02	14.17	14.17	15.06
Construction	31.87	27.57	45.66	51.41
Development finance	190.33	189.29	207.96	212.49
Development others	17.20	33.79	47.67	76.25
Goods transport	20.55	20.53	20.53	20.53
Manufacturing	100.75	105.85	129.76	129.22
Mining	19.27	24.52	24.52	24.52
Passenger transport	33.35	34.41	34.89	35.19
Trading	26.94	27.44	28.91	30.92
Miscellaneous	4.30	4.30	5.30	6.56
Total	458.58	481.87	559.37	602.15
Government Loans				
Agriculture and allied	8.91	5.47	10.93	12.58
Construction	3.91	2.12	3.56	5.84
Development finance	359.68	490.20	681.55	823.64
Development others	11.16	10.81	11.31	12.36
Goods transport	0.00	0.00	0.00	0.00
Manufacturing	38.78	17.52	72.46	227.64
Mining	0.08	0.06	3.89	6.27
Passenger transport	118.60	87.35	65.28	174.42
Trading	0.00	1.04	0.01	0.01
Miscellaneous	0.00	0.00	0.00	0.00
Total	541.12	614.57	848.99	1262.76
Total Government Investment				
Agriculture and allied	22.93	19.64	25.10	27.64
Construction	35.78	29.69	49.22	57.25
Development finance	550.01	679.49	889.51	1036.13
Development others	28.36	44.60	58.98	88.61
Goods transport	20.55	20.53	20.53	20.53
Manufacturing	139.53	123.37	202.22	356.86
Mining	19.35	24.58	28.41	30.79
Passenger transport	151.95	121.76	100.17	209.61
Trading	26.94	28.48	28.92	30.93
Miscellaneous	4.30	4.30	5.30	6.56
Total	999.70	1096.44	1408.36	1864.91

TABLE A.3

Tamil Nadu: Employment and Wage Emoluments of PSUs during 1991-96

(Rs crore)

	1991-92	*1992-93*	*1993-94*	*1994-95*	*1995-96*
Employees					
Agriculture and allied	10,177	11,544	10,859	10,067	10,605
Construction	974	1,155	1,202	1,153	1,190
Development finance	3,024	3,047	2,961	3,051	2,984
Development others	2,764	2,660	2,721	2,854	2,786
Goods transport	153	153	184	184	184
Manufacturing	8,891	8,448	7,965	10,482	11,627
Mining	4,401	4,396	3,655	3,755	3,643
Passenger transport	108,573	111,440	114,936	113,224	114,589
Trading	11,937	11,615	10,976	10,910	12,350
Miscellaneous	1,600	2,140	2,797	849	838
Total ('000)	152,494	156,598	158,256	156,529	160,796
Share of PSU employment in total state	25.34%	26.46%	25.34%	24.35%	24.22%
Share of PSU employment in total quasi and local	20.98%	21.22%	21.54%	21.21%	21.97%
Share of PSU employment in total State	11.48%	11.77%	11.64%	11.34%	11.52%
Emoluments					
Agriculture and allied	10.87	16.14	23.59	24.40	27.78
Construction	2.48	3.01	24.69	6.13	6.74
Development finance	11.07	12.83	15.44	16.89	18.22
Development others	9.63	10.55	11.93	13.66	15.78
Goods transport	1.85	2.19	2.36	1.24	1.40
Manufacturing	32.44	36.09	36.95	62.21	72.87
Mining	11.72	14.02	17.82	18.40	17.17
Passenger transport	386.95	473.74	530.60	587.64	750.16
Trading	36.94	42.21	47.51	55.32	59.94
Miscellaneous	2.21	2.54	2.84	3.44	4.50
Total	506.16	613.32	713.73	789.33	974.56

Per Employee Emoluments (Rs.)					
Agriculture and allied	10,681	13,981	21,724	24,238	26,195
Construction	25,462	26,061	205,408	53,166	56,639
Development finance	36,607	42,107	52,145	55,359	61,059
Development others	34,841	39,662	43,844	47,863	56,640
Goods transport	120,915	143,137	128,261	67,391	76,087
Manufacturing	36,486	42,720	46,390	59,349	62,673
Mining	26,630	31,893	48,755	49,001	47,131
Passenger transport	35,640	42,511	46,165	51,901	65,465
Trading	30,946	36,341	43,285	50,706	48,534
Miscellaneous	13,813	11,869	10,154	40,518	53,699
Total	33,192	39,165	45,100	50,427	60,608

TABLE A.4

Tamil Nadu: Company-wise Trends in the Profit/Losses during 1990-96

(Rs. lakh)

Public Sector Undertaking	*1990-91*	*1991-92*	*1992-93*	*1993-94*	*1994-95*	*1995-96*
1	2	3	4	5	6	7
A. PSUs that are consistently making profits						
I. Mining Group (1)	881	1511	1788	1952	1360	154
1. TN Minerals Ltd.	881	1511	1788	1952	1360	154
II. Manufacturing Group (3)	3678	4374	4300	5440	5671	7983
2. TN Zari Ltd.	0	5	2	11	33	28
3. TN Salt Corp Ltd.	33	87	46	24	6	131
4. TN Newsprint & Papers Ltd.	3644	4281	4252	5405	5631	7824
III. Construction Group (1)	0	0	1	8	3	2
5. TN Police Housing Corp	0	0	1	8	3	2
IV Development (Finance) Group (6)	505	923	792	2989	1326	2680
6. TN Industrial Investt Corp	154	206	157	2005	587	975
7. State Industries Promotion Corp of TN	17	154	210	350	440	424
8. TN Industrial Dev Corp	322	516	341	391	67	358
9. TN Tpt Dev Finance Corp	12	17	8	127	52	283
10. TN Power & Infra Dev Corp	0	14	40	115	177	635
11. TN Urban Fin. & Infra Dev Corp	0	17	35	1	2	5

V. Development (Other) Group (2)	13	60	55	15	15	47
12. TN Handicrafts Dev Corp	12	55	51	14	4	35
13. Dharmapuri Dt Dev Corp	1	4	5	1	11	12
VI. Miscellaneous Group (3)	41	90	180	219	194	213
14. TN Warehousing Corp	41	90	180	219	187	204
15. Pallavan Tpt Consultancy Services	0	0	0	0	1	1
16. TN Medical Services Corp	0	0	0	0	7	8
ALL PSUs (16)	8796	11331	11417	16063	14239	19062
B. PSUs that are usually but not consistently making profits						
I. Mining Group (1)	133	-237	136	-452	-570	317
1. TN Magnesites Ltd.	133	-237	136	-452	-570	317
II. Manufacturing Group (3)	-659	-946	-219	-168	-490	878
2. TN Small Industries Corp	-681	-967	-240	-182	-224	21
3. Electronics Corp of Tamil Nadu	23	21	21	14	-69	32
4. TN Cements Ltd.	0	0	0	0	-197	825
III. Trading Group (2)	-1496	-63	-7	-246	29	8
5. TN Civil Supplies Corp	-1497	-18	-14	-265	0	0
6. TN State Mktg. Corp	2	-45	7	20	29	8
IV. Agriculture and Allied Group (3)	-165	-329	52	-120	125	372
7. TN Agro Industries Corp	-198	-163	8	-132	-174	14
8. TN Forest Plantation Corp	-22	45	186	-30	132	27
9. Arusu Rubber Corp	56	-212	-141	42	167	331

(Contd.)

TABLE A.4 (*Contd.*)

1	2	3	4	5	6	7
V. Development (Finance) Group (1)	14	-64	-6	-79	82	116
10. TN Textiles Corp	14	-64	-6	-79	82	116
VI. Development (Other) Group (4)	-10	55	9	39	-32	171
11. TN Fisheries Corp	-26	42	25	3	-36	62
12. TN Backward Class Eco Dev Corp	4	1	-3	17	20	77
13. TN Corp for Dev of Women	12	12	-1	1	1	0
14. TN Corp FOR Industrial Infra Dev	0	0	-13	17	-16	32
VII. Miscellaneous Group (1)	-5	1	16	5	4	2
15. Overseas Manpower Corp	-5	1	16	5	4	2
ALL PSUs (15)	-2845	-2530	-239	-1189	-1343	2743
C. PSUs that are usually but not consistently making losses						
I. Passenger Transport Group (10)	-1442	-709	-2389	-1311	604	-6626
1. Anna Tpt Corp	-111	-16	-140	40	34	-1106
2. Cheran Tpt Corp	-529	-384	-1210	-528	236	-927
3. Dheeran Chinnamalai Tpt Corp	-85	-50	-74	-153	123	-591
4. Jeeva Tpt Corp	-114	-36	-134	-46	108	-595
5. Pandiyan Roadways Corp	-140	37	356	17	-416	-1467
6. Pattukkottai Azhagiri Tpt Corp	-202	-216	-473	-229	62	-345
7. Thanthai Periyar Tpt Corp	80	81	-271	33	18	-624
8. Rani Mangammai Tpt Corp	-228	-9	-172	-191	142	-310
9. Annai Sathya Tpt Corp	-113	-115	-270	-108	287	-140
10. Rajiv Gandhi Tpt Corp	0	0	0	-145	9	-520

II. Goods Transport Group (1)	790	1190	1236	2117	1240	-1398
11. Poompuhar Shipping Corp	790	1190	1236	2117	1240	-1398
III. Manufacturing Group (3)	115	198	-181	143	-373	-788
12. TN Sugar Corp Ltd.	-349	-279	51	248	-276	-676
13. Cheran Engineering Corp	1	3	-8	1	0	-14
14. TN Spirit Corp	463	474	-224	-106	-98	-98
IV. Agriculture and Allied Group (2)	135	-304	-221	98	-606	-156
15. TN Tea Plantation Corp	134	-289	-218	93	-611	-149
16. TN Medicinal Plant Farms & Herbal Med. Corp	1	-15	-3	4	5	-7
V. Construction Group (2)	6	212	219	-162	-350	-469
17. TN State Constn Corp	6	7	-85	-282	-247	-215
18. TN Adi Dravidar Housing & Development Corp	0	206	304	119	-104	-255
VI. Development (Finance) Group (3)	13	9	15	19	-196	-710
19. TN Small Ind. Dev Corp	10	13	17	29	19	-426
20. TN Handloom Dev Corp	2	-5	-4	-10	-13	-20
21. TN Film Dev Corp	0	1	2	0	-202	-264
VII. Development (Other) Group (3)	-10	88	45	23	-103	-378
22. TN Tourism Dev Corp	33	42	62	28	-63	-90
23. TN Poultry Dev Corp	12	-3	-39	-50	-49	-129
24. TN Leather Dev Corp	-55	49	21	44	9	-159
VIII. Miscellaneous Group (1)	-2	-1	2	-4	-23	-8
25. TN Ex-Servicemen Corp	-2	-1	2	-4	-23	-8
ALL PSUs (25)	-280	883	-1457	1065	-182	-11321

(Contd.)

TABLE A.4 (Contd.)

1	2	3	4	5	6	7
D. PSUs that are consistently making losses						
I. Passenger Transport Group (9)	-2752	-1797	-2777	-4676	-4560	-12925
1. Cholan Roadways Corp	-254	-256	-52	-737	-977	-1330
2. Kattabommen Tpt Corp	-338	-234	-393	-1098	-886	-2175
3. Marudhu Pandiyar Tpt Corp	-202	-11	-97	-396	-586	-1174
4. Nesamony Tpt Corp	-332	-237	-361	-434	-319	-1132
5. Pallavan Tpt Corp	-1547	-987	-727	-842	-183	-1834
6. Thiruvalluvar Tpt Corp	-81	-72	-876	-717	-847	-1909
7. PT MGR Tpt Corp	0	0	-272	-348	-193	-939
8. Dr. Ambedkar Tpt Corp	0	0	0	-51	-20	-1580
9. Mahakavi Bharathiyar Tpt Corp	0	0	0	-52	-549	-852
II. Manufacturing Group (2)	-829	-756	-872	-823	-1151	-768
10. Southern Structurals Ltd.	-829	-756	-872	-823	-962	-177
11. TN Steel Corp Ltd.	0	0	0	0	-189	-591
IV. Development (Other) Group (1)	-10	-3	0	0	0	0
12. TN Meat Corp (Defunct)	-10	-3	0	0	0	0
ALL PSUs (11)	-4419	-3311	-4520	-6321	-6861	-14461

TABLE A.5

Tamil Nadu: State Subsidies to Road Transport Corporations during 1990-96

(Rs. lakh)

Undertaking	*1990-91*	*1991-92*	*1992-93*	*1993-94*	*1994-95*	*1995-96*
Passenger Transport Group	1,147	2,273	3,243	4,067	4,049	4,116
1. Anna Tpt Corp	0	94	146	327	160	164
2. Cheran Tpt Corp	0	216	259	306	263	281
3. Cholan Roadways Corp	0	93	219	296	145	156
4. Dheeran Chinnamalai Tpt Corp	0	0	0	325	204	202
5. Jeeva Tpt Corp	0	85	116	226	115	136
6. Kattabommen Tpt Corp	0	100	0	250	140	112
7. Marudhu Pandiyar Tpt Corp	0	0	80	183	121	119
8. Nesamony Tpt Corp	0	0	102	72	158	155
9. Pandiyan Roadways Corp	0	8	378	372	193	218
10. Pallavan Tpt Corp	1,147	1,489	1,650	1,002	1,043	1,020
11. Pattukkottai Azhagiri Tpt Corp	0	94	184	89	93	100
12. Thanthai Periyar Tpt Corp	0	0	0	154	177	202
13. Rani Mangammai Tpt Corp	0	93	109	109	131	133
14. Annai Sathya Tpt Corp	0	0	0	114	129	120
15. POINT MGR Tpt Corp	0	0	0	72	129	124
16. Dr. Ambedkar Tpt Corp	0	0	0	169	825	849
17. Mahakavi Bharathiyar Tpt Corp	0	0	0	0	24	25
Total of CMA	1,147	1,489	1,650	1,172	1,867	1,869
Share of subsidy to CMA transport (%)	100.00	65.50	50.89	28.81	46.12	45.42

TABLE A.6

Tamil Nadu: Road Transport Fare Structure and Concessions during 1992-98

(Paise/km)

Particulars	*1992-93*	*1993-94*	*1994-95*	*1995-96*	*1996-97*	*1997-98*
1. Ordinary	12.50	14.00	14.00	14.00	14.00	20.00
2. Express	12.50	14.50	14.50	14.50	14.50	23.00
Deluxe	14.50	17.00	17.00	17.00	17.00	28.00
Super-Deluxe	-	-	-	-	-	33.00
Super-Deluxe A/C	-	-	-	-	-	50.00
3. Ghat/Hills	14.45	14.50	14.50	14.50	14.50	21.00
45 paise for every block of 30 kms.						
4. City/Town	12.71	13.02	14.64	14.76	14.76	21.28
5. Weighted Average	13.26	15.51	14.92	14.92	14.92	21.07
6. Date of effectiveness	1.11.91	1.11.93	1.12.93	1.12.93	1.12.93	9.9.97
7. A. Concessions/free travel facilities						
i. Students: (Number in 000)				1,569	1,778	1,893
Amount (Rs. crore)				48.54	65.46	99.35
ii. Physical handicapped: Number				5,977	6,422	7,177
Amount (Rs. crore)				0.71	1.00	1.38
iii. Freedom fighter: Number				7,643	8,637	8,837
Amount (Rs. crore)				1.97	2.19	2.20
iv. Journalists: Number				1,070	1,219	1,373
Amount (Rs. crore)				0.15	0.20	0.20
v. Language stir: Number				2,486	2,797	2,814
Amount (Rs. crore)				0.55	0.60	0.60
vi. Cancer Patients: Number				364	495	134
Amount (Rs. crore)				0.01	0.01	
vii. MLAs/ MPs: Number				234	234	234
Amount (Rs. crore)				2.50	2.50	2.50
viii. Drama Artists: Number				83	183	103
Amount (Rs. crore)				0.00	0.00	0.00
Total: (Number in 000)				1,587	1,797	1,914
Total: Amount (Rs. crore)				54.44	71.95	106.23
B. Reimbursement by Government, if any (Rs. crore)				36.19	54.90	42.66
C. Balance (Uncovered loss due to concessions—Rs. crore)				18.25	17.05	63.56
D. Balance as percent to total concession				33.53	23.70	59.84

Source: Govt. of Tamil Nadu, Finance Department, Resources for Annual Plan, 1998-99, Contribution of Road Transport Corporations, December 1997.

TABLE A.7

Tamil Nadu: State Road Transport Corporations as on 31.5.1998

Name of the Corporation	*Date of operation*	*Principal area of operation*	*Fleet (31.5.98)*
1	*2*	*3*	*4*
1. Metropolitan Transport Corporation Ltd., (Chennai Dn I), Chennai *(Pallavan Tpt Corpn Ltd., PTC)*	01.01.1972	Chennai Metropolitan Area (South)	1,523
2. Metropolitan Transport Corporation Ltd., (Chennai Dn II), Chennai *(Dr. Ambedkar Tpt Corpn Ltd., DATC)*	19.01.1994	Chennai Metropolitan Area (North)	1,337
3. State Express Transport Corporation Ltd , (Tamil Nadu Dn I), Chennai *(Thiruvalluvar Tpt Corpn Ltd. TTC)*	01.04.1980	Entire State of Tamil Nadu	829
4. State Express Transport Corporation Ltd., (Tamil Nadu Dn II), Chennai *(Rajiv Gandhi Tpt Corpn Ltd. RGTC)*	27.01.1994	Inter State service	255
5. Tamil Nadu State Transport Corporation Ltd., (Villupuram Dn I), Villupuram *(Thanthai Periyar Tpt Corpn Ltd. TPTC)*	16.01.1975	Villupuram and Cuddalore Districts	1,007
6. Tamil Nadu State Transport Corporation Ltd., (Villupuram Dn II), Vellore *(Pattukkottai Azhagiri Tpt Corpon Ltd. PATC)*	01.12.1982	Vellore and Thiruvannamalai Districts	830

(Contd.)

TABLE A.7 (*Contd.*)

1	2	3	4
7. Tamil Nadu State Transport Corporation Ltd., (Villupuram Dn II), Kanchipuram *(Puratchi Thalaivar MGR Tpt Corpn Ltd.)*	01.04.1992	Kanchipuram and Thiruvallur Districts	749
8. Tamil Nadu State Transport Corporation Ltd., (Salem Dn I), Salem *(Anna Tpt Corpn Ltd. ATC)*	15.02.1973	Salem and Dharmapuri Districts	957
9. Tamil Nadu State Transport Corporation Ltd., (Salem Dn II), Dharmapuri *(Annai Sathia Tpt Corpn Ltd. ASTC)*	01.04.1987	Dharmapuri Districts	692
10. Tamil Nadu State Transport Corporation Ltd., (Coimbatore Dn I), Coimbatore *(Cheran Tpt Corpn Ltd. CTC)*	01.03.1972	Coimbatore Districts	1,210
11. Tamil Nadu State Transport Corporation Ltd., (Coimbatore Dn II), Erode *(Mahakavi Bharathiyar Tpt Corpn Ltd. JTC)*	01.04.1983	Erode District	915
12. Tamil Nadu State Transport Corporation Ltd., (Coimbatore Dn III), Ooty *(Mahakavi Bharathiyar Tpt Corpn Ltd. MKBTC)*	18.02.1994	The Nilgiris District	409
13. Tamil Nadu State Transport Corporation Ltd., (Kumbakonam Dn I), Kumbakonam *(Cholan Roadways Corpn Ltd. CRC)*	01.02.1972	Thanjavur, Nagapattinam and Thiruvarur Districts	952
14. Tamil Nadu State Transport Corporation Ltd., (Kumbakonam Dn II), Trichy *(Marudhu Pandiyar Tpt Corpn Ltd. DCTC)*	01.04.1985	Thiruchirapalli, Karur and Perambalur Districts	971

15.	Tamil Nadu State Transport Corporation Ltd., Kumbakonam Dn III), Karikudi *(Marudhu Pandiyar Tpt Corpn Ltd. MPTC)*	01.04.1983	Sivaganga and Ramanathapuram Districts	593
16.	Tamil Nadu State Transport Corporation Ltd., (Kumbakonam Dn IV), Pudukottai *(Veeran Alagumuthu Tpt Corpn Ltd. VATC)*	16.03.1996	Pudukottai Districts	348
17.	Tamil Nadu State Transport Corporation Ltd., (Madurai Dn I), Madurai *(Pandiyan Roadways Corpn Ltd. PRC)*	17.01.1972	Madurai District	962
18.	Tamil Nadu State Transport Corporation Ltd., (Madurai Dn II), Thirunelvell *(Kottabomman Tpt Corpn Ltd. KTC)*	01.01.1974	Tirunelveli and Toothukudi Districts	877
19.	Tamil Nadu State Transport Corporation Ltd., (Madurai Dn III), Negerkoil *(Nesamony Tpt Corpn Ltd. NTC)*	01.04.1983	Kanyakumari District	674
20.	Tamil Nadu State Transport Corporation Ltd., (Madurai Dn IV), Dindigui *(Rani Mangammai Tpt Corpn Ltd. RMTC)*	01.04.1986	Dindigul District	755
21.	Tamil Nadu State Transport Corporation Ltd., (Madurai Dn V), Virudhunagar *(Veeran Sundaralingam Tpt Corpn Ltd. VSTC)*	01.05.1997	Virudhunagar District	382
	Total			**17,227**

SECTION II

Primary Sector Prism

13
CHAPTER

Utilisation of Irrigation for Sustainable Agricultural Development in Tamil Nadu

D. RUDRAPPAN

INTRODUCTION

Agriculture has a dominant role in the Indian economy. The contribution of agricultural sector to national income, foreign exchange, employment and industrial development is at maximum. Thus, the very economic structure of India rests upon agriculture. Agriculture contributes nearly 25 per cent of the GDP and accounts for about 18 per cent of the total value of the country's exports[1]. India ranks fourth in the world after USA, USSR and China. The country has the largest area in the world under pulse cultivation and it also stood first in the field of cotton. Of the total geographical area of about 329 million hectares cultivable area, net sown area and gross cropped area comprise 186 million hectares, 146 million hectares and 175 million hectares, respectively. By the end of the Ninth Plan, India has harnessed its vast water resources by creating an irrigation potential of about 70 million hectares[2]. The agricultural sector of Tamil Nadu, excluding forestry and fishing, contributed 27.9 per cent to the Gross Domestic Product of the State as on 2000. The contribution of this sector has been on the decline during the last three decades. During 1970-71, the share of agriculture in the economy was 45 per cent and this has declined sharply to 38 per cent in 1980-81 and to 27.9 per cent in 1999-2000[3].

Tamil Nadu is typically characterized by an ever increasing population pressure and declining man-land ratio. With the growth of population and the consequent need for larger agricultural production, the requirement of irrigation has increased a great deal. To inject dynamism in T.N's traditional agriculture, assured water supply is essential to inspire the agriculturist with hope in the farm business and to work with optimism. As water has magical properties of turning deserts into smiling fields, irrigation deserves top most priority in achieving agricultural development in any region or locality. It is not necessary to stress that irrigation is the most powerful source of generating employment in the rural areas. Like education for a man, irrigation is for land and agricultural development[4]. Irrigation provides livelihood for hundreds of millions of people in developing countries. In parts of South Asia, where it has seen a massive thrust in rural and national development, extensive irrigation networks coexist with the greatest concentration of rural poverty in the world.

Production and livelihood are linked, but poverty alleviation in the mid-1980s was partly because of food surpluses. The generation and support of livelihood is a higher priority than production *per se*. The key question is concerned with *'who gains and who loses'* from irrigation. Generally, the poor stand to gain from better managed irrigation—in employment and income, in security against impoverishment, in low out-migration and in quality of life. In South Asia, about 68 per cent of all irrigation is in India and 26 per cent is in Pakistan. Over half of the irrigation in the sub-continent is from dual-managed systems, controlled by official irrigation staff in their upper parts and by farmers lower down.

The most important input for agricultural development in India is irrigation, as it facilitates multiple cropping and increases crop productivity. These objectives can be achieved only by providing assured irrigation facilities to the cultivators. Agriculture forms the chief source of income-earning activity for the rural poor of the developing countries like India[5]. It offers livelihood to about 65 per cent of the rural farm households and it continues to dominate the farm economy.

Trevelyan has aptly remarked:

> "Irrigation is everything in India, water is even more valuable than land because when water is applied to land it increases the productivity at least six-fold and renders great extent of productive land, which otherwise would produce nothing or next to nothing."

But still Indian agriculture depends upon heavy monsoons, which are a gamble in nature. We find drought conditions in major parts of the country because of the failure of monsoons for consecutive years and result in famine or near famine conditions at various places. The vast areas still continue to be at the mercy of sufficient and timely rains to avoid drought and famine. About one-fifth of the total water derived from rainfall is naturally made use of for growing crops and remainder being either lost by erosion, evaporation or absorption by the soil. This additional supply of water through irrigation makes harvesting possible for two or three crops or cultivation of crops requiring perennial water supply. Irrigation produces higher yields and efficient use of agricultural land in areas of inadequate rainfall.

ROLE OF IRRIGATION IN ECONOMIC DEVELOPMENT

Irrigation plays an important role in generating employment in rural areas. The employment and income dynamics of irrigation goes beyond the farm sector. Irrigation expansion also plays a vital role in regional development. In India, the additional employment generation during the Eighth Plan is 8.7 million person-years (mpys) with 2.6 mpys in construction and operation and maintenance and 6.1 mpys in farm and rural non-farm activities. Estimates have it that a 100-rupee worth of irrigation-induced incremental agricultural output generates Rs. 105 worth of additional output in manufacturing and Rs. 114 in the tertiary service sector, implying a non-farm output multiplier of 2.19[6].

Irrigation has been the major source of agricultural growth in India and the pursuit of the country's goal of self-sufficiency has been based on massive investment on irrigation. The only means of increasing irrigated crop production is by increasing the efficiency with which every unit of the water resources is utilized in crop production. It is towards this goal, for example, that the Tamil Nadu's Water Resources Consolidation project was developed[7].

Great variation in the potential productivity between irrigation and rain dependent crop production emphasises the crucial role of irrigation towards maximization of crop productivity. Irrigation also has a favourable influence on the cropping pattern. In the rainfed areas, cropping pattern depends on the incidence and distribution of rainfall, climate and nature of the soil. Provision of irrigation to rainfed areas has brought radical changes in the cropping pattern. Irrigation increases the intensity of inputs utilization and irrigated crops require higher doses of inputs such as labour, manure, fertilizers and pesticides. Higher fertilizer use necessitates sufficient moisture in the soil. With assured irrigation, farmers in the irrigated tracts invest more on the inputs to enhance their productivity.

Irrigation acts as an instrument in the elimination of rural poverty as well. Agricultural labourers, small and marginal farmers and rural artisans constitute the largest bulk of the Indian people, for whom irrigation responds favourably with additional employment opportunity. The yield per acre in the irrigated crop is higher than in the rainfed crops. Irrigation thus generates farm income by increasing the productivity of land and favourable input-output ratio. Irrigation facilitates the growth of commercial and horticultural crops, which pay higher dividends.

Irrigation is a protective measure against drought, which affects crop production and often causes extensive drainage on human resources as well as cattle wealth. It contributes to the development of agro-based industries, which in turn help develop services and infrastructures. Above all, it promotes social change by improving the income and living standards of the people. In conclusion, irrigation plays a vital role in the economic development of a region through improvement in cropping patterns, increase in production and productivity, and promotes newer ideas and concepts in irrigation management.

The growth in agricultural production in Tamil Nadu is quite volatile, as a result of uncertain rainfall. Cropping is carried out during more than one season, depending upon the potential for crop rotation and the availability of irrigation facilities. The gross cropped area represents the area that is sown more than once. Cropping intensity which is described as the ratio of Gross Cropped Area to Net Sown Area has increased from 111.1 in 1950-51 to 132.7 in 1996-97, as a result of expansion in irrigation facilities[8]. In Tamil Nadu net area irrigated increased from 22 per cent of the sown area in 1970-71 to 52.7 per cent in 1997-98. In 1997-98, the area sown more than once accounts for 9.70 lakh hectares and the principal crop, paddy is grown in 22.60 lakh hectares in Tamil Nadu. In terms of area, the second place is occupied by groundnut which is raised in 8.77 lakh hectares and the third place by cereals, raised in 8.03 lakh hectares. With reference to irrigation in the State, the total net area irrigated accounts for 29.44 lakh hectares comprising 8.37 lakh hectares (28.43%) irrigated by Government canals; tanks 6.75 lakh hectares (22.93%); tube wells 2.08 lakh hectares; (07.09%) irrigation wells 12.03 lakh hectares (40.87%); and other sources provide irrigation to 18,740 hectares (0.68%) of land in the State. Gross area irrigated in the State has enhanced to 35.18 lakh hectares[9].

MODES OF IRRIGATION

The three main modes or sources of irrigation in Tamil Nadu are rivers, tanks and wells. Streams and spring channels are the other sources of minor importance. In the 1950s surface irrigation viz. canals and tanks registered a better rate of growth than wells. In 1960s and 1970s, canal irrigated area has stagnated and tank irrigation has declined, while there has been a striking increase in groundwater development. As a result, wells now contribute to more than 40 per cent of net irrigated area in Tamil Nadu as compared to about 25 per cent in the 1950s.

In spatial terms, canal irrigation is relatively more concentrated than the other modes. Thanjavur district alone accounts for nearly 51 per cent of net canal irrigated area. Five other districts account for a further 38.6 per cent, viz. Coimbatore and Periyar (14.5 per cent), Tiruchirapalli (9.2 per cent), Cuddalore (9.0 per cent), and Madurai (5.9 per cent). These are the districts watered by major rivers such as the Cauvery, Parambikulam—Aliyar, Palar, Pennaiyar and Periyar-Vaigai. In the case of tank irrigation, seven districts together account for more than 90 per cent of net irrigated area, viz. Ramanathapuram (23.3 per cent), Chengalpattu (18.6 per cent), Cuddalore (12.0 per cent), Pudukottai (9.9 per cent), North Arcot (9.8 per cent), Tirunelveli (9.7 per cent) and Madurai (7.0 per cent). These are the districts which benefit significantly from the North-East monsoon in which river systems, feed a number of tanks (North Arcot, Tirunelveli and Madurai). Well irrigation is prominent in eight districts: Coimbatore and Periyar (15.9 per cent), Cuddalore (14.8 per cent), Vellore and Tiruvannamalai (14.1 per cent), Madurai (11.8 per cent), Salem (9.3 per cent), Kancheepuram and Thiruvallur (8.2 per cent) and Tiruchirapalli (8.2 per cent)[10].

IRRIGATION AND THE CROPPING PATTERN

Paddy has remained the dominant one among irrigated crops in Tamil Nadu, accounting for 67 per cent of gross irrigated area in the late 1970s. The extension of irrigation, in the 1960s through 1970s, has resulted in part, in a shift from dry cereals to paddy, but a substantial portion of about 75 per cent of the additional area brought under irrigation, has been devoted to commercial crops such as sugarcane, cotton, oilseeds, chillies, fruits and vegetables. The relatively well-intensive districts are also the ones which irrigated commercial crops, such as sugarcane.

At the commencement of the First Five Year Plan, there were 23 major and medium irrigation projects benefitting 1.10 million hectares in Tamil Nadu. Against the ultimate irrigation potential assessed as 1.5 million hectares from major and medium irrigation projects by National Commission on Agriculture during 1976, the State has harnessed 1.47 million hectares from major and medium projects and 0.5 million hectares from minor irrigation schemes during the end of Eighth Five Year Plan (1992-97).

The following Table 1 on decadal trends of irrigation system describes the importance of ground water irrigation and points out that it has improved substantially from 23.48 per cent in 1950s to 47 per cent in mid-1970s and then to 48.71 per cent in 1997-98. However, diminishing trend has been observed with reference to surface irrigation systems; canal irrigation has declined from 37.57 per cent to 26.45 per cent and tank irrigation from 36.78 per cent to 22.94 per cent during the same period. The spurt in ground water exploitation has enhanced the per centage of area under crops irrigated to total cropped area from 40.87 per cent to 47.00 per cent leading to an increase in the area irrigated more than once from 6.19 lakh hectares in 1950 to 6.57 lakh hectares in 1995.

According to the assessment made by the Central Water Commission as on January 1992, the extent of ground water recharge and development in Tamil Nadu are worked out to be 60 per cent and it has increased to 63 per cent in 1997. The ultimate irrigation potential of the State as assessed by the Central Water Commission is presented in the following Table 2.

The Central Water Commission has reported that surface water has been tapped almost fully with a meagre remaining potential of ground water yet to be tapped which can irrigate an additional 2.36 lakh hectares only in Tamil Nadu in 1995.

Table 3 reveals that Tamil Nadu received an annual rainfall of 1080.4 mm during the year 1998-99 which was higher by 18 per cent over the normal rainfall of 981.3 mm. A decade earlier, the State received an actual rainfall of 714.5 mm as against the normal rainfall of 925 in the year, 1990-91. The season-wise rainfall and its contribution to the total rainfall has been described. As regards profitability of agriculture, it is pointed out that demand for irrigation is an inverse function of rainfall in a crop season.

The following Table 4 describes the irrigation pattern and changes in the sources of water supply in Tamil Nadu

TABLE I

Decadal Trends of Irrigation Systems in Tamil Nadu

Area irrigated source-wise	*Annual Average (in lakh Hectares) (Percentages in brackets)*					
	1950s	*1960s*	*1970s*	*1980s*	*1990s*	
					(1990-95)	*(97-98)*
Net area irrigated						
1. Canal system	7.92	8.83	8.94	8.23	8.24	8.37
	(37.57)	(35.62)	(33.16)	(32.99)	(30.53)	(28.45)
2. Tank system	7.76	9.12	8.49	6.15	6.15	6.75
	(36.78)	(36.79)	(31.49)	(24.69)	(22.83)	(22.94)
3. Well irrigation	4.97	6.45	9.18	10.38	12.19	14.11
	(23.48)	(26.02)	(34.05)	(41.81)	(45.16)	(48.71)
4. Other sources	0.46	0.39 24.79	0.35	0.19	6.40	0.18
	(2.17)	(1.50)	(1.30)	(0.08)	(1.48)	(0.60)
	21.11	24.79	26.96	24.96	26.99	29.44
	(100)	(100)	(100)	(100)	(100)	(100)

Source: Season and Crop Reports of Tamil Nadu, 1995 and 1997-98, Director, Department of Economics and Statistics, Chennai-6.

Area irrigated source-wise	*Annual Average (in lakhs Hectares)*				
	1950	*1960*	*1970*	*1980*	*1990 (1990-95)*
1. Area irrigated more than once	6.19	7.87	8.26	6.19	6.57
2. Gross area irrigated	27.30	32.66	35.22	31.15	33.56
3. Irrigation intensity (in per cent)	129.32	131.75	130.64	124.80	124.86
4. Percentage of area under crops irrigated to total cropped area	40.87	45.36	47.24	46.65	47.00

Figures in parentheses indicate percentage to total.
Source: Season and Crops Reports of Tamil Nadu, 1995, Director, Department of Economics and Statistics, Chennal-6.

consequent upon the introduction of green revolution programmes, which had a very extensive second innings during the early half of 1970s, after its introduction in the late 1960s. The number of canals which stood at 2,895 in 1976-77 increased to 2,422 in 1980-81 along with a spurt in other

TABLE 2

Irrigation Potentials of Tamil Nadu State: Year 1995

(In lakh hectares)

Name of the Sector	Surface water	Ground water	Total
I. Utimate irrigation potential available			
A. Major and Medium irrigation	15	—	15
B. Minor irrigation schemes	9	15	24
Total (A + B).	24	15	39
	(61.54%)	(38.46%)	(100.00%)
II. Potential created as on 1994	24.36	12.64	37
III. Potential yet to be tapped	Nil	2.36	2

Figures in parenthesis indicate percentage to total.

Source: Water and Related Statistics 1995, Central Water Commission, Government of India, New Delhi.

sources of water supply such as wells which has grown from 15,74,269 to 6,13,103 and the number of irrigation tanks increased from 38,296 to 40,487 during the same period. Thereafter during the year, 1983-84, the number of canals declined to 2,384 along with a reduction in the number of tanks to 37,716 due to insufficient attention paid to repairing and maintenance of canals and tanks by the Government.

Further, the fall in the number of canals and tanks forced the peasants to search for other sources of irrigation. Consequently, the number of wells had increased from 16,25,986 in 1981-82 to 16,54,193 in the year 1993 and the number of tube wells increased from 56,975 to 87,215 during the same period. Thereafter, it has been observed that there has been continuously an increasing trend in the number of irrigation wells to 16,57,022 and tube wells to 1,45,444 in 1997-98, due to continuous exploitation of ground water for agricultural use, in the context of negligence of public irrigation tanks and dwindling number of canals and canal length. Moreover, ground water offers considerable potential to enhance land productivity.

Gross area sown, gross area irrigated and total food grains production in Tamil Nadu over a period of 22 years

TABLE 3

Year	South West Monsoon		North East Monsoon		Winter Season		Hot Weather Season		Total	
	Normal Rainfall	Actual Rainfall	Normal Rainfall	Actual Rainfall	Normal Rainfall	Actual Rainfall	Normal Rainfall	Actual Rainfall	Normal Rainfall	Actual Rainfall
Tamil Nadu State										
1990-91	307.6	239.3	438.7	372.6	42.2	30.3	136.5	72.3	925	714.5
1997-98	324.6	286	460.8	783.3	47.3	5.5	143.9	78.4	976.6	1152.2
1998-99	326.2	340.1	470.5	602.4	447.3	21.5	137.3	116.4	981.3	1080

Source: Statistical Handbook of Tamilnadu, 1990-91, 1997-98, 1998-99, Department of Economics and Statistics, Government of Tamilnadu, Chennai-6.

TABLE 4

Irrigation Pattern and Sources of Water Supply in Tamil Nadu State

Year	*No. of Canals*	*Canal Length in Kms*	*No. of Tube Wells*	*No. of Wells*	*No. of Reservoirs*	*No. of Tanks*
1976-77	2895	15899	38719	1574269	33	38296
1977-78	2486	15227	44288	1550259	33	38695
1978-79	2392	11501	47734	1585272	34	38297
1979-80	2407	12257	49101	1607449	35	38294
1980-81	2422	12747	53295	1613103	42	40487
1981-82	2391	12626	56975	1625986	45	38304
1982-83	2383	12651	61478	1639344	45	37944
1983-84	2384	12632	63107	1642143	48	37716
1984-85	2438	12536	58751	1657409	49	37629
1985-86	2381	12561	62903	1672770	49	37645
1986-87	2290	12416	71895	1677185	58	37949
1987-88	2280	12550	82142	1644723	61	38229
1988-89	2280	12541	87215	1651193	62	38349
1989-90	2290	12611	88476	1657907	64	38483
1990-91	2296	12611	93074	1775260	64	38483
1991-92	2227	12611	99004	1682453	64	38752
1992-93	2229	12666	108342	1683492	66	38863
1993-94	2322	9668	109696	1690684	62	38863
1994-95	2323	9676	124213	1715541	62	38863
1995-96	2314	9720	137316	1690936	66	38706
1996-97	2314	9672	143207	1644946	66	39003
1997-98	2330	9720	145444	1657022	67	39003

Source: The Statistical Handbook of Tamil Nadu, Annual Issues from 1978-79 to 1997-98, Director of Economics and Statistics, Government of Tamil Nadu, Chennai-6.

have been traced in the following Table 5. The per centage of gross area irrigated hovered around 50 per cent, though there were some minor ups and downs by one or two per cent every year. Similarly, the total food grains production also varied from 60 to 80 lakh tonnes and the variation has taken place on account of natural factors such as, vagaries of monsoon, acute drought and flood havoc. Out of a gross sown area of 71.47 lakh hectares, 30.00 lakh hectares have been irrigated in the

TABLE 5

Gross Area Sown and Gross Area Irrigated in Tamil Nadu

(in hectares)

Year	*Total Food Grains Production (in 000 tonnes)*	*Gross Area Irrigated*	*Gross Area Sown*	*Percentage of Column (2) to (3)*
1	2	3	4	5
1976-77	6,337	3,000,165	7,147,018	42
1977-78	7,750	3,722,648	7,768,174	47.9
1978-79	7,598	3,818,565	7,684,230	49
1979-80	7,641	3,982,708	7,717,286	51.6
1980-81	5,651	3,294,000	6,470,000	50.9
1981-82	7,376	3,427,098	6,909,357	49.6
1982-83	4,975	2,732,054	6,030,476	45.3
1983-84	6,261	3,249,448	6,944,959	46.8
1984-85	6,888	3,506,707	7,088,209	49.5
1985-86	7,270	3,239,797	6,818,795	47.51
1986-87	7,181	2,844,314	6,508,349	43.7
1987-88	7,480	2,945,075	6,728,602	43.8
1988-89	7,329	2,873,178	6,450,959	44.5
1989-90	7,917	2,891,432	6,631,761	43.6
1990-91	7,496	2,891,432	6,631,761	43.6
1991-92	8,265	3,256,794	6,977,129	46.7
1992-93	8,358	3,384,718	7,067,217	47.9
1993-94	8,257	3,544,458	7,158,464	49.5
1994-95	9,081	3,587,547	7,025,988	51
1995-96	6,405	3,183,090	6,267,089	50.79
1996-97	6,930	3,347,401	6,456,686	51.8
1997-98	8,104	3,518,943	6,557,895	53.6

Source: The Statistical Handbook of Tamil Nadu, Annual Issues from 1978-79 to 1997-98, Director of Economics and Statistics, Government of Tamil Nadu, Chennai-6.

year 1976-77, accounting for 42%. Further, foodgrains production registered 63.37 lakh tonnes in the same year. The very next year, i.e. 1977-78 per centage of gross area irrigated to gross area sown has enhanced to 49%, as a result of which foodgrains production soared to the tune of 77.50 lakh tonnes. However, in the year 1979-80, the increase in per centage of gross area irrigated has increased to the level of 51.6% and this has not resulted in any gain in the production of meagre 75.98 lakh tonnes.

Although the per centage of gross area irrigated stood at 50.90% in 1980-81, the foodgrains production slumped to a low ebb of 56.51 lakh tonnes on account of unfavourable monsoon conditions. Similarly, it has been observed in the year 1982-83, the per centage of area irrigated dwindled to 45.3% resulting in the reduction of production to 49.75 lakh tonnes due to contraction in the gross irrigated area to 27.32 lakh hectares. The same momentum in irrigation has been maintained till 1990-91. Despite the fact that variation occurred to foodgrains production ranging from 6 to 8 lakhs of tonnes during the period 1984-85 to 1991-92. The year 1994-95 is a turning point in foodgrains production since, the output touched a record level of 90.81 lakh tonnes with 51% gross sown area irrigated. Subsequently, natural factors played havoc causing deceleration in the production to 64.05 lakhs in 1995-96 and 69.30 lakhs 1996-97. Invariably, scanty rainfall in some districts of the state seems to be the common phenomenon encountered by the farmers in the lean years. The year 1995-98 witnessed an increase in per centage of gross area irrigated to 53.60 resulting in the enhancement of production to 81.04 lakh tonnes.

However, the expansion of irrigated area *per se* is an inadequate measure of the irrigation development. More than this, timelines and assurance of water supplies; the extent of flexibility in adjusting water supply to crop water needs and the water use efficiency assume significance for a faster pace of agricultural development.

The following Table 6 on the cropping pattern of Tamil Nadu delineates an increasing trend towards the cultivation of commercial crops since the area devoted to food crops cultivation has been going down during the period starting from 1976-77 to 1997-98. The per centage area used for cultivating paddy has gone down from 35.9 per cent in 1976-

TABLE 6

Cropping Pattern in Tamil Nadu

Year	*Paddy*	*Cholam*	*Cumbu*	*Ragi*	*Cotton*	*Ground Nut*	*Others*
1976-77	35.9*	0.11	6.4	4.1	3.4	12.5	30.6
1977-78	35.8	9.7	5.6	3.7	4.2	11.9	29.1
1978-79	35.9	9	5.3	3.6	4.5	12.8	28.9
1979-80	37.3	9.2	4.7	3.2	3.6	12.8	29.2
1980-81	35.5	9.1	5.1	3.1	3.4	13	30.8
1981-82	36.2	10.2	4.8	3.1	3.1	12.5	30.1
1982-83	32.7	11.2	4.9	2.9	3.1	12.6	32.6
1983-84	34.8	11.2	4.9	2.9	2.7	12.8	30.7
1984-85	35.4	9.7	4.6	2.9	3.6	13.5	30.3
1985-86	33.2	10.7	4.5	4.6	3.7	13.7	30.1
1986-87	30	11.2	4.6	2.7	2.9	13.8	34.8
1987-88	29.1	10.2	4.3	2.5	3.6	14.7	35.6
1988-89	29.2	8.7	4.2	2.5	4	14.9	36.5
1989-90	28.8	8.6	3.8	2.5	4.1	14.8	37.3
1990-91	28	8.2	4.1	2.6	3.6	14.5	39
1991-92	30.3	7.3	3.5	2.3	3.7	15.7	37.2
1992-93	30.9	6.85	3.1	2.13	3.77	16.81	36.44
1993-94	32.2	7.1	3	2.2	3.2	16.2	36.1
1994-95	31.7	6.1	2.7	2.1	3.6	15.4	38.4
1995-96	31.12	6.12	2.75	1.94	4.16	14.89	39.02
1996-97	33.67	6.12	2.55	1.7	3.9	13.9	38.16
1997-98	34.47	5.8	2.57	1.63	3.47	13.23	38.83

* The data have been taken from official records of Tamil Nadu Government. As only one digit is given thereafter the decimal point, the same procedure is adopted here also.

** Separate data for each crop under the category 'others' is not available in the Table given by the Government of Tamil Nadu. However, under the category of "others", Sugar is the dominant crop.

Source: The Statistical Handbook of Tamil Nadu, Annual Issues from 1978-79 to 1997-98, Director of Economics and Statistics, Government of Tamil Nadu, Chennai-6.

77 to 34.47 per cent in 1997-98. The cultivable area used for bajra also has gone down from 5.3 per cent to 2.75 per cent, for ragi from 3.6 per cent to 1.94 per cent and for cholam from 9.0 per cent to 6.12 per cent during the same period.

Further, undulating variations have been observed in the

area pertaining to the cultivation of cotton from 4.5 per cent in 1978-77 to 2.9 per cent in 1986-87 and this had climbed up to 4.16 per cent in the year 1995-96. The Table shows the increased importance attached to groundnut cultivation in terms of enhanced per centage of land area from 12.5 in 1976-77 to 13.23 in 1997-98, over a period of 20 years. Further, the per centage area used for raising other commercial crops such as sugarcane also has gone up considerably from 30.6 per cent in 1978-79 to 38.83 in 1997-98.

There is competing demand on the available water resources. Possibilities for increasing the water resources for irrigation appear slender, hence water use efficiency and irrigation management will receive high priority. Reliability of public irrigation resources in Tamil Nadu is poor compared to the Northern river basins of the country. This introduces a certain risk element even in irrigated agriculture and makes it all the more important to have transparency in the management of reservoirs and public distribution network.

Water use efficiency is comparatively higher in ground water irrigation. But over mining of ground water in certain tracts is leading to disastrous consequences. The major constraints to the further expansion of irrigated areas are dwindling ground water resources, soil health problem and other fiscal constraints. Inter-cropping, multiple cropping, relay cropping, productivity improvement are the factors which might influence the cropping intensity and this has been estimated at 124.86 per cent in 1995.

FARMER'S MANAGEMENT OF IRRIGATION AND GOVERNMENT'S POLICY

Past experience would suggest that the inadequate attention paid to farm level irrigation water management is one of the reasons for the low performance of irrigation projects in the State. Consequently, the Tamil Nadu government considered farmers' organisation as the best possible one for the scientific and systematic development and maintenance of irrigation infrastructure. Hence, farmers' organisations have been given an effective role in the management and supply and distribution of water. For promoting the above stated objectives, Tamil Nadu Government passed an Act by name "Tamil Nadu Farmers' Management of Irrigation Systems Act, 2000" and this act received the assent of the President on February 25, 2001. Besides, over the years, the government has been trying to expand the irrigation base by providing increasing amount of electricity for irrigation pumping in rural areas, by specifically investing in rural electrification, watershed schemes and Million Wells Scheme. Under rural development programme as well as under rural credit programmes private households were extended loans along with subsidy to buy water extracting machines.

CONCLUSION

With the rapid growth of population and consequent slow growth of non-agricultural sectors, irrigation has to play a productive role than a protective role. Frequent recurrence of famine and drought has further enhanced the importance of irrigation to achieve agricultural growth with stability. The scope for increasing the net cultivated area being limited, further growth in agricultural production has to be achieved through diversified and multiple cropping and increased agricultural productivity.

The provision of irrigation facilities alone will not enhance the productive capacity of the region. The productivity of any irrigation project depends upon the several social and agro-economic conditions of the concerned region that have to be improved so as to maximize benefits per unit of water. Hence, irrigation is an instrument in the gradual elimination of poverty. It enhances the productivity of crop and generates farm income, employment and development of agro-based industries. Thus, irrigation contributes to economic development through agricultural development. Tamil Nadu is essentially an agricultural State depending on sufficient and equitable supply and distribution of water, which is a national wealth calling for the optimum utilisation by farmers for sustainable agricultural development. Hence, it is essential to promote and secure distribution of water among its users. Adequate maintenance of the irrigation system, efficient and the economical utilisation of water to optimize agricultural production by involving the farmers and inculcating a sense of ownership of the irrigation system in them in accordance with the water budget and the operational plan are most required.

Notes and References

1. India 2000, Agriculture: 402.
2. The Hindu Survey of Indian Agriculture, 1999.
3. Centre for Monitoring Indian Economy, Nov. 2000, Agriculture, p. 2.
4. D.L. Narayana, 1984, National Perspectives for Rural Development, Presidential address at the National Seminar on Bank Finance and Rural Development, S.V. University: Tirupathi (April): 5.
5. Report of Irrigation Commission, 1972, Volume 1, Government of India, Ministry of Irrigation and Power, New Delhi: 33.
6. Government of Andhra Pradesh, Sixth Five Year Plan, 1980-85, Draft Volume II, Finance and Planning Department, Hyderabad: 1.
7. Government of Andhra Pradesh, Statistical Abstracts, Directorate of Economics and Statistics, Hyderabad, 1997-98.
8. Centre for Monitoring Indian Economy, Nov. 2000, Agriculture, p. 2.
9. Statistical Handbook of Tamil Nadu, 1999, Department of Economics and Statistics, Government of Tamil Nadu, Chennai-6.
10. Madras Institute of Development Studies, 1988, Tamil Nadu Economy, Performance and Issues, Chennai, 1988, p. 172.

14

CHAPTER

Increasing Population and Decreasing Agricultural Land in Tamil Nadu

T. GOVINDARAJ AND R. RAJENDRAN

Agriculture occupies an important place in the economy of Tamil Nadu. It is the largest single source of state income which provides a strong and prosperous base to the state's economic growth. This paper attempts to analyse the increasing population and decreasing agricultural land in Tamil Nadu.

The population of Tamil Nadu was 48408077 in 1981 which increased to 55858946 in 1991 and 62110839 in 2001. The Annual growth rate of population in Tamil Nadu is lower than the All-India Population increase. This is due to the effective implementation of family welfare measures. Tamil Nadu was the first state to organise family planning campaign in the early 70's and thus effectively reduced the growth of population. Thanks to the efforts of the family welfare department of Government of Tamil Nadu. Every eligible couple both literate and illiterate is aware of the increasing population and the consequent economic impact. Small family norm is the order of the day both in rural and urban Tamil Nadu.

Even though the rate of growth of population and

growth rate of birth have come to a lower level compared to the All India growth rate, the increase in medical facilities and reduction in death rate have increased the life expectancy. This has contributed the net increase of population from 48.4 million in 1981 to 62.1 million in 2001. The net increase in the population warrants more food, housing, education and other amenities. The government efforts to provide all such things exhaust the revenue of the government.

Thanks to the efforts of the new strategy in agriculture introduced in early 60's, The combined effect of the chemical, biological and mechanical technologies have increased the food production throughout the country, an agrarian country which was importing more than 15 million tons food grains and exhausting the scarce foreign exchange resources attained the self-sufficiency during the process of green revolution. Thanks to the efforts of the agricultural scientists of this country with sincere efforts of the farmers under the leadership of the then central minister Late C. Subramaniam. India is not only self-sufficient in food front but also surplus in few crops.

The adoption of new technology in agriculture was widespread in Tamil Nadu. The single crop plants were converted into double cropping and paved the way for the Green Revolution. The Green Revolution has brought more food to the growing population and more raw materials to the expanding industries. The agrarian prosperity of 70's was responsible enhancing the economic status of the farmers. Due to the Cauvery dispute between the governments of Tamil Nadu and Karnataka, monopoly procurement of paddy in Delta region, ever increasing wage to the agricultural labourers, increase in the price of agricultural inputs like chemical fertilizers, pesticides and farm equipments and the continuous disputes between the landowners and the tenants made agriculture a less remunerative occupation. Many farmers raise one crop or leave the land fallow or switch over from paddy to long-term crops like coconut. In some parts of Trichy the most fertile paddy growing lands are used for Korai cultivation. Income elasticity and price elasticity are mainly responsible for decreasing agricultural lands.

The Table 1 illustrates the situation from 1987-88 to

TABLE I

(000' hectares)

Year	Cropping Intensity	Area Sown	Area sown more than once	Gross Cropped area
1987-88	116.4	5778	950	6728
1988-89	116.3	5547	904	6451
1989-90	120.5	5662	1160	6822
1990-91	118.0	5578	1054	6632
1991-92	121.8	5726	1257	6977
1992-93	121.6	5814	1253	7067
1993-94	121.3	5901	1257	7158
1994-95	121.3	5790	1236	7026
1995-96	117.7	5342	925	6267
1996-97	117.7	5486	970	6457

Source: Tamil Nadu - An Economic Appraisal.

1996-97. The cropping intensity in 1987-88 was 116.4, it reached the maximum of 121.8 in 1991-92 and has comedown to 117 in 1996-97. The area sown was 5778000 hectares in 1987-88, and it has gone up to 5901000 hectares in 1993-94 and it has come down to 5486000 hectares in 1996-97.

Similarly, the area sown more than once was 950000 hectares in 1987-88 increased to 1257000 hectares in 1993-94 but has comedown to 970000 hectares in 1996-97. The gross cropped area has a similar tendency. It was 6728000 hectares in 1987-88, increased to 7158000 hectares in 1993-94. But it has declined to 6457000 hectares in 1996-97.

The table explains how the cropping intensity, area sown, area sown more than once and gross cropped area declined in the last one decade starting from 1987-88 to 1996-97.

In Tamil Nadu, the net area sown in the total geographical area in 1971-80 was 47.2%. It has come down to 41.1% in 1995-96.

It has got its own impact on food grains production.

The food grains production in 1986-87 was 7181000 tons. it has steadily increased and reached the peak level of 9081000

TABLE 2

Production of Food Grains

(000'tons)

Year	*Production*
1986-87	7181
1987-88	7480
1988-89	7330
1989-90	7917
1990-91	7496
1991-92	8265
1992-93	8358
1993-94	8257
1994-95	9081
1995-96	6405
1996-97	6930

Source: Tamil Nadu—An Economic Appraisal.

tons in 1994-95. But declined to 6405000 tons in 1995-96 and 6930000 tons in 1996-97.

Since enough food is available to the population the people in general and administrators in particular are not worried about the changing agrarian scenario of Tamil Nadu. Migration of population from rural to urban areas is a continuous process in all parts of Tamil Nadu. Since agriculture has become less profitable and the rates of return from agriculture is meagre on one side, the growing demand for land for house construction and other non-agricultural purposes simultaneously with increasing land values changes the agricultural land to non-agricultural purposes. This is the main reason for the total decline of agricultural land to the tune of 6.1%. The reduction of agricultural land is followed by reduction of cropping Intensity.

The consequences are very serious in the long-run. If the change of land is not curtailed with an iron hand, the next decade will experience a severe food problem and the county may be forced to import food grains.

15

CHAPTER

Effect of Education in the Adoption of Agricultural Technologies in Tamil Nadu: A Micro-Level Analysis

J. GOVINDADASS

INTRODUCTION

Education is the key to economic development. It is not only a means to development measured by discount rates, rates of return and so on, but it also has broader socio-cultural dimension that needs to be taken into account when measuring its role in National Development. In this context the Report of the National Commission on Education (1966) recommended a National System of Education which would be a powerful instrument for the creation of democratic, secular and egalitarian society which would be based on Science and Spiritual values, wherein the evils of poverty, ignorance and ill-health would be eliminated through the humane use of scientific and technical knowledge.

In order to achieve this objective, the Report linked Education to productivity. In this context, the following observation of T.W. Schultz attracts our attention "The economics of development would be incomplete unless it could explain the emergence of new and better production possibility in agriculture; the economics of agriculture, in turn, would be incomplete unless it could explain this same economic behaviour".

Agricultural research and extension programmes complemented by the schooling of the farmers and farm workers are now widely acknowledged as important determinants of a farmer's efficiency and productivity. Education and productivity constitute a rising spiral whose different parts support one another. Education imparts specific knowledge and develops cognitive and non-cognitive skills. It improves the entrepreneurial ability of the farmers, which increases his utility function. Education affects the horizon of vision of the farmers. It is not just like any other input. It affects the way the farmer thinks about everything including production, and it also affects the attitude towards other inputs. Furthermore, the thoroughness with which the cultivator can investigate the economic opportunities of using modern inputs vary greatly with the extent of education. Hence, it is important to understand the role of education and adoption of improved technologies, and how farmers having different levels of educational background based in different resource endowments and stage of development are making use of the available and new information. In this context the need for initiating systematic studies in diverse agro-eco-regions to get a clear insight on the role of education at different stages of agriculture is widely recognized. Such studies are considered as essential and a prerequisite to design differential strategies for disseminating information for different regions.

However, the impact of education in the rural economy and in particular, on agriculture has been a matter of debate for sometime now. The traditional view is to regard formal education including literacy to be unimportant from the point of view of agricultural productivity and to argue all that matters is the traditional wisdom of the peasant. This view has been challenged by a number of studies (Lockheed *et. al.*, 1980), which reveal that differences in the level of education is related to differences in productivity and found in most cases a significant positive association.

Education affects productivity in two distinct ways; the allocative effect and the worker effect. The former distinction centres on better allocation decisions including adoption and diffusion of new technology; the latter relates to the technical efficiency aspect of production. The primary postulate of the allocative hypothesis is that education enhances the productive capabilities of farmers by helping them to adopt modern innovations.

In the present study, an attempt has been made to empirically test the allocative effect hypothesis of education in a dynamic setting in Tamil Nadu.

DATA AND METHODOLOGY

The focus of the present study is the paddy cultivating small and marginal farmers. The study was carried out in Thanjavur District during the year 1997-98. Cultivation of paddy accounts for 61% of the gross cropped area in the district. It is one of the seven districts in the country where the package programme was implemented. The programme not only involves adoption by cultivators of a package of improved practices, but also provision of a package of services consisting of technical staff, availability of credit, land and water improvement, adequate research information for basing extension recommendations thereon, storage and marketing which would enable the farmers to adopt scientific method of farming. The study was taken up in five sample villages in the Thiruvidaimaruthur Agricultural Division situated in close proximity to the Aduthurai Rice Research Station. This institution acts as a nucleus of disseminating paddy technology and other agricultural innovations to the farmers of this region. In all, 196 respondents were interviewed which was a little over 259% of the universe. Care was taken for including the small and marginal farmers with different levels of education.

RESULTS AND DISCUSSION

(i) Levels of Education and Adoption

Adoption of technologies in paddy farming was

measured by taking into account the overall adoption of nine selected farm practices recommended to the farmers in paddy cultivation. The extent of adoption was measured by an adoption index. Based on the mean (5.49) and standard deviation (1.95) of the adoption scores the respondents were classified into low, medium and high adoption categories.

The distribution of respondents on the basis of the levels of education and adoption of improved technologies was worked out and the result is presented in Table 1. The table clearly brings out that the high level of adoption of improved technologies in paddy cultivation increased along with the levels of education of both small and marginal farmers. The reason for this phenomenon may be that the more educated farmers had better knowledge in paddy technologies and their attitude towards adoption of such technologies was favourable.

(ii) Extent of Contribution of Education to the Adoption of Technologies

The objective of the study is to find out the effect of education in the adoption of agricultural technologies. The study takes into account the following independent variables for analysis: (i) age, (ii) Experience, and (iii) Education. The variable age refers to the chronological age of the respondents at the time of interview; experience refers to the actual number of years of experience of the respondents in agricultural operations; education refers to the number of years of schooling of the head of the household. Alternatively, the average years of schooling of all the adult members the respondent households was also taken into account for analysis since education may have externalities.

In order to find out the cause and effect relationship of the independent variable's age, experience and education and also to assess the extent of contribution made by such variables to the extent of adoption of technologies, multiple repression was worked out in four models and the results are presented in Table 2.

Model I: $Y = \beta_0 + \beta_1 \text{ AGE} + \beta_2 \text{ EDH} + \beta_3 \text{ AED} + U$

TABLE I

Levels of Education and Adoption of Paddy Technologies

Level of Education	*Adoption*							
	Small Farmers				*Marginal Farmers*			
	Low	*Medium*	*High*	*Total*	*Low*	*Medium*	*High*	*Total*
Illiterates	2 (2.3)	1 (1.15)	2 (2.3)	5 (5.75)	17 (15.6)	11 (10.09)	2 (1.83)	30 (27.52)
Primary	7 (8.04)	13 (14.94)	6 (6.9)	26 (29.88)	13 (11.93)	14 (12.84)	1 (0.92)	28 (25.69)
Middle	—	21 (24.14)	7 (8.05)	28 (32.18)	—	21 (19.27)	3 (2.75)	24 (22.02)
Secondary	1 (1.15)	3 (3.45)	8 (9.19)	12 (13.79)	—	15 (13.76)	1 (0.92)	16 (14.68)
Higher Secondary	—	—	16 (18.39)	16 (18.39)	—	—	11 (10.09)	11 (10.09)
Total	16 (11.49)	38 (43.68)	39 (44.23)	87 (100)	30 (27.53)	61 (55.96)	18 (16.51)	109 (100)

Figures in the parentheses denote percentages.
Source: Computed.

Model II: Y = b0 + b1 EDH + b2 D + b3 EXP + u

Model III: $Y = \beta_0 + \beta_1$ EDH $+ \beta_2$ AED + U

Model IV: $Y = \beta_0 + \beta_1$ AED $+ \beta_2$ EXP + U

where

Y= Adoption of recommended technologies in paddy forming.
EDU = Education of Head of the farm households.
AED = Average Education of adult member of the households.
EXP = Experience of the head.

In the Model I, the variable experience was not included since there was multi-collinearity among age and experience. All the three independent variables taken together, were able

TABLE 2

Estimated Regression Co-efficients of Education and other Independent Variables and Adoption of Paddy Technologies

Variables	*Model I*		*Model II*		*Model III*		*Model IV*	
	'b' Value	*SE of 'b'*	*'b' Value*	*SE of 'b'*	*'b' Value*	*SE of 'b'*	*'b' Value*	*SE of 'b'*
Constant	7.1123	1.5623	4.8823	1.0411	4.1151	0.3633	10.2963	0.7837
Age	-0.0506 (1.972)	0.0256	—	—	—	—	—	—
Education of Head	0.3148 (4.946)*	0.0636	0.3884 (7.032)*	0.5525	0.4242 (13.056)*	0.0314	—	—
Average Education	-0.1567 (2.474)	0.0634	-0.1778 (2.824)	0.0629	-0.1851 (2.976)	0.0622	0.0232 (0.371)	0.0627
Experience	—	—	0.0196 (0.786)	0.0249	—	—	-0.1637 (10.321)	0.0158
R^2	0.5373		0.5278		0.5287		0.4093	
F-Value	76.003		73.667		110.409		68.576	
D.F	3		3		2		2	

to explain 53.57 per cent of the variation in the dependent variable viz., adoption of technologies. However, only education of head had a positive and statistically significant 'b' value at 1 per cent level. The result indicates that one unit increase in the education of the head would increase 0.31 units in the adoption. The lower level of education of the small and marginal farmers may be the cause for lower levels of adoption of technologies. The lack of externalities of education of the adult members in the farm operator households, the risk factor and the high cost of adoption of the paddy technologies may be the cause for the negative effect of average education in adoption.

In the Model II, the variable age was excluded and experience of the farm operator household was included. All the three variables taken together were able to explain 52.76 per cent variation in the dependent variable, viz., adoption. However, the education of the head had a positive and statistically significant 'b' value at 1 per cent level. This indicates that one unit increase in the education of household would increase 0.3884 units in adoption. The negative 'b' value of experience shows that experience of the farmers did not contribute to the level of adoption.

In the Model III, only education of head and average education were taken into account and they were able to explain 52.87 per cent of the variation in adoption. While the average education had negative 'b' value, the education of head had a positive and statistically significant coefficient at 1 per cent level. This result indicates that one unit increase in education would increase the extent of adoption by 0.42 units. This result has led to infer that only education of head had a positive effect on adoption of technologies and no externalities of education was created as could be seen from the negative coefficient of average education.

In the Model IV, only average education and experience were considered and these two variables taken together were able to explain only 40.93 per cent of the variation in the extent of adoption. However, in contrast to the earlier models the average education had a positive 'b' value indicating one unit increase in the average education would increase 0.00232 units in adoption. Hence, all the models taken together, education had a positive and statistically significant effect in the level of adoption. However, the effect of average education was not significant.

CONCLUSION

It is known from the findings, that the high level of adoption of technologies in paddy cultivation increased along with the increase in the levels of education of the small and marginal farmers. The educated farmers make perceptible improvement in productivity with their allocative skills acquired through education. The percentage of small farmers who had higher adoption levels was higher when compared with the marginal farmers. Since the size of holding of the small farmers is larger than that of the marginal farmers, their economic condition could be relatively better which would have enabled them to have a higher level of adoption of technologies. It is evident from the four models that the education of the farm households has a positive and statistically significant association with the extent of adoption of technologies.

References

Blaug, M. (Ed.), *Economics of Education*, English Language Book Society, Vol. 1, 1972.

Chandra, Suman K., *Education and Develoipment: A Study of Human Capital Formation*, Discovery Publishing House (New Delhi) 1997.

Feder, Gerson and Roger Slade, "The Acquisition of Information and the Adoption of New Technology, *American Journal of Agricultural Economics*, Vol. 66, No. 3, August 1984.

Hand Book of Agriculture, Indian Council of Agricultural Research (New Delhi), 1992.

Lockhoed *et. al.*, "Farmers Education and Farm Efficiency: A Survey", *Economic Development and Cultural Change*, Vol. 29, No. 1, October 1980.

Lin, Justin Yifu, "Education and Innovation Adoption in Agriculture: Evidence from Hybrid Rice in China", *American Journal of Agricultural Economics*, Vol. 73, No. 3, August 1993.

Narayanamoorthy, A., "Impact of Farmers' Education, Age and Experience on Fertilizer Use and Yield", *Productivity*, Vol. 34, No. 4, January-March, 1994.

Pandey, K.N., *Adolption of Agricultural Innovations: A study of small and Marginal Farmers of Varanasi (U.P.)*, Northern Book Centre, (New Delhi), 1989.

Report of the National Commission on Education, Government of India (New Delhi), 1966.

Schultz T.W., *The Economic Organisation of Agriculture*, Tata Mcgraw-Hill Publishing Company, 1953.

16

CHAPTER

Development Prospects of Fisheries Sector in Tamil Nadu

K. PAZHANI

Like other sectors of the economy, fisheries sector also plays an important role in the economic development of all maritime states in India. Malnutrition is a problem faced by most of the Third World Countries like India. As supplier of cheap animal protein, the fishing industry plays a predominant role to fill the problem of 'protein gap' in India and other less developed countries. Fisheries development is essential, both as a means of increasing levels of food production in most developing countries and as a means of improving the quality of diet in developing countries, as a source of protein, vitamin and essential minerals, fish provides an ideal supplement to the poor and monotonous diet which is the daily fare of the inhabitants of many tropical and sub-tropical countries.

Fisheries development mainly depends on the socio-economic and cultural development of fishermen who are the heart and soul of this industry. But, the fisher people who are responsible for bringing a huge foreign exchange (Rs. 1450 crores) to the state live below poverty line. Though the Central as well as the State Governments have been taking various steps to increase fish production, export of fish products and to the socio-economic uplift of the fishermen, the actual benefits have not yet reached the toiling fishermen who are in the lowest rung of the social ladder.

IMPORTANCE OF THE FISHING INDUSTRY

Fisheries occupy an important place in the economy of Tamilnadu. Next to 'agriculture' and 'hand loom' sectors, fisheries provide employment avenues to a larger section of the population in the state. It is observed that 1,94,470 fishermen are employed, out of which 87.67 per cent are directly engaged in fishing activities, 3.77 per cent on diving, net making, fish trade and other allied activities. The total fisher women employed has increased from 24,812 in 1986 to 37,343 in 2000.

Tamil Nadu contributes 10 per cent of India's total marine fish production by producing 3.77 lakh tonnes of fish. By way of exporting 45,026 tonnes marine products the state has earned is 1379.01 crores which forms 29.8 per cent of India's export earning by exporting fish and fishery products.

Earlier studies (Anugraham: 1940, Warrior: 1967, Blake: 1970, Norr: 1972, Selvaraj: 1975, Sathiadhas: 1978 and 1991, Siva Kumari : 1979, Durairaj: 1981, Brewes: 1982, Pazhani: 1988 and 1998, Stephen: 1993, Devarajan: 1995) dealt with socio-economic conditions of the fisher folk, motorization of traditional crafts, problems in marketing of fish and fish products, economics of mechanized fishing and also export of fishery products at a micro level (village, taluk or district level). Macro-level studies encompassing all the above-mentioned constituents of the marine fishing industry are conspicuous in their absence and necessitate the study of this nature. A comparative analysis of available data for a period of ten years (1989-90 to 1998-99) will serve the purpose to explain the status of fishing industry in Tamil Nadu, its contributions in the past and the developmental necessities of this industry.

OBJECTIVE

This paper attempts to:

1. Present an overview of the fishing economy of Tamil Nadu;
2. Analyse the growth trends in fish production in Tamil Nadu;
3. Study the growth of marine products exports in Tamil Nadu;
4. Analyse the adequacy of infrastructural facilities for fisheries development; and
5. To identify the major problems of fishermen and fisheries development in the State.

It is a temporal study for a period of ten years. The study is based on purely secondary data.

FISHERIES IN TAMIL NADU—A PROFILE

Tamil Nadu is one of the important maritime states on the South East Coast of India, extending between latitude 8' 5' N and 13' 35' N and longitudes 76' 15' E and 80' 20' E by the Bay of Bengal, Palk Strait and Gulf of Mannar, in the South by Indian Ocean and in the West by the Arabian sea and the states of Kerala and Karnataka.

Tamil Nadu has a coastline of 1076 kms. It covers both East and West coasts which constitute 15 per cent of India's total coastline. About 6.8 lakh of marine fisher folk live in 13 coastal districts. The fishery resources spread over the continental shelf of 41412 kms. The State is rich in fish resources. There are 591 fishing villages and 1,41,340 fishermen households in the State. The total fishermen population was 6,79,711 in 2000. 2/3rd of the fisher folk are literates, 56.79 per cent are having primary level education, 34.01 per cent upto high school level. Only 3.34 per cent are employed in Government and other private sector establishments. Compared to the 1986 census, the income per fishermen family has increased from Rs. 2915 to Rs. 6573 in the year 2000.

DEVELOPMENT OF FISHERIES IN TAMIL NADU

Fishing, along with agriculture, is one of the oldest human occupations, and a great part of the fish economy of the state, as also. of the country, is still 'traditional,' depending on human energy and wind power without any kind of mechanisation. In this paper an attempt has been made to ring to light some of the important facts by analysing the following factors.

(i) Financial Outlay,
(ii) Active Fishermen Population,
(iii) Equipments used,
(iv) Trends in fish production,
(v) Trends in fish exports,
(vi) Coastal Infrastructure developments, and
(vii) Fishermen welfare activities.

(i) Financial Outlay

The State's Fisheries Policy is to:

1. Achieve sustainable fish production and thereby standards of population;
2. Achieve improved management of capture fishery in the marine fishery sector;
3. Ensure scientific management of inland fisheries in devoirs, irrigation tanks, village ponds and to bring in additional area under fish culture;
4. Generate employment and income in rural areas through inland fishing; and
5. Establish viable fishermen co-operatives.

To achieve these objectives the Government of Tamil Nadu's budget estimates and actual expenditures have been increasing year after year.

(ii) Active Fishermen Population

Any sector is considered as developed or developing depending on the nature of employment it provides, number of people depending on it for their livelihood, its contribution

TABLE I

Budget Estimates and Actual Expenditures for Fisheries Development

(Rs. in lakhs)

Year	*Budget Estimates*			*Actual Expenditure*		
	Plan	*Non-Plan*	*Total*	*Plan*	*Non-Plan*	*Total*
1990-91	422.31	667.45	1089.86	942.7	669.06	1611.76
1991-92	750.24	779.71	1529.95	864.83	746.09	1610.92
1992-93	788.18	823.82	1612	1813.92	791.45	2605.37
1993-94	1249.76	842.33	2092.09	1733.37	900.61	2633.98
1994-95	1661.35	873.72	2535.07	2719.46	1364.12	4083.58
1995-96	1978.38	944.73	2923.11	2215.26	969.76.	3185.02
1996-97	2411.03	1018.28	3429.31	4210.7	1210.04	5420.74
1997-98	1545.37	1188.41	2733.78	3418.36	1450.25	4868.61
1998-99	2726.36	1674.86	4401.22	3820.22	1851.1	5671.32
CGR			16.51			18.15
Projected Value for 2009-10			8388.42			11569.5

Source: Data obtained from the Directorate of Fisheries, Chennai.

to GDP. Fisheries sector provides employment to a neglected section of the people who will be out of employment otherwise. Those employments are seasonal in nature and the number of people depending on it for their livelihood has increased considerably. For instance, the active fishermen population has increased from 1.09 lakhs in 1991 to 2.60 lakhs in 1999 registering an average annual growth (AAG) of 11.5 per cent. This industry remains as a training ground for getting similar type in foreign countries.

(iii) Equipments used

Fishermen use different types of crafts and gears as equipements for fishing in the turbulent sea. They use traditional catamarams, canoes and mechanized boats. As a mark of development motorisation of crafts with different subsidy the Central as well as the Government of Tamil Nadu encouraged schemes. Under the scheme, 50 per cent of the cost of engine is given as subsidy limited to a ceiling of Rs. 12,000 or Rs. 10,000 for buying inboard engines or outboard motors respectively. The balance cost is to be borne by the beneficiary. From 1987-88 to 1999-2000, 12,837 such engines have been distributed to the traditional fishermen. They are also given a subsidy of Rs. 6000 per head for the purchase of fishing nets under the scheme. So for 163 nets had been distributed to the fishermen. The number of mechanised fishing boats operating Tamil Nadu coasts increased from 2514 in 1986 to 8009 in 2000. There is about 218.58 per cent increase. There are 41770 crafts operating in TN coast, out of which 15,106 crafts are motorized. This is because of utilization of 50 per cent subsidy for motorizing the crafts.

(iv) Trends in Fish Production

The quantity of output produced is also a better indicator of the development of any industry. The total fish production in the state has increased from 3,64,000 tonnes of fish during 1989-90 to 4,65,610 tonnes during 1997-98 showing an AAG rate of 3.1 per cent. The following Table 1 shows the target and achievements of marine and inland fish production in Tamil Nadu.

Table 2 shows that fish production has increased from 3,64,000 tonnes in 1989-90 to 4,65,610 tonnes in 1997-98. The ratio of marine fish catch and inland fish production to total fish production of the State remained stable at 3:1 during the study period. Total fish production grew at a compound growth rate of 3.39 per cent during 1997-98. The compound growth rate (CGR) of marine fish production (2.90) is lower than that of inland fish production (3.39). Further, the per centage of share of marine fish production in total fish production has decreased from 79.4 per cent in 1989-90 to 76.48 per cent in 1997-98. This situation may be attributed to:

(a) Monsoon failures,
(b) Over-crowding of fishing crafts in the inshore area;
(c) Conflict between the traditional and mechanized craft operators and fall in the fishing days;
(d) Migration of fishermen to other states for fishing;

TABLE 2

Marine and Inland Fish Production

(Units in '000 tonnes)

Year	*Marine*		*Inland*		*Total*
	Achievement	*Percentage to totals*	*Achievement*	*Percentage to totals*	
1989-90	289	79.4	75	20.6	364
1990-91	292	78.07	82.93	21.93	374
1991.92	299.94	84	84	21.88	383.94
1992-93	307.72	75.75	98.4	24.25	405.75
1993-94	317.72	74.77	107.2	25.23	424.92
1994-95	330.73	75.38	108	24.62	438.73
1995-96	341.32	75.96	108.05	24.04	449.37
1996-97	350.79	76.29	109	23.71	459.79
1997-98	356.11	76.31	109.5	23.69	465.61
CGR	(2.9)		(5.06)		(3.39)
Projected Production for year 2010					
	458.25		167.21		625.46
	(73.27)		(26.73)		(100.00)

Source: Data obtained from the Directorate of Fisheries, Chennai.

and

(e) Fluctuations in the financial outlay and actual expenditures.

These situations necessitate government intervention to frame appropriate policy measures to improve fish production. Through the projected marine fish production for the year 2010 (4,58,250 tonnes) shows an increase of 1,02,140 tonnes over a period of twelve years the share of marine fish production has been showing a further decline from 76.48 per cent in 1998-99 to 73.27 per cent during 2009-10.

For promoting inland fisheries, Fish Farmers' Development Agencies' numbering 13 are functioning since 1976. Total number of fish farmers benefited were 1264 in 1997-98. Per hectare fish production had increased from 1251 kilograms during 1996-97 to 1488 kilograms during 1997-98 registering a growth of 18.9 per cent.

(v) Export of Fish and Fish Products

Export of fish and fish products remain as an important source of foreign exchange earning to Tamil Nadu. Among the varieties of fishes caught in the State a few varieties of fish like prawn, squid, scrab, etc., are in great demand in the foreign countries. Though there are only two ports (Madras and Tuticorin) available throughout its long coastline, there has been an increasing trend in the export of fish and fish products.

Table 3 reveals that the volume of fish exported from Tamil Nadu has increased from 18,509 tonnes during 1989-90 to 45,026 tonnes during 1998-99, registering an average annual growth of 11.8 per cent. It constituted 16.79 per cent of India's export of fish products during 1989-90 and decreased to 14.86 per cent during 1998-99. This situation may be attributed to:

TABLE 3

Trends in the Export of Marine Products from 1989-90 to 1998-99

Year	*India*		*Tamil Nadu*	
	Quantity	*Value*	*Quantity*	*Value*
1989-90	110243	634.99	18509	99.74
			(16.74)	(15.70)
1990-91	139419	893.39	27340	165.88
1991-92	171820	1375.89	25084	230.53
1992-93	208602	1767.43	30963	337.45
1993-94	243960	2503.62	20473	461.88
1994-95	307337	3575.27	28831	780.88
1995-96	296277	3501.11	31330	919.19
1996-97	378199	4121.36	40878	1075.67
1997-98	385818	4697.48	41052	1220.05
1998-99	302934	4626.87	45026	1379.01
			(14.86)	(29.80)
CGR	13.88	25.43	8.64	34.45
2020	709060	10526	7063	3032.56
			(9.96)	(28.81)

Source: Data obtained from the Directorate of Fisheries, Chennai.

(a) Migration of fishermen in large numbers from Kanyakumari district to Kerala for fishing;
(b) Sales of major portion of fish catches to Kerala merchants; and
(c) Absence of port, (though planning to construct a harbour at Colachel) for export of fish at present.

The export of fish products in value terms has increased from 15.71 per cent to 29.8 per cent during the same period. This situation may be attributed to:

(a) The export of high valued species like prawn, squid and scrab;
(b) An increase in the volume of fish export (by 3,974 tonnes) in Tamil Nadu during 1998-99; and
(c) Increasing demand for Indian fish products from the Western countries like U.S.A.

But there is a fear that the war between U.S.A. and Afghanistan may affect our export sizably. By improving the marketing infrastructures in the coastal districts, especially in Kanyakumari District (since it has more than 25 per cent of fishermen population and produces 1/3rd of total fish production of Tamil Nadu) and procuring fish for exports through Tuticorin Port, the export of fish and fish products from the State could be increased to a greater extent.

(vi) Infrastructure Development

Provision of quality infrastructure services at a reasonable cost is a necessary condition for achieving sustained economic growth. In view of the long coastline and large fleet of mechanized fishing boats, Tamil Nadu needs considerable landing and berthing facilities. The existing facilities are inadequate, considering the needs based on the momentum of mechanized fishing. But even after 15 years the same situation remains unchanged. The fishing infrastructure of the State basically consists of 362 landing centers, 3 major fishing harbours, 4 medium harbours and 6 fishing landing jetties. Considering the number of coastal districts, fishing villages and the number of crafts (both traditional and mechanized) the coastal infrastructure of the State is not adequate to achieve desired growth of this industry.

(vii) Fisheries Co-operative Societies

Development of fisheries can also be understood by taking into account the trends in the growth of fishermen and fisherwomen co-operative societies and their membership and their involvement in co-operative activities. In most of the coastal villages, these societies are functioning only as fair-price shops and recover old loans. They are also collecting member contributions to Savings-*cum*-Relief Fund and distribute them (including the contribution of Centre and State Governments) to the fishermen during the lean season. The involvement of fisherwomen in co-operative activities is an important development in this sector.

TABLE 4

Growth of Fisheries Co-operatives and Membership

Year	*Fisheries Co-operatives*	*No. of Societies*	*Membership*
1991	Marine FMCS	405	152013
	Inland FMCS	251	
1996	Marine FMCS	646 (6.00)*	
	Inland FMCS	263 (0.6)*	311416 (9.40)*

Source: Compiled from Marine Fisheries Statistics, Department of Fisheries, Chennai.

$$*AAG = r - \text{Anti}\log\frac{(\log Pn\ -\ PI)}{n-1} - 1\times 100$$

Pn = Value of the variable at the nth year,

P = Value of the variable at the initial year,

r = Relative increase per year expressed as per centage, and

n = Number of years.

Table 4 shows that the growth rate of the number of

marine and inland fisheries co-operative societies as 6 per cent and 0.6 per cent respectively. This may be attributed to the existence of one fishermen co-operative society in each coastal village and absence of such development in the inland sector. The Saving-*cum*-Relief Fund Scheme has made the marine fishermen to joint and get benefit from these co-operatives. The State Government has allotted only Rs. 0.01 lakh for fisheries co-operative during the Annual Plan, 2000-01. This financial outlay is inadequate to provide financial assistance to member of these co-operatives (both marine and inland).

(viii) Fishermen Welfare Programmes

- ❑ In order to help in the 'motorisation of traditional fishing crafts the State has been providing loans with subsidies. Upto 1995-96, 7296 traditional crafts have been motorized. During 1996-97, the State has sanctioned Rs. 11 crores to motorise 6100 traditional crafts. During the Ninth Five Year Plan period Rs. 2 crores have been allotted to motorise 2000 crafts. An outlay of Rs. 1 crore is provided for the purchase of 5000 units of fishing nets and Rs. 3 to purchase 7500 traditional crafts during the same period.
- ❑ Under the Savings-*cum*-Relief Fund Scheme Rs. 1080 has been given to the fishermen during the lean season. The fishermen have to contribute Rs. 45 per month for 8 months. The Central and State Governments grant Rs. 360 each per fishermen. Despite the withdrawal of support by the Central Government for this purpose, the State government has allotted Rs. 15 crores to benefit Rs. 1.25 lakh marine fishermen annually during the Ninth Plan period.
- ❑ Under the Group Insurance Scheme, in case of death/total disablement, a sum of Rs. 15,000 is paid to the fishermen family and incase of partial disablement a sum of Rs. 7500 is given. The insurance payable on behalf of a fisherman is Rs. 4. It is fully met by the State Government. For the

year 2000-01, an amoumt of Rs. 14.50 lakh is provided for this scheme.

- Under the Fishermen Group Accident Insurance Scheme, in case of accident resulting in death/total disablement Rs. 25,000 is given and in case of partial disablement Rs. 12,500 is paid to the fishermen. For this insurance premium of Rs. 9.75 per fisherman is paid equally by the Centre and the State.
- During the 9th Plan, the State Government has allotted Rs. 20 lakh to 20 Fishermen Co-operative Societies (FMCS) as share capital assistance at Rs. 1 lakh each. The remaining FMCS is left without any such assistance. The State has also decided to contribute Rs. 160 lakh (20 per cent of total cost) to Tamil Nadu Fisheries Development Corporation Ltd. for the purchase of 4 deep sea fishing vessels and the Centre's contribution will be Rs. 520 lakh during the 9th Plan.
- Under Ma. Singaravelar Memorial Free Housing Scheme 16,000 houses were sanctioned for 4 years. 12,603 were completed. A sum of Rs. 1242.15 lakh is provided during 2000-01 to construct 4000 houses for fishermen with a unit cost of Rs. 37,000.
- In order to help the fisherwomen to carry fishes to the interior villages in hygienic way aluminium containers are supplied with 50 per cent subsidy. The State Government has proposed to supply 2000 such containers at a total cost of Rs. 3.02 lakh during the year 2000-01.
- In addition to the above, link roads to coastal villages, fish landing platforms, fishing harbours and jetties and guide lights are the on-going schemes.

SUMMARY OF FINDINGS

- Marine fishing is one of the important industries of Tamil Nadu, which provides employment, income and livelihood for the rural masses in the Coastal villages of the State.

- The per centage of financial outlay to fisheries sector to total plan outlay (0.4 per cent is less than the outlay made by the Central Government (0.5 per cent). The Outlay made by the Tamil Nadu Government has decreased to 0.37 per cent to the total plan outlay during 2000-01. This insufficient financial outlay is the main cause for the existing poor, financial, marketing and other basic infrastructure facilities.
- The active fishermen population has increased from 1.09 lakh in 1,989,89 to 2.60 lakh in 1998-99. This situation may be attributed to the absence of other sources of employment in the coastal areas.
- Though the active fishermen population registered an AAG rate of 11.5 per cent, the trend in fish production is 3.1 per cent growth. The ratios of marine fish catch and inland fish production remained stable at 3:1 during the study period. The compound growth rate of marine fish production (2.90 per cent) is lower than that of inland fish production (3.39 per cent).
- Though the volume of fish exported from the State has increased from 18,509 tonnes during 1989-90 to 45,026 tonnes during 1998-99, its share in India's export of fish products has decreased from 16.79 per cent to 14.86 per cent during the same period. But the export in value terms has increased from 15.71 per cent to 29.8 per cent.
- The AAG rate of number of Fishermen Co-operative Societies, both marine and inland remains at 6 per cent and 0.6 per cent respectively. The growth rates of membership in the co-operative societies remain at 9.4 per cent.
- Most of the earlier studies reveal that finance is the major constraint for fisheries development in our country. Most of the formal institutions are reluctant to give liberal credit to the poor fishermen to speed up the process of mechanization and purchase of gears of various types to continue fishing throughout the year.

POLICY IMPLICATIONS

Considering the importance of fisheries as a source of employment, income, supplier of cheap animal protein and foreign exchange earner in Tamil Nadu, the State has to allocate at least 1 per cent of its Plan outlay to fisheries sector.

At present the Parathavar community in Chenkottai Taluk of Thirunelveli district and Kanyakumari District is declared as Backward Community. This remains a problem getting for education and employment by this neglected sections of the society. The Government of Tamil Nadu should come forward to announce all those who are involved in fishing activities as Scheduled Castes irrespective of their caste, religion and place of residence.

The Government should take steps to provide alternate sources of employment during the lean season. They cannot live by using the amount (Rs. 1,080) released under the Savings-*cum*-Relief Fund Scheme. Absence of such steps will push the poor fishermen into 'debt trap'.

Though there is an increase in the active fishermen population there is no corresponding increase in fish production. This can be solved by making appropriate changes in the technology used in fishing and increase the number of working days by solving the conflict between the traditional and mechanized craft operators.

The study necessitates increase in investment in basic infrastructures (production, marketing, financial and public health) in the coastal villages by the Government.

With a view of sustainable fisheries development the Tamil Nadu Government has imposed 45 days (from April 15 to May 29) ban on fishing operations in the entire State. It deprives thousands of crews and mechanized boat operators from employment. During this period the Government evolve a policy to curtail- <mailto:curta@l->trawling operations along the without affecting employment and livelihood of any sections of the society.

The State Government should ask the Central Government to implement the recommendations of the Murari Committee recommendations on Deep-Sea Fishing with its full spirit so as to provide adequate and effective protection to the traditional fishermen from encroachment of the mechanized trawlers into the inshore water and to prevent the depletion of marine resources through indiscriminate fishing.

Fisheries Co-operatives can be made viable only through proper guidance, financial help and follow-up actions by the authorities in the Fisheries Department. As stated by Umre (1982), a composite plan for the development of fisheries co-operatives can be attempted with the inputs like education of fishermen, training of secretaries, better catch of fish, proper marketing of fish and also full financial and promotional support by the Government and financial institutions.

To increase the export of fish, processing centers should be established at least in few villages in each district. This arrangement is permanently needed to provide employment opportunities to fisherwomen who are without gainful employment.

Like agricultural commodities, the Agriculture Costs and Prices Commission should fix prices for fish to provide stable income to the fishermen.

Giving subsidies of various types to the poor and downtrodden is a world-wide phenomenon. The Central as well as the State Governments should take necessary steps to provide fuel at a subsidized rate to fishermen in the traditional and mechanized sectors.

Government should adopt policies to encourage and help voluntary agencies like Kanyakumari District Fishermen Sangams' Federation to make financial arrangement and to undertake marketing of fish to protect fishermen from exploitation by village moneylender and middlemen.

References

Arockiasamy, M.S. (1996), 'Fisher People Struggle against Foreign Vessels', *Main Stream*, 33 (34).

Hand Book of Fisheries Statistics, 1996, Ministry of Agriculture, Fisheries Division, Government of India, New Delhi.

India 2001—A Reference Annual, Publications Division Ministry of Information and Broadcasting, Government of India, New Delhi.

John Kurien (1996), *'Towards A New Agenda For Sustainable Small- Scale Fisheries Development',* South Indian Federation of Fishermen Societies, Trivandrum.

Krishnan, M. and Sharma, B.M. (1994), 'Development Prospects of Fisheries Sector in India with Special Emphasis on Marine Products Export,' *MIDS Bulletin*, Vol. XXIV, No. 7, July.

Narrative Notes on Plan Pogrammes, Annual Plan, 2000-01, State Planning Commission, Chennai, August 2000.

Ninth Five Year Plan, Tamil Nadu 1997-2000, Discussion Papers, State Planning Commission, September, 1997.

Pazhani K. (1998), *'Marine Fisheries Finance in Kanyakumari District—An Economic Study'* (Ph.D Thesis Submitted to Manonmaniam Sundaranar University) Thirunelveli, Tamil Nadu.

Report of the National Workshop on "Fisherfolk and the Eight Plan: Challenges and Opportunities for the Voluntary Sector and Recommendations adopted at the Workshop", 28th and 29th June 1990, Madras.

Report of the Committee to Review Deep Sea Fishing Policy, Headed by Shri P. Murari, submitted to Ministry of Food Processing Industries, New Delhi, February 1996.

Richard Bailey (1989), 'Third World Fisheries: Prospects and Problems', *World Development*, Vol. 16, No. 6.

Study Report on Techno-Socio-Economic Survey of Fishermen Households in Tamil Nadu (1986), The Institute of Techno-Economic Studies, Madras.

Tamil Nadu Economy: Performance and Issues (1998), Madras Institute of Development Studies, Oxford & IBH Publishing Co. Pvt. Ltd, New Delhi.

Tamil Nadu Marine Fisherfolk Census Year, 2000, Tamil Nadu Fisheries Department, Chennai.

Tamil Nadu: An Economic Appraisal, 1997-98, Department of Evaluation and Applied Research (DEAR), Government of Tamil Nadu, Kuralagam, Chennai.

SECTION III

Services Sector Signals

17

CHAPTER

Reforms in Power Sector: An Analysis

K.T. Rengamani and P. Ganesan

Ever since India attained Independence, development of electricity sector has largely been the responsibility of the Government. Electricity consumption is often considered as a mark of a society's progress. Though the installed capacity and electricity generated have registered a quantum jump, the demand has also been ever increasing. The demand for power in 1947 was merely 1400 MW. With increasing growth rate in the population and the economy, the demand presently is about 1,20,000 MW. The gross installed capacity is around 92,000 MW.

In India, the share of State Electricity Boards (hereafter SEBs) in terms of power generation is 54-55 per cent and the rest 46-45 per cent is contributed by Central sector (38-39 per cent), Private power utilities (5-6 per cent) and Private IPP (3-4 per cent). But, the SEBs are afflicted by a plethora of problems and all the SEBs without exception suffer from huge accumulated losses, which has brought them to a critical condition. This article is intended to study: (a) the current scenario of power sector in Tamil Nadu with reference to some critical indicators, (b) the policy initiatives proposed by the Central Government with reference to SEBs, and (c) the current status of the implementation of the policies in Tamil Nadu.

CURRENT SCENARIO OF SEBs

The functions of State Electricity Board involves generation of power at power house, transmission of power and distribution of power to the ultimate user. For ensuring best results, the three functions must work in tune with each other.

Generation and transmission of power involves heavy investment. Historically the power plants have been built by way of resources allocated through budget. The special feature of power is that it cannot be stored or warehoused like physical goods. It has to be fed to the transmission system, popularly known as grid. An efficient grid system minimizes power wastage and enables the allocation of power from surplus centres to deficient ones. The next stage is the distribution process where the power is supplied to the retail customer or end user. Certain amount of losses during the transmission stage and distribution stage are inevitable. This results in direct revenue loss and power managers must endeavour that such losses are kept to the minimum. Hence all power produced is not being sold to the end user.

Apart from this inevitable losses, faulty administration by State Electricity Boards in the following forms escalate the losses:

1. Large scale thefts of power. It is accounted as transmission losses.
2. Poor quality of transmission and distribution system.
3. Poor maintenance and administration.
4. Populist measures like free power to agriculture sector.
5. Large scale over staffing.

The SEBs have continued to suffer from high T&D losses which stood from 25 per cent in 1998 to 26 per cent in 1999. The net subsidy after accounting for amount received from state governments was Rs. 540 crore in 1992, which has gone up to Rs. 2290 crore in 2000. The hidden subsidy for agriculture and domestic sectors has increased from Rs. 745

crore in 1992 to Rs. 3810 crore in 2000. The gross subsidy of the state power sector as a percentage of gross fiscal deficit of state government was about 36 per cent in 2000. The Central Government decided to unbundle the three service arms of SEBs and corporatize them to improve their operational systems and financial situation.

POWER SECTOR IN TAMIL NADU

The performance of the power sector in Tamil Nadu with generation, transmission and distribution indicators is presented in the following Table 1. It is observed that the period between 1966-67 and 1996-97, the installed power generating capacity was witnessed high growth rates. During 1990s and 2000-2002, non-availability of hydel-potential, very high cost of establishing thermal stations, the time lag involved in engaging private agencies in power generation, absence of any new Central Sector projects etc. may be the reasons attributable for the tardy growth in the additions to the installed capacity during late 1990s.

The power availability in terms of generation and purchase in Tamil Nadu has registered a reasonable growth rate during the decenial periods 1966-97 and during late 1990s. The availability of power was 4103 MU in 1966-67 and has increased to 38313 MU in 2001-02. The energy sales also witnessed the same pattern as witnessed by power availability.

The position of percentage of line loss power sector in Tamil Nadu is 16.25 in 2001-02 and which was 16.5 per cent in 1966-67, which is comparatively lower than the other states.

The per-capita power consumption recorded a significant growth during the period under study. It was 98 Kwh in 1966-67 and has risen to 567 Kwh in 2001-02. The annual growth rate of per-capita consumption was 48.98 per cent during 1976-77 and increased to 81.03 per cent during 1996-97. The late 1990s witnessed an average growth rate of 6-11 per cent. The distribution indicators viz., EHT and HT sub-stations and lines, LT lines and Distribution transformers' performance of the power sector in Tamil Nadu also witnessed similar scenario.

The electrification in Tamil Nadu is shown in Table 3.

TABLE I

Installed Capacity, Power Availability, Energy Sales and Line Loss in Power sector of Tamil Nadu

	Installed Capacity (MW)	*Annual Growth Rate*	*Generation and Purchase (MU)*	*Annual Growth Rate*	*Energy Sales (MU)*	*Annual Growth Rate*	*Line Loss (%)*	*Annual Growth Rate*
1966-67	1470		4103		3360		16.5	
1976-77	2364	60.82	8350	103.51	6576	95.7	18.34	11.15
1986-87	3987	68.65	14853	77.88	11999	82.5	18.65	1.69
1996-97	6908	73.26	32700	120.16	25805	115	16.9	-9.38
1997-98	6916	0.12	34065	4.17	26943	4.41	16.9	0.00
1998-99	7120	2.95	35172	3.25	28394	5.39	16.8	-0.59
1999-00	7203	1.17	38313	8.93	30090	5.97	16.75	-0.30
2000-01	7513	4.30	41764	9.01	33290	10.63	16.5	-1.49
2001-02	7905	5.22	43923	5.17	38313	15.09	16.25	-1.52

The number of towns, villages and hamlets electrified are 43874 during the period between 1966-67 and 2001-02. However, during late 1990s, the electrification is stagnant. The pumpsets electrified were more in the period 1966-67 to 1976-77 and the growth rate has decelerated since 1976-77 and the growth rate was around 2 per cent in the period 1996-97 and 2001-02. The number of consumers were 14.83 lakhs and 151.88 lakhs in 1966-67 and 2001-02 respectively, thus registering growth rate of 5 to 7 per cent during 1990s and 2000-02.

POLICY INITIATIVES AND IMPLEMENTATION BY SEBS

Restructuring of State Electricity Boards:

1. State Electricity Regulatory Commissions

Each State/Union Territory shall constitute SERC before 31st March, 1999 to enable rationalization of tariff and improvement of the financial health of State Electricity Boards and to avail the interest subsidy on loans by the Power Finance Corporation as well as other incentives available. Most of the SEBs including Tamil Nadu Electricity Board (TNEB) have implemented this.

TABLE 2

Per Capita Consumption and Power Distribution in Tamil Nadu

	Per capita consumption (Kwh)	*AGR*	*EHT and HT sub-stations (Nos.)*	*AGR*	*EHT and HT lines (ckt Kms)*	*AGR*	*LT Lines (lakh ckt Kms.)*	*AGR*	*Distn. transformers (Nos.)*	*AGR*
1966-67	98		219		42482		0.80		18500	
1976-77	146	48.98	304	38.81	71569	68.47	2.14	167.50	42499	129.72
1986-87	232	58.90	475	56.25	91908	28.42	3.00	40.19	68826	61.95
1996-97	420	81.03	734	54.53	124991	36.00	4.01	33.67	111522	62.03
1997-98	430	2.38	782	6.54	127419	1.94	4.06	1.25	114830	2.97
1998-99	452	5.12	831	6.27	130533	2.44	4.09	0.74	120813	5.21
1999-00	480	6.19	876	5.42	136883	4.86	4.15	1.47	129554	7.24
2000-01	510	6.25	913	4.22	162524	18.73	4.23	1.93	135457	4.56
2001-02	567	11.18	948	3.83	165524	1.85	4.35	2.84	140710	3.88

TABLE 3

Electrification in Tamil Nadu

Year	Towns, Villages and Hamlets (Nos.)	Annual Growth Rate	Pumpsets (Lakhs)	Annual Growth Rate	Consumers (Lakhs)	Annual Growth Rate
1966-67	20250		2.9		14.83	
1976-77	63274	212.46	7.85	170.69	32.23	117.33
1986-87	63755	0.76	11.16	42.17	64.86	101.24
1996-97	64063	0.48	15.67	40.41	112.14	72.90
1997-98	64091	0.04	16.08	2.62	119.07	6.18
1998-99	64091	0.00	16.43	2.18	124.03	4.17
1999-00	64093	0.00	16.79	2.19	133.3	7.47
2000-01	64099	0.01	17.22	2.56	143.51	7.66
2001-02	64124	0.04	17.62	2.32	151.88	5.83

2. Power Sector Reform Bill

Each State/Union Territory shall announce Power Reform Policy and initiate steps for drawing up a Reform Bill wherever necessary in a time bound manner. Orissa, Haryana and Andhra Pradesh have already enacted the Reform Bills outlining a reform plan for their power sectors. Most other states including Rajasthan, Tamil Nadu, Karnataka are in the process of implementing this.

3. Corporatisation

State/Union Territories will endeavour to take steps to corporatise and commercialize generating companies, transmission companies and distribution companies so that they are able to operate on commercial principles, generate the required resources and ensure availability of reasonable priced power to the common man. Orissa was the first state in India to corporatise its generation, transmission and distribution function. Tamil Nadu is in the process of doing this.

4. Distribution Reforms

In view of the urgent need to reduce transmission and distribution losses, facilitate higher investments in system improvement and ensure availability of reliably power to the consumers, reform of the distribution sector will be initiated by establishing distribution companies in different regions of each state. The entry of private investors will be encouraged wherever feasible. To begin with, atleast 25% of the state will be taken up for distribution reform. The whole state will be covered in 4 years. Tamil Nadu Electricity Board is in the process of complying with this.

5. Mega Projects

To take advantage of the benefits of mega projects, each State/Union Territory will take steps to facilitate setting up of mega projects in accordance with the guidelines issued by Government of India. Once the corporatisation process is completed and effectively enforced, the concerned State can opt for mega projects where the Central government gives concession in customs duty. Since Tamil Nadu Electricity Board has not completed the corporatisation process they can not opt for the mega-projects at this stage.

CONCLUSION

Corporatisation of the SEBs and entrusting the generation, transmission and distribution function to separate corporations is a step in the right direction. As this will professionalise the operation and administration function. The corporates will have total autonomy and will be totally freed from the policy directions of respective State governments. The management of the corporations should be in the hands of experts, professionals, and proven administrators. The companies should be run on commercial lines. The pricing of power will have to take into account all commercial considerations like direct materials, direct labour and direct overheads. The Electricity (General) Act, 1948 guarantees a return of 16 per cent on the net fixed assets deployed by the generating companies. The companies have the freedom to fix tariff after considering all input cost and guaranteed returns as above. This will directly result in the increased sale price per unit of power sold. This is a necessary evil and a price the consumers have to pay for the mistakes committed by SEBs all these years.

Efficiency of the corporations can be improved by adopting the following measures:

- Creating new capacity involves high investments and long gestation period. While capacity addition is a must to meet extra demand, by increasing the efficiency of the generating plants, the quantum of power produced can be increased. Average Plant Load Factor (PLF) of Power Plants of Tamil Nadu is around 65-68 per cent. The average PLF of existing private sector companies like BSEs, Tata Electric, etc., is around 72-75 per cent. The 'unbundled' generating corporation should aim at achieving higher PLF. This extra power produced will help in increase the revenue realisation and improve the financial health of the corporation.
- Transmission loss control is another potential area for savings. This has been a long neglected area. This has been the responsibility of the Central government all along. The advent of Power Grid Corporation has been a big step forward to bring down the transmission losses. There is need for maintaining the equipments in the first place and over a period have a modernisation plan. If the point of generation and area of distribution to be covered is nereby short distances, transmission loss can be minimised
- The third major area where improvements can be effected by the unbundled corporation is in the Distribution segment. At present large scale power thefts are a common place occurrence. This may be with the connivance of the concerned officials as well as without their knowledge. The existing system has to be thoroughly overhauled by the new 'distribution corporaton'. Steps have to be initiated to ensure that all power used is meterd and billed.
- Agricultural consumers who were hitherto beneficiaries of the largesse of various state

governments will be billed for their use of power. There is a need for creating a awareness in the rural/semi-urban/agricultural users about the choice of getting free power but for very short uncertain durations in a day or getting assured and quality power continuously and pay for that.

- The argument that if the agricultural users is billed, it will result in the large scale increase in the price of agricultural produce and bring down the margins to the farmers, does not hold water as in reality the continuous availability of quality power will result in increased production and better price realisation.
- Once the SEBs are restructured and become functional, they can opt for mega projects with fiscal incentives. This will help the unbundled generating company to reap the economies of scale.
- A transmission and distribution company with financial and operational efficiency will attract large scale private sector companies into the power generating sector. On hind sight, may be the Ministry of Power should have taken up the restructuring of SEBs first and only after achieving that they should have invited Foreign direct investment. This might have resulted in robust capacity addtions and could have avoided embrassment like Cogentrix and Enron.

References

Tamil Nadu Economic Appraisal, 1996-97, Evaluation and Applied Research Department, Government of Tamil Nadu.

Economic Survey, Government of India, Various Issues.

www.tneb.org

Central Electricity Authority Reports.

Planning Commission Reports, Government of India.

18 CHAPTER

Pricing of Bus Transport Services: A Case Study of Tamil Nadu Transport Corporations

P. Jegadish Gandhi

Public Transportation is an important utility service in any country. In India, most of the public utility services are the monopolies of either the Central Government or the State Government or the Local bodies. In foreign countries, utility services are rendered by the private organizations as monopolies and they are under the full control of the Government.

PRICING POLICY

Pricing a public sector service is a controversial and complicated subject. It is difficult to lay down any general principle on pricing policy in a public enterprise. The general perception is that a public enterprise is ridden with surplus labour, low production, higher wage rate, under-utilisation of capacity and low overall managerial effectiveness. Fare fixation in State Transport Undertakings (STUs) is a difficult exercise. Since there are no clear-cut spelt-out policies on pricing essential services of public enterprises, the guidelines of UN Study Team on "Financing of Public Enterprises in Developing Countries" is recapitulated for policy decisions:

(i) Prices should cover necessary operating costs and replacement of assets plus contribution to the cost of public service and to the expansion of public enterprise sector.

(ii) They should be so set that surplus generation is maximum in respect of amenity goods and lowest in respect of basic consumption goods and key investment inputs.

(iii) Cross-subsidisation between higher and low surplus generation products should be organized in such a way as to ensure minimum distortion in production and investment and also undesired shift in consumption.

PRICING MECHANISM

Bus Transport pricing is regulated under Section 67(1) of the Motor Vehicles Act, 1988 under which the State Government can issue directives to the State Transport Authority regarding fixing of fares including the minimum and maximum for stage carriers and contract carriers. There are a number of fare systems in stage carriages throughout the world such as straight line scale method, tapered scale method, zonal fare, flat fare, etc. The prevalent fare structure for each type of bus service in different states of our country is the combination of one or more of the above mentioned fare systems. A few states like Tamil Nadu, Punjab, Haryana, West Bengal (North Bengal STU), etc., are adopting different fare rates according to the terrain of bus operation such as plain, ghat road, metalled-plain, unmetalled-plain, metalled-hill, unmetalled-hill, etc. The different pricing was aimed at recovering the additional cost of vehicles that is needed in procurement of superior class of vehicles, higher depreciation amount to be recovered, higher interest on cost payable besides loss of capacity owing to superior class of services and reduction in the seating capacity. Since the superior class clientele is expected to cross-subsidise the other types of loss-making services, *an average plus margin* is normally built into the pricing mechanism. Generally, the fixation of fare ordinary service is done taking into account the average cost of passenger kilometer in as much as the basic fare corresponds to revenue per passenger km.

State Transport Corporations (STCs) in Tamil Nadu like their counterparts in other states are peculiar in their operations since they have to dovetail the commercial consideration with social obligatory objectives. In view of this backdrop, pricing of public transport service in Tamil Nadu is suggested on the *break-even pricing policy* so that the cost of operation is recovered in full including the cost of capital employed.

POLITICAL DECISIONS

In an election, people vote for a political party with a whole set of policies set out in their election manfestioes and public platforms. The political process of voting every five years is a relatively poor method for the public to express its preferences. In making decision our elected/formed Government has a number of motives. They may honestly be trying to promote the public interest or at least what they believe to be the public interest. The desire to be re-elected also leads politicians to favour policies with a cost that is hidden and benefit that is obvious and will be realised before the next election. We have to ponder over the fact that why should politicians promote a policy that the public won't understand or a policy that will provide benefits after the next election? One of the reasons that politicians can take this limited short-run view that a busy public cannot be adequately informed about the countless issues on which politicians must decide in the cabinet. Thus politicians tend to put-off tough, unpleasant long-run economic decisions and when they finally do take action, it is often in response to a inescapable crisis. The recent hike in petroleum prices and Railway freight charges of the Central Government and the Bus fare hike in Tamil Nadu are hard decisions.

OPERATIONAL ECONOMICS

While the aggregate revenue of all STCs in Tamil Nadu multiplied by 3.3 times, i.e., from Rs. 18235 lakhs in 1980-81 to Rs. 61459 lakhs in 2000-01, the overall cost escalated by 3.4 times, i.e., from Rs. 19553 lakhs to Rs. 67641 lakhs in the same period. This shows a critical relationship between the revenue potentials and the cost pressures in public utility bus service system. A dichotomy between the cost of operation and fare level has been attributed as the main cause along with uncontrollable cost escalation of various inputs, for the spill-over effect of losses in the successive years. The STCs have incurred a cumulative loss of Rs. 2035 crores as on 31st March 2001 (See Table 1).

TABLE I

State Transport Corporations in Tamil Nadu
Operational Losses

(Rs. in crores)

Year	*Current Year Loss*	*Cumulative Loss*
1989-90	—	122
1990-91	42	164
1991-92	22	186
1992-93	50	236
1993-94	48	284
1994-95	41	326
1995-96	207	533
1996-97	311	844
1997-98	229	1073
1998-99	411	1484
1999-2000	318	1802
2000-2001	233	2035

Source: *White Paper on Tamil Nadu Government's Finances*, Government of Tamil Nadu, August 18, 2001.

COST DYNAMICS

(1) A comparison of expenditure patterns during the last decade shows that the establishment costs of the STCs grew from Rs. 336 crores in 1990-91 to Rs. 1316 crores in 2000-01. Similarly, the expenditure on HSD oil shot up from Rs. 195 crores to Rs. 916 crores during the same period.

(2) Frequent revisions in the cost of HSD oil without a concomitant increase in the fare being collected have added to the growing deficit of the STCs. Inadequacies in material management and cost management and the consequent high procurement cost of materials and spares have contributed to the financial miseries of the STCs.

(3) The STCs provide free travel facility based on the policy of the Government to certain categories of people. These include free travel for students, freedom fighters, accredited journalists in Tamilnadu, former and sitting Members of Parliament and State Legislative Assembly, physically handicapped, etc. A 50 percent fare subsidy is also provided to students in self-financing engineering colleges, polytechnics and select drama artists, etc. The Government has not been able to reimburse the expenditure on account of these subsidies to the STCs in time because of its poor state of finances.

IMPACTIONAL SYNDROME

(1) Crippled Daily Services

The STCs are finding it impossible to maintain their daily services. The STCs have been unable to purchase spare parts to maintain daily operations and have now begun cannibalizing spares from road worthy buses and transferring them to those under repair, in order to keep them running. Nearly 812 buses are awaiting replacement of spares in different workshops across the State.

(2) Heavy Borrowing

The STCs have borrowed heavily from the Transport Development Finance Corporation (TDFC). The outstanding loan liabilities of the STCs are pegged at Rs. 995.85 crores as on 31.5.2001. As a result, TDFC has stopped lending to all the defaulting STCs.

(3) Outstanding Dues

The immediate outstanding dues of the STCs are Rs. 308.32 crores and this includes: Rs. 73.8 crores to oil companies, Rs. 41.27 crores to the suppliers of spare parts, Rs. 193.25 crores towards accident compensation, gratuity and credit dues among others.

(4) Increased Compensation

The most worrisome trend is the phenomenal growth in accident-related compensation being paid by the STCs—this amount has increased from Rs. 10.51 crores in 1990-91 to Rs. 68.30 crores in 2000-01.

(5) Replacement

In addition, the backlog in replacement of over-aged buses is 4962 accounting for 29 percent of the fleet.

Break-Even Cost Analysis

The level of productivity of operation is relatively high among most of the State Transport Undertakings (STUs) in the country. Likewise the physical performances of Tamil Nadu STCs in recent years has been quite satisfactory. The financial losses in these STCs have therefore been the result of the pricing policy adopted by the State Government with a view to fulfilling the social responsibilities in favour of poor and the concessions extended to the various sections of the society.

Break-even is that point at which the total operating revenue just meets the total operating cost. It is a point at which neither a profit nor a loss is made. Break-even cost (BEC) can be calculated as follows:

$$\text{Cost per seat km.} = \frac{\text{Total cost per km. (in paise)}}{\text{Average seat capacity}}$$

$$\text{BEC per seat km.} = \frac{\dfrac{\text{Cost per seat km.}}{\text{Seating capacity}}}{100} \times \text{Occupancy ratio}$$

To illustrate:

$$\text{The BEC for the year 1990-91} = \frac{540.0}{51 \times 80 / 100}$$

= 13.23 paise per km.

Assuming the occupation ratio at 80 per cent, the break-even cost per seat km. for the two years 1988-89 and 1989-90 were 11 paise and 12 paise per km. respectively. During the same period, the bus fare charged by State Transport Corporations was sticky at 10.5 per km. that is below the sustainable fare by 0.5 paise in 1988-89 and 1.5 paise in 1989-90 and 2.7 paise in 1991. In 1994-95 and 1995-96 BEC is 20.36 paise and 21.0 paise respectively, but the actual fare is 14.0 paise. Therefore, the sustainable fare is below by 6.3 paise per km. Between December 1993 and September 1997 there were hikes five times in the price of diesel and spare parts while the personnel cost and the welfare expenses on employees mounted without any corresponding increase in bus fare. Apart from the bloated losses since 1991-92, it was disheartening to note that STCs had incurred cash loss from 1995-96 onwards. This resulted in heavy borrowing even for meeting the working capital requirements with a disproportionate debt-equity ratio. It put hurdles in the way of replacement of overaged buses and augmentation of fleet strength to cope with the increase in traffic growth.

FARE REVISIONS

Normally, the fixation of fare for ordinary service is done taking into account the average cost of passenger kilometer in as much the basic fare corresponds to revenue per passenger km. Much water has flown under the bridges of Coovam and Thamaraparani, since the last bus fare revision in December 1993. It is pertinent to analyse the changes in the cost structure of public transport corporation so as to perceive the need for rationalization as well as revision of bus fare for all types of bus service. The bus fares had remained almost static in Tamil Nadu, since 1972 at 5 paise per km., prior to the upward revision effected in November 1980 at 6.25 paise per km. The fare was raised to 7.5 paise in June 1981, 8.0 paise in 1985, 9.5 paise in March 1987, 10.50 paise in October 1989, 12.50 paise in November 1991, 14.0 paise in December 1993 and to 20.0 paise in September 1997 after a gap of four years. (See Table 2).

TABLE 2

Bus Fare Revisions in Tamil Nadu

Month/Year	*Fare Per Km. (Paise)*	*Marginal (Paise) Rate of Hike (MRH)*	*Upward revision gap (Months/ Years)*
1972	5.0	-	-
1980 (Nov.)	6.25	1.25	8 years
1981 (June)	7.0	1.25	7 months
1985	8.0	1.0	4 years
1987 (March)	9.5	1.5	2 years
1989 (Oct.)	10.50	1.0	2 years
1991 (Nov.)	12.50	2.0	3 years
1993 (Dec.)	14.00	1.5	2 years
1997 (Sep.)	20.00	6.0	4 years
1998 (April)	18.00	(-)2.0	7 months
1999 (October)	22.00	4.0	14 months
2001 (1st December)	30.00	8.0	18 months
2001 (6th November)	28.00	(-) 2.0	5 days

Source: Compiled.

Strangely, the fare was forced to bring down to the level of 18 paise per km. in April 1998 due to political pressures. However, it was hiked to 22 paise per km. in October 1999 and to 30 paise on 1st December 2001 taking into cost escalation between these periods. Again, the fare was scaled down (within 5 days) to 28 paise per km. on 6th December 2001 due to political pressure and public protest. It should be noted that every one paise fare reduction the government will lose its transport revenue by Rs. 100 crores and *vice versa*. On the other hand, there is always a direct correlation between the hike in fare and the subsequent reduction in the current year losses. For example, the loss margin was reduced from Rs. 411 crores in 1998-99 to Rs. 318 crores in 1999-2000 and to Rs. 233 crores in 2000-2001 (Vide Column 2 in Table 1 and 2).

POLICY PRESCRIPTIONS

Having scanned the pathological causes of the chronic losses of STCs in Tamil Nadu, it is imperative to take the following remedial steps.

Privatisation was not a panacea for the financial ills of the State transport corporations (STCs). All city and town bus services should not be privatized in order to sustain the State's social commitment in providing common public utility services at affordable cost to the poor and middle income sections; inter-State express bus service could be operated exclusively by the State government; all long-distance routes and mofussil short routes should be handed over to private operators with proven records of performance; to avoid corrupt practices and political pressures, the route permits should not be given to private operators for fixed lease charges. The administrative set-up of the regional transport divisions should be restructured into three operational divisions, namely, the Chennai Metropolitan Transport Corporation, the Tamil Nadu State District Transport Corporations, and the Tamil Nadu Inter-State Express Transport Corporation. This down-sizing would help scale down administrative expenses and boost managerial efficiency.

A Permanent Bus Fare Fixation Committee could be constituted to monitor the periodical increase in input costs and modify the fare level accordingly to avoid possible losses in earnings. In view of the time lag and the resultant accumulation of losses, it was suggested that the fare revision for the corporation should be linked with the annual Budget proposals presented in the Assembly on the analogy of the Railway budget presented in the Parliament every year. Such an arrangement, the authorities thought, would minimize the gap between the mounting cost and the economic fare so as to run the corporation on business principles as envisaged in section 22 of the RTC Act, 1950.

Transport labour unions could be encouraged to form road transport cooperatives to own and operate bus service on the eve of possible privatization and retrenchment. Instead of recommending straightaway privatization of uneconomic routes, the committee should prioritise remedial steps to avoid losses and increase operational revenues. It should analyse the causes for the continuation of uneconomic routes. If the routes' operational input cost was more than the revenue accruals for two successive years, those routes should be given to private operators.

If the routes were incurring losses due to leakage of revenue, less occupancy ratio, inadequacy of trips, irregular service, poor maintenance of vehicles, mismanagement at depot level etc., those routes should be brought under surveillance for two years to make them economically viable. Opening of new routes should be based on real economic consideration. The government could follow the policy of cross-subsidisation of non-economic routes with the earnings from the economic routes. The Motor Vehicles Act could be modified so as to facilitate mini-bus operators to extend their services to inadequate and non-viable 'served areas' of STCs. Lastly, unconventional methods such as advertisement in buses, courier postal service, carrying of authorized light luggage for educational institutions, hospitals and service organizations could be attempted to increase the non-traffic revenue of the STCs.

In fact that both the DMK and AIADMK Governments are responsible for the incremental increases in bus fare in Tamil Nadu since 1980. It is not politics, but pragmatic economics that should dominate any genuine policy decision. The protest of labour union leaders is not justifiable considering their penchant attitude for higher wages and other pecuniary benefits. They should remember that the personnel-cost-push factors are primarily responsible for the bloated total cost of transport corporations. The public should also know that an essential service like bus transport cannot be subsidized at all times at the cost of the State's exchequer. In short, pricing of bus service should be based only on economic rather than on political compulsions.

References

Amartya Sen: Choice, Welfare and Measurement, Oxford University Press, Delhi 1993.

Amitava Bose, et al: Issues in Economic Theory and Public Policy, Oxford Publishers, Delhi 1997

Anand Swaroop, B.: "A Mechanism for Fare Fixation in STUs—A Case Study of APSRTC", *Journal of Transport Management*, January 1994.

Jegadish Gandhi, P.: "State Transport Corporation: Still long way to go", *Business Line*, May 8, 1995.

———: Paper on "Road Transport in Tamil Nadu" at the Silver Jubilee Seminar Madras Institute of Development Studies, April 2, 1996.

———: Expert Member's paper on "An Overview of the Performance, Problems and Potentials for development in the Passenger Road Transport in Tamil Nadu", State Planning Commission, May 1996.

———: "State Transport Corporation: Any way out to avoid losses? *Dinamani*, Tamil News Paper, October 14, 1996.

———: "Bus fare hike to tide over revenue loss", *Indian Express*, November 16, 1996.

———: "Bus fare hike Justified" *The Hindu*, September 10, 1997.

———: "Economic Professor defends fare hike", *Indian Express*, September 14, 1987.

———: Paper on "STCs in Tamil Nadu at the cross roads: An Overview" at the Infrastructure Development Seminar, Karpagam Arts & Science College, Coimbatore, October 1, 1997.

———: "Public Bus Transport in Tamil Nadu at the Crossroads: An Overview," *Peninsular Economist*, Vol. X, No. 2, 1998-99.

———: "Bus Nationalisation in India: Retrospective-*cum*-Prospective Reflections", *Indian Journal of Transport Management*, March 1999.

———: "Public Passenger Road Transport in Tamil Nadu: Pricing Policy—Fair and Farce Syndrome?", *Southern Economist*, October 1, 1999.

———: "Bus Revision in Tamil Nadu: Ostrich-like Approach must change", *Business Line*, October 15, 1999.

———: A Pre-Budget *Memorandum* submitted to the Chief Minister of Tamil Nadu to Stream State Finances, March 20, 2002.

———: *Memorandum* submitted to the Chief Secretary, Govt. of Tamil Nadu and Chairman of the High level Committee on Privatization on Road Transport Sector, May 30, 2002.

Jegadish Gandhi, P., John Gunaseelan, G.: Indian Transport System: An Appraisal of Nationalised Bus Services (Eds.), Mittal Publications, 1994.

———: "Political Economy of Bus fares in Tamil Nadu" in Regional Economic Development in India (Eds.) Susheela Subrahmanya and Srinivasa Gowda, Deep & Deep Publications, New Delhi, 1995. *Memorandum* submitted to the State Transport Minister, Government of Tamil Nadu for improving the operations efficiency and the financial viability of STCs, June 18, 1996.

———: "Public Bus Transport Service in Tamil Nadu: An Appraisal", *Indian Journal of Transport Management*, October 1996.

19

CHAPTER

Asymmetrical Performance of Scheduled Commercial Banks in Tamil Nadu

P. GANESAN AND P.N. RAVI

In the post-independent economic history of India, 1991 is an important landmark year. The country went through a severe crisis triggered by a serious balance of payment situation. The crisis was converted into an opportunity to introduce some fundamental changes in the content and approach to economic policy of India (Dr. Rangarajan, 2001).

Banking is an important segment of the country and is the lifeblood of economic progress and prosperity by playing the role of a catalyst agent in development of developing countries like India. Nationalisation of Indian Scheduled Commercial Banks (hereafter SCBs) have brought sea changes in the objectives and its operations. However, Indian banking sector suffered from drawbacks like low productivity and efficiency, poor customer service, low capital base, lack of modernisation, deterioration in loan portfolio, etc. The then three major Committees' recommendations strengthened the operations and brought efficiency to the SCBs. Of which, Financial Sector Reform Committee (1991 & 1998) made landmark recommendations on several deregulatory measures in the banking system like reduction in the credit allocation to the directed credit programmes, directed investment programmes, deregulated interest rate, new accounting and prudential norms related to income recognition, provisioning and capital adequacy, in line with international standards, new private sector banks provided they confirm to RBI guideline for such banks. These major reform prescriptions of Narasimham Committee have been implemented by the SCBs since 1992-93.

The successes of any reform process introduced at national level highly depend on the implementation by the State economies in a federal system like India. Tamil Nadu is ranked among the developed states in India and is one of the six fastest growing states judged by per capita income and several other social and economic indicators (Palanidurai, 2001).

The purpose of this paper is to examine and compare the crucial banking indicators of Scheduled Commercial Banks with respect to Tamil Nadu by population group-wise: branch expansion, deposit mobilisation, credit deployment, CD ratio, deposit per branch and credit deployment per branch. In order to study the objective, time series data for the period between 1993-2000 was collected from Economic Survey, Government of

TABLE I

Branch Expansion of SCBs

(in Numbers)

Year	*Rural*	*Semi-Urban*	*Urban*
1993	1942	1054	1386
1994	1957	1093	1406
1995	1933	1120	1463
1996	1844	1178	1565
1997	1846	1177	1619
1998	1849	1186	1641
1999	1839	1198	1690
2000	1830	1211	1721
CGR	-1.02	1.92	3.41

India and Tamil Nadu Economic Appraisal, and Tamil Nadu Government official web-site.

The details on branch expansion of Scheduled Commercial Banks (hereafter SCBs) in Tamil Nadu is presented in Table 1. During the period 1993-2000, the number of additional branches opened was 380 in Tamil Nadu during the study period 1993-2000. The growth rate of rural branch expansion showed a negative trend as against semi-urban and urban areas. That is, the number of rural branches was 1942 in 1993 and declined to 1830 branches in 2000.

TABLE 2

Deposit Mobilisation by SCBs

(Rupees in Lakhs)

Year	*Rural*	*Semi-urban*	*Urban*
1993	230294	411672	1289409
1994	266987	468867	1433239
1995	309975	539209	1707694
1996	341002	608678	2020919
1997	402662	696833	2297561
1998	487142	842771	2725990
1999	547617	963456	3103452
2000	650312	1152990	3791015
CGR	15.88	15.75	16.66

The growth of branch expansion and closure of unremunerative branches as per the recommendation of Financial Sector Reforms Committee (1991 & 1998) attributed to tardy growth rate of deposit mobilization in rural and semi-urban areas compared to the rate of growth achieved by the urban branches at the state level (Table 2). The rate of growth of deposit mobilization by population group-wise in Tamil Nadu was around 16 per cent per annum. In Tamil Nadu, the additional deposit mobilized between 1993-2000 was Rs. 36662942 lakhs, of which rural branches contributed only 12 per cent as against 20 per cent and 68 per cent of semi-urban and urban areas respectively.

SCBs deployed Rs. 3250964 lakhs additional loans and

TABLE 3

Credit Deployment by SCBs

(Rupees in Lakhs)

Year	*Rural*	*Semi-urban*	*Urban*
1993	213240	246585	1212177
1994	230631	274638	1376491
1995	265877	338600	1866132
1996	292038	404049	2257939
1997	320584	442329	2516978
1998	365519	487551	2840073
1999	370908	541525	3378466
2000	402572	591152	3929243
CGR	9.82	13.58	18.26

advances into the Tamil Nadu Economy (Table 3). Growing fear on Non-Performing Assets (NPAs), objectives on higher profit and profitability of bank as well as branches, higher rate of overdues influenced the lower growth rate of loans advances deployed by the SCBs to Tamil Nadu's rural economy. Annual Rate of growth of advances made by SCBs in Tamil Nadu during the period was 18.26 per cent per annum in urban areas which was around two time compared to rural area branches (9.82 per cent) and semi-urban accounted only 13.58 per cent per annum.

Though the growth rate of deposits is almost the same among population group-wise, the deposit per branch showed laurels achievements by the SCBs in Tamil Nadu (Table 4). The rural people highly habituated and safety seekers rather like semi-urban and urban people who invest their money in Non-Banking Financial Corporations by looking higher rate of interest attributed to higher annual growth rate of average deposits of rural branch was 17.07 per cent in Tamil Nadu compare to the growth achieved by the semi-urban and urban centre branches of SCBs of Tamil Nadu.

The policy compulsion from Reserve Bank of India and Government of India paved the way for higher rate of advances per branch of SCBs in Tamil Nadu. The progressive

TABLE 4

Deposits per Branch of SCBs

(Rupees in Lakhs)

Year	*Rural*	*Semi-urban*	*Urban*
1993	118.586	390.5806	930.3095
1994	136.4267	428.9726	1019.373
1995	160.3595	481.4366	1167.255
1996	184.9252	516.7046	1291.322
1997	218.1268	592.0416	1419.124
1998	263.4624	710.5995	1661.176
1999	297.7798	804.2204	1836.362
2000	355.3617	952.0974	2202.798
CGR	17.07	13.56	12.82

variation in the advances per branch is witnessed between population group-wise in Tamil Nadu, India. For instance, the ratio between rural and semi-urban was 1:2.13 and between rural and urban was 1:8 and at the close of 2000 the ratios stood-up to 1:2.22 and 1:10, thus the credit deployment tilting toward urban and semi-urban centres.

Another disquieting feature noticed is that the rate of

TABLE 5

Advances per Branch of SCBs

(Rupees in Lakhs)

Year	*Rural*	*Semi-urban*	*Urban*
1993	109.80	233.95	874.59
1994	117.85	251.27	979.01
1995	137.55	302.32	1275.55
1996	158.37	343.00	1442.77
1997	173.66	375.81	1554.65
1998	197.68	411.09	1730.70
1999	201.69	452.02	1999.09
2000	219.98	488.15	2283.12
CGR	10.95	11.44	14.37

TABLE 6

Credit-Deposit SCBs

Year	*Rural*	*Semi-urban*	*Urban*
1993	0.93	0.60	0.94
1994	0.86	0.59	0.96
1995	0.86	0.63	1.09
1996	0.86	0.66	1.12
1997	0.80	0.63	1.10
1998	0.75	0.58	1.04
1999	0.68	0.56	1.09
2000	0.62	0.51	1.04

Credit-Deposit ratio with respect to rural and semi-urban areas *versus* urban of Tamil Nadu. The rate of disparity is widening considerably as period progressed from 1993 to 2000. The flow of funds diverted from rural and semi-urban centres to urban centres indicating that more credit deployment over and above the deposits mobilised therefrom.

FINDINGS AND CONCLUSION

- Noticeable Branch expansion by SCBs with respect to semi-urban and urban areas, but in rural areas, negative growth is witnessed which means considerable unremunerative branches have been closed after the introduction of reform both at State level.
- Deposit mobilization by population group-wise centered around 16 per cent per annum. However, rural branches have not made any impressive additional deposit mobilization during the period under review.
- Even after the reform, SCBs have been unenthusiastic in credit disbursement to rural economy as witnessed by growth rate of rural areas credit deployment.
- Though the deposit mobilized per rural branch is higher than the semi-urban and urban branches,

the flow of funds tilting towards urban centres shows that rural prosperity is afflicted by the urban branches after the reform process.

- CD ratio also supported the above argument that more credit deployment over and above the deposit mobilized by urban centre branches.

The Narasimham Committee is handy for the SCBs for closure of unremunerative rural and semi-urban branches, but it has caused heavy damages on the credit deployment and other developmental schemes to these areas. The real doubt arises on the basic objectives of the nationalisation of banks that uplifting the poor and downtrodden people who suffers for basic needs. Adequate earnings might be one of the criteria for branch closure, but not the only criteria. Due consideration could be given to achieve the social objectives.

It is clear from the analysis that there is a unsymmetrical performance of schedule commercial banks in Tamil Nadu. It is suggested that there is an urgent need for further strenghtening the comprehensive policy measures with respect to retail banking facilities to farming and allied sectors, enlarging and effective distribution of micro-finance to rural masses without rigid conditionalities, motivating Self-Help Groups (SHGs), proper attention on customer relationship, need-based and employment-oriented loans to the neglected sectors of the rural economy, etc and the alike rather than measures for political gains. This would give real benefit not only to the rural people, but also to the SCBs at national and State level.

References

Palanidurai, K.V., "Tamil Nadu Economy: Progress During Nineties and Challenges Ahead", in Dr. P. Jegadish Gandhi and Dr. P. Ganesan (Ed.), Special Session on Tamil Nadu Economy, Shortlong Papers (Abstracts), 84th Annual Conference of Indian Economic Association, December, 28-30, 2001, pp. 1-4.

Dr. Rangarajan, "Indian Economy", Inaugural Address delivered during the 84th Annual Conference of Indian Economic Association, December, 28-30, 2001

Dr. P. Ganesan, "Public Sector Banks and Priority sector Advances—A Critical Analysis", *Southern Economist*, Vol. 37(8), August 15, 1998, pp. 12-16.
Economic Survey, Ministry of Finance, Government of India, various issues.
Tamil Nadu Economic Appraisal, 1996-97 and 1997-98.
www.tn.gov.in.

20

CHAPTER

Dyanmics of IT Industry in Tamil Nadu

B. MURALI MANOHAR AND S. GANESH

NEED FOR THE STUDY

Information Technology has become the magic *mantra* of the day. Needless to say that every administrator in the country needs to be aware of the emerging trends. Tamil Nadu has jumped into the foray lately after the pioneering efforts by the southern states of India like Karnataka and Andhra Pradesh.

Information Technology covers all spheres, including Government Departments, Educational institutions, Banking, Shopping, Entertainment and a whole gamut of other consumer applications, in Tamil Nadu as in other southern states. As per the 9th Five Year Plan projections by the year 2001-02, IT revenue in Tamil Nadu will be of the order of Rs. 13,000 crores (Rs. 5,000 crores in Hardware and Rs. 8,000 crores in Software). The industry has predicted that this can be achieved provided the State Government announces and implements an industry-friendly IT policy, with the aim of achieving the goals spelt out in the 9th Plan and by focusing attention on the IT industry as a striving force of growth. The paper brings out the dynamics of IT development in Tamil Nadu.

OBJECTIVES OF THE STUDY

Keeping in mind the above mentioned aspects, the authors have set out to study the following:

- Progress of IT sector—Tamil Nadu.
- Role of Software Technology Park India (STPI).
- Information Technology Policy of Tamil Nadu.

A STUDY ON PROGRESS OF IT SECTOR IN TAMIL NADU

From the Diagram 1, we can understand the progress of IT industry in Tamil Nadu. It is understood that the growth in this sector is primarily attributed to the efforts of many private organisations/entrepreneurs. The authors have calculated the Compounded Annual Growth Rates (CAGR) for total exports, STP and other units from the above data. Total exports have grown by an impressive 179.30%; STP units by 103.15% whereas other units by 150.31%. So, it is clear that the growth of IT industry is attributed to the efforts of many organisations/entrepreneurs, who are either operating from STPs or other geographical areas of the state. This is also evident from the following tables:

TABLE I

Growth of Software Industries in Tamil Nadu and Pondicherry: 2000-01

Years	*Others*	*STP Units*	*Total No. of Units*
1993-94	0	10	10
1994-95	0	23	23
1995-96	0	34	34
1996-97	4	65	69
1997-98	17	91	108
1998-99	45	121	166
1999-2000	65	536	601
2000-01	92	674	766

DIAGRAM I

Software Export Growth—Tamil Nadu

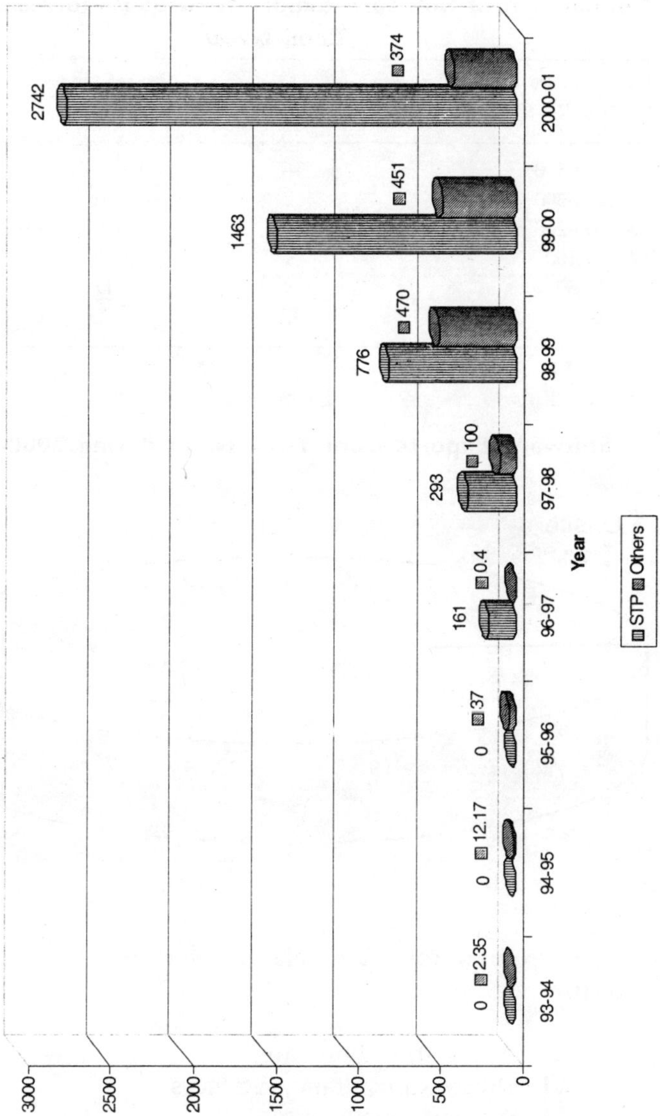

TABLE 2

Comparison of Software Export Growth Performance from Tamil Nadu

Sl. No.	Software Export Turnover (in Rs. Crores)	No. of Units 1998-99	1999-00	2000-01
1.	400-500	—	—	2
2.	200-300	2	2	1
3.	100-200	2	2	5
4.	50-100	1	2	1
5.	10-50	9	17	18
6.	1-10	37	70	97

DIAGRAM 2

Software Exports from Tamil Nadu during 2000-2001

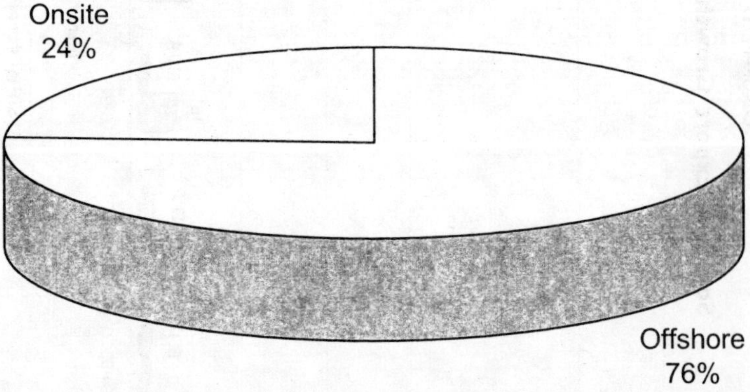

IT exports from Tamil Nadu cover the following areas of expertise, viz.

- Application Software,
- Onsite Consultancy Services,
- Systems Software,
- IT Enabled Services, and
- Web Applications and Product/Packages.

This diagram gives a break-up of revenue assignments for various IT organisations in Tamil Nadu for the period 2000-2001. A major part of the revenue comes from offshore projects.

The authors are interested in projecting the IT exports from Tamil Nadu for the next decade (Annexure 1) by using the method of least squares.

SOFTWARE TECHNOLOGY PARKS OF INDIA (STPI)

STPI is a non-profit society set-up in 1991 by the Ministry of Information Technology, Govt. of India to promote and facilitate Software Exports from India.

STPI Scheme

STPI scheme is a 100% export-oriented scheme for undertaking software development for export using data communication link or in the form of physical media including export of professional services.

Benefits under STPI Scheme

- Approval under single window clearance,
- An STP project may be set-up anywhere in India,
- Sales in Domestic Tariff Area (DTA) permissible upto 50% of the export in value terms,
- No corporate income-tax till 2010,
- Reimbursement of CST,
- Full convertibility of Indian Rupee on Current Account,
- Tax exemption on export profits, and
- Depreciation on IT product @ 60%.

TAMIL NADU IT POLICY—INCENTIVES AND INITIATIVES

Tamil Nadu's contribution to the IT industry has been significant. The key elements which have made TN an important player in this area—are availability of skilled and educated manpower, comparatively higher standard of educational institutions, reasonably good infrastructure, and lower costs of operation. Apart from these, the presence of an International Airport and a major Seaport in Chennai have also helped the growth of IT industry in Tamil Nadu.

The potential for growth of Information Technology in Tamil Nadu is enormous with IT penetrating all spheres, including Government Departments, educational institutions, Banking, shopping entertainment and a whole gamut of other consumer applications. The industry, while drawing up the program for the 9th Five Year Plan has projected that by the year 2001-02, IT revenue in Tamil Nadu will be of the order of Rs. 13,000 crores (Rs. 5,000 crores in Hardware and Rs. 8,000 crores in Software). The industry has predicted that this level of achievement can be obtained provided the State Government announces and implements an industry-friendly IT policy. With the aim of achieving the goals spelt out in the 9th Plan and by focusing attention on the IT industry as an engine of growth in the State, it has been decided to formulate an industry-specific policy for the IT industry.

The objectives of the IT policy are as follows:

- to encourage and accelerate the growth of hardware and software industries and associated services in the State and to remove the bottlenecks for starting and running of such units in Tamil Nadu;
- to increase both domestic and export earnings of software and hardware sectors in the State;
- to upgrade and develop manpower skills required for the IT industry by facilitating training, to accelerate the use of IT in schools, colleges and educational institutions with a view to providing skills and knowledge to the youth to make them fit for employment in this sector;
- to upgrade the quality of life the citizens of the State by facilitating access to consumer application of Information Technology; and
- as part of the above objectives, the Government will also encourage the use of IT in Government institutions and Departments with a view to improving productivity and efficiency of

Government services, revenues and tax collections, and assist in the process of decision-making by Government services, and monitoring of Government programs.

INCENTIVES AVAILABLE TO THE INDUSTRY

- There is no system of Entry Tax or Purchase Tax in Tamil Nadu.
- Facility of uninterrupted power will continue to be offered to IT industry.
- Fiscal and Tax concessions for investments of various slabs.
- Capital subsidy as applicable to electronics industries @ 20% of fixed assets subject to a maximum of Rs. 20 lakhs will be available to all IT industries.

NEW INITIATIVES

- The State Government will set-up IT parks (ITPs) at Chennai, Coimbatore, Tiruchirapalli and Madurai in a phased manner.
- Apart from ITPs in the Government and joint sectors, Government will facilitate setting up of ITPs by the private sector in potential locations for the development of IT industries.
- The Government will provide assistance to VSNL and Department of Telecommunications to expand communication links in the State and also provide the land and power wherever required by such agencies.
- All ITPs set-up by private promoters will have the same status as ITPs promoted by Government.
- In all the Technology Parks set-up by Government and joint ventures, there will be an Executive Authority of the Park which will function as the single window for all statutory clearances required for the units, within the Parks.
- Apart from development of software and hardware industry through ITPs/STPs the Government will

also encourage software development outside the Parks by giving such stand-alone units the same incentives as the unities in the ITPs/STPs.

- All software industries including Services and Training Institutions in IT will be entitled to enjoy "Industry" status. Such units shall be eligible for all concessions and incentives applicable to Industries.
- Government will provide continuous power supply in industry rates to all IT units .
- Government will encourage setting up of Venture Capital Fund for development of IT Industry through TIDCO in association with private sector partners.
- Government will set-up an Information Technology Institute of Tamil Nadu (TANITEC) to take care of the training and technology upgradation aspects of IT in the State.
- Training Institutes for hardware, software, servicing and maintenance will be deemed to be "Industries" and will be eligible for all facilities offered to Industries including Bank finance and SSI or IEM registration.
- Basic training in computers will be introduced in all schools from the high school level.
- Government of Tamil Nadu will encourage IT industries to obtain ISO 9000 process certification.
- Government of Tamil Nadu will offer relaxation of FSI (Floor Space Index) in metropolitian areas to the extent of 50% for IT Parks.
- Government of Tamil Nadu will co-ordinate with Government of India to facilitate the setting up of an 'Internal Container Depot' to take care of exports of specified industrial products through Chennai Port, including products of electronic and hardware units.
- Government of Tamil Nadu will facilitate setting up an Air Freight City near Chennai Airport, for improving cargo movement for imports and exports from Chennai Airport.

CONCLUDING REMARKS ABOUT IT INDUSTRY IN TAMIL NADU

Strengths

- The IT industry has grown at an impressive rate of 179.30% over a period of time.
- Highly developed infrastructure in the form of International Air Port, sea port and high band width telecommunication networks are available
- Size of the IT industry estimated to be Rs. 5000 Crore in the year 2001.
- TN is among the top 5 states in IT industry.
- Software exports to the tune of Rs. 3116 Crore in the year 2000.
- Computer Hardware exports worth Rs. 576 Crore in 2000.
- 30,000 IT professionals will graduate every year from about 230 engineering colleges in a few years.
- 200 private computer training institutes are present
- Largest private internet service provider—Satyam Online.
- Installed base of 150,000 PCs in 1996 has increased 7-fold in 5 years.
- Industry estimates that about 1000 PCs are sold everyday throughout the State.
- The State pioneered the introduction of computer science courses at the school level.

Weaknesses

- The absence of a dynamic political personality in the form of a Chief Ministers like in Andhra Pradesh and Karnataka, hence no high profile foreign investor visited the state in the recent past.
- No concrete measures on e-governance which is successfully implemented in several key areas of administration in the states like Andhra Pradesh and Karnataka.

References

http://www.tidco.com
http://www.tanitec.com
http://www.stpi.com
http://www.investopedia.com

Annexure I

Projected IT Exports from Tamil Nadu for the next 10 Years

Year	*Projected Sales (in Rs. Crores)*
2001-2002	2743.9
2002-2003	3162.5
2003-2004	3581.1
2004-2005	3999.7
2005-2006	4418.3
2006-2007	4836.9
2007-2008	5255.5
2008-2009	5674.1
2009-2010	6092.7
2010-2011	6511.3

Note: YC = a + b(x), where a = 860.2 and b = 418.6.

ANNEXURE 2

TABLE 1

Software Export Performance, 2000-01 from Secondary Cities of Tamil Nadu

Cities	*Type*	*Rs. Crores*	*Total*
Coimbatore	STP (14)	19.19	
	Others(3)	1.28	Rs 20.47 Crs
Thirunelveli	STP (2)		Rs 1.68 Crs
Vellore	STP (1)		Rs. 85,000
Trichy	STP (1)		Rs. 2.64 Crs
Thanjavur	STP (1)		Rs. 25,00,000

TABLE 2

Spread of Software Export Units Across Tamil Nadu and Pondicherry

Place	*STP*	*Others*	*Total*
Chennai	591	85	676
Coimbatore	63	3	66
Madurai	3	2	5
Trichy	2	—	2
Tirupur	2	—	2
Vellore	1	—	1
Dindugal	1	—	1
Thirunelveli	2	—	2
Erode	1	—	1
Thanjavur	1	—	1
Pondicherry	7	2	9
	674	92	766

TABLE 3

Software Export Performance, 2000-01 (Tamil Nadu and Pondicherry)—Area of Expertise

Sl No.	*Area of Expertise*	*1999-2000*			*2000-2001*		
		Exports (Rs. Cr)	*%*	*No. of Units*	*Export (Rs. Cr)*	*%*	*No. of Units*
1.	Application Software	1223	64	105	1167	39.47	138
2.	Onsite Services	470	25	26	739	25	30
3.	Systems Software	139	7	30	626	21.20	32
4.	IT Enabled Services	68	4	58	260	9	71
5.	Web Applications	9	0.5	44	121	4.1	56
6.	Product/Packages	5	0.3	20	43	1.5	25

TABLE 4

Software Export Performance—STPI—Chennai, 2000-01

(Rs. in crores)

Certified by STPI	2956
MEPZ	160
Total Software Exports	3116
From EHTP units	576
Total Software and Hardware Exports	3692

SECTION IV

Financial Facets

21
CHAPTER

Tamil Nadu State Finances: Some Crucial Issues

R. BALAJI

THE BACKDROP

In a federation, financial powers and responsibilities are distributed between the federal and regional governments. An ideal federation is one in which each governmental unit has adequate and independent financial resources to perform its exclusive functions and responsibilities effectively. Financial adequacy and autonomy, thus, constitute the core principles underlying a sound federal fiscal system.

The federal structure of the Indian Constitution provides for a division of functions and resources between the Centre and the States, under which the former is vested with the most productive sources of revenue with relatively fixed functions *vis-a-vis* the States. The founding fathers of the Constitution, great visionaries as they were, rightly thought of a strong Centre for a large sprawling country like India. However, the expansion of the activities of the States in diverse fields such as development and social welfare coupled with inelastic sources of revenue at their disposal for funding their ever-increasing expenditures has widened the fiscal imbalance between the Centre and the States. Thus while the Centre has access to a large number of productive, elastic and buoyant tax and non-tax revenue sources, the States are endowed with the most expensive and expansive development and non-developmental expenditure functions. The Constitution has taken into consideration the need for alleviating fiscal imbalances, both vertical and horizontal, by providing for federal fiscal transfeRs. But owing to several factors, the States in the 'Indian Union' have found it increasingly difficult to bridge the gap between their revenue resources and expenditure commitments.

The problem that is assuming alarming proportions ever since 1987-88 is the 9 burgeoning deficits, particularly on the revenue account of the state budgets. This is reflected in the enormous growth of gross fiscal deficit of the states. As pointed out by Govinda Rao, the higher growth of revenue expenditure in relation to the growth of revenue receipts has created an explosive cycle of expenditure growth. The use of borrowed funds for meeting revenue expenditure, while increasing interest liability, does not create corresponding sources of revenue. In addition to this, as even the borrowed funds used for capital spending are not efficiently utilised, interest liabilities feed back into the growth of expenditures requiring even larger diversion of borrowed funds[1]. Tamil Nadu is no exception to all these depressing and disturbing trends in states' finances. It is in this backdrop that this pursuit has sought to examine critical trends in Tamil Nadu state finances over the decade 1990-2000, identifying in the process, crucial issues that need to be addressed with all seriousness in the years to come. Only if a well-intentioned programme of fiscal correction and restructuring is carried out, can there be sustained and accelerated growth in the state economy in an era of second generation economic reforms ushered in for strengthening the process of liberalisation.

MOUNTING FISCAL DEFICIT OF TAMIL NADU

Fiscal deficit, a concept widely applied by the International Monetary Fund, is known to Indian public finance for a decade now. While the conventional budgetary deficit captures only a part of the shortfall in the government's fiscal operations (which is made good by drawing down its cash balances, and/or resorting to ways and means advances and overdrafts from the Reserve Bank of India[2]. Thus gross fiscal deficit captures the entire shortfall that is to be made good through borrowings, withdrawals of cash balances and/or resorting to ways and means advances and overdrafts from the Reserve Bank of India. Thus, gross fiscal deficit (GFD) depicts the *total resource gap* in the fiscal operations of the state government. It is the gap between total expenditure (revenue expenditure + capital outlay + net lendings) and total revenue receipts. Putting it differently, gross fiscal deficit is equal to the gap in the revenue account + capital outlay + net lendings. In fine, it represents the total borrowing requirements of the government.

Tamil Nadu's gross fiscal deficit was of the order of Rs. 1126 crore in 1990-91; it stood at Rs. 1255 crore in 1995-96 to reach a staggering figure of Rs. 5382 crore in 1999-2000. These figures when expressed as a ratio of total expenditure serve a useful purpose of distinctly measuring the total resource gap faced by the State in the respective years. The uncovered portion of total expenditure (that is, total expenditure not covered by the receipts on the revenue account, but met by borrowings) which stood at 18 per cent in 1990-91 fell to 11 per cent in 1995-96, only to rise to 25 per cent in 1999-2000. The GFD-SDP ratio, considered to be the best indicator of the fiscal health of a state, declined from 4.1 per cent in 1990-91 to 2.1 per cent in 1995-96, to rise to 4.0 per cent in 1999-2000 (Table 1).

The figures of gross fiscal deficit of Tamil Nadu show that the borrowings of the State have, indeed, been alarmingly high, calling for sterner measures to check the trend. The phenomenal rise in the gross fiscal deficit resulted in a seemingly untenable outstanding debt (Table 2). A high level of debt inexorably increases the interest burden which, in turn, claims a sizable portion of the revenue receipts (Table 3).

ALARMING REVENUE DEFICIT

Effective management of revenue account of the budget

TABLE 1

Gross Fiscal Deficit of Tamil Nadu, 1990-2000

Year	*GFD (Rs. in Cr.)*	*GFD as % of Total Expenditure*	*GFD-SDP Ratio*
1990-1991	1126	18	4.1
1991-1992	1375	17	4.2
1992-1993	1824	21	4.8
1993-1994	1433	15	3.1
1994-1995	1496	14	2.8
1995-1996	1255	11	2.1
1996-1997	2445	17	2.7
1997-1998	2122	14	2.0
1998-1999	4777	25	4.0
1999-2000	5382	25	4.0

Source: Government of Tamil Nadu, Budget Memoranda; Reserve Bank of India, *Monthly Bulletins*.

TABLE 2

Outstanding Debt of Tamil Nadu, 1990-2000

Year	*Outstanding Loans and Liabilities (Rs. in Crore)*
1990-1991	5501
1991-1992	6527
1992-1993	7724
1993-1994	9290
1994-1995	11174
1995-1996	12552
1996-1997	14183
1997-1998	16406
1998-1999	19939
1999-2000	23840

Source: Reserve Bank of India, *Report on Currency and Finance*, Vol. II, Various Issues.

TABLE 3

Interest Burden of a High Outstanding Debt

Year	*Interest Payments of TN*	*Interest Payments as % of*
		(Rs. in Crore)
1990-1991	483	9
1991-1992	557	8
1992-1993	688	10
1993-1994	957	12
1994-1995	1090	12
1995-1996	1293	12
1996-1997	1476	12
1997-1998	1763	13
1998-1999	2122	15
1999-2000	2711	17

Source: Government of Tamil Nadu, Budget Memoranda; Reserve Bank of India, *Monthly Bulletins.*

implies mobilisation of adequate funds for feeding the revenue and investment expenditures of the state and/or compression of the revenue expenditures well within the revenue resources. But when the state fails to find sufficient revenues to cover even the revenue expenditures the strain on the budget increases, affecting eventually the funding of larger investment expenditures.

Revenue deficit, which is the gap between revenue receipts and revenue expenditures, has become a common feature of Tamil Nadu state finances. While there was a minimal point in 1995-96, the gap widened to such an extent that it touched the all-time high of Rs. 4400 crore in 1999-2000 (Table 4). There were times when revenue budgets used to generate surpluses for financing investment expenditures. However, with the gap between revenue receipts and expenditures growing alarmingly, the state is forced to borrow even more in order to finance not only its investment expenditures but its revenue deficits too.

Revenue deficit, which is a component of GFD, when expressed as its ratio indicates the extent to which the borrowing of the government is used to finance its revenue expenditure. As seen, large gaps in the revenue account of the state budget absorbed major portions of borrowed funds in the decade 1990-2000, punctuated, of course, by peaks and troughs (Table 4). In 1990-91, revenue deficit of Tamil Nadu formed about 50 per cent of the state's gross fiscal deficit. In 1995-96, it fell to 25 per cent only to peak at 82 per cent in 1999-2000. Thus, the contribution of the revenue account gap to the total resource gap had accentuated from one-half at the beginning of the decade to four-fifths at the end of the decade. This points to the worrisome state of Tamil Nadu state finances. It is imperative, therefore, to contain revenue deficit. Otherwise, revenue deficit and gross fiscal deficit by mutual reinforcement would lead eventually to a larger accumulation of debt with all its attendant problems. The point of concern is that as observed in other states in the Indian federation, fiscal deficits in Tamil Nadu have been driven more and more by revenue deficits. C. Rangarajan notes that borrowing to fill revenue deficit implies that current consumption of the government is financed by private savings, even though in some cases, revenue expenditures as defined in the budget documents may lead to the creation of assets.

The absorption of larger portions of borrowed funds by revenue deficits adversely affected the availability of resources for investment expenditures, namely, capital outlay and loans given by the government for developmental purposes (Table 4). This reinforces the need for controlling revenue deficit for enhancing capital outlays and net lendings by the state government. Moreover, the wider the gap in the revenue account, the larger would be the total resource gap and greater the need for borrowed funds, and more serious the strain on the state budget. Greater investment expenditures would be possible in the state only through substantial reduction of revenue deficit. And, this is possible only if concerted efforts are made by the state in the direction of pruning revenue expenditures, specifically the non-developmental component, while at the same time attaining greater buoyancy in the revenue receipts.

TABLE 4

Total Resource Gap Borrowing Requirements of Tamil Nadu

Year	*Revenue Deficit*	*Investment Expenditure*	*Gross Fiscal Deficit*
1990-1991	553	573	1126
	(49)	(51)	(100)
1991-1992	1904	529*	1375
	(138)	(-38)	(100)
1992-1993	1526	298	1824
	(84)	(16)	(100)
1993-1994	692	741	1433
	(48)	(52)	(100)
1994-1995	416	1080	1496
	(28)	(72)	(100)
1995-1996	311	944	1255
	(25)	(75)	(100)
1996-1997	1104	1341	2445
	(45)	(55)	(100)
1997-1998	1364	758	2122
	(64)	(36)	(100)
1998-1999	3436	1341	4777
	(72)	(28)	(100)
1999-2000	4400	982*	5382
	(82)	(18)	(100)

* indicates excess of recoveries over loans and advances given by the government.

Source: Government of Tamil Nadu, Budget Memoranda.

PROFILE OF REVENUE SOURCES OF TAMIL NADU

The revenue receipts of Tamil Nadu comprises own revenue receipts and central transfers on the revenue account. Own revenue receipts formed more than two-thirds of the total revenue receipts; a third was transferred by the Centre.

Own revenue receipts fall under two categories, namely, tax and non-tax revenues. Tax revenues accounted for more than 80 per cent of the gross own revenue receipts; the contribution of non-tax revenues at less than 20 per cent pointed to the presence of a grey area in Tamil Nadu state finances.

Tax revenues for the state come from direct and indirect tax sources. The share of indirect taxes at 98 per cent during 1990-2000, focussed sharply on the direct taxes' dismal performance at just 2 per cent of the total tax revenues of the state. Thus, the state's indirect taxes constituted the single largest source of tax revenue, playing a significant role in the mobilisation of development finance in Tamil Nadu. This reflects the pattern of tax system that has emerged in all the states in the Indian federation.

There are three components of the direct tax structure in Tamil Nadu: agricultural income tax, land revenue and urban land tax, all of which are non-performers from the productivity point. Interestingly, the state's direct taxes are being grossly underutilised at a time when the state is yearning for larger resources to meet its ever-increasing revenue requirements.

Among the indirect taxes of Tamil Nadu, sales tax emerged as the major contributor to the state exchequer by providing two-thirds of total indirect tax revenues. The remaining share was collectively held by taxes such as state excise duties, motor vehicles tax, entertainment tax, stamp duties and registration fees. This again is reflective of the typical pattern obtaining in other states where there is excessive reliance on sales tax as a tool of mobilising indirect tax revenues (in fact, of total tax revenues).

Among the non-tax revenue heads, interest receipts on loans and advances given by the state government, and receipts from economic services emerged the major contributors to total non-tax revenues, followed by general services and social services. The share of the component, dividends and profits of state public enterprises was negligible.

There are two components of central transfers on the revenue account: tax devolutions and grants. Tax devolutions recommended by the Finance Commissions constituted two-thirds of total transferred resources; the remaining one-third was in the form of statutory grants recommended by the Finance Commissions, plan grants as sanctioned by the

Planning Commission, and non-plan non-statutory grants provided by the central ministries using their discretion. One of the thorny issues in Indian fiscal federalism has been the grants that are discretionary in character.

ISSUES IN REVENUE AUGMENTATION

An important dimension of fiscal restructuring in Tamil Nadu is revenue augmentation to reduce the deficits on the revenue account. Options seem to be fewer and difficult to exercise; but courageous and imaginative steps that could usher in long-term fiscal correctives need to be undertaken for larger benefit of the state.

The sphere of agriculture for taxation purposes finds place in the State List in the Seventh Schedule of the Constitution. Time and again it has been pointed out by several experts that there is need and scope for placing greater reliance on the farm sector. The Planning Commission had expressed itself strongly in favour of a highly progressive agricultural taxation. Thanks to the new technology and resultant green revolution, agriculture has improved considerably in terms of productivity and output leading to increased farm disposable incomes. Also, taking into consideration the fact that governments have put enormous resources into the agricultural sector, not to mention the power, water and fertilizer subsidies, there is justification and scope for raising agricultural taxation and tapping the tax-paying ability of the higher-income fanning community. No longer can the farm sector claim tax immunity citing absence of a comprehensive crop insurance scheme or non-availability of adequate inputs in time. So far, States in the Indian federation had displayed laxity and lacked the political will in this regard. It is expected that Tamil Nadu would set the lead in mobilising additional resources from the farm sector given the shape of its finances. An all-party consensus is important in this matter. The Eleventh Finance Commission had also suggested better exploitation of land-based taxes for reducing the budgetary deficits.[3]

In the post-independence period, public sector enterprises came into existence to fulfil certain socio-economic objectives. Huge investments were made in these enterprises, which, over time, acquired commanding heights of the Indian economy. While they attained the socio-economic goals, most of the enterprises have become a burden on their creatoRs. Since efficiency and effectiveness were never the core of their operations, either they have registered deplorably low profits or have incurred heavy losses. Far from being self-financing and profit-making, the enterprises have been relying heavily on budgetary support, adding to government deficits. In order to fill these deficits, the governments have been increasingly resorting to borrowings, resulting in high outstanding debt and large interest payments. These, in turn, have been eating into the very vitals of state resources. In Tamil Nadu, aggregate investments in the form of share capital assistance and loans in sixty-plus public sector undertakings rose from Rs. 789.47 crore in 1990-91 to Rs. 1991.85 crore in 1999-2000. The number of profit-making enterprises declined from 33 in 1989-90 to 26 in 1999-2000. These enterprises suffered a net loss of Rs. 298.08 crore in 1999-2000 as against a net profit of Rs. 1.07 crore in 1989-90. Their total accumulated loss as on 31.3.2000 was at Rs. 2292.40 crore, which far exceeded the paid-up share capital of Rs. 1298.14 crore of the government. The rate of return (ratio of earnings to capital employed) was negligible at 1.56 per cent in 1999-2000, implying that while the government has had to resort to high-cost borrowings from the market its investments in the public sector undertakings fetched insignificant receipts[4]. Statistics speak for themselves. Criticism of the working of state-level public sector undertakings cannot be more severe than that of the Centre for Monitoring Indian Economy: It is the losses of the Central Government enterprises which have generally received maximum publicity. It is not realised, however, that the worst culprits in this respect are to be found among state governments. There, the state electricity boards, the irrigation works, the road transport corporations and other state government-owned enterprises have the most scandalous record of making losses[5]. There is an urgent need, therefore, for a radical restructuring of the state-level public sector undertakings for upgrading their performances and wiping-off the accumulated losses. Reasonable upward revision of user charges in public utilities, though politically sensitive, should be taken up boldly and decisively to reduce the subsidy component and the resulting strain on the state budget. The advice of the Planning Commission to the State Government in this regard is timely. The Eleventh Finance Commission had also suggested that user charges should be index-linked to input costs and process of periodic revision become automatic. Further, there should be a regular revision of royalties on minerals. The task of making recommendations on royalty rates should be entrusted to an independent body.

Sales tax is the single largest source of revenue for Tamil Nadu; in fact, it constitutes the bulwark of Tamil Nadu state finances. Rationalisation of the sales tax structure should result in netting additional revenues through reduction of tax evasion, arrears and litigation, and abolition of tax exemptions/deferrals for attracting investment. A welcome step in tax reforms in Tamil Nadu was the introduction of Value Added Tax (VAT) in the budget for 1996-97, to be only suspended for want of adequate administrative preparation and failure to enlighten traders on the system. It is intended to introduce VAT all over the country in April 2002. However, successful implementation of the system would require creation of awareness about the beneficial effects that VAT would have for manufacturers, traders, consumers and the tax administratoRs. It is expected that once the system is properly implemented, leakages would have gone and tax base widened. Amaresh Bagchi observes that buoyancy of sales tax can improve if a full-fledged VAT is put in place; however, its introduction will require certain immediate changes that cannot come about without strong conviction among policy-makers[6].

In order to augment the resources of the states and reduce fiscal imbalances, the Constitution has provided for central transfeRs. However, states like Tamil Nadu feel that the mechanism of resource transfers in India is not sound and rational and is not conducive to cooperative federalism. The contribution of tax devolution to Tamil Nadu's total revenue receipts had declined from 20 per cent in 1990-91 to 16 per cent in 1999-2000. Similarly, the share of all central grants fell from 11 per cent to 8 per cent. Demanding rationalisation of criteria that determine central devolutions Tamil Nadu had submitted memoranda before successive Finance Commissions, but to no avail. In fact, successive Finance Commissions had denied the State its due share in the devolution of central taxes/duties. Tamil Nadu's share in the divisible pool of central taxes/duties fell persistently to reach a low of 5.385 per cent in the award of Eleventh Finance Commission. The reduction in the share of tax devolution for Tamil Nadu from 6.637 per cent (TFC award) to 5.385 per cent (EFC award) is because of the modification in the formula for determining *inter-se* share of central devolution. As a consequence of the EFC award, the State has to forego a whopping sum of Rs. 2946 crore during the period 2000-05[7]. This, indeed, is a big loss for the state to bear. In the case of states like Maharashtra the loss in devolution is estimated to be still larger. At this rate, some progressive states are apprehending real danger of being denied any devolution from Central funds in another 15-20 years[8]. Highlighting the penalising nature of the EFC award, Tamil Nadu in collaboration with other affected states presented a joint memorandum to the Prime Minister in August 2000. It is imperative, therefore, that central devolutions are made taking into consideration the fiscal needs and problems of all the states; otherwise, centre-state financial relations in the years to come would be marked by escalated conflict and tension. After all, the Constitution has provided for the appointment of a Finance Commission every five years for easing the financial difficulties of the states in the Indian Union.

The alternative scheme of devolution suggested by the Tenth Finance Commission is a positive step towards strengthening of centre-state financial relations in the country. The commission recommended a 26 per cent states' share in the aggregate central tax revenues (inclusive of corporation tax) enabling, thereby, the states to share the aggregate buoyancy of central taxes and enjoy at the same time greater certainty of resource flows. It also recommended an additional 3 per cent of aggregate tax receipts as the share of the states, in lieu of additional excise duties. It suggested that the scheme be reviewed every fifteen years. Ideally, constitutional amendments in respect of these recommendations would put

TABLE 5

Criteria and Weights for Determining *Inter-se* Share of Tax Devolution—A Comparison

Criterion	*Tenth Finance Commission*	*Eleventh Finance Commission*
1. Population	20.00%	10.00%
2. Distance	60.00%	62.50%
3. Area	5.00%	7.50%
4. Index of Infrastructure	5.00%	7.50%
5. Tax Effort	10.00%	5.00%
6. Fiscal Discipline		7.50%
Total	100.00%	100.00%

enhanced resources at the disposal of the states and remove much of the irritants in federal financial relations. The suggestion of the West Bengal Memorandum for an automatic transfer of 75 per cent of the central tax receipts to the divisible pool of the states, or the demand raised by the Tamil Nadu Legislature for a one-third share in all central taxes, or that raised by the Northern States' Finance Ministers' Zonal Conference (October 1997) for a 50 per cent share in the gross central tax receipts has not found favour with the Centre. In the context of current economic reforms, particularly in the domain of taxation, the Centre should seriously consider the question of bringing in amendments to the Constitution for implementation of the Tenth Finance Commission's alternative scheme of devolution.

ISSUES IN EXPENDITURE MANAGEMENT

As part of the programme of fiscal restructuring, expenditure management assumes even more significance than revenue augmentation efforts. Since revenue deficits, a component of gross fiscal deficit, reflect a mismatch between revenue receipts and revenue expenditures, states should strive to live within their means. Second, the proportion of investment expenditure to total expenditure (investment plus current/revenue) has been phenomenally low. This shows the extent and type of expenditure the states are committed to. The share of revenue expenditure in total expenditure of Tamil Nadu was as high as 93.9 per cent in 1999-2000. Therefore, governments of the present should focus on amending the composition of expenditures for the larger benefit of posterity.

In developing economies like India, subsidies are necessitated by certain basic social objectives. They create positive effects on production and distribution in the economy. However as growth gathers momentum, subsidies need be gradually minimised so that more resources get deployed in infrastructure expansion and installation of capital projects. The Discussion Paper on subsidies[9] viewed that these are justified only in the case of merit goods such as primary education, public health and scientific research and do not have any justification in the case of non-merit goods like food, fertilizers, etc. There are, of course, points and counter-points on this issue. Nevertheless, in the face of severe resource constraints confronted by governments, subsidies should get more and more target-oriented, with the implicit component-type drastically cut. Again, the temptation of the states to introduce populist schemes in order to satisfy the vote banks should be avoided. Such expenditures ultimately become instruments of political patronage and do not have a positive impact on fiscal efficiency.

The last decade in Tamil Nadu witnessed a phenomenal increase in explicit/implicit subsidies to the tune of Rs. 2861 crore in 2000-2001 as against Rs. 641 crore in 1991-92, recording a jump of nearly four and a half times[10]. They formed 9 to 17 per cent of the total revenue receipts of the state during the decade. Explicit subsidies are direct and transparent. In such cases, there is a clear identification of beneficiaries and budgetary allocation. Payments to TNEB for free supply of power to farmers, reimbursement of losses incurred by TNCSC for procurement and supply of food articles under PDS, payment to TNCSC towards difference in cost of rice supplied under CM's Noon Meal Scheme, production incentive to farmers in cauvery delta for the supply of paddy to TNCSC, rebate on sale of handloom cloth, distribution of free sarees and dhoties, assistance to central cooperative banks towards waiver or refund of interest and penal interest on loans, and relief to agriculturists, and free bus pass for students belong to this category. Implicit subsidies, on the other hand, are indirect and hidden; they arise on account of non-recovery of user charges for services provided by the government and also includes non-recovery of loans given to public sector undertakings, cooperative societies, etc. Given the precarious condition of Tamil Nadu state finances, the following correctives become imperative:

- The food subsidy regime should target determinedly only people below poverty line; otherwise it will be a drain on state finances.
- Power sector reforms has become a necessity. Power tariff should be appropriately amended to bring in all categories of consumers, so that electricity board functions atleast on a "no profit no loss basis".
- The policy of transport subsidy must be reviewed. In the face of growing losses of state transport undertakings, populist schemes like free travel facility have to be desisted. A committee should be set-up to examine the question of functional management in the transport undertakings and suggest measures for implementation to enhance their operational efficiency and reasonably hike up the user charges.
- While announcing "free schemes", it has to be ensured that economic considerations outweigh the political compulsions; otherwise, scarce resources would get frittered away affecting badly the state's finances.
- The existing free saree and dhoti scheme should be made available only to families below the poverty line. This scheme also aims at protecting the handloom industry. But the present policy of the government does not seem to fulfil even this objective.
- The policy of providing grants (implicit subsidies) for the sustenance of cooperative mills and

societies should be reviewed. The time has come for these institutions, which are virtually in a debt trap, to stand on their own levels. A drastic reorganisation of the cooperative sector is imperative for improving their finances and thereby state's finances.

- Another form of implicit subsidy is the loans which stand irrecoverable from the loss-making public sector undertakings. Given the condition of Tamil Nadu state finances it is impossible for these enterprises to be helped with budgetary support. A radical restructuring should make these institutions generate resources not only for their own growth and expansion, but also for contributing positively to the state exchequer.

A matter of serious concern is the increase in the wage bill and pension liability of the state government. Rising from Rs. 3040 crore in 1991-92 to Rs. 11.492 crore in 2000-01, salaries and pensions worked out, on an average, to 54 per cent of the total revenue receipts. Revisions of pay for employees subsequent to the recommendations of the Pay Commissions and the University Grants Commission, and regular enhancement of dearness allowance based on the revisions effected by the Central Government for its own employees have been the major reasons for the spurt. The option lies in either mobilising additional resources for funding government pensions and salary growth or resorting to such measures as a freeze in dearness allowance and/or a freeze in further direct employment by the state government.

As pointed out earlier, the unsustainably wide revenue deficit resulted in enormous growth of debt and increased interest payment liabilities. During the decade 1991-92 to 2000-01, interest payment commitments of the State worked out, on an average, to 13 per cent of total revenue receipts. Add to this, subsidies (14 per cent) and pensions and salaries (54 per cent), the quantum of revenue account resources available for other components of the revenue budget was indeed small. This explains the dire necessity for the state to resort to borrowings on an increasing scale not only for meeting the capital account obligations but unfortunately revenue account commitments too. This again leads to increased interest payment obligations, higher growth of revenue expenditure in relation to the growth of revenue receipts and, in turn, increased need for borrowed funds. Therefore, the solution lies in attaining greater buoyancy in revenue receipts, while at the same time, restraining and pruning the revenue expenditures, specifically the non-developmental component.

CONCLUSION

In any federation it has proved impossible to effect a clear separation of finances of the several layers of government[11]. Federal systems across the world, including the older federations, have come to be characterised by fiscal imbalances. India is no exception to this state. The working of the institutional mechanisms created by the Constitution of India to reduce the vertical and horizontal imbalances has led to a situation where the States are neither satisfied with the quantum of resources transferred, nor their distribution *inter-se*, nor the controls that go with the transfer[12].

The discretionary element in the non-statutory refers has put the States at the doorstep of the Centre. Even the statutory Finance Commission's role in the reduction of fiscal imbalances has come in for sharp disagreements. Thus, sound fiscal federalism demands proper and justifiable criteria for Finance Commission devolutions, and elimination of discretionary content in the non-statutory resource transfeRs. The States, on their part, should display greater fiscal discipline and prudent management of their finances. In the case of Tamil Nadu, appropriate fiscal correctives and restructuring should put the State's finances on a sound track. In other words, a time has come for the State of Tamil Nadu and its people to choose between tightening the belt or losing the pants.

NOTES AND REFERENCES

1. Govinda Rao M., "Proposals for State-Level Budgetary Reforms", *Economic and Political Weekly*, February 1, 1992, p. 211.

2. Rangarajan C., Anupam Basu and Narendra Jadhav, "Dynamics of Interaction between Government Deficit and Domestic Debt in India", *RBI Occasional Papers*, Vol. 10., September 1989, p. 170.
3. Rangarajan C., "Better Expenditure Management will Accelerate Growth", Keynote Address at Conference on India: Fiscal Policies to Accelerate Economic Growth, New Delhi, May 21, 2001.
4. Government of Tamil Nadu, Finance Department, "White Paper on Tamil Nadu Government's Finances", August 18, 2001, p. 41.
5. Centre for Monitoring Indian Economy, "Public Sector in the Indian Economy", August 1990.
6. Bagchi, Amaresh, "Fiscal Reform", *The Hindu*, July 18, 2001.
7. Government of Tamil Nadu, Finance Department, White Paper, *op. cit.*, p. 16
8. Godbole, Madhav, "Finance Commissions in a Cul-de-sac", *Economic and Political Weekly*, January 6, 2001, p.29.
9. Government of India, Ministry of Finance, *Discussion Paper*, "Government Subsidies in India", May 1997.
10. Government. of Tamil Nadu, *White Paper, op. cit.*, pp. 23-24.
11. Sastri, K.V.S., Federal-State Fiscal Relations in India, Oxford University Press, Bombay, 1966, p. 5.
12. Venkataraman, K., States' Finances in India: A Perspective Study for the Plan Periods, George Allen & Unwin Ltd., London, 1968, p. 81.

22

CHAPTER

A Recursive Macro Fiscal Adjustment Model for Tamil Nadu

GAUTAM NARESH AND J.V.M. SARMA

INTRODUCTION

Growing fiscal imbalance and its adverse effects on macro-economic equilibrium in the country has been receiving wide attention by policy-makers as well as researchers. However, the issue of fiscal imbalance at the State level has not so far been adequately analyzed.

It is a fact that, just like the Centre, several States are also facing deteriorating budgetary positions, with serious implications on their developmental efforts. Insufficient revenue sources, uncontrolled growth of current expenditures, and failure of central transfers to grow as fast as the States' own revenues have been the sources of the imbalances. In many respects, the fiscal situation in the States is more critical than that at the Centre as the States have the primary Constitutional responsibility for providing basic social and economic services.

At the same time, while the elasticity of own revenues of the Centre and the States are broadly the same, the States' expenditures have been growing at rates faster than that of the

Centre particularly in recent years. There is not only a shrinking of capital expenditure, but the maintenance of existing capital assets is also not getting its due. Other signs are rising trend of non-developmental consumption expenditure, high cost of government employees' especially after the implementation of the Fifth Central Pay Commission. At the State level, there is an increasing trend in the volume in government employment thereby burgeoning rise in wages and salary bill apart from rise in debt servicing. From the receipts angle, poor tax collections, poorly targeted cost recovery policy and lack of desired tax reforms adversely affect the income-buoyancy of the taxes that put constraints on expenditure needs from own revenue sources of the States. This leads to dependence on higher-level governments for larger fiscal transfers and also on ways and means advances. Besides, public sector enterprises (PSEs) are largely in a financial mess requiring huge doses of budgetary support to sustain them. These are some of the worrisome factors among others. If the same fiscal trends follow, the fiscal deficit is likely to assume disquieting proportions due to an increasing component of revenue deficit to be financed from borrowings. Hence, there is need to strengthen the revenue-effort and restructuring of expenditure for sustainability. It is a tough challenge to all the governments. Therefore, a suitable fiscal correction at this level needs an integrated and concerted effort on all fronts of the economy with an iron-will.

Further, the States do not have the same ability to finance their growing fiscal imbalance. Unlike the Centre, the States do not have independent power to borrow from the market, nor can they take recourse to borrowing from the central bank because of the regulation of the overdrafts. Given these constraints on borrowings, the burden of adjusting to the imbalance has tended to fall mainly on capital and maintenance expenditures with adverse implications in terms of infrastructural constraints, declining productivity of public sector investment and deceleration in long-term growth of the economy.

These issues are persistent over the years as brought out by various studies such as Aiyar and Kurup (1992), Bajaj and Aggarwal (1992), Guhan (1992), Jetha (1992), Rajaraman,

Mukhopadhyay and Amarnath (1998), Rao and Sen (1993), Sarma, Naresh and Bohra (1999), Sen and Rao (1998), Srivastava, Chattopadhyay and Jena (1998), Srivastava, Chattopadhyay and Rangamannar (1998), Rao and Sen (1993) pertaining to the States of Andhra Pradesh, Gujarat, Haryana, Kerala, Punjab, Tamil Nadu and Uttar Pradesh.

Since most of the issues are common to all States, it is possible to have a common package of reforms. In this paper an attempt has been made to suggest a plausible package of State level fiscal reforms using State finances of Tamil Nadu as an example, using a recursive model the impact of the suggested reform package on the future of the finances has been estimated. The paper is organized as follows: In section 1 a brief review of the fiscal imbalances and the suggested fiscal correction strategy pertaining to Tamil Nadu. In section 2, a simple recursive macro-economic model with the twin objectives of forecasting and policy simulations has been developed. In section 3, fiscal forecasts for the period 1998-99 to 2001-05 based on this model have been presented with the *status quo* scenario depicting where the fiscal situation will be if no corrective measures are taken. In section 4 the results of the alternative scenario with the suggested fiscal reform strategy are presented. Finally section 5 gives a summary.

FINANCES OF TAMIL NADU STATE: AN OVERVIEW

Tamil Nadu is the southernmost seventh largest populated State in the Indian subcontinent covering about 4 percent of the India's geographical area and also one of the most densely populated States in India. The modest natural resource base makes economic development an arduous task. Yet, the overall growth performance of Tamil Nadu has not been unimpressive during the last one-and-a-half decades. The headway in the sphere of infrastructure already achieved during the British rule, particularly in the irrigation and agricultural sector, partly explains the fast growth. In recent years, however, the growth performance seems to have been confined to only tertiary sectors such as trade, transport, banking, and public administration. The Ninth Plan aims at achieving 7 percent growth and the resource requirement is estimated to be at Rs. 25,000 crore. The State government share is put at Rs. 16,000 crore, the remaining being expected from private sector and foreign direct investment.

The public finances of Tamil Nadu are relatively well managed but still there is room for selective fiscal correction. The ratio of total expenditure to GSDP is contained within limits, but there is need for reprioritization towards specific areas, particularly infrastructure—both in terms of creation and maintenance of assets. During 1990-98, there was a significant rise in revenue expenditure, particularly, in employees' compensation, subsidies and interest payments. The rise in these components has cut into the growth of capital expenditure. With the exception of education, the pattern of government expenditure has not been exactly in line with the socio-economic needs. The expenditure shares of agriculture, irrigation as also infrastructural sectors and public health are falling. There is also a need for better control and monitoring of current expenditure.

In financing the expenditure, the revenue-raising effort has so far been concentrated only on tax revenue and attempts to augment non-tax revenues through cost-recoveries has been a neglected area. The dependence on own sources, particularly, sales tax, State excises, stamp duties and registration fees, and motor vehicles tax has been high. Yet, there are certain factors that hamper the productivity of the State taxes. The problem areas in sales taxation have been high tax rates, ineffective tax incentives, regressiveness, and the cascading effect arising from taxation of intermediates and inputs.

Besides, there is scope for improving the buoyancy of stamp duties and registration fees, motor vehicles tax, land revenue and agricultural income tax. In the case of stamp duties and registration fees, there is considerable under-reporting of sale values and, consequently, substantial tax leakage. Although this has been tackled through the adoption of normative values and through coordination with valuations arrived at by the income tax authorities, there is need to strengthen these systems. In the case of motor vehicle tax, the scope for sizable increases in the revenue through rate revisions is limited. The ratios of non-tax revenues and Central transfers have been either stagnant or falling. As for cost-recoveries, it is clearly necessary to contain the growth of unrecovered costs and to improve recoveries from services provided by the State government. Studies show that on the whole, the recoveries come to about only 1.2 percent of net State expenditure. The cost-recovery rate is particularly low for social sector services, and varies from 2 percent to 3 percent. Fiscal balance for the most part of the period of 1980-98 was negative and also on the decline because of fast growth of revenue expenditure and the signs of improvement in recent years have not proved to be long-lasting.

The selected key sectors have played important role in the State's economy. Their performance has resulted in fiscal stress and strain. These sectors are power, irrigation, roads and bridges, education, health, transport and public sector enterprises.

1. Power

Until recently, there seems to be laxity in providing the required additional investment to meet the State's energy demand. By the year 2002 this requirement would be much more than the outlay provided in the Ninth Plan. Notwithstanding the operational efficiency, there have been continual increases in costs. Yet, institutional factors have prevented charging of remunerative tariffs. Consequently, the financial position of Tamil Nadu Electricity Board (TNEB) has been precarious. The tariff subsidy for agriculture has particularly serious impact on TNEB revenues. In addition to the capital transfers, every year TNEB receives direct budgetary subsidy to make-up for the net operating loss.

2. Irrigation

Tamil Nadu's endowed irrigation potential is less than half of the all-India average. Except for river Cauvery the State has no perennial water resources. Most of the water potential is already exploited. As regards cost recoveries in the irrigation sector, water charges are based on the classification of land and dependability of the source. Yet, the receipts add up to only a negligible proportion of the total current expenditure on irrigation and these proportions have come down over the years.

3. Roads and Bridges

Road network in Tamil Nadu has increased five-fold since Independence and almost all the villages and hamlets are now accessible by roads. There has been a corresponding increase in the road density. Yet, total expenditure on the road sector, as a ratio to GSDP, has come down during the last 15 years. Although three-fourths of the roads are surfaced, the maintenance of the roads has not been receiving adequate attention. Financial constraints prevent renewal of riding surfaces as frequently as needed, and consequently, expenditure on maintenance is far below the normative requirement. The deficiency in maintenance is reflected in the premature ageing of roads.

4. Education

Literacy level in Tamil Nadu is better than the all-India average, and the State ranks only below Kerala and Maharashtra. Projections show that if the decline in the birth rate as well as the efforts of the Government continues, gross enrolment may cover all the children of 6-11 years age group by the turn of the century itself. In secondary education, schemes such as free bus pass, free hostel facilities, free supply of books and equipment have helped to arrest the dropout rate. The flip side effect of this improvement is the increased demand for more schools and more teachers at the middle and secondary level. In addition, up-gradation of present level schools to one stage up is also being contemplated. Although there has been a considerable increase in expenditure on education, most of it is in the nature of the current expenditure. About 80 percent of the expenditure are met from non-Plan resources and the remaining from State, Central and shared Plan schemes.

5. Health and Family Welfare

Tamil Nadu seems to have achieved most of the targets set in the National Health Policy. General health indicators such as the total fertility rate (TFR), the infant mortality rate (IMR) and the crude birth rate (CBR) have improved and are better than the all-India averages. Yet, government expenditure on health as a ratio to GSDP in Tamil Nadu is declining over the years. The decline is particularly sharp in the share of capital expenditure during the 1990s. Though cconsiderable progress has been made in the last several decades in expanding the public health system and in reducing the incidence of diseases. Yet, there remains certain area such as child and maternal morbidity and communicable diseases where the government needs to pay more attention.

6. Transport

The public transport sector is also severely sick financially like power sector. There is a prior need to evolve a mechanism for periodic revision of passenger fares to compensate for the increases in the input costs (as being attempted in the case of irrigation tariffs). In addition, with a view to making the public transport corporations compete with the private counterparts, it is necessary to compensate them for tariff concessions and losses due to plying on uneconomic routes, particularly in metro areas.

7. Public Sector Enterprises (PSEs)

As in the case of many States, the performance of PSEs in Tamil Nadu has been a cause for concern. Except for the development finance corporations, the financial performance of the 67 PSEs has been poor with no significant contribution to the State. Not only the return on the investment by way of dividends and interest is nil or negative, they block roughly over Rs. 5,000 crore (of which 38 percent or roughly Rs. 2,000 crore invested by the Government of Tamil Nadu) from being put to more productive alternative uses. The Gross State Domestic Products (GSDP) originating from the PSEs at Rs. 1,500 crore is an insignificant proportion of the total GSDP. Thus, the PSEs in Tamil Nadu have not had a great impact on the economy of the State, as expected, except for direct employment of 1.6 lakh persons.

The review brings out that although the fiscal deficit appears to be under control the fact that about half of it is due to the revenue deficit that is somewhat disquieting. The low level of capital expenditure indicates that most of the borrowings are frittered away in current spending. The asset maintenance is far from satisfactory. In the roads sector there is a noticeable spending gap in the O&M expenditure. In the case of irrigation, although the operation and maintenance expenditure has been in line with the norms prescribed by the successive Finance Commissions, most of the assets need replacement rather than maintenance. There exists room for improving the revenue-effort by rationalizing certain taxes, stepping up non-tax revenues through better-cost recoveries, and restructuring of the PSEs. The aspect that needs immediate government attention is infrastructure — power, irrigation, roads and bridges, and transport. It is also imperative that expenditure on social sectors such as education and health are stepped up and preferably targeted so that vulnerable sections benefit rapidly and can participate in the development process. In order to do this; the authorities have to step up revenue-efforts including adequate cost recoveries in public utilities and effect economy in spending programs.

In what follows, an attempt is made to examine policy options available to the government and quantify their impact for the period 1998-2006. Creation of fiscal space for this purpose should comprise augmentation of the revenue efforts along with growth-inducing rationalization of the tax system in the State. Simultaneously, the spending pattern shall also be restructured with emphasis on productive sectors including human capital. Specifically, the measures shall include:

- ❑ Strict restriction on recruitment to government services,
- ❑ Pruning and improved targeting of welfare schemes to help achieving better results,
- ❑ Revamping of cost recovery policies in roads, irrigation and power sector,
- ❑ Harmonizing sales tax rate-structure in conjunction with neighbouring States,
- ❑ Scraping of tax deferral scheme and simplifying the industrial incentive schemes,
- ❑ Preparing an agenda for the gradual introduction of VAT,
- ❑ Revamping of excise rate structure by integrating vend fees into the rate, and

- In the case of stamp duties and registration fees, strengthening the system of normative valuation and coordination with income tax authorities.

If the same fiscal trends follow, the fiscal deficit is likely to assume disquieting proportion due to increasing component of revenue deficit. In addition, capital expenditure is shrinking, use of borrowings in consumption, and O&M expenditure is also not getting its due.

From the review of the government finances of Tamil Nadu, it is clear that so far they are relatively well managed as compared to many other States. Yet, there exists room for strengthening the fiscal sustainability as:

- Review shows that although the fiscal deficit appears to be under control the fact that about half of it is due to the revenue deficit is somewhat disquieting.
- The low level of capital expenditure indicates that most of the borrowings are frittered away in current spending.
- The asset maintenance is far from satisfactory. In the roads sector there is a noticeable spending gap in the operation and maintenance expenditure. In the case of irrigation, although the operation and maintenance expenditure has been in line with the norms prescribed by the successive Finance Commissions, most of the assets need replacement rather than maintenance.
- There exists room for improving the revenue-effort by rationalizing certain taxes and stepping up non-tax revenues through better cost-recoveries and restructuring of the PSEs. In this paper an attempt is made to examine policy options available to the Government and quantify their impact for the period 1998-2006.

Though the fiscal management seems comparatively better, yet there is scope for and need to strengthen its revenue-effort and restructuring of expenditure for sustainability. If the same fiscal trends follow, the fiscal deficit is likely to assume disquieting proportion due to increasing component of revenue deficit. In addition, capital expenditure is shrinking, use of borrowings in consumption, and operation and maintenance expenditure is also not getting its due.

A simulated fiscal scenario, with a set of reform package, if implemented to set right the upward rising trends of fiscal/revenue deficits emerges in which the fiscal balance turns into surpluses. To follow the path of growth-inducement through Government capital expenditure, this surplus can be ploughed back into the economy resulting in income-augmentation, rise in capital expenditure and better asset maintenance, particularly infrastructure sectors. The fiscal deficit may be capped within a tolerable limit, say, at 2.5 percent of GSDP to reduce the need for high revenue receipts and high expenditure.

MACRO FORECAST MODEL

We set-up a simple recursive macro-economic model with the twin objective of forecasting and policy simulations. The assumed mechanism underlying the model is as follows: State income (GSDP) is endogenously determined on the basis of government expenditure—capital expenditure (CAPEX) and also certain components of revenue expenditure such as that on human development, broadly proxied as non-interest expenditure. For the base line or *status-quo* simulations, capital expenditure of the government (CAPEX) is assumed to be driven by the aggregate demand within the State as proxied by GSDP. However, for the reform scenario government capital expenditure is assumed to be guided basically by the availability of resources as also government policy regarding the role of private sector. Since expenditure restructuring involves reduction in employees' compensation (WAGES), subsidies (SUBSIDIES) and transfers (TRANS), and stepping up expenditure on operation and maintenance (OM), it is imperative to examine their responsiveness to increases in population (POP) representing the growth in demand for public goods and services. Own tax revenue [comprising revenue from taxes on income (INCTAX), taxes on capital transactions (CAPTAX) such as stamp duties and registration fees and taxes on commodities (COMTAX) such as sales tax and State excise], and non-tax revenues (NONTAX) including net lending are assumed to move with the GSDP. Transfers from the Center are in accordance with the Tenth Finance Commission award. New borrowings (BORROW) including public account balances are assumed to be equal to the fiscal deficit or the difference between total revenue and total expenditure. The stock of debt outstanding (DEBT) is basically an accumulation of past borrowings. However, the debt-stock function is not an identity as the stock includes the public account balances. Interest and debt-servicing expenditure moves with the accumulated debt.

The structural model in equation form is as follows:

1.	Ln (GSDP)	= ln (CAPEXt–1) + (TRD)
2.	Ln (INCTAX)	= ln (GSDP)
3.	Ln (CAPTAX)	= ln (GSDP)
4.	Ln (COMTAX)	= ln (GSDP)
5.	Ln (NON-TAX)	= ln (GSDP)
6.	Ln (WAGES)	= ln (SEMPLOYMT)
7.	Ln (SEMPLOYMT)	= ln (POP)
8.	Ln (OM)	= ln (GSDP)
9.	Ln (SUBSIDIES)	= ln (POP)
10.	Ln (TRANS)	= ln (POP)
11.	Ln (CAPEX)	= ln (GSDPt–1)
12.	DEBT	= DEBTt–1 + BORROW
13.	INTEREST	= DEBTt–1
14.	BORROW	= WAGES + SEMPLOYMT + OM + SUBSIDIES + INTEREST + TRANS + CAPEX – INCTAX – CAPTAX – COMTAX – NONTAX + CENTRAN

Key:

GSDP : Gross State Domestic Product

TD : Time trend

REVEX : Revenue expenditure other than interest

	(debt-servicing) expenditure
WAGES :	Employees compensation
OM :	Operation and maintenance (expenditure on goods and services)
SUBSIDIES :	Direct subsidies
TRANS :	Current transfers including grants to local bodies
INTEREST :	Debt servicing expenditure
CAPEX :	Capital expenditure
TAXREV :	Tax revenue
INCTAX :	Taxes on income such as agricultural income tax
CAPTAX :	Taxes on capital transactions such as stamp duties
COMTAX :	Taxes on commodities such as sales tax and excises
NONTAXREV :	Non-tax revenue including interest receipts on loans and advances
BORROW :	New borrowings (fiscal deficit)
DEBT :	Stock of outstanding debt including public account balances
POP :	Population
CENTRAN :	Central transfers
SEMPLOYMENT :	State Government employees' number

The macro fiscal mechanism is as depicted in the Figure shown below. The model is estimated by Generalized Least Squares (GLS) procedures with necessary adjustments for possible auto-regressive error structures. Several alternative specifications with other possible independent variables are experimented with. The model retained for forecasting and simulations along with trend growth rates of the variables employed are as in Table 1.

STATUS-QUO SCENARIO

The broad consequences of allowing the revenues, the expenditure and the debt to grow at the same pace as in the past without any major policy changes during the next five years (1998-99 to 2005-06) are as shown in Table 2. In

TABLE I

Estimated Parameters of the Macro–Fiscal Model

		State Income
Gross State Domestic Product		
Ln (GSDP)	=	8.34 + 0.08 ln (CAPEXt–1) + 0.14 (TRD)
		26.33 1.5 32.63
		Revenue Side
Taxes on income such as agricultural tax		
Ln (INCTAX)	=	– 4.91 + 0.72 ln (GSDP)
		– 3.2 4.8
Taxes on capital transactions such as stamp duties		
Ln (CAPTAX)	=	– 6.06 + 1.12 ln (GSDP)
		–19.6 36.8
Taxes on commodities such as sales tax and excises		
Ln (COMTAX)	=	– 2.89 + 1.04 ln (GSDP)
		–12.3 45.4
Non–tax revenue including loan recoveries		
Ln (NONTAX)	=	– 0.86 + 0.74 ln (GSDP)
		– 1.8 8.1
		Expenditure Side
Employees compensation		
Ln (WAGES)	=	20.99 + 4.48 ln (SEMPLOYMT)
		13 8.3
State Government employees' number		
Ln (SEMPLOYMT)	=	– 6.69 + 2.23 ln (POP)
		– 16.6 9.4
Operation and maintenance, i.e. expenditure on goods and services		
Ln (OM)	=	– 0.19 + 0.63 ln (GSDP)
		– 0.2 11.1
Direct subsidies		
Ln (SUBSIDIES)	=	– 26.91+19.10 ln (POP)
		– 7.2 8.9
Current transfers including grants to local bodies		
Ln (TRANS)	=	– 5.75 + 7.23 ln (POP)
		– 5.8 12.4
Capital expenditure@		
Ln (CAPEX)	=	1.68 + 0.53 ln (GSDPt–1)
		1.7 9.0
Stock of outstanding debt including public account balances		
DEBT	=	119.73 + 0.79 DEBTt–1 + 1.77 BORROW
		0.3 7.5 2.6

Debt servicing expenditure#

INTEREST	=	0.11 DEBTt–1 27.7
BORROW	=	WAGES + EMPLOYMT + OM + SUBSIDIES + INTEREST + TRANS + CAPEX – INCTAX – CAPTAX – COMTAX – NONTAX + CENTRAN

Growth Rates of Fiscal Variables: 1981–98 (Per cent per annum)

1.	GSDP	15.42
2.	REVEX	16.31
3.	WAGES	18.72
4.	OM	09.62
5.	SUBSIDIES	29.69
6.	TRANS	10.36
7.	INTEREST	19.44
8.	CAPEX@	07.71
9.	TAXREV	16.24
10.	INCTAX	10.99
11.	CAPTAX	17.41
12.	COMTAX	16.17
13.	NON–TAXREV	12.62
14.	BORROW	14.23
15.	DEBT	13.66
16.	POP	01.37
17.	CENTRAN	14.07
18.	SEMPLOYMT	03.08

Figure: Macro fiscal flows.

@ Capital expenditure is guided by availability of borrowings. Non–tax revenue is not a factor for capital expenditure. Tax revenue is not relevant.

Current debt moves over 80% and barely 20% with current borrowings.

Note: Figures below the coefficients are t–statistics.

particular, the income-buoyancy of major taxes is assumed to remain the same as in the past. Own non-taxes will grow at the historical pace. Transfers from the Center will be in accordance with the Tenth Finance Commission award. The State government salary bill will grow at the average rate of growth observed in the recent past. Also, the growth of the other expenditure components will be the same as in the past. The additional expenditure due to the recommendations of the

FIGURE
Micro Fiscal Flows

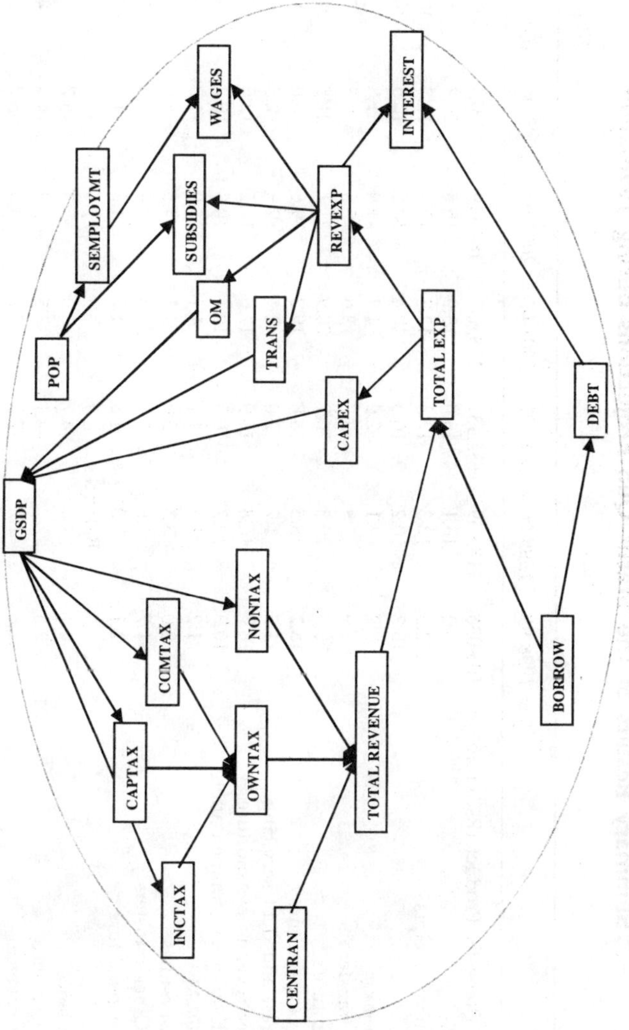

TABLE 2

Summary Results of the Status Quo Projections during 1998-2006

(Percent to GSDP)

	1998-99	*1999-00*	*2000-01*	*2001-02*	*2002-03*	*2003-04*	*2004-05*	*2005-06*
Gross State Domestic Product (Rs. crore)	103,036	118,959	137,431	158,637	183,119	211,373	243,986	281,630
Total receipts	16.2	16.1	16.0	15.9	15.8	15.8	15.8	15.7
Own source receipts	12.3	12.3	12.3	12.3	12.3	12.3	12.3	12.3
Tax	10.2	10.2	10.3	10.4	10.5	10.5	10.6	10.7
Non-tax	2.2	2.1	2.0	1.9	1.9	1.8	1.7	1.7
Central transfers	3.9	3.8	3.7	3.6	3.5	3.5	3.4	3.4
Total expenditure	20.3	20.5	20.7	20.9	21.1	21.5	21.9	22.4
Revenue expenditure	18.2	18.5	18.8	19.2	19.5	20.0	20.5	21.1
Interest and debt servicing	1.5	1.7	2.0	2.1	2.3	2.5	2.7	2.9
Other revenue expenditure	16.7	16.8	16.9	17.0	17.2	17.5	17.8	18.2
Employees' compensation	10.8	10.7	10.5	10.4	10.3	10.2	10.0	9.9
O&M	1.2	1.2	1.1	1.1	1.0	1.0	0.9	0.9
Subsidies	3.0	3.3	3.7	4.1	4.5	5.0	5.6	6.2
Other transfers	1.7	1.6	1.6	1.5	1.4	1.3	1.3	1.2
Capital expenditure	2.1	2.0	1.8	1.7	1.6	1.5	1.4	1.3
Balances								
Fiscal balance	-4.1	-4.4	-4.7	-5.0	-5.3	-5.7	-6.1	-6.7
Revenue balance	-2.3	-2.7	-3.1	-3.5	-3.9	-4.4	-4.9	-5.5
Primary balance	-2.6	-2.7	-2.7	-2.8	-3.0	-3.2	-3.5	-3.8
Debt outstanding	18.4	20.6	22.5	24.3	26.1	28.1	30.2	32.7
Debt servicing/revenue (%)	8	9	10	11	12	12	13	14

Note: Projections based on actualize for 1997-98.

Pay Commission, and the State Finance Commission are borne by the State government in a phased manner and therefore, is subsumed in the trends.

The base line scenario shows that during the next eight years, the total receipts to GSDP ratio is likely to come down from 16.2 percent to 15.7 percent basically owing to the likely fall in the non-tax revenues and Central transfers. Own source receipt-GSDP ratio is likely to remain constant at 12.3 percent. There is likely improvement in own tax-GSDP ratio whereas other sources of receipts will fall. Consequently, there will be a steep deterioration in the fiscal balance. The fiscal deficit will reach a high 6.7 percent of GSDP by 2005-06, most of it being accounted by the revenue deficit. Because of the steady rise in the new borrowing, the debt-stock is likely to show a rising trend. The total expenditure as a ratio to GSDP is likely to rise from 20.3 percent to 22.4 percent. This will be basically due to steep rise in the interest and debt-servicing expenditure and subsidies. The O&M expenditure ratio is likely to be negligible and falling. Current transfers including grants to local bodies are also likely to fall. Capital expenditure is going to fall consistently below 1.3 percent of GSDP.

THE REFORM STRATEGY

The reform strategy to achieve fiscal sustainability aims at restructuring expenditure to make it more productive, and at strengthening the revenue-raising machinery to maximize the yield from the existing revenue sources. It relies on improving cost-recoveries on current assets, broadening the tax base and rationalizing the tax structure to make it more revenue-productive. More specifically, the reform strategy could comprise the following:

The most important source of rising current expenditure has been wages and salaries. Fiscal reforms should aim at reducing the rate of growth of government employment to at least the same level as the rate of growth of population. Currently, the rate of growth of government employees in Tamil Nadu is over 3 percent per annum while population growth rate is just 1.37. The reforms will aim at bringing the current elasticity of government employment with respect to population from the existing 2.25 to unity.

The second important source of growth of current expenditure has been the numerous direct subsidies. Expenditure on subsidies grew over 29 percent per annum during 1980-81 to 1996-97. In recent years, that is, from 1993-94 onwards, however, the rate of growth has been only about 6 percent per annum. Under the reform scenario, the annual growth rate of subsidies is to be brought down to 1.3 percent so that the expenditure on subsidies grows exactly in tandem with the size of population. This will be achieved by phasing out subsidies to PSEs, TNEB and the Road Transport Undertakings. Particularly, the latter two will be allowed to revise their tariffs for breaking-even and reduce their dependence on the Government.

As regards transfers, over 70 percent of current transfers other than subsidies and other transfers are grants to local bodies. Even so, compensation and assignments to local bodies formed less than 2 percent until 1996-97. The First State Finance Commission has recommended devolution of 8 percent of State's own tax revenues net of collection costs to local bodies for 1997-98, gradually increasing by one percent annually to 12 percent in 2001-02. The reform scenario is worked out on the assumption that these recommendations will be adhered to.

There is also a need to step up the operation and maintenance expenditure for replacement of aged, and worn out assets particularly, in the irrigation and roads sectors. It is assumed that one of the reforms will be to see that the present low elasticity of operation and maintenance expenditure at around 0.62 will be gradually doubled by 2005-06. This will considerably reduce the spending gap in respect of maintenance of roads and bridges.

On the revenue side, the buoyancy of the taxes on agricultural sector will be stepped up from the present 0.71 to unity level. As regards the commodity taxes (sales tax and state excise), without widening the base and adopting the VAT system applicable to goods as well as services, it may not be possible to raise more revenue. Revenue yield is likely to improve with the introduction of VAT because of improved transparency leading to better compliance. With these reforms, it is assumed that the commodity tax buoyancy will be raised up from 1.05 to 1.2. Tax base-broadening and rate-structure rationalization will be supplemented by administrative tightening to improve their productivity and curb evasion.

As regards non-tax revenue, the cost-recovery strategies will be revamped such that the buoyancy with respect to GSDP is gradually raised to unity. For example, in the irrigation sector the recoveries could be made to equal the expenditure on operation and maintenance along with a one per cent additional return. The reform strategy is as depicted in Table 3.

REFORM SCENARIO

The impact of the reform process can be divided into two stages. In the first stage, we tried to quantify to what extent the fiscal restructuring can improve the fiscal balance. In the event of the fiscal balance turning out to be a surplus, we attempted in the second stage, to examine two of the available options of using the fiscal surplus. The first option is to divert the fiscal surplus to step up capital expenditure in the government sector. The second option is to retain the government capital expenditure to grow at the present trend and downsize the tax revenue to match the compressed government expenditure by revamping the tax system with a view to lowering the tax burden on the society. The lower tax burden will help boosting up private savings and private sector investment that could result in higher economic growth.

Stage I: Reform and Fiscal Balance

The summary results of the first stage of reform scenario are shown in Table 4. The simulation shows that with the suggested reforms, the revenue deficit is going to turn positive from 2001-02 itself. Consequently, fiscal deficit is likely to come down and will indeed, turn into a surplus by the year 2002-03. The decline in outstanding debt will also be considerably faster than in the base-line scenario.

With expenditure restructuring, the ratio of expenditure to GSDP will be fast declining from 19 percent to as low as 12.5 percent by 2005-06. With restraints on new recruitment,

TABLE 3

Assumed Strategy for Fiscal Reforms during 1998-99 to 2005-06

Year	*O&M elasticity w r t GSDP*	*Subsidies (Elasticity w r t population)*	*Transfers (mainly to local bodies) as percent to own revenue*	*Taxes on income (Buoyancy w r t GSDP)*	*Taxes on commodities (Buoyancy w r t GSDP)*	*Non-tax revenue (Buoyancy w r t GSDP)*	*Government employment (elasticity w r t population)*
1999	0.62	5.1	9%	0.71	1.05	0.82	2.25
2000	0.70	5.0	10%	0.75	1.07	0.90	2.00
2001	0.80	4.0	11%	0.80	1.09	1.00	1.75
2002	0.90	4.0	12%	0.85	1.10	1.00	1.50
2003	1.00	3.0	12%	0.90	1.10	1.00	1.25
2004	1.10	2.0	12%	0.95	1.15	1.00	1.00
2005	1.20	1.0	12%	1.00	1.20	1.00	1.00
2006	1.25	1.0	12%	1.00	1.20	1.00	1.00

employees' compensation is likely to be below 9 percent of GSDP by 2001-02. Similarly, the ratio of direct subsidies will also be restricted to a modest level of 2 percent. With fiscal deficit under control, the need for new borrowings will be less and the interest liability will be lower than that under the no-reform scenario. In fact, the fiscal balance will turn into a surplus by 2001-02. Consequently, the outstanding debt will be nil by 2004-05.

Stage II: Growth through Government Capital Expenditure

The fiscal surplus can be gainfully utilised for additional capital expenditure to improve the overall economic growth. As a first option we examined the consequences of diverting the fiscal surplus to finance additional capital expenditure that will result in higher GSDP. We simulated the model by deriving capital expenditure as a residual after pegging fiscal deficit at 2.5 percent of GSDP. The results of this simulation are as given in Table 5.

The cap on the fiscal deficit of 2.5 percent of GSDP is

TABLE 4

Reform Scenario—Summary of Projections: 1998-06

(Percent to GSDP)

Variable	*1998-99*	*1999-00*	*2000-01*	*2001-02*	*2002-03*	*2003-04*	*2004-05*	*2005-06*
Gross State Domestic Product (Rs. crore)	103,036	118,959	137,431	158,637	183,119	211,373	243,986	281,630
Total receipts	16.3	16.3	16.3	16.4	16.4	16.6	16.8	17.0
Own source receipts	12.5	12.5	12.6	12.8	12.9	13.1	13.4	13.7
Tax	9.9	10.0	10.1	10.3	10.4	10.6	10.9	11.1
Non-tax	2.6	2.5	2.5	2.5	2.5	2.5	2.5	2.5
Central transfers	3.9	3.8	3.7	3.6	3.5	3.5	3.4	3.4
Total expenditure	19.0	18.6	18.0	17.3	16.2	15.0	13.7	12.5
Revenue expenditure	16.9	16.6	16.2	15.6	14.7	13.5	12.4	11.2
Interest and debt servicing	1.5	1.5	1.4	1.3	1.0	0.7	0.2	
Other revenue expenditure	15.4	15.1	14.8	14.3	13.6	12.8	12.1	11.5
Employees compensation	9.9	9.7	9.3	8.8	8.3	7.6	7.0	6.5
O&M	1.2	1.2	1.1	1.1	1.1	1.1	1.2	1.2
Subsidies	2.5	2.3	2.1	1.9	1.7	1.5	1.3	1.2
Other transfers	1.8	2.0	2.2	2.5	2.5	2.5	2.6	2.7
Capital expenditure	2.1	2.0	1.8	1.7	1.6	1.5	1.4	1.3
Balances								
Fiscal balance	-2.6	-2.3	-1.7	-1.0	0.2	1.6	3.1	4.6
Revenue balance	-0.8	-0.6	-0.1	0.5	1.6	2.9	4.3	5.7
Primary balance	-1.1	-0.8	-0.3	0.3	1.2	2.3	3.3	4.2
Debt outstanding	15.8	15.0	13.4	11.0	7.3	2.3		
Debt servicing/ revenue	9	9	9	8	7	5	2	

TABLE 5

Simulation Results of Pegging Fiscal Deficit at a Specified Level along with the Fiscal Reforms

(Percent of GSDP)

Variable	*1998-99 (BE)*	*1999-00*	*2000-01*	*2001-02*	*2002-03*	*2003-04*	*2004-05*	*2005-06*
Gross State Domestic Product (Rs. crore)	103,036	118,294	138,332	162,907	191,945	226,944	267,883	315,173
Total receipts	16.3	16.4	16.2	16.0	15.7	15.5	15.4	15.4
Own source receipts	12.5	12.6	12.6	12.5	12.4	12.3	12.3	12.3
Tax	9.9	10.1	10.1	10.0	10.0	9.9	10.0	10.1
Non-tax	2.6	2.5	2.5	2.5	2.4	2.3	2.3	2.2
Central transfers	3.9	3.8	3.7	3.5	3.4	3.2	3.1	3.0
Total expenditure	18.8	18.9	18.7	18.5	18.2	18.0	17.9	17.9
Revenue expenditure	16.9	16.7	16.2	15.4	14.4	13.4	12.5	11.5
Interest and debt servicing	1.5	1.5	1.4	1.4	1.4	1.3	1.3	1.3
Other revenue expenditure	15.4	15.3	14.7	14.0	13.1	12.1	11.2	10.2
Employees' compensation	9.9	9.7	9.3	8.6	7.9	7.1	6.4	5.8
O&M	1.2	1.2	1.2	1.2	1.1	1.1	1.2	1.0
Subsidies	2.5	2.3	2.1	1.9	1.6	1.4	1.2	1.1
Other transfers	1.8	2.0	2.2	2.4	2.4	2.4	2.4	2.4
Capital expenditure	1.9	2.1	2.6	3.1	3.8	4.6	5.4	6.3
Balances								
Fiscal balance	-2.5	-2.5	-2.5	-2.5	-2.5	-2.5	-2.5	-2.5
Revenue balance	-0.8	-0.6	-0.2	0.3	1.1	2.0	2.8	3.7
Primary balance	-1.0	-1.0	-1.1	-1.1	-1.1	-1.2	-1.2	-1.2
Debt outstanding	15.5	15.3	14.9	14.5	14.3	14.1	13.9	13.9
Debt servicing/ revenue	9	9	9	9	9	10	10	11

likely to reduce the need for high revenue receipts and high expenditure. The diversion of additional resources to capital formation results in higher GSDP growth of about 17 percent per annum. On the whole, the suggested macro fiscal correction along with sectoral reforms suggested in the earlier sections can put the State financial position on a stronger track.

CONCLUSIONS

Though the fiscal management of Tamil Nadu seems comparatively better, yet there is scope for and need to strengthen its revenue-effort and restructuring of expenditure for sustainability. If the same fiscal trends follow, the fiscal deficit is likely to assume disquieting proportion due to increasing component of revenue deficit. In addition, capital expenditure is shrinking, use of borrowings in consumption, and O&M expenditure is also not getting its due.

A simulated fiscal scenario, with a set of reform package, if implemented to set right the upward rising trends of fiscal/revenue deficits, emerges in which, the fiscal balance turns into surpluses. To follow the path of growth-inducement through Government capital expenditure, this surplus can be ploughed back into the economy resulting in income-augmentation, rise in capital expenditure and better asset maintenance, particularly infrastructure sectors. The fiscal deficit may be capped within a tolerable limit, say, at 2.5 percent of GSDP to reduce the need for high revenue receipts and high expenditure.

References

Aiyar, R.R. and K.N. Kurup (1992), *State Finances in Kerala* in Bagchi A., J.L. Bajaj and W.A. Bird (1992), *State Finances in India*, New Delhi: Vikas Publishing House.

Bajaj, J.L. and O.P. Aggarwal (1992), *State Finances in Uttar Pradesh 1965-90* in Bagchi A., J.L. Bajaj and W.A. Bird (1992), *State Finances in India*, New Delhi: Vikas Publishing House.

Bennett, S. and V.R. Muraleedharan (1998), *The Role of Government in Adjusting Economies*, Paper 28 on "Reforming the Role of Government in Tamil Nadu Health Sector", The University of Birmingham, Development Administration Group, School of Public Policy.

CMIE (1997). *Profiles of States.* Economic Intelligence Series. New Delhi: Centre for Monitoring Indian Economy Private Ltd. (March)

India, Government of. *India.* (Various issues), Ministry of Information & Broadcasting, New Delhi.

India, Government of (1993), *Report of the Expert Group on Estimation of Proportion and Number of Poor,* New Delhi: Planning Commission.

India, Government of (1988), *First Report for 1989-90,* New Delhi: Finance Commission.

India, Government of (1989), *Second Report for 1990-95,* New Delhi: Finance Commission.

India, Government of (1994), *Report for 1995-2000,* New Delhi: Finance Commission.

India, Government of Planning Commission, *A Study on the Performance of State Road Transport Undertakings,* New Delhi, September.

India, Government of (1993), *Report of the Committee on Norms for Maintenance of Roads,* New Delhi: Ministry of Surface Transport (Road Wing), (March).

India, Government of, Planning Commission (1997), *Annual Report on the Working of State Electricity Boards & Electricity Departments,* New Delhi: Power & Energy Division, (February).

India, Government of (1997), *Task Force Report* (Modified Expert Group), New Delhi: Planning Commission, (March).

Guhan, S. (1992), *State Finances in Tamil Nadu 1960-1990* in Bagchi A., J.L. Bajaj and W.A. Bird (1992), *State Finances in India,* New Delhi: Vikas Publishing House.

Guhan, S. (1986), *State Finances in Tamil Nadu, 1960-85: A Survey,* Working Paper # 77, Chennai: Madras Institute of Development Studies.

Jayanth, V. (1998), *"Restructuring of the Tamil Nadu PSEs", The Hindu,* November, 20.

Jetha Nizar (1992), *Gujarat State Finances* in Bagchi, A., J.L. Bajaj and W.A. Bird (1992), *State Finances in India.* New Delhi: Vikas Publishing House.

Madras Institute of Development Studies (1988), *Tamil Nadu Economy: Performance and Issues,* New Delhi: Oxford and IBH Publishing Co. Pvt. Ltd.

Musgrave, S. and N. Stern (1985), *Alcohol Demand and Taxation in South India in the 1970s,* University of Warwick.

NIPFP (1994), *Economic Reforms and the Stamp Act: An Interim Report,* New Delhi: National Institute of Public Finance and Policy, (July).

NIPFP (1995), *Annual Estimates of Population by Age and Sex 1901-2006 as on October 1,* New Delhi: National Institute of Public Finance and Policy.

NIPFP (1995), *Annual Estimates of Population by Age 1991 to 2006 as on October 1,* New Delhi: National Institute of Public Finance and Policy.

Raghavan, S.N. (1994), *Public Sector in India,* New Delhi: Asian Institute of Transport Development.

Rajaram, Indira, H. Mukhopadhyay and H.K. Amarnath (1998), *State Fiscal Studies: Punjab,* New Delhi: National Institute of Public Finance and Policy.

Ramesh, J. (1998), *"Three Bundles of Joy—Kerala, Tamil Nadu, Andhra Pradesh: India's Population Revolution"*, *India Today*, August 10.

Rao, M.G. and S. Mundle (1991), *The Volume and Composition of Government Subsidies in India: 1987-88*, New Delhi: National Institute of Public Finance and Policy, (Mimeo).

Rao, M.G. and T.K. Sen (1993), *State Finances in Kerala: Selected Issues*, New Delhi: National Institute of Public Finance and Policy.

Reserve Bank of India, *Bulletin* (Various Issues).

Roth, Gabriel (1988), *The Private Provision of Public Services in Developing Countries*, EDI Series in Economic Development, World Bank: Oxford University Press.

Sarma, J.V.M., G. Naresh and O.P. Bohra (1999), *State Fiscal Studies: Tamil Nadu*, New Delhi: National Institute of Public Finance and Policy, (Mimeo).

Sen, T.K. and R. Kavita Rao (1999), *State Fiscal Studies: Haryana*, New Delhi: National Institute of Public Finance and Policy, (Mimeo).

Srivastava, D.K. and T.K. Sen (1997), *Government Subsidies in India*, New Delhi: National Institute of Public Finance and Policy.

Srivastava, D.K., S. Chattopadhyay and TS Rangamannar (1998), *State Fiscal Studies: Assam*, New Delhi: National Institute of Public Finance and Policy.

Srivastava, D.K., S. Chattopadhyay and P.R. Jena (1999), *State Fiscal Studies: Kerala*, New Delhi: National Institute of Public Finance and Policy.

Tamil Nadu, Government of, *(1990), Tax on Entry of Motor Vehicles into Local Areas Act, 1990 with Rules, Forms and Notifications.*

Tamil Nadu, Government of, (1993), *Tamil Nadu Motor Vehicles Taxation Act and Rules 1974*, Transport Department.

Tamil Nadu, Government of, (1997), *Ninth Five-year Plan Tamil Nadu—1997-2002*, State Planning Commission, (September).

Tamil Nadu, Government of, (1997), *Planning and mobilization of Farmers Organization and Turnover, Tamil Nadu Water Resources Consolidation Project*, Water Resources Organization, Public works Department. Final Report, (December).

Tamil Nadu, Government of, (1997), *Policy Note on Medical and Public Health*, 1998-99.

Tamil Nadu, Government of, (1997), *Survey of State Taxes 1996-97*, Finance Department, (February)

Tamil Nadu, Government of, *Budget Document* (Various issues).

Tamil Nadu, Government of, *Economic and Functional Classification of Tamil Nadu Budget Analysis* (Various issues).

Tamil Nadu, Government of, *FOT Manual.*

Tamil Nadu, Government of, *Note on Policy on Road Transport Services and Shipping, 1997-98.*

Tamil Nadu, Government of, *Policy Note on Irrigation and Buildings, 1998-99.*

Tamil Nadu, Government of Tamil Nadu, *Policy Note on Rural Development 1997-98.*

Tamil Nadu, Government of, *Policy Note on Social Welfare Programs, 1997-98.*

Tamil Nadu, Government of, *Report on Gross Fixed Capital Formation of Tamil Nadu, 1992-93,* Directorate of Economics and Statistics.

Tamil Nadu, Government of, *Resources For Annual Plan—1998-99, Contribution of Roads Transport Corporations,* (February).

Tamil Nadu, Government of, *Review of State Public Sector Enterprises in Tamil Nadu* (Various issues).

Tamil Nadu, Government of, *Tamil Nadu—An Economic Appraisal* (Various issues).

Tamil Nadu, Government of, *Water Policy of Tamil Nadu, 1997-98.*

SECTION V

Gender Dynamics

23

CHAPTER

Gender and Employment in Tamil Nadu: Some Observations

A. MUTHURAJA

INTRODUCTION

Tamil Nadu is the southern most part of peninsular India with a 1000 miles long coast line on the east and the states of Andhra Pradesh, Karnataka and Kerala on the north and west respectively. Its population of 55.64 million is about 7% of the total population of India. The growth rate of female population in Tamil Nadu is 27.42 as against 28.22 of males as per 1991 census. The rural-urban sex ratio is 983 and 951 respectively. There are more females per males in rural Tamil Nadu.

In the mid-twentieth century, there was a persistent change in the structure of work force in the state of Tamil Nadu with many people moving away from agriculture towards industry and services, the shift occurring largely in terms of the decline in the category cultivators. The proportion of agricultural labourers has increased but not to a striking degree. The proportion of agricultural labourers has increased but not to a striking degree. The performance of Tamil Nadu in comparison with the country as a whole is remarkable only

TABLE 1

Labour Force in Tamil Nadu (1981-91)

(in million)

		Total		Rural		Urban	
		1981	1991	1981	1991	1981	1991
Total	Persons	48408	55368	32456	36611	15952	19027
Population	Males	24488	28217	16334	18466	8153	9751
	Females	23920	27420	16122	18145	7798	9275
Main Workers	Persons	18909	22972	13931	16523	4978	6448
	Males	13520	15757	9416	10556	4104	5201
	Females	5389	7214	4515	5967	873	1247
Other Workers	Persons	6434	8326	2450	3037	3983	5289
	Males	5465	6868	2005	2415	3459	4453
	Females	969	1458	444	622	524	836
Marginal Workers	Persons	1667	1584	1350	1438	316	146
	Males	511	330	320	285	191	44
	Females	1155	1254	1029	1151	125	107
Non-workers	Persons	27722	22756	17089	15613	10633	7144
	Males	10389	5262	6544	5190	3844	53
	Females	17334	17494	10545	10405	6788	7085

Source: Tamil Nadu Economic Appraisal, 1991, Government of Tamil Nadu, Chennai.

TABLE 2

Male-Female Participation Rate—Tamil Nadu (1971-91)

(in percentage)

	1971	1981	1991
Male	55.4	56.0	57.01
Female	15.1	22.6	30.88

Source: Tamil Nadu Economic Appraisal, 1991, Government of Tamil Nadu, Chennai.

in respect of female work force growth. With regard to women, employment it is significant despite the fact that the

TABLE 3

Cultivators and Agricultural Labourers in the Working Force—1971-91

Category		*1961*		*1971*		*1981*		*1991*	
		TN	*India*	*TN*	*India*	*TN*	*India*	*TN*	*India*
Cultivators	Male	41.87	50.97	34.51	45.73	31.98	43.77	26.59	53.81
	Female	42.45	55.32	29.73	29.73	22.93	19.16	21.33	46.38
Agricultural Labourers	Male	14.30	13.73	24.15	21.70	23.16	19.77	25.98	16.86
	Female	26.36	24.63	54.39	50.99	52.25	45.57	52.02	35.13

Source: Tamil Nadu Economic Appraisal, 1991, Government of Tamil Nadu, Chennai.

TABLE 4

Employment of Women in Industrial Classification (as on 31st March 1991)

Sl. No.	Industry	Public Sector	Private Sector	Total
1.	Agriculture, Hunting, Forestry, Fishing, etc.	2.3	37.8	40.1
2.	Mining and Quarrying	2.8	0.9	3.7
3.	Manufacturing	5.7	87.4	93.1
4.	Construction	4.2	0.6	4.8
5.	Electricity, Gas, Water and Sanitary Services, etc.	3.7	-	3.7
6.	Trade and Commerce	5.3	2.0	7.3
7.	Transport, Storage and Communication	18.5	0.2	18.7
8.	Service	280.0	50.5	330.5
	(a) Finance, Insurance, Real Estate, Business Service	16.1	1.3	17.4
	(b) Community Social and Personal Services	263.9	49.2	313.1
	Total	322.5	179.4	501.9

Source: Yasoda Shanmugasundaram (1993), "Women Employment in India", Institute for Advanced Studies & Research, Madras.

Female Crude Work Participation Rates (CWPR) are generally lower than the male rates, the female CWRP role sharply for rural females from 17.62 to 28.06 per cent between 1971 to 1981.

Women in Tamil Nadu in the recent past have emerged as potentially significant contributors to the country's growing labour force. The proportion of women in total workers increased from 26.5% in 1981 to 30% in 1991. With regard to work participation rate (WPR) for women in 40.82%, the state occupied the fifth place among the states during 1991.

WOMEN WORKERS: SOME ISSUES

At the end of United Nations' decade for women, a World Conference was held in Nairobi in 1985. The conference adopted the forward looking strategies for the advancement of women from 1986 to 2000 AD, empowerment is the most recent approach (women's empowerment phase: 1986 to date), articulated by the third world women. It seeks to meet women

TABLE 5

Change in the Proportion of Household Sector Workers in the Non-Agrarian Workforce—1981-91 in Selected Districts in Tamil Nadu

Districts	*Males*			*Females*		
	HW as % of TNAW (1981)	*HW as % of TNAW (1991)*	*Increase (+)/ Decrease (–)*	*HW as % of TNAW (1981)*	*HW as % of TNAW (1991)*	*Increase (+)/ Decrease (–)*
Madras	2.67	1.62	–	11.58	4.38	–
Chengalpattu	8.66	7.15	+	19.59	17.09	–
North Arcot	12.24	13.59	+	35.18	4.20	–
South Arcot	5.06	5.16	+	12.65	12.73	+
Dharmapuri	3.58	2.53	–	9.13	7.92	–
Salem	16.44	16.78	+	31.72	38.73	+
Periyar	4.31	3.92	–	10.40	11.45	+
Coimbatore	5.27	3.73	–	7.53	4.79	–
Nilgiris	0.70	8.02	+	0.47	0.74	+
Madurai	6.05	3.47	–	19.82	8.54	–
Tiruchy	5.79	5.66	–	22.57	20.58	–
Thanjavur	6.86	6.98	+	21.44	19.54	–
Pudukkottai	3.65	2.92	–	10.15	8.96	–
Ramanathanpuram	8.35	9.78	+	36.26	41.26	+
Tirunelveli	7.23	9.38	+	49.84	175.18	+
Kannyakumari	4.16	4.55	+	25.09	35.30	+
Tamil Nadu	6.60	5.50	–	22.63	18.85	–

HW: Household Sector.
TNAW: Total Non-Agricultural Workers.
Source: Yasoda Shanmugasundaram (1993), "Women Employment in India", Institute for Advanced Studies & Research, Madras.

strategic gender needs, due to their subordinate position to men, through bottom up mobilization around practical gender needs according to their accepted role in society. It aims at increasing women's power in terms of their self-reliance and internal strength to determine choices in life and to influence the direction of change.

Women's participation in employment is not only mediated by gender, but also by caste, ethnicity, age and

TABLE 6

Unemployment Rate in Tamil Nadu—1987-88

Category		*Male*		*Female*	
		Tamil Nadu	*India*	*Tamil Nadu*	*India*
Rural	Usual Status	4.0	2.8	4.5	3.5
	Current Weekly Status	7.7	4.2	6.7	4.4
	Current Daily Status	8.4	4.6	10.7	6.7
Urban	Usual Status	7.3	6.1	9.1	8.5
	Current Weekly Status	8.1	6.6	9.4	9.2
	Current Daily Status	12.3	8.8	13.2	12.0

Source: Tamil Nadu Economic Appraisal, 1991, Government of Tamil Nadu, Chennai.

marital status. Dalit and tribal women have significantly higher work force participation rates than the rest of Indian women. In the upper caste and Muslim households women are withdrawn from the labour force as soon as their economic status improves. In the export processing zones, being promoted under the new economic policy, women entry into the labour market is also determined by age. Employers prefer to employ young single women. Marriage results in retrenchment becaue it is assumed that they cannot work for long hours, especially after child birth.

The direct impact of new economic policies on women's work are:

- ❑ Cut back in the funds allotted for employment generation programs for women. As two-thirds of the work force constitute poor women, their employment opportunities would be drastically cut.
- ❑ Decrease in employment opportunities in industries arising out of easier retrenchment and closure laws, on the unwritten principle of women first.
- ❑ Decrease in employment opportunities for women workers in the public sector arising out of privatization.

- The increase in unemployment has not been accompanied by a parallel increase in employment opportunities in the private sector. The increase in employment in private sector is largely in export processing zones, where in young educated single women are recruited in the bottom rungs of the ladder in industries.
- They are paid low wages, and are retrenched when they get married and have children. Moreover, sexual harassment at the work place is a serious problem.
- Expansion in contract labour system in contrast to self-employment opportunities.
- Decrease in wages in real terms, and wage freeze in selected sectors.
- Increase in girl child labour.
- Lack of right to unionise.

Several factors account for this situation. Among these the significant are the absence of appropriate skills. Women also tend to get easily displaced by new technologies and are either pushed out or pushed down when job requirements call for skilled and trained persons. With the introduction of new macro-economic policies, skill and vocational training for women assume key importance.

WOMEN WORKERS: PARTICIPATION AND EMPLOYMENT PATTERN

Womanpower in Tamil Nadu as in India is one-half of the total labour power. The 1991 census put the total population of Tamil Nadu at 55.64 million. Out of this, women constituted 27.42 million more than 50% of the population constituting the womanpower. The 1981 census has included 1667 millions as marginal workers in Tamil Nadu, the major part being women marginal workers (1554 mn.) and they form 3.5% of the total population. Particularly in the case rural workers, the marginal worker concept has accounted for 135 millions in workforce out of whom 1030 mn. are women. In 1991 the total of marginal workers was 1.58 million with 1.25

as female marginal workers.

The femal work participation rate in Tamil Nadu has shown a marginal increase between 1971 and 1991. The performance of females in the workforce is relatively higher than male participants. The male-female work force ratio is almost reaching 2:1 in Tamil Nadu. Female participation rate has significantly increased between 1971 and 1991 from 15% to 30%. The employment of female under usual status reveals that the urban female employment has increased significantly compared with rural employment. Both rural and urban unemployment rate were more pronounced in Tamil Nadu than the all India rates. A comparision of current weekly and current daily status shows that the fall in female employment rates is one the whole higher than the male employment rates.

Women employment in the organized sector is a recent phenomenon and is caused by the factors of Urbanization. The total employment in public and private sectors was 2.289 mn. of which women employment accounted for 0.50 mn. The male-female employment ratio in public and private sectors is approximately 5:1. Community, social and personal services offer bulk of the employment opportunity ie., 62% of total employment of women in public and private sectors.

WOMEN WORKERS: AGRICULTURE, NON-AGRICULTURE AND INDUSTRY

It is to be noted that majority of female workers in many districts are agricultural labourers. In the predominantly agricultural district of Thanjavur, nearly 73% of female workers are agricultural labourers. Sizeable percentage of female working in household industry is noticed in the district of Tirunelveli, Kannyakumari and Chennai. Among the districts, Tirunelveli ranks first with 46.43% female workers, while Chennai ranks last with 9.41%.

The incidence of agricultural female workers is higher in Tamil Nadu than in the country as a whole, while the incidence of cultivators among male was higher than that of agricultural labourers. In the case of females, the incidence of agricultural labourers was double the incidence of cultivators. Regarding the relative growth of male-female agricultural labourers at the district level, the general tendency has been to widen the disparity in sex ratios of the agricultural labourers. Female casual labour is an important type of labour. They provided nearly 50% of the labour time in the farm. Women involvement in agriculture operation is tasks specific. There is also a decline in the days of work on farm for female agricultural labourers. The percentage decrease among women was nearly double that of men. Wage employment, therefore, shows a similar decline.

Women in rural non-agricultural labour force were 10.65 lakhs or 17.8% of the total female labour force in 1981. This has declined to 6.22 lakhs in 1991, forming only 10% of the female main workers. Casual wage employment in non-agriculture activities is available for women at certain time facilitating their occasional, participation in such work. In the rural economy of Tamil Nadu, non-agriculture activities offer considerable work opportunities for women.

In the household sector, incidence of work is higher for both males and females in Tamil Nadu than the all India levels. There is a decline in the proportion of household sector in the non-agrarian work force for both male and females between 1981-91. But the proportion of females was above that of males during the same period. On the other hand, in the non-household industry there is considerable increase in the incidence in Tamil Nadu, which was above the all India incidence. The district which have registered large increase are Periyar, Chengalpattu, Sale, South Arcot, Nilgiris and Trinelveli. The incidence of female workers has increased considerably in Tamil Nadu.

Regarding the female employment in the tertiary sector, the dominant groups in 1961 were personal services, educational and scientific services and retail trade. The tertiary sector employment was considerably increased from 1981 to 1991 for both male and females in Tamil Nadu. Increased in female employment (17.5% to 20.21%) was higher than male employment during this period (34.33% to 36.24%). Urban female employment recorded the highest increase of 5.16%. In the organized sector, female employment occupies the largest in agriculture (45.94%). In services, 20.04% are females. Manufacturing and mining employ around 13% each.

Electricity, gas, transport, storage, communication services and construction categories in public sector absorb a large percentage of female workers.

In the organized sector, the proportion of women in total employment improved from 14.6% (1970) to 15.9% (1980) and further to 21.2% in 1990. The share of women further went upto 25.2% in total organized sector employment during 1995. Not only is the employment of women and the increase in the unemployment among women going up but also the differences between the employment situation in Tamil Nadu and that of entire country may be noted.

- Higher labour force participation rate and male workers rate among female in Tamil Nadu.
- The low labour force participation rates among male in the state should be undertook as highlighting the higher figure for females rather as being low in itself.
- Relatively lower dependence of workers on the primary sector of a living.
- A higher percentage of workers among agricultural labour than among cultivators.
- Smaller percentage than the all India figure of workers depending on livestock, forestry, etc.
- Relatively higher percentage of workers depending on other industries.

WOMEN WORKERS AND UNEMPLOYMENT

The magnitude of educated unemployment is rather high in Tamil Nadu, paradoxically with the literacy level also being high. Unemployment rate has increased among the urban males and females under the usual status category is higher in Tamil Nadu than in India. This indicates that those participating occasionally in work exceeded those who temporarily withdraw.

The difference in the unemployment situation as between Tamil Nadu and India may be noted.

- Low incidence of unemployment among female in

Tamil Nadu.

- Relatively low unemployment among females of the state in the 15-49 age group as compared to that for the country as a whole.
- Higher proportions of new entrants in the total unemployed.
- Educated unemployment among males as well as females are high.
- Low percentage of illiterates seeking jobs.

AGENDA FOR FUTURE ACTION

What is not yet recognized is effort to improve women's position the need to focus on women as economic factors. Measures to enhance women's access to productive resources are critical as directed and self-targeted means to reduce poverty. Many economists have formulated the problem exclusively as employment generation. For the point of women, it is not enough to provide employment but change to bring about an attitude to women. Though women's issues have moved center stage in our thinking and women's participation is now an inseparable part of theory of planning. Gender equality and gender justice is still distant dreams. The following are the suggestions and policy prescriptions to improve the conditions of women's employment and empowerment:

- State interventions to redress the problems of gender imbalances in employment need to clearly distinguish between the short-term palliatives and long-term solutions. In the long-run, improving the resource and skill endowments of women to widen their options and opportunities alone could bring in gender equity in employment. In the short-run, program could alleviate their current handicap *vis-a-vis* men, by checking overt discriminations in searing employment, placement and earning through positive discrimination and affirmation action. The choice between and combination of interventions to enable women to possess productive assets *versus* cash income /through wage-employment assistance *versus* empowerment through legal and economic means, become important in this contest.

- ❑ This is powerful demonstration of how market forces can radically change patriarchal norms through economic incentives. The same process has happened in poorer households in those areas where new job opportunities have come for young women as, for example, in the export promotion zones. The families have agreed to postpone the marriage of the girls and allowed them to travel and migrate above to job location.
- ❑ Better infrastructure facilities need to be provided for encouraging self-employment among the educated unemployed women.
- ❑ Efforts have to be made to bring the development of different skills in line with social need and give opportunities for unemployed women. Special entrepreneurship courses should be run for women unemployed. Larger variety of vocational courses particularly for girls, who do not intend to continue their general education beyond elementary or secondary stage, should be introduced.
- ❑ Lobby with government to cut back its expenditure on defense and increase its expenditure in public distribution system, health, housing and employment and recognize the above as rights of people which cannot be abrogated to the private sector.
- ❑ Not only have additional employment opportunities to be generated by using the suitable structure of investment and production, but distributive justice must be done.
- ❑ Organize and train poor, dalit and tribal women to take part in the economic activities.
- ❑ Evolve a gender disaggregated data on the above issue so as to lobby effectively with the government and plan development projects which

are sensitive to survival needs and strategic gender interests.

- Evolve alternative development paradigm sensitive to gender caste, class, religious identities and environment.
- Over and above all, through these measures special educational facilities are to be provided for the women.

REFERENCES

Arun Bandhopadhyay (1992), "The Agrarian Economy of Tamil Nadu", K.P. Bagchi and Company, Calcutta.

Banarjee, N. (1995), "Women Employment and All that", *The Administrator*, Vol. 40, No. 3.

Kalpagam, U. and Usha, P. (1980), "Female Workforce in Tamil Nadu", *MIDS Bulletin*, Vol. 10, Nos. 5 and 6, March and June.

MIDS (1988), "Tamil Nadu Economy", IBH & Oxford Publication, Madras.

Muthuraja, C. (2001), "Gender and Employment in India: An Agenda for the 21st Century" in Murthy S. (ed.), *Women and Employment*, RBSA Publishers, Jaipur.

Muthuraja, C. (1990), "Rural Women in Indian Agriculture", *Khadi Gramodyog*, Vol. 36, No. 8.

Rajalakshmi, N. (1999), "Tamil Nadu Economy", Business Publications Inc., Mumbai.

Ramachandran, V.K. and Subramanian (1982), "Agricultural Labourers in the Working Population of Rural Tamil Nadu", *MIDS Bulletin*, Vol. 12, Nos. 5 and 6, May-June.

Ranjani, K. Murthy (1994), "Economic Development of Tamil Nadu", S. Chand and Company, Delhi.

Perumalsamy, S. (1995), "Economic Development of Tamil Nadu", S. Chand and Company, Delhi.

Shanthi, K. (1989), 'Sectoral Distribution of Women Employment in the Organized Sector in Tamil Nadu' in Mahajan V.S. (ed.), 'Women Contribution to India's Economic and Social Development', Deep & Deep Publications, New Delhi.

World Bank (1997), 'Gender and Poverty in India', A World Bank Country Study, Washington, D.C.

Yasodha Shanmugasundaram (1980), 'Urban Workforce: A Tamil Nadu Profile", *MIDS Bulletin*, Vol. 10, No. 4, April.

Yasodha Shanmugasundaram (1993), 'Women Employment in India', Institute for Advanced Studies & Research, Madras.

24

CHAPTER

A Study on Women Empowerment in Tamil Nadu

S. Lakshmi

> It is quite clear that the 21st century will be a century of much greater gender equality than the world has ever seen before.
>
> —*Mahbub ul Haq*

Now-a-days the role of women in the society has changed. The role of women could be seen in all walks of life. For centuries, only men acted as the bread winner of the family and women looked after the household activities. But slowly the situation has changed and women have also become the bread winner of the family, along with men. Realising the need for women empowerment in economic, social and political spheres, the government had taken various measures. For instance: 1. gender-focussed District Primary Education Programme (DPEP) implemented to increase the enrolment of girls and to increase the retention rate in primary schools, 2. one-third of the jobs in government sector reserved for women, 3. one-third of total number of seats in all panchayats reserved for women, and 4. in the case of IRDP scheme larger weightage given for women compared to men.

In this context it is significant to have a study on the status of women in Tamil Nadu in the case of education, participation in the labour force etc., so that appropriate steps can be taken to improve the status of women in the society.

The concept 'Empowerment' is defined as comprising increased power in the economic (material), social, political and/or psychological realms, and consider this in conjunction with people's identification of their own problems and needs (Human Development in South Asia, 2000). Ackerley states Empowerment can be considered a change in the context of a woman or man's life that enables her/him increased capacity to lead a fulfilling human life, characterized by external qualities such as health, mobility, education and awareness, status in the family, participation in decision-making, and level of material security, as well as internal qualities such as self-awareness and self-confidence (Ackerley, 1995).

Some of the instruments through which empowerment can be attained are: improving literacy, expanding educational opportunities, providing gainful employment, enhancing skill by training and offering health and nutrition support. Here an attempt has been made to look into the indicators namely literacy rate of men and women and participation of men and women in the labour force in various fields, in order to find out the presence of gender differences, so that appropriate measures can be taken to eleminate the gender differences for the sake of improving the status of women in the society.

Female population constituted a significant proportion of the total population in Tamil Nadu. For instance, in Tamil Nadu out of the total population of 55.9 million, female population was 27.6 million in 1991. In 2001, out of the total population of 62.1 million, female population was 30.8 million (2001 census) (Table 1).

Regarding the literacy rate in Tamil Nadu, the female literacy rate is lower than the male literacy rate, eventhough the rate of increase in the literacy rate of women is more than the rate of increase in the literacy rate of men in 2001 compared to 1991 (Table 2). The enrolment of girls in the primary schools is less than the enrolment of boys in the primary schools, and it is a pitiable state that the drop-out rate of girls is more than the drop-out rate of boys in the primary

TABLE 1

Population and Sex Ratio in Tamil Nadu

Year	Population (in Millions)			Sex ratio*
	Male	Female	Total	
1991	28.3	27.6	55.9	974
2001	31.3	30.8	62.1	986

* No. of females per 1000 males.

Sources: 1. Primary Census Abstract for General Population—1991, Directorate of Census Operation, Tamil Nadu, Chennai.

2. Census of India 2001, Series-34, Tamil Nadu, Provisional Population Totals, Paper-1 of 2001, Directorate of Census Operation, Tamil Nadu, Chennai.

TABLE 2

Literacy Rate in Tamil Nadu

Year	Male	Female	Combined
1991	74	51	63
2001	82	65	74

Sources: 1. Directorate of Census Operation, Tamil Nadu, Chennai.

2. Evaluation and Applied Research Department, Chennai, Various Census.

schools (Tables 3 and 4).

The enrolment of boys and girls in the primary school has done down in 1997-98 compared to 1994-95. But in the classes from VI to VIII the enrolment of girls showed an increase in 1997-98 compared to 1994-95 and the enrolment of boys has gone down during that period. In the case of IX to X and Plus Two classes, the increase in the enrolment of boys is more than the increase in the enrolment of girls in 1997-98 compared to 1994-95 (1,65,784), whereas for women there was an increase in the enrolment i.e., from 1,38,417 in 1994-95 to 1,66,671 in 1997-98. Again in the case of special education, eventhough there was an increase in the enrolment of men (4408) and women (4907) in 1997-98 compared to 1994-95

TABLE 3

Enrolment of Children in Primary Schools in Tamil Nadu

(in lakhs)

Year	*Boys*	*Girls*	*Total*
1990-91	29.80	25.70	55.50
1996-97	34.91	32.49	67.31
1997-98	35.19	32.95	68.14

Source: Various issues of Policy Notes on School Education

TABLE 4

Drop-out in Primary Schools in Tamil Nadu

Year	*Boys*	*Girls*	*Total*
1990-91	18.27	22.68	20.32
1995-96	14.88	16.97	15.85
1996-97	14.05	16.20	15.06
1997-98	13.99	16.18	15.05

Source: Various issues of Policy Notes on School Education.

(men—3994, women—4154), the increase in the enrolment was more in the case of women than men (GOT, 1997-98).

Regarding work participation in Tamil Nadu, there was an increase in the member of men and women in 1993-94 compared to 1991, but the work participation rate of women is less than that of men in both the periods (Table 6).

It is significant to note that in the case of organized sector employment, women lag behind men in public as well as private sector industries, except in agriculture, hunting, forestry etc., where the participation of women is more than that of men in the private sector. In the case of agriculture, hunting, forestry and construction industries the participation of women in the private sector has gone down in 1998 compared to 1991. But it is appreciable to note that the employment of women in the public sector in all the categories of industries, except mining and quarrying, has gone up in

TABLE 5

Enrolment by Age Groups in Tamil Nadu

Sl. No.	*Age Group*		*1994-95*	*1995-96*	*1996-97*	*1997-98*
1.	6-11	(I-V)				
		Boys	4347	4389	3490	3519
		Girls	3763	3807	3240	3295
2.	11-14	(VI-VIII)				
		Boys	2044	2102	1894	1930
		Girls	1614	1680	1612	1664
3.	14-18	(XI-X) and plus Two				
		Boys	1168	1220	1270	1309
		Girls	802	842	883	907

Sources: 1. Directorate of School Education, Chennai
2. Directorate of Elementary Education, Chennai.

TABLE 6

Work Participation Rates in Tamil Nadu

(in percent)

Rural/Urban	*1991*	*1993-94 (NSS—Usual Status)*
Rural		
Male	58.28	60.2
Female	38.50	47.8
Persons	48.49	53.9
Urban		
Male	52.78	57.5
Female	13.10	23.0
Persons	33.34	40.2
Total		
Male	56.39	59.3
Female	29.89	39.3
Persons	43.31	49.4

Source: 1991 Census and NSS 50th Round.

1998 compared to 1991. The extent of participation of women in the manufacturing industries in the private sector is higher compared to the employment of women in the private sector in all other categories. Again, only in the community, social and personal services the extent of employment of women in the public sector is higher compared to the employment of women in the public sector in all other categories (Tables 7 to 15). At this juncture it is imperative to look into the steps taken by the government for increasing the participation of women in the labour force and thereby to improve the status of women in Tamil Nadu.

The Government of Tamil Nadu has implemented various Poverty Alleviation programmes in order to raise the living status of women in the society. For instance, in the case of IRDP programme, it has been stipulated that 40 per cent of the beneficiaries should be women beneficiaries who got assistance under IRDP in the year 1997-98. They accounted for 42.5 per cent of the total (1.81 lakh) beneficiaries in the state (GOT, 1997-98).

Development of Women and Children in Rural Areas (DWCRA) has been implemented exclusively for economic development of women. The scheme helps the poor women to organize themselves into groups to undertake economic activities. Each group is provided with a one time grant of Rs. 25,000. During 1997-98, 2206 women groups and since inception 9537 groups have been formed (GOT, 1997-98).

The scheme called TRYSEM (Training of Rural Youth for Self-Employment) was started in rural area to impart training to rural youths to equip the trainees with skills and technology under various employment-oriented trades, in order to enable them to be self-employed. Out of 10972 rural youths trained during 1997-98, women trainees constituted 49.6% (5444) (GOT, 1997-98).

The Tamil Nadu Corporation for Development of Women Limited was established in 1983. The objective of this Corporation is to provide better employment avenues for women particularly in self-employment ventures. The Tamil Nadu Women's Development Project has been implemented through the network of Women's Self-Help Groups which are established with the support of the NGOs at the village level.

TABLE 7

Employment of Men and Women in Public and Private Sector in Agriculture, Hunting, Forestry etc., in Tamil Nadu

Years	Public			Private		
	M & W	M	W	M & W	M	W
1990	26.4	24.2	2.2	66.2	28.1	38.1
1991	26.7	24.4	2.3	64.7	26.9	37.8
1992	26.0	23.6	2.4	65.7	28.4	37.3
1993	26.8	23.9	2.9	61.0	26.4	34.6
1994	27.6	24.5	3.1	61.4	25.9	35.5
1995	27.2	24.2	3.0	59.3	24.7	34.6
1996	27.5	24.3	3.2	60.4	25.4	35.0
1997	27.5	24.2	3.3	64.5	26.8	37.7
1998	27.4	24.0	3.4	61.6	25.3	36.3

Source: Director of Employment and Training, Chennai.

TABLE 8

Employment of Men and Women in Public and Private Sector in Mining and Quarrying in Tamil Nadu

Years	Public			Private		
	M & W	M	W	M & W	M	W
1990	29.8	27.0	2.8	5.4	4.5	0.9
1991	30.9	28.1	2.8	5.4	4.5	0.9
1992	30.9	28.2	2.7	5.3	4.4	0.9
1993	30.0	27.3	2.7	5.1	4.3	0.8
1994	28.7	26.2	2.5	4.9	4.3	0.6
1995	27.2	24.8	2.4	4.7	4.2	0.5
1996	26.2	23.8	2.4	5.2	4.7	0.5
1997	26.2	23.8	2.4	5.4	4.9	0.5
1998	25.9	23.5	2.4	4.2	2.9	1.3

Source: Director of Employment and Training, Chennai.

Initially this project was in operation in selected 75 blocks of 8 districts of Tamil Nadu. The project aims at encouraging the poor women to save and rotate the sum among the group members. In 1997-98, about 1,20,276 women were covered

TABLE 9

Employment of Men and Women in Public and Private Sector in Manufacturing in Tamil Nadu

Years	Public			Private		
	M & W	M	W	M & W	M	W
1990	120.0	114.0	6.0	436.3	351.7	84.6
1991	117.6	111.9	5.7	451.7	364.3	87.4
1992	118.0	112.1	5.9	445.7	354.5	91.2
1993	116.5	110.2	6.3	451.3	364.8	92.5
1994	114.2	107.9	6.3	476.2	372.3	103.9
1995	112.2	105.6	6.6	481.3	377.3	104.0
1996	110.7	104.1	6.6	525.2	399.5	125.7
1997	110.7	104.1	6.6	601.5	404.0	197.5
1998	114.5	107.4	7.1	616.6	416.2	200.4

Source: Director of Employment and Training, Chennai.

TABLE 10

Employment of Men and Women in Public and Private Sector in Construction Industries in Tamil Nadu

Years	Public			Private		
	M & W	M	W	M & W	M	W
1990	52.3	48.1	4.2	9.4	9.4	0.5
1991	52.3	48.1	4.2	9.7	9.7	0.6
1992	50.3	46.0	4.3	10.1	9.1	1.0
1993	51.1	46.8	4.3	10.0	9.5	0.5
1994	51.8	47.2	4.6	9.9	9.4	0.5
1995	50.0	45.4	4.6	10.3	9.9	0.4
1996	51.6	46.7	4.9	11.3	10.8	0.5
1997	77.7	73.0	4.7	11.6	11.2	0.4
1998	47.4	42.9	4.5	11.7	11.3	0.4

Source: Director of Employment and Training, Chennai.

through a network of 5101 Women's Self-Help Groups (GOT, 1997-98).

The project called TANWA (Tamil Nadu Women in Agriculture) assisted by the Danish International Development

TABLE 11

Employment of Men and Women in Public and Private Sector in Electricity, Gas, Water and Sanitary Services, etc., in Tamil Nadu

Years	Public			Private		
	M & W	*M*	*W*	*M & W*	*M*	*W*
1990	84.2	80.5	3.7	0.6	0.6	-
1991	82.7	79.0	3.7	0.6	0.6	-
1992	82.2	78.4	3.8	0.6	0.6	-
1993	79.7	75.9	3.8	0.6	0.6	-
1994	81.9	77.8	4.1	0.5	0.5	-
1995	78.9	74.5	4.4	0.5	0.5	-
1996	77.7	73.0	4.7	0.7	0.68	0.02
1997	51.6	46.6	5.0	0.7	0.5	0.2
1998	79.3	73.9	5.4	0.7	0.68	0.02

Source: Director of Employment and Training, Chennai.

TABLE 12

Employment of Men and Women in Public and Private Sector in Trade & Commerce, Wholesale and Retail Trade and Restaurants and Hotels in Tamil Nadu

Years	Public			Private		
	M & W	*M*	*W*	*M & W*	*M*	*W*
1990	44.3	38.4	5.9	38.1	36.0	2.1
1991	45.3	40.0	5.3	36.0	34.0	2.0
1992	45.2	38.9	6.3	34.6	32.5	2.1
1993	45.4	39.0	6.4	34.1	31.9	2.2
1994	46.4	40.0	6.4	38.9	35.3	3.6
1995	46.5	39.9	6.6	40.4	36.7	3.7
1996	47.4	40.9	6.5	46.6	42.3	4.3
1997	47.4	40.4	7.0	40.0	31.7	8.3
1998	46.3	39.1	7.2	44.2	39.6	4.6

Source: Director of Employment and Training, Chennai.

Agency aims to impart training to farm women on the latest agricultural techniques and thereby induce them to take part in agricultural activities. During the first phase of the project

TABLE 13

Employment of Men and Women in Public and Private Sector in Transport, Storage and Communication in Tamil Nadu

Years	Public			Private		
	M & W	M	W	M & W	M	W
1990	295.5	278.1	17.4	8.0	7.7	0.3
1991	295.7	277.2	18.5	8.0	7.8	0.2
1992	292.6	273.8	18.8	7.6	7.2	0.4
1993	296.8	276.9	19.9	7.6	7.1	0.5
1994	293.3	273.2	20.1	8.0	7.4	0.6
1995	292.5	271.3	21.2	8.3	7.7	0.6
1996	291.4	269.6	21.8	10.4	9.8	0.6
1997	291.4	269.6	21.8	10.4	9.9	0.5
1998	293.3	270.6	22.7	8.0	7.6	0.4

Source: Director of Employment and Training, Chennai.

TABLE 14

Employment of Men and Women in Public and Private Sector in Services in Tamil Nadu (Finance, Insurance, Real Estate and Business Services)

(in '000)

Years	Public			Private		
	M & W	M	W	M & W	M	W
1990	129.8	114.5	15.3	11.7	10.5	1.2
1991	131.0	114.9	16.1	12.3	11.0	1.3
1992	135.3	118.3	17.0	12.7	11.2	1.5
1993	137.6	120.1	17.5	13.4	11.6	1.8
1994	134.5	116.3	18.2	15.1	13.0	2.1
1995	138.9	119.5	19.4	16.1	13.7	2.4
1996	138.5	114.5	24.0	18.9	15.3	3.6
1997	138.5	117.8	20.7	19.3	16.3	3.0
1998	136.0	115.5	20.5	19.6	16.5	3.1

Source: Director of Employment and Training, Chennai.

period (1986-93) about 14,000 farm women were covered (GOT, 1997-98).

TABLE 15

Employment of Men and Women in Public and Private Sector in Services in Tamil Nadu (Community, Social and Personal Services)

(in '000)

Years	Public			Private		
	M & W	*M*	*W*	*M & W*	*M*	*W*
1990	780.8	537.2	243.6	123.3	73.2	50.1
1991	797.2	533.3	263.9	121.6	72.4	49.2
1992	792.7	521.7	271.0	119.0	70.4	48.6
1993	816.7	530.1	286.6	129.5	74.0	55.5
1994	842.2	528.2	314.0	142.7	79.9	62.8
1995	860.3	537.6	322.7	147.0	80.8	66.2
1996	874.7	508.2	366.5	153.0	80.5	72.5
1997	838.8	508.2	330.6	156.4	82.4	74.0
1998	858.5	523.7	334.8	165.5	87.5	78.0

Source: Director of Employment and Training, Chennai.

In Tamil Nadu as per 1996 elections, out of the elected Presidents for village panchayats of 12,584, SC/ST women presidents were 1,107 and women Presidents (General) were 3,150. Out of the elected ward members of 97,026, SC/ST elected women ward members were 6,250 and women (General) elected ward members were of the order of 26,164. In case of Panchayat Unions, the total numbers of elected ward members were 6,499. The number of SC/ST women elected ward members were 549 and women (General) elected ward members were 1,736. Again, out of the 648 ward members of the District Panchayats, SC/ST women elected ward members were 54 and the elected women (General) ward members were 171 (GOT, 1997-98).

It can be stated that due to the introduction of various measures by the government for women empowerment, the literacy rate and the participation of women the labour force might have increased over the years. But even then women are lagging behind men in literacy and employment. We have to go a long way to achieve women empowerment in Tamil

Nadu. So what is needed in the present day context is the steps to popularize the programmes implemented by the government for the benefit of women through different means. Awareness has to be created among women to come out of the clutches of age old, blind customs and traditions and to come forward to gain knowledge, education and to increase their participation in the labour force in all possible fields, in order to achieve sustainable economic development for the betterment of themselves and for the society as a whole. In our march to empower women co-operation from both men and women is needed.

References

Ackerley, B. (1995), 'Testing the Tools of Development: Credit Programmes, Loan Involvement, and Women's Empowerment', *IDS Bulletin*, 26 (3): 56-57.

GOT (1997-98), Tamil Nadu—An Economic Appraisal, Chennai.

GOT (1998), Statistical Hand Book of Tamil Nadu, Department of Economics and Statistics, Chennai.

Human Development Report (1998, 1999 and 2000), Oxford University Press, New York.

Human Development in South Asia (1998, 1999 and 2000), Oxford University Press, Karachi.

SECTION VI

Social Sector Skewness

25

CHAPTER

Economic Reforms and Social Sector Development in Tamil Nadu

M. NAGANATHAN AND K. JOTHI SIVAGNANAM

INTRODUCTION

The macro-economic reforms launched from 1991 onwards are expected to alter drastically the basic parameters of erstwhile Indian economic policies that were followed since Independence. The national economy has been waned away from a regime of state stabilization through which a planned economy is charged into a market driven competitive economy along with the creation of the basic institutional framework of a full-fledged market economy constitutes 'the first generation reforms'. All these reforms aimed at placing the Indian economy at a 'higher growth trajectory'. For instance, Kirit S. Parikh (1997) once thought "the reforms have put the Indian economy on higher growth path . . . with more sensible policies, we have an opportunity to accelerate our growth further and takeoff into a higher growth trajectory". However, the dreams of becoming a new tiger, a fast growth miracle economy remain elusive—reports Kirit S. Parikh in the Indian Development Report, 1999-2000. This is the state of affairs after having completed almost a decade of first generation reforms. It needs to be noted that during the reform period the 'Asian Tigers' have been reduced to just 'cats' and the 'miracle' became a 'crisis'. And that is what happened to Indian economy. Thus, the 'first generation' not merely failed to achieve its objective of accelerating the growth of output all around, they have also failed even to maintain the growth rate of eighties.

However, the pro-reforms economists, though tacitly recognized the failure of the reform on growth front in general and industrial sector in particular, claimed success in other counts. The sponsors of the 1991 reforms claimed that gains in foreign investments, balance payments, etc. But one should not forget that the aim of the reform was to place the economy on higher growth trajectory, with the hope that it would help the poor.

The so-called 'second generation reforms' have to be viewed in this background. Our development strategies and programmes particularly the ongoing variety placed much stress on balance of payment and economic growth and almost ignored the issues of human well-being. Whereas, Amartya Sen shifted the growth centered debate to that of the more 'fundamental problems' of human well-being. Amartya Sen and J. Dreze (1997) assert that there must be an attempt to link the strategies of development to something more fundaméntal, in particular, the ends of economics and social development. How are the success and failures of policies to be judged? It is only with an explicit recognition of the basic ends that debates on means and strategies can be adequately founded. R.B. Norgaard also expressed similar views. According to him, 'Economics systems exist to provide for people, not *vice-versa*, markets should be turned to reach socially determined ends and not promoted *per se* . . . Now, simply keeping our economies going faster and faster has become an end in itself. And what growing economies might provide for us is secondary, if addressed at all (R.B. Norgaard, 1999).

Human development has emerged as a prime candidate that requires our immediate attention and adequate effort not only from the Indian policy-makers and the public but also from the world community. And growth of social sector is of paramount importance in this regard.

For the Indian policy-makers, it took several decades to realize that economic growth is not an 'end' in itself. In fact, human development is the 'end' and economic growth a 'means'. So the purpose of growth should be to improve the standard of living of the people by enlarging their choices—choices that are created by expanding human capabilities and functioning—what people do and can in their lives. At all levels of developments, a few capabilities are essential for human development without which, many choices in life would not be available. These capabilities are to lead long and healthy lives, to be knowledgeable and to have access to the resources needed for a decent standard of living (Paul Streeton, 1999).

At the initial stage, reformers made attempts to convince the Indian mass that they have to bear the initial strain of stabilization measures till it delivers the results. Further, achieving higher growth would reward them and the benefit would percolate to poor people. Thus the policy-makers promised that the higher growth would "trickle down" to the classic Indian poor living in some remote villages. However, there are no takers to such traditional and elusive doctrine. In fact, poverty, illiteracy and ill-health still remain major problems, and are aggravated by worsening environment (K.S. Parikh, 1999). The so-called Second Generation Reforms have to be perceived in this background. Social sector, the sector in which we have failed not only during the 'first generation reforms' period but also many generations, should be given top most priority. Let us see the trend of social sector expenditure in Tamil Nadu. The following section focuses on the trend and composition of social sector expenditure in Tamil Nadu from 1980-81 to 1999-2000 and the pre-reform and post-reform periods are examined.

GROWTH OF SOCIAL SECTOR EXPENDITURE IN TAMIL NADU

Most of the recent studies on social sector expenditure have focused their attention either by taking total budget (Union and States) or by examining the budgets of all the states together. Guhan (1995) has justified his concentration on the Union Budget of the following grounds:

- It can be argued that in as much as it is the center that has initiated the new policies, the primary responsibility is also that of the center for cushioning their impact on the poor;
- The food subsidy and central and centrally-sponsored programmes for poverty alleviation, employment generation and basic needs are especially relevant because they are sizeable and have a nation-wide impact; and
- Practical constraints have operated to confine most of the discussion to the central level although the states have a much larger share in social expenditure; date in regard to the latter is less accessible in a timely and sufficiently desegregated form; besides, wide variations among the states make it difficult to arrive at conclusions of general interst.

However, in a country where wide variations and disparities in income, expenditure, development—both economic and human, political commitment are apparent, distinctive policy and specific programme focus become more essential and sensible. Furthermore, most of the social sector comes under the State list and the share of states' expenditure on social sector is more than that of the Union Government. That is the state share is more than 76%. Guhan has acknowledged this fact.

Finally, state level studies are of interest in so far as the states are distinct political and administrative units, ruled by different political parties and leaders with different ideologies; different levels of administrative efficiency; and they have their own priorities, programmes, policies, schemes and expenditure decisions on social sectors.

In India, Tamil Nadu is a middle income state and ranks fourth according to CMIE composite index of development (1993). The state ranks first in terms of per capita income and sixth in terms of HDI indicators. According to the South India Human Development Report [2001], 'The development performance of the state is more impressive against social rather than economic indicators'. The Tamil Nadu state domestic product (SDP) at current prices increased from Rs. 7218.16 crores in 1980-81 to Rs. 66133.82 crores in 1996-97 recording a nine-fold increase with an average annual growth rate of 15.14%. The average annual growth recorded a steady increase from 13.85% during the Sixth Plan to 14.78% during the Seventh Plan and further increase to 15.30% during the Eighth Plan.

However, the average annual growth rate at constant prices during the Sixth Plan period was 6% (Table 1). It went down to 4.94% during the Seventh Plan and again that went up to 6% during the Eighth Plan period with individual years showing marked differences. It is interesting to note that the extreme variations are noticeable during the different periods of study. On an average, the growth rate between 1980-81 and 1987-88 was 4%, which went up to 7.85% in the succeeding

TABLE I

Year	*AGR*
1981	—
1982	10.98
1983	-5.4
1984	5.41
1985	13.07
1986	3.97
1987	-0.86
1988	6.26
1989	8.49
1990	6.85
1991	8.22
1992	2.7
1993	4.9
1994	9.36
1995	9.54
1996	0.1
1997	5.94
1998	5.74
1999	—
2000	—

period (1988-89 -1990-91). Again it further declined to 5% during the next period 1991-92 to 1996. Subsequently, it got recovered to 6% during the first two years i.e. 1997 and 1998. These figures test@ the popular opinion on the financial and administrative ability of the then leadership. This nature of the development experiences of Tamit Nadu has certain implications on social sector development. As a whole, Tamil Nadu is well-known for its social sector schemes in general and social security schemes in particular during the study period.

Tamil Nadu State Planning Commission's Ninth Five-year Plan (1997-2000) has adopted the strategy to attain the social sector objectives. The plan aims at achieving a growth rate of 7% during the plan period. Having declared that 'human development as a means to growth will receive priority attention' the Plan spells out explicitly, the following objectives to be adopted towards the social sector.

- To improve the living conditions of the people and provision of basic minimum services like drinking water, road connectivity, elementary education, health care, nutrition, housing and public distribution system for essential commodities.
- Emphasis on poverty alleviation through well targeted programmes.
- Effective implementation of safety net programme for disadvantaged sections of the society.
- To decentralise the planning process by assigning a key role to rural and urban local bodies in local level planning.

In addition to these, strategies, education, health, rural development, basic minimum needs like 100% coverage of safe drinking water, and primary education, literacy and housing assistance to all shelterless poor families, improvement of nutritional status; decentralised planning; social welfare, Ad-dravidar and Tribal welfare, and the welfare of Other Backward Classes have been declared as priority and thrust areas. To achieve these social sector objectives, the Ninth Plan has allocated 44.12% of its total outlay. This is a more than two-fold increase from the First Plan allocation (Table 2)

TABLE 2

Sectoral Composition of the Plan Outlay in Tamil Nadu: 1951-2002

Sector	*First Plan* 1951-56	*Second Plan* 1956-61	*Third Plan* 1961-66	*Annual Plan* 1966-69	*Forth Plan* 1969-74	*Fifth Plan* 1975-79	*Sixth Plan* 1980-85	*Seventh Plan* 1985-90	*Eighth Plan* 1992-97	*Ninth Plan* 1997-2002
Agriculture & Allied activities	12	17.3	23.1	26.1	20	15	21.2	12.2	10.04	10.41
Social and Community Services	20	20.2	23.1	19.7	25.6	25.2	33.5	36	41.9	44.12
Irrigation	25	9.3	9	4.8	4.4	6.4	4	5.7	5.74	5.56
Power	37.7	42.2	34.4	39.1	38.2	35	26.3	35	29.56	24.08
Industry & Minerals	1.9	7.5	6.8	6.2	5.9	6.3	6.6	5	5.39	5.23
Transport & Communication	3.4	2.9	3.4	3.9	5.5	11.3	7.5	4.8	6.93	10.04
Others	0	0.6	0.2	0.2	0.4	0.8	0.9	1.3	0.44	0.56
Total	100	100	100	100	100	100	100	100	100	100

The total expenditure in nominal terms has increased around eighteen-fold from 1980-81 to 1999-2000. In terms of the proportion of the combined state's expenditure, the share of total social sector expenditure, both revenue and capital account put together, increased from 27.26% in 1980-81 to a peak of 40.46% in 1988-89. During the period 1988-91, total social sector expenditure steadily increased from 8.96 to 10.31%. The ratio of social sector expenditure in Net State Domestic Product (NSDP) ten-ns started a steady declining trend from its peak (10.31%) to the level of 7.94% during the five years (1991-96). However, the growth rate again started a steady increasing trend and reached 10.02% in 1999-2000.

It is easy to ascribe the marked downward trend of social sector expenditures during the five years (1985-90) prior to the New Economic Policies. However, the reversal of the trend during the post-reform period, clearly shows the political will and commitment of particular governance. Similar trend in other indicators also helps to strengthen this view.

Table 3 also presents the revenue and capital expenditure trends in Tamil Nadu. The proportion of capital expenditure, being below one percent, has not been significant enough during the entire period (1980-2000). The share of revenue expenditure presents some clear trend. The revenue expenditure of the state in nominal terms has increased sixteen times during the reference period. However, social sector expenditure on revenue account has increased eighteen times. In NSDP terms, the revenue expenditure of the state has increased from around 15% to 23%. The proportion of social sector expenditure in SDP terms was 8.03% during the pre-reform period and 8.61% during the post-reform period. However, the above increase may not be attributed to economic reforms as such. In terms of political regimes, the proportion was 7.54% during the period of 1980-88 and it has steadily increased from 7.54% to 10.12% during the next 3 years. Again, the downward trend was set in during the subsequent period, the proportion gradually declined from the peak of 10.12% to 7.55%. It is interesting to note that since 1996 there has been a gradual increase from the low of 7.55% to 9.71%.

TABLE 3

Social Sector Expenditure in Tamil Nadu: 1980-2000

Year	*1981*	*1982*	*1983*	*1984*	*1985*	*1986*	*1987*	*1988*	*1989*	*1990*	*1991*	*1992*	*1993*	*1994*	*1995*	*1996*	*1997*	*1998*	*1999*	*2000*
Sector																				
a. Social Sector (R.A.)	43256	53171	71082	83866	88372	110488	117220	160376	179085	220059	279851	301396	329165	376508	416354	435044	552030	614522	700752	786729
Social Sector (2.C.A.)	1973	3286	3111	3553	3328	2257	2700	2951	3829	4378	5204	9451	9094	9068	10786	22983	23853	24723	17216	25308
Total (1+2)	45229	56457	74193	87419	91700	112743	119920	163327	182914	224437	285055	310847	338259	385576	427140	458027	57588	639245	717968	812037
1 as % of revenue expenditure	38.44	39.1	45.1	43.89	39.98	45.1	42.23	47.52	47.59	46.52	49.61	34.72	42.92	45.36	43.21	39.87	42.25	41.1	38.83	42.53
1 as % of NSDP	5.99	6.13	8.06	8.2	7.35	8.08	7.66	8.83	8.77	9.19	10.12	9.26	8.69	8.17	7.84	7.55	8.35	8.68	9.25	9.71
2 as % of capital expenditure	3.7	5.09	4.35	4.22	4.5	2.63	3.23	3.81	5.05	4.7	5.31	10.27	7.54	6.96	6	14.18	13.23	10.38	7.77	10.28
2 as % of NSDP	0.27	0.38	0.35	0.35	0.28	0.16	0.18	0.16	0.19	0.18	0.19	0.29	0.24	0.2	0.2	0.4	0.36	0.35	0.23	0.31
3 as % of toal expenditure (R.A. + C.A.)	27.26	28.15	32.37	31.76	31.08	34.07	33.2	39.37	40.46	39.64	43.05	32.38	38.11	40.15	37.36	36.35	38.73	36.88	35.43	38.74
3 as % of NSDP	6.27	6.51	8.41	8.55	7.62	8.24	7.84	8.99	8.96	9.38	10.31	9.55	8.93	8.36	8.04	7.94	8.71	9.03	9.46	10.02

The distribution of total social sector expenditure among the major heads in NSDP terms is presented in Table 4. Around fifty percent is spent on education, 25 percent on health and the rest on housing, social security and others.

Different political parties ruled the Tamil Nadu both during the pre-form and post-reform period. The change in policies has not brought about any significant difference in the quantum of social sector expenditures, whereas the change in governments have certainly made some significant changes in the social sector expenditures.

More increase in budget resources alone may not bring about changes in social sector and improvement in human development. Meticulous care is necessary to revamp the delivery mechanism and administrative structures for several programme to make them more responsive to the targeted group. Leakages and malpractices have to be curbed and coverage has to be extended. While the increased public expenditure plays an important role in the social sector, the former depends purely on the decisive role and strong political will of the ruling party as well as its leadership.

Tamil Nadu in general is well-known for its social sector schemes. The government has implemented several innovative social sector schemes and some of the schemes were implemented at the national level (Guhan, 1995). They are :

1. *Moovalur Ramamritham Ammaiyar Ninaivu Thirumana Nidhi Udhavi Thittam.* (Marriage Financial Assistance Scheme in memory of Moovalur Ramamritham Ammaiyar).
2. *Dr. Muthulakshmi Reddy Ninaivu Thirumana Mahapperu Nidhi Udhavi Thittam.* (Marriage and Maternity Financial Assistance Scheme in memory of Dr. Muthulakshmi Reddy).
3. Old-age Pension Scheme.
4. Tamil Nadu Integrated Nutrition Project.
5. *Periyar Ninaivu Samathuvapuram* (Equality Village in Memory of Pedyar).
6. *Namakku Naamea Thirram* (Self-Help Scheme).
7. *Anna Marumalarchi Thittam* (Anna Renaissance Scheme).

TABLE 4

Revenue Expenditure on Social Sector in Tamil Nadu

Year	1981	1982	1983	1984	1985	1986	1987	1988	1989	1990
1. Education	23816	26870	34505	38116	44546	56036	60636	69357	78632	106356
2. Health	10480	14774	18293	26501	21897	26314	28303	44131	44330	61351
3. Housing	1196	1701	3458	1246	3063	2872	5428	4193	5184	5506
4. Social Security	6419	8173	13435	13021	14639	17838	20396	22285	26642	29172
5. Others	1345	1653	1391	4982	4227	7426	2457	20410	24297	17674
6. Total	13256	53171	71082	83866	88372	110486	117220	160376	179085	220059
As % of Total										
Education	55.06	5054	48.54	45.45	50.41	50.72	51.73	43.25	43.91	48.33
Health	24.23	27.79	25.74	31.6	24.78	23.82	24.15	27.52	24.75	27.88
Housing	2.76	3.2	4.86	1.49	3.47	2.6	4.63	2.61	2.89	2.5
Social Security	14.84	15.37	18.9	15.53	16.57	16.15	17.4	13.9	14.88	13.26
Others	3.11	3.11	1.96	5.94	4.78	6.72	2.1	12.73	13.57	18.03
As % of NSDP										
Education	3.3	3.1	3.91	3.73	3.7	4.1	3.96	3.82	3.85	4.44
Health	1.45	1.7	2.07	2.59	1.82	1.92	1.85	2.43	2.17	2.56
Housing	0.17	0.2	0.39	0.12	0.25	0.21	0.35	0.23	0.25	0.23
Social Security	0.89	0.94	1.52	1.27	1.22	1.3	1.33	1.23	1.3	1.22
Others	0.19	0.19	0.16	0.49	0.35	0.54	0.16	1.12	1.19	0.74
6 as % of NSDP	5.99	6.13	8.06	8.2	7.35	8.08	7.66	8.83	8.77	9.19

Year	1991	1992	1993	1994	1995	1996	1997	1998	1999	2000
1. Education	128388	133874	150143	180200	192034	218059	248536	289316	351666	411024
2. Health	75367	88441	94722	106154	97519	98932	147516	60591	171852	180119
3. Housing	7667	10626	12038	7294	9494	10890	14157	10666	10929	16531
4. Social Security	31608	34063	38513	44673	50705	32021	69071	78612	97996	111413
5. Others	36821	34392	33749	38187	66602	45142	72750	75337	68309	67642
6. Total	279857	301396	329165	376508	416354	435044	552030	614522	700752	786729
As % of Total										
Education	45.88	44.42	44.61	47.86	46.12	50.12	45.02	47.08	50.18	52.24
Health	26.93	29.34	28.78	28.19	23.42	22.74	26.72	26.13	24.52	22.89
Housing	2.74	3.53	3.66	1.94	2.28	2.5	2.56	1.74	1.56	2.1
Social Security	11.29	14.3	11.7	11.87	12.18	14.26	12.51	12.79	13.98	14.16
Others	13.16	11.41	10.25	10.14	16	10.38	13.18	12.26	9.75	8.6
As % of NSDP										
Education	4.64	4.11	3.97	3.91	3.61	3.78	3.76	4.09	4.64	5.07
Health	2.73	2.72	2.5	2.3	1.84	1.72	2.23	2.27	2.27	2.22
Housing	0.28	0.33	0.32	0.16	0.18	0.19	0.21	0.15	0.14	0.2
Social Security	1.14	1.05	1.02	0.97	0.95	1.08	1.04	1.11	1.29	1.38
Others	1.33	1.06	0.89	0.83	1.25	0.78	1.01	1.06	0.9	0.83
6 as % of NSDP	10.12	9.26	8.69	8.17	7.84	7.55	8.35	8.68	9.25	9.71

8. *Uzhavar Santhai* (Farmer's Market).

The above schemes are evidences that the Tamil Nadu government has been implementing the several social sector schemes to improve the living standards of the weaker section in Tamil Nadu. The level of success that these schemes have achieved is evident from the widespread acceptance and appreciation they received from the general public in Tamil Nadu.

CONCLUSION

Tamil Nadu Experiences in social sector development may differ from that of other states such as Orissa or Bihar. Therefore, the recognition of such diversities should be the basis to formulate policies at the Union Government level. Uniform policies or schemes that have been framed by bureaucrats in New Delhi may not reach the people of Kannyakumari or Kottaiyam. Even if it reached, how effective the implementation, targeting and monitoring shall be? Who will account for whom? What will be the quality? There are several questions like these and the list of goes on without any answers.

Moreover, the size of the Indian states in terms of area and population is equivalent to that of many European countries. Liberalisation has reduced the degree of control exercised by the Union Government in many ways leaving much greater scope for state level initiatives. Analysis and understanding of the policies and performance of states may help us to formulate the strategy for other states. However, State level performance and policies have not received the attention that they deserve (Montek S. Ahluwalia, 2000).

Hence, the Union Government, instead of formulating its own schemes and spending on uniform programme throughout India without taking into account of the inter-regional and intra-regional variations, diverse aspirations regarding the quantity and quality of a particular service, the Union Government can make conditional transfers directly to sub-national governments which are nearer to the people to whom the services are meant. In a similar way, the state governments also should come forward to decentralise powers, functions and funds at the district and village level. In other words, to achieve the social sector development the process to be undertaken on the basis of 73 Amendments instead of concentrating the power either at the centre or state level. In such cases the quality of a particular social service can be tailored to meet the needs and preferences and evidences shows that quality of such service dramatically improves when local government implement the programmes.

References

Ahluwalia, Montek S. (2000), 'Economic Performance of States in Post-Reform Period, *Economic and Political Weekly*, May 6-12.

Berg, A. (1987), Malnutrition: What can be done? Lessons from the World Bank Experience, Baltimore, Johns Hopkins Press.

Chelliah, Raja J. (1999), 'Economic Reform Strategy for the Next Decade', *Economic and Political Weekly*, September 4.

Guhan, S. (1995), 'Social Security for the Poor in the Unorganised Sector : A Feasible Blueprint for India' in Kirth S. Parikh and R. Sudharshan, *Human Development arid Structural Adjustment*, Macmillan, Madras.

Guhan, S. (1995), 'Social Sector Expenditure in the Union Budget : 1991-96', *Economic and Political Weekly*, May 6-13.

Norgaard, R.B. (1999), 'Beyond Growth and Globalisation', *Economic and Political Weekly*, September 4.

Parikh, Kirit S. (1999), India Development Report, 1999-2000, Oxford University Press, New Delhi.

Sen, Amartya and J. Dreze (1997), India Development: Selected Regional Perspectives, Oxford University Press, New Delhi.

Streeton, Paul in UNDP (1999), Human Development Report, 1999, Oxford University Press, New Delhi.

26

CHAPTER

Public Expenditure and Social Sector Development in Tamil Nadu

REKHA JAGANATHAN

Social sector development is the touch-stone of success of any Government for it translates economic growth into development by improvement of quality of life of the people. The Govermnent is the harbinger of social sector development through public expenditure. The welfare objectives of the State are better suited to execute social sector development than private sector motivated by self-interest. With federal structure of Governance, State government is allotted with the responsibility of developing social sector. Most of the social sector development programs are funded and executed by the state Government. There are schemes funded partially or wholly by the Government of India but executed by the State government. Several schemes are also funded or collaborated by international bodies. This study concentrates on the expenditure of the state government of Tamil Nadu on social sector. The indicators taken for social sector development are: (a) Extension of minor irritation, (b) Nutrition, (c) Health facilities, (d) Provision of education, (e) rural electrification, (f) Provision of drinking water, and (g) Road length.

Tamil Nadu economy has made strides in State

Domestic Product between 1983-84 and 1994-95 when the state's income grew by more than 4% unlike several other states during the period. It was also a great change over its dismal. Growth rate of less than 1% in the previous decade. But in the 1990s fiscal deficit has increased. Revenue expenditure in all areas has risen by abominable rates. This paper is concerned about social sector expenditure from this angle too.

Tamil Nadu's total expenditure and expenditure on social sector are given in Table 1. Further, a disintegrated picture of social expenditure into revenue and capital expenditure is also given to measure the progressiveness of social sector expenditure. It is observed that the social sector expenditure is rising slowly.

On the *revenue account,* state spending has risen from Rs. 3586.1 crores in 1993-94 to Rs. 5613.4 crores in 1997-98. It has risen to an impressive extent in 2000-2001 to Rs. 81604 crores.

Out of the above amount, medical and health expenditure has risen from Rs. 549.1 crores in 1993-94 to Rs. 746.0 crores in 1997-98. There is a leap in public expenditure on this sector in 2000-2001 to Rs. 1056 crores. On nutrition it was Rs. 282.5 crores in 1993-94. It rose to 405.8 in 1997-98. In 2000-2001 it increased marginally to Rs. 581.2 crores.

Expenditure on water supply and sanitation has declined through the time of analysis. During 1993-94 it was Rs. 327.7. In 1997-98 it declined to Rs. 218 crores. In 2000-2001 it further declined to Rs. 154.6 crores.

On energy the allotment of the state has always been low. It has also declined through time. In 1993-94 it was Rs. 4.6 crores. In 1997-98 it was Rs. 1.2 crores. In 2000-2001 there was a marginal rise to Rs. 2.8 crores.

On transport and communication the state has allotted relatively higher amount than the other items of revenue expenditure. In 1993-94 the State spent Rs. 238.4 crores for this sector. The amount remains stable around the same figure throughout the 1990s. It was Rs. 239.8 crores in 2000-2001.

On rural development the State allots much more than on education and health. But the allotment has declined from

TABLE I

Social Sector Revenue Expenditure of the Government of Tamil Nadu

(Rs. in crores)

Year	*Social Services total*	*Minor Irrigation*	*Health and Medical*	*Education*	*Water and Sanitary*	*Transport and Communication*	*Rural Development*	*Energy*
1993-94	3586.1	—	549.1	45.8	327.7	238.4	419.2	4.6
1994-95	3847.6	—	610	46.2	287.4	252.2	315.9	4.2
1995-96	4332.9	46.0	575.8	53.9	244.1	302.5	327.3	4.8
1996-97	5121.4	41.8	670	86.4	324.1	353.4	398.9	2.5
1997-99	5613.4	51	746	74.6	218.0	397.7	531.8	1.2
1998-99	7101.3	67.5	908.2	81.7	263.3	339	566.6	1.2
1999-00	7626.9	55.3	945.2	128.2	256.7	300.7	542.3	2,3
2000-01	8160.4	45.3	1056.2	103.6	154.6	239.8	552.8	2.8

Social Sector Capital Expenditure of the Government of Tamil Nadu

(Rs. in crores)

Year	*Social Services total*	*Minor Irrigation*	*Health and Medical*	*Education*	*Water and Sanitary*	*Transport and Communication*	*Rural Development*	*Energy*
1993-94	90.7	86.2	14.2	1.1	29.8	68.7	-	200.2
1994-95	107.6	91.0	24.1	1.6	21.8	1443.7	0.2	205.0
1995-96	229.4	68.5	14.3	1.4	18.1	171.4	0.4	-
1996-97	208.0	27.4	20.4	1.3	13.3	385.6	0.6	133.8
1997-98	246.9	66.2	39.4	2.0	14.1	393.7	0.4	574.3
1998-99	228.0	226.0	67.0	3.1	11.9	440.6	0.3	-57.5
1999-2000	288.9	499.6	76.8	2.5	55.4	470.7	0.4	-726
2000-2001	617.5	483.8	32.2	2.2	507.1	463.2	81.2	100

Rs. 419 crores in 1993-94 to 398.9 crores in 1996-97. The very next year it rises to Rs. 531.8 crores.There is a marginal rise in 2001 to Rs. 552 crores.

Thus it could be observed that there is a gradual rise in revenue expenditure of the state Government on social sector on the whole and decline in expenditure on some items of social sector. Capital expenditure on social service is Rs. 90.7 crores in 1993-94. It increases to Rs. 246.9 crores by 1997-98. In 2000-2001 it is Rs. 617.5 crores. Capital expenditure on medical and public health was Rs. 14.2 crores in 1993-94. It was Rs. 39.4 crores in 1997-98. In 1998-99 it was Rs. 670 crores. In 1999-2000 it was 76.8 crores. It falls the next year to Rs. 32.2 crores in 2000-2001. On water supply and sanitation the state spent Rs. 29.8 crores in 1993-94 in this account. It declined to Rs. 14.1 crores in 1997-98. The next year there is a sudden rise to Rs. 507.1 crores. Capital expenditure on education has been low and is also stable at that level through the period of analysis. It was Rs. 1.1 crores in 1993-94. In 1997-98 it was Rs. 2.0 crores. In 2000-2001, it was Rs. 2.2 crores. On energy the state spends more compared to the other areas. State expenditure on this area stood at Rs. 200.2 crores in 1993-94. It increased to Rs. 574.3 crores in 1997-98. But the allotment declined to Rs. 100 crores in 2001. On transport and conununication the allotment of the state Government was Rs. 68.7 crores in 1993-94. State Government spending increased to 219.2 crores in 1997-98. There was a further rise to Rs. 463.2 crores during 2000-2001. Capital expenditure on rural development has been less during the 1990s compared to other areas. It was Rs. 0.2 crores in 1994-95. It was Rs. 0.4 crores in 1997-98. But it has risen to Rs. 81.2 crores in 2000-2001.

Observation of the data during the period as above shows clearly that overall expenditure on social sector is increasing gradually in both revenue account as well as capital account. But there is very big rise on the revenue account compared to capital account in all the items. This unhealthy fiscal trend is observed in Tamil Nadu like in several other states. It is also a matter of concern that the gap between the expenses on both the accounts is widening over the years. It indicates asset creation in all the areas is very low compared to the administrative expenditure. It makes public expenditure a burden on the Government making sustainable economic development difficult as future budgets of the state are normally expected to cut further on social sector spending to reduce the fiscal deficit, as the easy way out.

With the allocation as above, by the state, several changes were brought about in the social indicator of the state. The plight of the small and marginal farmers largely depends on water supply as on finance. In this direction *minor irrigation* has played a major role in the State. Tamil Nadu has the largest number of wells in the country. During the 1990s the number of wells increased marginally. In 1995-96 there were 16,90,936 wells. This was a small rise compared to their number in 1989-90 which was 16,57,905. The number of canals remained stable during the period of analysis. It was 2290 in 1989-90. There were 2322 canals in 1996-97. Total cropped area has declined during the period. It was 68.2 lakh hectares in 1989-90. In 1995-96 it declined to 62.7 lakh hectares. But the area under minor irrigation has increased from 35.81% of the cropped area in 1989-90 to 41.3% of the cropped area.

Health Facilities

Number of hospitals in the state has increased from 267 in 1989 to 382 in 1996-97. The number of dispensaries during the same time has declined from 884 to 313. It is also a good trend that the number of patients per hospital has declined from 209925 to 152592. But the number of people per dispensary has decreased during the same time from 63405 to 186230. Number of beds has increased marginally from 44901 to 47638 between 1989-90 and 1996-97. The population covered per medical institution is 5880 in 2000-2001. The number of people per bed is 1155 during the same year. The number of people per doctor is 6300 and the number of people per nurse is 3436. The health facilities compared to the other states places Tamil Nadu as a moderately developed state.

The state has noon meal program started in 1982 for providing nutrition to children between 2 years and 10 years. Initially it catered to 7 million children. It is the largest State sponsored program anywhere in the world. The state spends 45 paise per child and 5 paise on administration. Nutrition is distributed through 'Child Welfare Centres' and elementary schools. The success of health facilities is reflected in the following indicators. The Infant mortality rate (WM) is 58 now. It was 59 in 1989-90. Death rate is 8.2, it was 8.5 in 1989-90.

Birth rate is 19.2 now. It was 21 in 1989-90. Life expectancy at birth has risen from 60.85 in 1989-90 to 62.85 at present for males and 60.80 in 1989-90 to 63.05 for females at present.

Education

The number of primary schools in the state has risen from 29491 in 1989-90 to 30619 in 1996-97. During the same years, the number of middle schools has decreased marginally from 5651 to 5503. The number of high schools has increased from 4949 to 6308 during this period. Student enrolment for primary school has declined during the period from 5446096 to 4586276. For middle school it fell from 2997620 to 2571890. For high school and higher secondary schools enrolment increased from 3824452 to 5231561.

Average number of students per institution was 196 during the year 1999-2000 at primary. It was 583 at middle school and 408 at high school stage. At higher secondary stage the number of students per institution was 1009. The student-pupil ratio during 1999-2000 was fairly good at 35 for primary stage, 40 for middle school, 38 for high school and 35 for higher secondary school.

The success of the state in this direction is seen in its literacy level of 63.58%. It is higher than the literacy rate at the national level. Male literacy is at 74.28% and female literacy at 61.38%. It has a sex ratio of 972 showing good status of women in the state

Drinking Water

The number of villages having drinking water facility in 1989-90 was 72380 out of the total number of villages 75831. Now Tamil Nadu is one of the few states where all the 75831 villages have access to drinking water.

Rural Road Length

The total road length was 165734 Kilometers in 1989-90. It has increased to 174645 Kilometers in 1996-97. The proportion of rural road length out of the total road length was 61.9% in 1989-90. In 1996-97 it increased to 67.1%.

Rural Electrification

In 1989-90 out of the 75831 villages 75813 were electrified. In 1995-96 out of the then 76780 villages 75822 were electrified. Now all the villages of the state are electrified.

Success

There is increased social sector expenditure on both revenue and capital account indicating priority to the sector. It has achieved 100% electrification and drinking water access to the villages. Its demographic indicators—death rate, birth rate infant mortality rate and life expectancy are those of a developed state of India in terms of human development, compared to the other states. Good status of women is shown by the sex ratio. Employment is given to 1730 lakh people in regularly working factories. 99.25% of the villages are connected through villages. In terms of the number of hospitals the state stands 5th in ranking with 382 hospitals. With these achievements Tamil Nadu could be foreseen among the first five states in tens of human development in the next human development index of the states if the difficulties in its way are overcome successfully.

Challenges

Revenue expenditure of the state in this sector like in the other states is rising many times more than the capital expenditure. There is need to down size the Government and to apply the cannon of economy in reducing administrative expenditure. Capital expenditure particularly in education, transport and energy has to be stepped up. As the state is reeling under serious fiscal deficit, it has to generate funds from external and private sources. There is very slow growth and in very small proportion in all the indicators in the 1990s.

It is good that the number of hospitals is high. But the medical infrastructure has to be improved. There is one medical institution for 5880 people. The number of people per bed is 1155. There is just one doctor for 6300 people and one nurse for 3436 people. The quality of treatment in the hospitals therefore needs to be upgraded. Birth rate and death rate are certainly good by inter-regional comparison. But it has to reach the ideal birth rate of 15. Infant mortality rate of 58 is not the desirable rate. It exhibits need for improving prenatal and care of mother and child.

Literacy rate is better than the national standards and one among the best states by inter-regional comparison. Female literacy has to be improved. But there is a lot to be done to improve the standard of education.

Drop out rate is very high at all levels. It is marginally higher for females. 15% of the enrolled children drop out of primary schools. There is naturally highest drop out rate at high school level with boys taking up some job and girls being married off. About 35% of the enrolled children drop out at middle school level. It indicates several problems of the parents. Most important is poverty of the parents. More self-employment, wage employment and asset build in opportunities have to be generated by the state. There is need for awareness about the importance of education in improving the standard of living. There is also need to introduce more link between education and jobs.

There is also need for imparting elementary education through audio-visuals and during convenient time for the agricultural families as the most important occupation is agriculture. There is also need to introduce education computers. This could make education interesting to village folk through animation and games. There could be one computer per village. The state has 51 primary schools, 9 middle schools and 5 secondary schools for 1 lakh population. At the outset it seems there is need to increase the number of schools at all levels with more stress on primary schools. But this statement would be inconsistent when one looks at the number of schools not working in full capacity. The average student strength per institution is 196 at primary level, 583 at middle school level, 408 at high school level and 1009 at higher secondary level. At this juncture it would be appropriate to improve commutation facilities and also improve other infrastructure in these schools.

The total road length itself needs to be improved. Surface road length for every 10,000 population is 26.02 kilometers. There is also need to connect all villages with some kind of road. The existing roads also need to be upgraded as all weather roads.

When one observes the economy it reminds us of former finance minister Chidambaram's budget statement, "There is a lot that has been done and there is a lot that has to be done." Social development in Tamil Nadu qualifies the state as a moderately developed state when compared with other states. Its achievements are commendable in terms of health facilities, demographic indicators, rural electrification and potable water provision to rural areas. Revenue expenditure in the sector has to be reduced and capital expenditure has to be increased. Otherwise there will be cuts in social sector expenditure in future budgets of the state. There is a lot to be done in the area of transport and education. Moreover, all the social indicators have to be improved qualitatively. The shortage of funds has to be met by attracting Multinationals, Non-resident Indians and domestic Industrialists to invest in these areas. Political fluctuations and difficulties in governance are increasing the revenue expenditure. If these aspects are tackled on war footing, it should not be difficult for the state with such good agricultural record, industrial performance and hard working labour to reach the highest ranking among the states in the decades to come.

27

CHAPTER

Economic Growth and Decline of Poverty in the Post-Reform Period of Tamil Nadu

A. BARATHAN

INTRODUCTION

The performance of the Indian economy in recent years in terms of rate of growth of national income is remarkable. "Economic reforms initiated in 1991 would be the cause for such growth. The growth rate of GDP was very stagnant at the mean level of 3.5 per cent before 1980s and at 5.8 per cent during 1980-90 had jumped to 6.1 per cent in 1990-98" (R. Nagaraj, 2000: 2831)

The economic growth banishes the intensity of poverty and provides relief to the poor by offering various opportunities. Jagdish Bhawaty has pointed out "Growth helps to reduce poverty because of three central reasons . . . It creates jobs that 'pull up' the poor into gainful employment . . . It provides the revenues with which we can build more schools and provide more health facilities for the poor . . . It creates the incentives that enable the poor to access these facilities and also for the advancement of progressive social agendas . . . (Jagdish Bhagawaty, 2001: 844)

The inverse relationship between economic growth and decline in poverty level has been witnessed in Indian economy too.

"India's experience in the 1960s and most of the 70s showed that poverty reduction was negligible when per capita GDP growth was below 2 percent, but it began to decline when per capita growth accelerated to 3 per cent and more in the late seventies and eighties. Generalising from the experience one should expect that poverty reduction should have occurred . . ." (Montek S. Ahluwalia, 2000: 1640) However, there is a dispute about the tale of poverty reduction. Deepak Lal and others (2001: 1019) found that NSS (National Sample Survey) indicates the stagnation of poverty around 37-38 per cent throughout 1990s. Whereas NCAER's (National Council for Applied Economic Research) data reveal significant reduction of poverty along with higher economic growth in the 1990s.

That is the story of nation. What about the case of individual States? Ahluwalia feels that economic performance of the individual States in the post-reform period has received less attention. Liberalisation has reduced the degree of control exercised by the centre in many areas leaving much greater scope for the State level initiatives. This is particularly true as far as attracting investment, both domestic and foreign is concerned. Therefore, State level performance deserves more attention. This paper focuses the performance of the State of Tamil Nadu in post-reform period in the area of growth and poverty.

ISSUES OF THE STUDY

The growth rate of State Domestic Product (SDP) of Tamil Nadu, as observed by Montek Ahluwalia has been better during the reform period. For instance, the growth rate of SDP during 1991-92 to 1997-98 is 6.22 per cent as compared to 5.38 per cent in the period 1980-81 to 1990-91. Similarly, the poverty level is also considerably reduced in the State. The percentage of population in poverty has fallen from 43.39 per cent in 1987-88 to 35.03 per cent in 1993-94. The figures indicate that the growth rate improved as a result of economic reforms and the improved growth rate has reduced the poverty level.

The performance of Tamil Nadu economy during the post-reform period leads one to raise the following questions. Is the growth significant or not? Which sector contributes more for the growth? Has the growth really reduce the poverty level? This paper tries to examine these issues.

DATA SOURCES AND METHODOLOGY

This study mostly employs the National Accounts Statistics (NAS-State level) down loaded from the website wwwcircon india.com. Recently, a new series of NAS has been introduced with the base year 1993-94, replacing the earlier one with the base year 1980-81. However, similar revision has not yet been done for SDP at the State level. Hence, this work is done on the data which are based on 1980-81 as base year. Data on poverty and employment are collected from NSS, Economic Appraisal of Tamil Nadu—1994-95 and from articles.

In India the estimates of poverty have been done by two sources—NSS and Market Information Survey of Households (MISH) of NCAER1. The Planning Commission estimates the population below poverty line using the expenditure distribution of NSS. The estimates of poverty by Planning Commission, NCAER and K. Sundaram (2001) are used here to study the level of poverty in the State.

Linear growth model is used in analysing growth rate. Linear regression and correlation are employed to find out relationships of certain variables.

GROWTH OF THE STATE

The sectoral contribution to the growth in NSDP (Net State Domestic Product) of Tamil Nadu at constant prices (1980-81) is dealt with below. Table 1 provides estimated growth rates for NSDP and its main sectors between pre-reform (1980-81 to 1990-91) and post-reform (1991-92 to 1996-97) period.

From Table 1 we can understand that the growth rate of

TABLE 1

Growth Rate of Principal Sectors and NSDP

(per cent per annum)

Sector	*1980-81 to 1990-91*	*1991-92 to 1996-97*
Primary	8.9*	4.9NS
Secondary	1.82*	3.6*
Tertiary	4.42*	7.1*
NSDP	5.56*	9.91*

* Significant at 1% level.
NS—Not significant.
Source: National Accounts Statistics

NSDP is significantly increased in the post-reform period. It lauds the reforms are working well in the state. Though the primary sector is not performing well, the other two sectors namely secondary and tertiary are doing the job better in the state during the post-reform period.

GROWTH AND POVERTY

Since reforms are positively influencing the NSDP, we can expect the level of poverty would be reduced rapidly. This has been explained in Table 2.

TABLE 2

Percentage of Population below Poverty Line

Year	*MISH*	*Planning Commission*
1987-88	43.98	43.98
1993-94	24.63	35.03
1997-98	11.54	—

Source: Deepak Lal *et. al.*, (2001: 1021).

Table 2 shows that Tamil Nadu has experienced a decline in poverty over the 10 year period. Both MISH and Planning Commission data indicated the fact. However, MISH data show a faster decline than the Planning Commission data. This is due to methodological differences of the sources.

The problem of poverty must be analysed by taking rural-urban division into account. Then only one can understand the impact of growth on the reduction of poverty at different regions. Table 3 deals with the issue of rural-urban poverty.

TABLE 3

Percentage of Population below Poverty Line between Rural and Urban Sreas

Year	*MISH*		*Planning Commission*		*Sundaram*	
	Rural	*Urban*	*Rural*	*Urban*	*Rural*	*Urban*
1987-88	45.60	38.04	45.60	38.04	—	—
1993-94	26.30	21.66	32.48	39.77	37.27	37.83
1997-98	13.54	8.00	—	—	—	—
1999-2000	—	—	—	—	39.37	29.82
Mean	28.48	22.57	39.04	38.90	38.32	33.82
S.D.	16.14	15.04	9.27	1.22	1.48	5.66
C.V.	56.67	66.63	23.74	3.13	3.86	16.70

The data presented in Table 3 are inconsistent with each other. The calculated coefficient of variation shows that the data of Planning Commission and Sundaram are more consistent than MISH data. The average size of rural poverty is higher in all sources than urban poverty. Therefore, we can conclude that there is rural-urban divide in the process of growth of Tamil Nadu economy. The probable reason for more poverty in rural area is the poor performance of agriculture in the State. We know agricultural development and falling down of rural poverty are closely related.

To find out the inverse relationship between growth and poverty, the correlation coefficient has been worked out between per capita income of the State and the level of poverty as measured by MISH. The picture has been presented in Table 4.

TABLE 4

Relation between Growth and Poverty

Year	MISH	Per capita Income (1980-81 price)
1989-90	34.72	2235
1993-94	24.63	2410
1997-98	11.54	3220*

Correlation coefficient -0.99**

* Estimated.

** Significant at 1% level.

Source: Deepak Lal *et. al.*, (2001: 1021), Tamil Nadu—An Economic Appraisal (1994-95:5).

The correlation coefficient is -0 99. It significantly confirms the inverse relationship. It leads to draw a conclusion that the reforms initiated in Tamil Nadu produces prosperity to the State in terms of economic growth and poverty reduction.

TRENDS IN EMPLOYMENT

Reduction in poverty means increase in the scope of employment. When the level of poverty of the State has fallen one would expect the employment opportunities in the State to increase. To examine this fact, the growth trend of organised sector employment is discussed in Table 5.

TABLE 5

Growth Trend in Organised Sector Employment

(Annual Average Growth Rate in per cent)

Year	Public Sector	Private Sector	Total
1985-89	1.9	0.11	1.32
1990-94	1.02	1.95	1.31

Source: Tamil Nadu—An Economic Appraisal (1994-95: 155).

The annual average rate of growth for total employment has remained more or less same in the two periods. The private sector employment has accelerated from 0.11 per cent to 1.95 per cent in the post-reform period. However, the public sector employment has decelerated in the post-reform period. These accelerations and decelerations balanced the total growth rate.

The growth of employment can also be measured through elasticity of employment. Since output is a function of employment, the elasticity of employment to the output indicates the change in employment. Here, industrial output and employment in factor sector are taken as proxy to find out the elasticity. Table 6 reveals the employment elasticity.

TABLE 6

Employment Elasticity of Output in Factory Sector

Year	*Net Value Added (Rs. in Crores)*	*Employees (No. in Lakh)*
1980-81	1229	7.9
1985-86	2402	8.5
1990-91	5793	9.6
1994-95	11698	11.6

Employment elasticity 3.46*
Correlation coefficient 0.99.

Source: *Economic and Political Weekly*.

The employment elasticity shows that to produce 1 unit of output, 3.46 labourers are required. It means more labour is employed in the process of production. Thus in Tamil Nadu, the employment growth in relation to output is at a satisfactory level over a period of time. The correlation coefficient (0.99) also reveals a strong positive relationship between output and employment.

CONCLUSIONS

The domestic economy of Tamil Nadu has grown

significantly at the rate of 9.91 per cent during reform period as compared to 5.56 per cent before the reform period. Though the primary sector is not performing well, the other two sectors namely secondary and tertiary have done the job better.

The economic growth reduces the number of the people who live below the poverty line. However, the level of rural poverty is greater than urban poverty. This is due to the poor performance of primary sector.

It is found that, the growth of the State is associated with the growth of employment.

Note and Reference

1. MISH was started in 1985-86 by NCAER to estimate the size of market for a variety of consumer goods both durables and non-durables.

References

Deepak Lal *et al.*, (2001): "Economic Reforms and Poverty Alleviation", *Economic and Political Weekly*, Vol. XXXVI, No. 12, March 24-30.

Evaluation and Applied Research Department (1995): *Tamil Nadu: An Economic Appraisal, 1994-95*, Government of Tamil Nadu, Chennai.

Jagadish Bhagwati (2001): "Growth, Poverty and Reforms", *Economic and Political Weekly*, Vol. XXXVI, No. 10, March 10-16.

Montek S. Ahluwalia (2000): "Economic Performance of States in Post-Reforms Period", *Economic and Political Weekly*, Vol. XXXV, No. 19, May 6-12.

Nagaraj, R. (2000): "Indian Economy Since 1980—Virtuous Growth or Polarisation?" *Economic and Political Weekly*, Vol. XXXV, No. 32, August 5-11.

Sundaram, K. (2001) : "Employment and Poverty in 1990s", *Economic and Political Weekly*, Vol. XXXVI, No. 32, August 11-17.

Website—www.circon.india.com

SECTION VII

Economic Externalities

28

CHAPTER

Role of Leather Industry in the Economy of Tamil Nadu

P. MOHAMMED YOUSUF

India is naturally endowed with a large, domesticated animal population comprising cattle, buffaloes, sheep and goat. The last animal census indicates a cattle population of 220 million head count with buffalo standing at 94 million head count. The head count of sheep and goat are 58 million and 123 million respectively and our country has 15% of the world livestock head count. We have 56% of the buffalo, 16% of the cattle, 18% of the goat and 5.5% of the sheep population *vis-a-vis* the world. With the completion of the animal life cycle, the by-product, skin or hide of the animal had spawned the leather industry in India as in all part of the world.

Even though the tanneries in Tamil Nadu took root about one hundred and fifty to two hundred years ago, the bulk of the hides and skins that were available within the country were exported to the European continent in the salted or semi-tanned form. It was only as late as 1972 that the E.N. Murthy Committee suggested to the Planning Commission that valuable foreign exchange was being lost in this practice of exporting a quality raw material without sufficient value-addition. The shift from the traditional vegetable tannage was

TABLE 1

World Livestock Headcount Vis-à-vis India's Position

Livestock (Headcount)	*World 2001*	*India 2001*	*%age Share*
Buffalo	167,611,168	94,132,200	56.2
Cattle	1,360,136,890	219,642,000	16.1
Goat	693,456,713	123,000,000	17.7
Sheep	1,059,107,230	57,900,000	5.5
Total	3,280,312,001	494,674,200	15.1

Source: FAO.

TABLE 2

World Leather Production *vis-a-vis* India's Production

Leather Production (Kilograms)	*World 2001*	*India 2001*	*%age Share*
Buffalo	819,623,000	510,000,000	62.2
Cattle	7,329,153,000	466,000,000	6.4
Goat	823,225,000	128,340,000	15.6
Sheep	1,608,966,000	52,110,000	3.2
Total	10,580,697,000	1,156,450,000	10.9

Source: FAO.

made due to exigencies demanded by the end-product manufacturers. The new technology of tanning was effected using chromium salts that, by then, had become a universal practice and the "wet-blued" raw material became a world-wide industry standard. The early seventies saw the export of chrome-tanned skins but inevitably this export was shut down keeping in mind the value-addition desired by the E.N. Murthy Committee. The eighties saw the full-scale promotion of ready-in-use leathers for product manufactures and the Central Government had identified the leather industry as a "thrust" area.

TABLE 3

Small-Scale Tanneries in India

State	*Large and Medium Scale Tanneries*	*Small Scale Tanneries*	*Total Number of Tanneries*	*Percentage Share of SSI Tanneries*	*Percentage share of Tanneries in the State*
Tamil Nadu	58	775	833	93	52.5
West Bengal	11	350	361	97	22.7
Uttar Pradesh	9	179	188	95	11.8
Punjab	0	79	79	100	5.0
Maharashtra	3	30	33	91	2.1
Andhra Pradesh	5	19	24	79	1.5
Haryana	0	17	17	100	1.1
Bihar	0	17	17	100	1.1
Karnataka	1	15	16	94	1.0
Other States	0	20	20	100	1.3
Total	87	1501	1588	95	100

TABLE 4

Export of Leather and Leather Products from India

(in US$)

Category	*Period*		*Variation*
	April 1999-March 2000	*April 2000-March 2001*	*(in percentage)*
Finished Leather	239.82	381.86	59.23
Leather Footwear	377.39	384.47	1.88
Footwear Components	215.09	238.06	10.67
Leather Garments	347.28	460.55	32.62
Leather Goods	376.52	443.83	17.87
Saddlery & Harness	34.11	42.72	25.24
Non-Leather Footwear	14.12	19.50	38.09
Total	1,604.35	1,970.98	22.85

TABLE 4

Production Capacity of Leather and Leather Products from India *vis-a-vis* Tamil Nadu

Category	*Units Per Day*	*India*	*Tamil Nadu*	*%age share*
Leather	Pieces	681,388	517,854	76
Leather Footwear	Pairs	534,722	96,250	18
Footwear Components	Pairs	440,000	184,800	42
Leather Garments	Pieces	50,111	16,035	32
Leather Goods	Pieces	333,055	23,314	7

TABLE 5

Export of Leather and Leather Products from India *vis-a-vis* Tamil Nadu

Product	*Period 2000-2001*		*%age share of Tamil Nadu*
	India	*Tamil Nadu*	
Leather	17,445.16	10,248.24	58.7
Leather Footwear	17,564.16	7,255.53	41.3
Footwear Components	10,875.43	8,528.72	78.4
Leather Garments	21,040.01	6,099.47	29.0
Leather Goods	23,118.00	3,688.98	16.0
Total	90,042.76	35,820.94	39.8

TABLE 6

Share of States in Export of Leather and Leather Products

States	*%age Share*
Tamil Nadu	39.8
West Bengal	20.0
Uttar Pradesh	32.0
Delhi & Punjab	-
Maharashtra	5.0
Karnataka	3.2
Total	100

TABLE 7

World Trends in Leather Exports

(in million US$)

Details	*1995*	*1996*	*1997*	*1998*	*1999*
World Imports	70,167.12	74,743	75,927.67	70,374.47	68,243.88
Exports from China	9704.34	9993.42	11741.75	11246.65	11321.84
	(13.83)	(13.37)	(15.46)	(15.98)	(16.59)
Exports from Italy	12690.81	14163.31	12770.07	12100.31	10870.63
	(18.09)	(18.95)	(16.82)	(17.19)	(15.93)
Exports from Korea	3495.54	3152.18	2823.01	2188.39	2210.00
	(4.98)	(4.22)	(3.72)	(3.11)	(3.24)
Exports from Brazil	2089.75	2345.70	2361.17	2088.66	1984.37
	(2.98)	(3.14)	(3.11)	(2.97)	(2.91)
Exports from Indonesia	2191.18	2319.33	1624.27	1310.22	1702.10
	(3.12)	(3.10)	(2.14)	(1.86)	(2.49)
Exports from India	1762.97	1618.27	1671.90	1654.89	1604.35
	(2.51)	(2.17)	(2.20)	(2.35)	(2.35)
Exports from Thailand	2656.62	1844.28	1645.60	1312.32	1226.15
	(3.79)	(2.47)	(2.17)	(1.86)	(1.80)
Exports from Argentina	1130.92	1041.88	1152.28	927.18	832.48
	(1.61)	(1.39)	(1.52)	(1.32)	(1.22)
Exports from Mexico	470.32	582.21	705.38	697.79	719.89
	(0.67)	(0.78)	(0.93)	(0.99)	(1.05)
Exports from Turkey	629.54	547.59	680.35	606.65	476.29
	(0.90)	(0.73)	(0.90)	(0.86)	(0.70)
Exports from Bangladesh	214.97	179.11	152.87	145.07	N.A
	(0.31)	(0.24)	(0.20)	(0.20)	

Figures in Parentheses are share of respective countries in world imports

The leather industry grew by leaps and bounds over the last three decades with a remarkable shift from the traditional, conttage-type of unit to the modern and sophisticated industry producing products that were basically designed for and consumed by the developed countries. The demand for Indian leather and leather products in the developed countries spurred the forward-integration of tanneries with the product sector. Starting from a paltry Rs. 28 crore in 1956-57, India's exports of leather and leather products for the year ending

March 2001 was nearly Rs. 9,000 crore, fetching the country its valuable foreign exchange. It is one amongst the top 8 export earners for the country. The share in the export of leather and leather products from the state of Tamil Nadu is about 40% while the estimated share In the production capacity (*vis-a-vis* the country) for finished leather garments and goods at about 40%. The slides depicting the monetary share of the industry in Tamil Nadu *vis-a-vis* the rest of the country clearly indicates that we produce products with a much higher value than our brethren in the north, east and west. Take the case of footwear for example—even though the capacity in Tamil Nadu represents just 18% of the capacity of the whole country, the share of footwear in exports is 41%! Similarly, in footwear components, the installed capacity is 42% whereas the share in exports is close to 80%! In the fast-paced global competition that we witness today, it is the quality-product manufacturer who survives. The leather industry has left its indelible mark in the economy of Tamil Nadu. Further and in addition to this feather in the cap, its measure of importance could be gauged while looking at certain all-India industrial output data. The share of auto-components is 35% in Tamil Nadu; cotton yarn 32%; software stands at 42%; heavy commercial vehicles at 27%; software stands at 42%; heavy commercial vehicles at 27%; newsprint at 17% and whereas the share of leather and leather products is about 70%! It needs no further emphasis of the important position held and the role played by the leather industry in the economy and industrial development of Tamil Nadu.

The leather industry in India is predominantly in the small-scale sector and 95% of the tanneries fall under this category. The industry is a large employment provider with more than 5 million being directly and indirectly employed. The downstream product sector is employment-intensive and women occupy 80% of the jobs. A capital investment of Rs. 20,000 can create a job and not many industries can match this figure. Further, the ratio between the capital employed and the turnover value generated is at a level that is the envy of many an entrepreneur.

The decades of the seventies and eighties saw the growth of environmental consciousness on a global level. A summit was conducted by the World Commission on Environment and Development in the year 1972 at Stockholm. In 1987 an international conference was held with the theme "OUR COMMON FUTURE" in Norway and the BRUNDTLAND REPORT was adopted as the basis for the propagation of a new concept called SUSTAINABLE DEVELOPMENT. This was further elucidated by the famous EARTH SUMMIT of 1992. India was also a signatory to all these summits and hence the Department of Environment was opened by the Government of India as per the recommendation of the TIWARI COMMITTEE. The Tamil Nadu Pollution Control Board was formed in the year 1982. All the industries in our state were put on notice to instal proper pollution control devices that would safeguard the local environment. The leather industry in Tamil Nadu was the first to respond to this call. It negated the general idea that small-scale industries like tanneries can never stand up to fulfil this statute. Rather, they held many brain-storming sessions and came out with the concept of Common Effluent Treatment Plant (CETP). The year 1986 saw the amorphisation of the first CETP for tanneries in India and this was located at Vaniyambadi.

In this context and in the present scenario, the leather industry has in place 12 Common Effluent Treatment Plants (CETPs) for multiple plants for stand-alone tanneries all built at a cost of about Rs.120 crore in the state of Tamil Nadu. These effluent treatment plants are designed to comply with the standards set for discharge of treated industrial effluents into public water bodies except in the case of total dissolved solids. All the 734 operating tanneries in Tamil Nadu are either connected to CETPs or have their own, dedicated effluent treatment plants that are constantly monitored by the Tamil Nadu Pollution Control Board for compliance of parameters set for final discharge. In addition to these facilities, 12 more CETPs are under construction and once completed, would then permit the 167 closed tanneries to operate as per the orders of the Supreme Country in 1996.

Ongoing investments are being made in acquiring know-how from within and outside the country while implementing cleaner technologies at the process floor. The leather industry in Tamil Nadu signed a Memorandum of Understanding, at a cost of Rs. 4 crore, with the CSIR laboratories—the Central Leather Research Institute, Chennai and the National Environmental Engineering Research Institute, Nagpur—in which the former was to provide the tanneries with improved methods of leather processing that would wrest on the proven foundation of cleaner technologies. An offshoot of this effort was the formation of Waste Minimistation Circles (WMCs) that would promote inter-technical dissemination of clean, shop-floor practices. With regard to the expertise of the scientists of the NEERI, the plant managers and chemists were educated in the critical aspect of evaluating their respective CETPs/ETPs performance. Systematic monitoring of the individual units in the wastewater treatment plant/s helps the technical personnel in obtaining advance warnings of possibly upset conditions that may arise. These personnel have gained valuable inputs from the scientists and have proved their mettle in the field while working in this system personified by the 24-7-365 paradigms.

No efforts have been spared in acquiring additional technical expertise for the optimum operation of the wastewater treatment plants. The industry has appointed a full-time German expert under its umbrella organisation who has been deputed under the GTZ scheme of the German Government. His vast experience is being put to the best of use in the endeavour to optimize the performance of the existing wastewater treatment plants.

Through the office of the UNIDO's Regional Programme for Pollution Control in the Leather Industry in South East Asia, a number of European experts have visited the CETPs/ETPs in Tamil Nadu while providing their deep insights in the technical and administrative management of such entities. For an industry that was hardly aware of the concept of wastewater treatment more than a decade back, these edifices represent a tribute to environmental protection at the local level.

Delegations from the leather industry that visit other countries during the course of exploring markets for their products do not fail to keep abreast of the happening in the environmental front pertaining to wastewater treatment practices and technologies adopted in the developed countries. Today, it has become a practice for such teams and delegations to sell not only their wares abroad but also to look for technological advances and equipment related to wastewater treatment that would further augment the performance of their facilities.

The CETPs/ETPs operated by the tanning industry in Tamil Nadu spend a sum of Rs. 25 crore annually while maintaining these systems in order. And these costs have been rising with every passing year. The recent hike in electricity tariff alone would increase this expenditure by another Rs. 1 crore.

The tanning industry has already made a start in addressing the solid wastes generated by the tanneries. Solid wastes, predominantly, thrown out of the process of leather manufacture are organic in nature and are, therefore, biodegradable. This quality is conducive to the biomethanation of solid wastes and its conversion into useful methane gas has been demonstrated (currently being monitored by CLRI, Chennai and CTC, France) at one cluster in Melvisharam. Replication and implementation in other areas are expected to follow after a "due diligence" of the project is carried out.

The industry is tirelessly working out the ways and means to achieve the standard set for the Total Dissolved Solids in a way that will be feasible both technically and economically. The ultimate in the re-cycling and re-use of treated tannery effluents is contemplated with an industrial scale pilot-plant that is slated to be in place by the end 2002, using membrance filtration technology. The results from this project would provide the industry its future course of action. We are confident that this inexorable march of technology into the future would support us in a venture to turn every drop and ounce of waste into a valuable resource. And there would be no re-writing a history on this account.

We are confident that the inexorable march of technology into the future would support us in our venture to turn every drop and ounce of waste into a valuable resource. And there would be no re-writing of history on this account.

The growth potential of the leather industry in India is accentuated by the fact that the developed countries of the world have lost their competitiveness in certain sections and consumer areas. Countries like China, Thailand, Indonesia and India are filling the vacuum thus created. In this race for market capture, the Indian leather industry could pluck a prime place for itself if it is supported by the Central and State Governments on the multifarious issues pertaining to industrial and fiscal policies, infrastructure development and labour laws.

29

CHAPTER

Environmental Assessment of Industrial Effluent in River Cauvery

N. Rajalakshmi, D. Janagam, J. Sacratees and R. Annadurai

The term water pollution is referred to the addition of an excess material or heat, that is harmful to man, animals or aquatic life or otherwise causes significant changes from normal activities of various living communities in or near water bodies[1] (Dr. V.N. Naidu, 1992).

Water pollution is the mixing of objectionable material like water, inorganic impurities, etc. in the natural water bodies such river streams, lakes, wells, etc. According to our president knowledge the total water resources of the world amount to 26.6 trillion. Out of this 98.9% in seas, 1.077% is shared by polar and mountain ice and snow, 0.02% of water is bound in lithosphere i.e., in other words ground water, fresh water contribution is 0.002% and the rest of 0.001% is water vapor in our atmosphere. The term water pollution refers to any type of aquatic contamination between two extremes: (1) a highly enriched over productive biotic community such as river or lake with nutrients from sewage or fertilizers otherwise called as cultural eutrophication, and (2) a body of water poisoned by toxic chemicals which eliminate or devastated all forms of life.

Water found in different conditions in nature is not pure in the chemical sense, but natural waters are not regarded as polluted, impurities in traces are universal for water. Even the freshly falling rainwater is never nearing distilled. It contains measurable quantities of dissolved nutrients and other chemicals, which the rainwater gets from the atmospheric dust and nitrogen fixed due to lighting in the clouds. Rainwater pH is generally less than 7 while that of distilled water is 7. We get concerned about the quality of water, in its physical, chemical and/or biological characteristics or its quality deteriorates and becomes harmful to man, his domestic needs or other aquatic life or to a balanced functioning of the aquatic ecosystem. Such a situation is referred to an aquatic pollution. The physical aspects of water pollution may be in the form of change in: (i) the colour or the water leading to modification of light quality and quantity, (ii) the odour due to several factors leading to foul smell unfit for drinking, bathing and washing, (iii) temperature which may be harmful directly as a primary pollutant and indirectly through driving out the dissolved oxygen leading to death of fishes, (iv) turbidity which reduces light and dissolved oxygen, and (v) density of the water which changes with the change in temperature and causes upturning of water. The causes of chemical aquatic pollution are of numerous types such as the dissolved solids, suspended solids, hardness of water, acidity or alkalinity, pH changes, dissolved oxygen, carbon dioxide and other gases, metal ions like iron, copper, arsenic, manganese, lead, cadmium, mercury, sodium, potassium, calcium, magnesium, and other ions like sulphates, nitrates, phosphates, chloride, fluoride, silicate ammonium, etc. Soaps and detergents such alkyl benzene sulphonates are also pollutants organic chemical pollutants like sugars, starches, fats, proteins on decomposition cause pollution. A large variety of new synthetic chemical in form of pesticides and other non-biodegradable chemicals are also very harmful and have long lasting effects. Radioactive matters are also reaching water bodies and causing pollution. Further, there are a variety of aspects for the biological characteristics of pollution such as the presence and preponderance of harmful and disease causing bacteria (*Ibid.*).

TYPES OF WATER POLLUTION

The water pollution are of three types, namely, Physical Pollution, Chemical Pollution, Bacteriological Pollution.

STANDARD OF WATER QUALITY

The following standouts of quality of drinking water are based on U.S. Public Health Service Standards or World Health Organisation (WHO) recommendations.

Colour	10 to 2 ppm. Preferable; less than 10 ppm (Platinum cobalt scale)
Odour	0 to 4 P Value
Taste	No Objectionable Taste
Temperature	10 to 16C
Turbidity	5 to 10 ppm, Preferable; less than 5ppm (Silica scale)[2] (Marimuth & Balasubramanian)

PHYSICAL POLLUTION

They are due to the presence of inorganic substancel, like clay, pebbles, sand, silt, algae, fungi, bacteria, etc., in water in finely divided conditions. Lighter substances float, heavier substances settle and of equal specific gravity mix with water (Marimuthu & Padmini). Factors of Physical pollution are colour, foam, taste and odour, temperature, turbidity, radioactivity and suspended matter.

Chemical Pollution: They may either organic or inorganic. They may be present in their suspended or dissolved form. Pollution is due to Organic Chemicals. It is caused by the presence of fats, proteins, carbohydrates and other organic substances. Organic chemicals are of two forms: (a) Suspended Organic Substances; and (b) Dissolved Organic Substances.

(a) Suspended Organic Substances

This is due to the presence of certain industrial wastes, vegetables or animals. Vegetables are algae, decayed leaves, fungi, etc. They impact acidity, colour and taste of water.

Animals are insects, dead animals, etc. They grow bacteria in water. They contain large quantity of albuminoidal ammonia, small quantity of free ammonia and chlorides. Such waters are dangerous as they contain bacteria.

(b) Dissolved Organic Substances

This is due to the presence of certain industrial wastes or due to decay of vegetables and animals. They contain large quantities of albuminoidal ammonia, free ammonia and chlorides. Such water may contain pathogens. Hence, it is highly dangerous to public-to-public health.

POLLUTION DUE TO INORGANIC CHEMICALS

Inorganic or mineral pollution of water is of five forms:

Acids
Alkalies
Toxic inorganic compounds
Dissolved inorganic substances
Suspended inorganic substances

CHEMICAL CHARACTERISTICS OF WATER QUALITY

1.	Arsenic	0.65 ppm. (maximum)
2.	Alkalinity (carbonate)	120 ppm.
3.	B.O.D.	Nil
4.	Chlorides	250 ppm. (maximum)
5.	Copper	1 to 3 ppm.
6.	Dissolved Oxygen	5 to 6 ppm.
7.	Fluorides	1.5 ppm. (maximum)
8.	Hardness	75 to 115 ppm. (Hardness as carbonate equivalent)
9.	Hexavalent Chromium	0.05 ppm (maximum)
10.	Iron and manganese	0.3 ppm (maximum)
11.	Lead	0.1 ppm (maximum)
12.	Magnesium	125 ppm (maximum)
13.	Nitrite nitrogen	Nil
14.	Nitrate nitrogen	45 ppm (maximum)
15.	Organic nitrogen	0.3 ppm (maximum)

16.	Oxygen absorbed	3 ppm (maximum)
17.	pH Value	6.5 to 8.5
18.	Phenolic compounds in terms of Phenol	0.001 ppm (maximum)
19.	Residual Chlorine	0.05 to 0.2 ppm
20.	Sulphate	250
21.	Total solids	500 to 1000 ppm
	Preferable	Below 50 ppm[4] (*Ibid.*)

BACTERIOLOGICAL POLLUTION

The bacteriological pollution is caused in water by presence of bacteria. The bacteria may be harmful or harmless. Harmless bacteria are called non-pathogens. They are not dangerous. However, their presence is an indication of pathogens, which are otherwise known as disease producing bacteria. Pathogens are dangerous and are mainly responsible for waterborne diseases. Hence, such impurities are to be carefully identified and removed to avoid out-break of epidemics.

WATER POLLUTION AND HEALTH HAZARDOUS

Water pollution is significant only when it influences living systems directly or indirectly. Water is the most preponderant chemical found within any freely metabolizing cell and in bacterial cells the content ranges from 75.09 percent. Although pollution is produced by the activities of organisms (including man), it is recognized only when it adversely affects other living organisms, that is fish and killed algal growth is enhanced people contract a disease. Generally the reference point for identifying and assessing pollution is the impact it has on human interests. However, we have become sophisticated enough to realize that any thing which indirectly influences man's well-being is as important as man himself and that the pollution which ultimately influences man's well-being, although indirectly is also a matter of survival[5] (P.C. Mishra).

Water as a part of the human environment, occurs in four main forms as, groundwater, in fresh water surface masses, in the sea and a vapor in the atmosphere human health may be affected by ingesting water directly or in food, by using it is personal hygiene or for agriculture, industry or recreation and by living near it. Two main categories of water associated health hazards deserve consideration. Hazards from biological agent that may affect man following ingestion of water or other forms of water contact, or through insect vectors and hazardous from chemical pollutants usually resulting from discharge of industrial wastes.

WATER RELATED DISEASES (CAUSATIVE ORGANISMS)

Group	*Causative Organism*	*Disease or Symptom*
Viruses	Rota virus	Vomiting, diarrhea,
	Potio virus	Potiomyelitis, Fever,
	Entero virus	Diaarrhea, Respiratory Disease, Meningitis
Bacteria	Hepatitis A	Infections hepatitis
	Salmonella typhi	Typhoid fever
	Shigella spp	Bacillary dysentery
	Vibro Cholerae	Cholera
	Escherichia coli	Gastro anterites
	Leptospira ictero Hemorrhage	Well's syndrome
Protozoa	FntAMOWH hiarolytic	Amoethic dysentery
	Garida Lambia	Malabsorption, diarrhoea
Helminthes	Disphyllobothrium latum	Tapeworm infection
	Faciolopsis busket	Infection of small intestine
	Schistosoma mansoni	Bill harzia
	Schistosoma haematihium	(lonorchiasts) (trematode
	Colorchis sinensis	infection)
	Dracumculus Medinensis	Guinea worm.[3]

POLLUTION OF RIVER CAUVERY

Cauvery the lifetime of Tamil Nadu is the 8th largest river in the country originating 1355 meter above the mean sea level in the western giants (Sahyadris) at Talaikaveri in Brahmagiri hills Karnataka. With a running cause of 765 kms the river joins the sea at Poompuhar in Tamil Nadu. The river

TABLE I

Details of the Population in the Cauvery Basin Industries in Tamil Nadu

Sl. No.	*District*	*Population of the district*	*Rural*	*Urban*
1.	Cuddalore & Villupuram	42,01,869	4,53,664	98,979
2.	Dharmapuri	19,97,060	9,04,302	1,06,430
3.	Salem	34,41,717	21,23,860	3,64,954
4.	Coimbatore	30,60,184	11,69,884	12,98,226
5.	Periyar	20,68,462	16,13,194	4,55,268
6.	Trichy	36,12,320	15,43,618	2,45,268
7.	Pudukkottai	11,56,813	69,144	5,140
8.	Thanjavur	40,63,545	26,19,879	5,48,052
9.	Anna	15,64,825	9,00,109	2,68,712
10.	Nilgiris	6,30,169	2,76,454	2,62,368
	Cauvery Basin	1,58,19,907	1,16,66,108	41,53,798
	Tamil Nadu	4,84,08,077	3,24,26,202	1,59,51,875

Source: Danida, Studies for the Environment of river Cauvery and Vaigai in Tamil Nadu, p.13.

is polluted when it passes through major urban areas. Industrial establishments at Mettur, Pallipalayam discharge all types of effluents to the extent of 5082 lakh LPD. Sago mills, engineering industry, water tanneries, distilleries, pulp, paper, fertilizer, viscose and rayon wastes are the chief pollutants in the river Cauvery.

In Tamil Nadu we have observed the cauvery water from Pallipalayam and Musiri. It is observed that 90 to 95% of the water flow is purpose fully utilized and it is one of the best-regulated rivers in the country. There are 1139 industries comprise major, medium and small scale sited in the Cauvery basin.

The Cauvery cuts across the center of Tamil Nadu and is fed by both the monsoons. The Cauvery delta consists of gently sloping alluvial plan covering an area of 11,600 sq. km.

There are 51 towns located on the banks of the river Cauvery and its tributaries and distributors. These towns draw water from the rivers for all beneficial purposes and discharge them back into the river. It is found that these towns are not sewered. Hence, the wastewater passes through open drains and ultimately joins the river. A few municipalities which are on the banks of the river use treated water and apart of the untreated wastewater for raising guinea grass. Still a part of the waste joins the river.

Tamil Nadu Pollution Control Board has recently made a survey of the types of industries located in the Cauvery Basin. A total of some 1100 registered industries are located in the basin. To estimate that a total of 16,200 m(3)/day of effluent is discharged from the factories within the basin, out of which a total of approximately 87,000 m(3)/day is discharged directly into the cauvery river or its main tributaries[6] (Danida).

TABLE 2

Water Consumed and Waste Water Discharged

Sl. No.	*District*	*Total Quality of Water Consumption (in Kilo Litres)*	*Total Quantity of Waste Water Discharged*
1.	Dharmapuri	5893	3704
2.	Nilgiris	17015	11585
3.	Coimbatore	9970	5773
4.	Periyar	5292	4865
5.	Salem	101686	63996
6.	Anna	8805	8061
7.	Trichy	102294	57664
8.	Pudukkottai	533	265
9.	Thanjavur	5895	6137
10.	South Arcot & Villupuram	-	-
	Total	2,57,391	1,62,051

Source: *Ibid*., p. 14.

Tables 1 and 2 represents the volume of water consumed by the industrial towns and the volume of the wastewater discharged into the river Cauvery.

TABLE 3

Water Quality Report in Terms of Annual Mean Values
Location: Cauvery at Pallipalayam, Tamil Nadu

Year	*1986*	*1987*	*1988*
Temperature	30.1	30.1	31.5
pH	7.9	8.1	8.0
Total Alkalinity (mg/1)	176	190	181
d.o. (mg/1)	6.3	6.1	6.0
b.o.d. (mg/1)	2.6	2.8	2.9
c.o.d (mg/1)	25.3	26.8	20.9
Nitrites Nitrates (mg/1)	0.006	0.019	1.659
Total Kjeldhal Nitrogen (mg/1)	0.763	0.346	1.659
Chlorides (mg/1)	65	55	63
Sulphates (mg/1)	25	26	27
Sodium (mg/1)	28	49	48
Hardness Caco3 (mg/1)	147	154	180
Fecal Coliform (MPN/1000ml)	58	1402	8.620
Total Coliform (MPN/100ml	276	2387	10.680

We have explained fourteen parameters, namely, temperature, hydrogen ion (pH), alkalinity, chlorides, dissolved oxygen, biological oxygen, chemical oxygen, nitrates, kjeldahl nitrogen, sulphates, sodium, hardness, fecal and total coliform. The parameters are explained in the next section.[7]

Temperature

Temperature means the degree of hotness. Water temperate changes seasonally. The main source of heating the water of an ecosystem is through the discharge of hot or warm effluent from industries and from burning of dead bodies on riverbanks and washing down of the hot ash, burn wood and coal form the pyre. The sources heat the water in localized segments of lake or river where the heated effluent joints it.[8] (R.S. Ambasht).

PH (Hydrogen Ion)

PH means hydrogen ion. It denotes the symbol of pH. Hydrogen means an inflammable light gaseous element obtained from water (ion—a minute part of an atom charged with electricity). pH is among the most important and commonly studies property of natural water. pH regulates most of the biological process and bio-chemical reactions. The speed and direction of forward or backward reactions is also required by pH. pH in waters, sewage or effluent can be measured calorimetrically using standard indicator or pH papers or electrometrically using sensitive electrodes[9] (*Ibid.*).

Alkalinity

Alkalinity in water due to the presence of the compounds of calcium, magnesium, potassium or sodium. Alkalinity is the measure of the hydroxide, carbonate or bicarbonate content of the above compounds, it is expressed in PPM should exceed 120 ppm.

Chlorides

Sodium Chloride is the chief substance in chloride water. The presence of chlorides is an indication of contamination by sewage. Sodium chloride may be regarded as a normal constituent to long as it does not exceed the permissible value of 2.50 ppm. Its amount beyond this limit is injurious. The chlorides can be determined by titrating water with silver nitrate and potassium dichromate. If chlorides are present, reddish colours will be formed[10] (Padmini).

Sulphates

Sulphate is of widespread occurrence and is present in most waters ranging from trace to thousand of mg/1. Industries and sewage and domestic waters also contribute significant quantity of sulphates to lakes and rivers.

Hardness

The hardness is expressed in terms of degree of hardness. Naturally occurring waters are usually classified into hard and soft water. Hard water does not form lather with soap as the dissolved calcium and magnesium carbonates and bicarbonates present in hard water, precipate the soap hardness is usually not regarded as pollution because it does not harm the health in a major way. But hardness causes a number of economic hardships, hardness is of two types temporary hardness and permanent hardness.

Dissolved Oxygen

A measure of the amount of oxygen available for biochemical activity in a given amount of water. When wastes discharged into water increases dissolved oxygen decrease. In water, however, free oxygen is available from a small stock held in dissolved form. This quantity is far too title as compared to oxygen content in the air being 8 - 10 ppm or mg/1. The saturation level of dissolved oxygen or DO is 14-15 ppm at OOC in fresh clean water.

Bio-Chemical Oxygen Demand (B.O.D)

The dissolved oxygen required decomposing organic matter in water. It is a measure of pollution because the demand for oxygen increases when there is an increase in effluent discharged into water. To study the sewage pollution load is through the analysis of biochemical oxygen demand that the bacterial and other decomposer organisms make is a polluted aquatic system. More BODS means more micro-organisms, which are, turn means the present of more organic waters or sewage pollution.

Chemical Oxygen Demand (C.O.D.)

Chemical oxygen demand or COD is the measure of oxygen equivalent to the requirement to oxidizing organic matter content by a strong chemical-oxidizing agent. A number of such agents can be used by dichromate is superior oxidant for most kinds of organic wastes found in waters.

Mineral Constituents

Five indicators, namely, Alkalinity, Sulphate, Chloride, Hardness and Sodium are testing mineral constituents.

CONCLUSION

In Tamil Nadu Pallipalaya and Musiri the level of DO is 6.0 and 7.1 mg/l. The saturat n level of DO is 14-15 ppm at OOC in fresh clean water, here it is not like that so in these areas water is slighted polluted due to industries.

The environmental pollution and environmental awareness is passing through a very existing phase in the short history of its development.

Man's activities affect his environment in many ways what we destroy we can not replace, millions of years for nature to stickup our present supply of minerals and fossils fuels but it will take us only a few centuries to run through them. As pillagers and predators, we surpass all other species just as we do as thinkers and creators. Creative ability are poor compared to our capacity for curtailing destruction.

Gothe has rightly said, "we must earn again for ourselves what we have inherited. It becomes therefore a duty for all to maintain the nature's ecological balance and preserve environmental heritage of a kind while we seek progress of man and society in partnership with nature". The cause of pollution includes chemical industries, textile, pulp and paper distilleries, and power plants. At Pallipalayam, the bio-chemical oxygen demand level varies between 2.6 and 2.9 mg/l in 1988. At Musiri in Tamil Nadu the bio-chemical oxygen demand has come down from 3.5 mg/1 in 1986 to 1 mg/1 in 1988. The required level of bio-chemical oxygen demand in 3 mg/l or more. The water purity level has to be increased by implementing pollution control measures. At Pallipalayam dissolve oxygen level is 6.3 mg/l in 1986 and it has come down to 6 mg/l in 1988.[11]

At Musiri the level has increased from 6.8 mg/l in 1986 to 7.1 mg/l in 1988. The required level of dissolved oxygen is 4 mg/l or more. As per the criteria the quality of water is good at Pallipalayam and Musiri in Tamil Nadu (Gothe, 1972).

Development activities affect environment in many ways. What we destroy, we cannot replace, nor can nature not at this speed. It has taken millions of years for nature to stickup our present supply of water resource but it will take us only a few centuries to run through them. Environmental is not static, it is dynamic and changes occur even if there is no human. Comervalas of water resource is the need of the day.

The pollutant and emission into the country have to be checked in view with the demanding alternative uses of it. Conflick in shorting Cauvery water for development can be settled by checking emission and keeping them under control.

The river faces serious pollution problems as a result of both domestic and industrial effluent discharge (untreated, partly treated or fully treated, as well as non-point pollution from agriculture fertilizers and pesticides). Being also the source for irrigation and domestic water supply (as well as industrial supply), the river and its main tributaries present a serious threat to public health conditions, especially in the day season, if no action is taken to reduce pollution[12] (*Ibid.*).

To effectively control the water pollution to some extent effort should be to avoid industrial pollution's large scale factories should not be permitted near the river.

Each industrial organization must appoint environmental manager to advise and steps should be taken to solve environmental problems of the locality both by government and non-government agencies.

Notes and Reference

1. Dr. V.N. Rayudu, Tamil Nadu Pollution Control Board, Lecture Notes on Aquatic Pollution derived at Bharathiyar University, Coimbatore 1992.
2. Marimuthu and Balasubramanian, Environmental Engineering and Pollution Control, p. 94.
3. Marimuthu and Balasubramanian, Environmental Engineering and Pollution Control, p. 73.
4. *Ibid.*, pp. 13 and 15.
5. P.C. Mishra, Fundamentals of Air and Water Pollution, p. 15.
6. Danida, pp. 13 and 15.
7. *Ibid.*, pp. 13 and 15.
8. R.S. Ambasht, Environment and Pollution, p. 40.
9. *Ibid.*, Chlorides, p. 50.
10. P. Padminis, Environmental Engineering Pollution, p. 83.
11. Goethe, cited in Era J. Winn, ed., Basic Issues in Environment (Ohio, 1972), p. 241.
12. *Ibid.*, p. 1.

30

CHAPTER

Tannery Pollution: Its Impact on Tamil Nadu Economy

P.S. SUBRAMANIAN

The environmental degradation caused by the billions of liters of highly toxic effluents including manganese, zinc, sulphur, nitrates, phosphates, large quantities of chlorides, chromium and other 175 chemicals discharged by hundreds of tanneries and the damage suffered to the Tamil Nadu economy in terms of pollution of water, agricultural lands, human and animals lives.

The magnitude of the shocking damage caused by tannery effluents in Ambur in Vellore District, a very leading leather export zone in India was exhibited by the gathering of more than 20000 people in June 1984 and taking out a big procession demanding supply of potable water since all the water sources including Palar river water were polluted by tannery effluents. There were petitions galore reaching Tamil Nadu Government followed by personal representations including that of a voluntary organization called Community Action for Development (CAD) under the chairmanship of Mr. Narayanamurthy (Nani) of Alangkuppam. The Tamil Nadu government requested the Tamil Nadu Legal Aid and Advice Board to assess the damage caused by tannery effluents and the methods to be adopted for preventing them. The Board entrusted the matter to the North Arcot District Legal Aid and Advice Committee (now known as Vellore District Legal Service Authority). The Committee deputed two panel lawyers, one myself and Mr. M.R. Ramanan to visit Ambur and the nearby villages and after meeting the people and experts file the report within two months from November, 1984. We visited all the affected places with the help of Mr. Nani and the Magistrate of Ambur who look very great interest of arresting damage by the effluents we filed our report on 18.02.1985 containing eight pages suggesting for the closure of the tanneries and stop the licenses issued to them. The Supreme Court while deciding our Forum's case W.P. No. 914 of 1991 in the Tamil Nadu Tannery Pollution case (as reported in All India reported 1996 Supreme Court, p. 2715) in the interlocutory order passed on April 9, 1996 expressing great anguish on the unabated discharge of the tannery effluents causing environmental and health hazards said, "The tanneries in the five districts of Tamil Nadu (Trichy, Erode, Dindigul, Kancheepuram and Vellore) referred above in this order have been operating for a period of more than two decades. All this period, these tanneries have been polluting the area. Needless to say that the total environment in the area has been polluted. We issue show cause notice to these industries through their learned counsel who are present in court why they not be subjected to heavy pollution fine. We district the state of Tamil Nadu through the Industry Ministry, the Tamil Nadu Pollution Control Board and all other authorities concerned and also the Government of India through the Ministry of Environment and Forests not to permits the setting up of further tanneries in the State of Tamil Nadu". Needless to say this mandatory order is honored more in breach and flagrantly and deliberately violated with active collusion between the polluters and the Central and State Governments.

'Economic' means "spending frugally for useful purposes", a term used relating to reasonable and purposeful use of funds by individual person, industries and the nation as a whole. 'Economists' is a person who guides the nation in the spending of funds collected from the tax paying public within reasonable limits for achieving, perfecting and excellence of the concerned projects. Here frugality does not mean 'miserly'. It implies regulated proper spending applicable for individuals and the several schemes and budget estimates and spending at State, National and International levels with coexistence of sustainable human development. It is worthwhile to note that the dictionary word 'economic' is preceded by the word 'ecology', which is a study thing in their surrounding. A mistaken impression is created by leading industrialists who always pronouncedly declare that the strong economy and the resources generated always came through them by defining 'ecology' as referring only to flora and fauna and human beings can simply watch the damage caused to agriculture, water sources. Article 21 of the Constitution of India States, "No person shall be deprived of his life or personal liberty except according to procedure established by law". Right to livelihood and Right to health are integral right to life. They are held to be fundamental rights. The Supreme Court in the Vellore Citizens' Welfare Forum case applied these rights and directed the Tamil Nadu Government and the district collectors of the five districts to provide potable water and medical facilities to the people living in the tannery belts in the interlocutory order passed on April 20, 1992. It is another thing that these people are still reeling under acute water scarcity with the available water sources heavily polluted by the tannery effluents and most of the people including the workers in the tanneries are suffering from skin and respiratory diseases and as per the report of the Tamil Nadu Government, Ministry of Health there is one doctor to attend on workers of 700 tanneries.

The Tamil Nadu Agriculture University Research Centre at Virinchepuram, Vellore in its report released through the Vellore District Collector (March 6, 1992) had stated, "The preliminary survey of tannery pollution and revealed that nearly 35,000 to 40,000 hectares of agricultural lands have become practically or tally unfit for cultivation. Particularly area under cultivation has been practically reduced by 40 per cent in the tannery belt being substituted by other cash crops like ragi, ground nut and sugarcane and reduction in cropping intensity is 43% to 56.5% . The yield in the remaining paddy area is reduced to 50% of the normal yield. Even the substituted crops the establishment is poor and yield unsatisfactory. The loss in revenue ranged from Rs. 5000 to Rs. 16061 per hectare depending upon crops. The cost of expenditure on inputs also increased due to application of soil amendments, trashmulching, application of higher doses of organic measure, fertilizer and higher seed rate. The land value in tannery belt is on the decreasing trend". This report also stated that most of the women in the tannery belt areas are suffering from the disease called "Milk diarrhoea" and the young men had become impotent. In the article entitle, "Tamil Nadu Agriculture—slipping down" by Mr. S. Viswanathan published by *The Hindu* in June, 2000 had observed that, "prior to the green revolution Punjab and Tamil Nadu with a total annual food grain production of 44 lakh tones against Tamil Nadu 56 lakh tones. Thirty two years later food grains production in Punjab shot up five fold to 219 lakh tones, registering an average growth of over 12.5 per cent. In these years, foodgrains production in Tamil Nadu grew to 84 lakh tones, working out to an average growth of less than 1.6 per cent. Its record has been the lowest among the major agriculture producers in the country. He had further observed that, "even the modest growth of agriculture in Tamil Nadu has been sustained through massive subsidies. Free power supply to agriculture is costing the exchequer around Rs. 1600 crores a year. Add this to the poor recoveries on irrigation facilities, extended incentives given for procurement and other benefits estimated to cost nearly 20 per cent of the total size of the budget".

The Department of Environmental Sciences, Tamil Nadu Agricultural University, Coimbatore, in its Final report on Assessment of loss of Ecology in Palar river basin released on September 30, 1999 had stated, "the reduction due to tannery pollution was maximum in the case of paddy (75%), followed by coconut (52%) and sugarcane (48%)". The loss of Ecology (Prevention and Payments of Compensation) Authority constituted by the Central Government under section (3) of the Environment Protection Act, 1986 on the direction of Supreme Country in our Forum's case had determined the rate of compensation payable to affected agriculturists to tannery effluents in Vellore district as per the Total Dissolved Solides (TDS) in well water used for irrigation upto 4900 mg/l at Rs. 14000 per hectare per year calculating for the limited period from August 12, 19991 (the date of filing of the Writ Petition of our Forum) to December 31, 1998. It is not known as why the compensation for the earlier period was not assessed and why after December 31, 1998 the affected parties are not entitled to claim the amount. Further even as per the admission of the Tamil Nadu Pollution Control Board the TDS in most of the Well Water had exceeded 13000 mg/l. Dr. G. Thiagarajan, the former Managing Director of the Central Leather Research Institute had observed that while the international standard for concentration of chromium was only 2 ppm (particles per million) the concentration of chromium had exceeded 5000 ppm in the tanning yards. The Authority had identified 29193 individual/families affected in Vellore district by tannery effluents were entitled to get Rs. 26,82,02,328 for the stated period and the corresponding extent of affected agricultural lands was 15,14,96.76 hectares. It is significant the Authority did not refer to the damaged lands due to tannery effluents to the extent of 35,000 to 40,000 hectares pointed out by the Tamil Nadu Agricultural University Research Centre, Vellore in its report. The Authority had fixed the reversal of the damage due to tannery effluents during the above period in Vellore district for embarking on various schemes to restore the ecology at Rs. 122 crores fixing the liability on the polluters to pay only Rs. 3.66 crores being three percent on the total expenditure. For Dindigual the damage of agricultural lands was estimated at 2004.14.0 hectares with the sum payable by the tanners at Rs. 3,93,38,613 to be distributed to 6863 agriculturists. For Vellore district 546 tanners were named with amounts payable by them. For Dindigual 107 tanners were asked to pay the amount. For Dindigual the period fixed was from 12.08.1991 to 31.12.2000. The amount fixed for reversal of ecology was only Rs. 24,56,957. For Kancheepuram, it is shocking no individual compensation was awarded even though there are more than 200 tanneries funding here. For reversals of ecology, the total sum of the merge sum of Rs. 7.5 lakhs was ordered to be recovered from the tanners. In respect of Tiruvalluvar district eighteen tanneries situated in Madhavaram the shockingly low sum of Rs. 75,000 only and this was only for reversal of ecology and no individual compensation was ordered to be paid to the affected agriculturists. The Authority is yet to submit its report and award for Trichy and Erode district even though. The time extended for it had expired on September 30, 2001.

The Tamil Nadu Pollution Control Board has fixed the TDS standard for 2100 mg/l. But the Tamil Nadu Government through its Environment Department Secretary had announced that TDS in well water and other sources could exceed even 7500 mg/l and the tanneries will have this concession till March 2002. If the Government itself should violate the norms fixed for pollution standards where can the people go for the redressal of their grievances? The Supreme Court had observed, "the standards stipulated by the TNPCB is justified" and the tanneries and other industries should note exceed these limits in Tamil Nadu. According to our Forum even the standard fixed for TDS, COD and BOD by the TNPCB are highly inadequate and not in conformity to the international standards. It may not be out of context to mention here that the Union Minister for Environment during the year 1992 Mr. Kamal Nath admitted in the Rajya Sabha that Palar river was critically polluted river and Vellore District topped the list among the nineteen highly polluted places in India due to tanneries. Dr. G. Thiagarajan of CLRI had admitted that there was no violable methods found any where in the world for safe disposal of the chrome sludge.

The leather tannery is one of the major industries in India and Tamil Nadu stands first accounting for more than 75% of country's export of finished leather and its products. There are more than 3000 tanneries big, medium and small sized in Tamil Nadu alone apart from those functioning in Uttar Pradesh, West Bengal, Andhra Pradesh, Maharashtra states in India. The economy of Tamil Nadu depends mostly on the increased earnings from the leather sector in which Chennai city limits, Vellore, Trichy, Erode, Dindigual, Kancheepuram and Tiruvalluvar districts are deeply and vitally involved with growth of tanneries like mushrooms. But of these places Vellore district with the contributon of 60 per cent of Indian export of leather has the location of several hundreds of tanneries in Ambur, Vaniyambadi, Vellore, Wallaja, Arcot, Kaveripakkam, Pernambut, and Ranipet. The Tamil Nadu G.O. No. 213 of 1989 dated March 30, 1989 makes mention of fourteen hazardous industries including tanneries which are prohibited from being located within the one kilometre from rivers, reservoirs and other water sources. This distance by later amendement was increased to five kilometers. But there are more than five hundred tanneries situated within one kilometer from Palar. According to TNPCB, nearly one thousand five hundred dyeing industries are located from the rivers and reservoirs in Erode, Tirupur and other places. Increasing human population lead to more production and distribution of food with sustainable development being encouraged in agricultural activities and preventing damage of agricultural lands and the source for their increased fertility through agencies like pollution water supply, harmless and hazardous free manure's and pesticides, India, striving hard to emerge as the leading player in global market for leather products has according to the Union Commerce Ministry touched Rs. 7500 crores during April 2000 to December 2000 and by the end of December 2001 shall be touching Rs. 9000 crores. Tamil Nadu's contribution in this final figure is Rs. 6750 crores and Vellore district shall be making it share of Rs. 5400 crores.

In the Final Report on Assessment of Loss Ecology in Palar River Basin by the Department of Environment Science pointed out that, "in Tamil Nadu, particularly in Vellore, the damage done to soil, agriculture, water resources and ecosystems is extensive and irreversible. Tannery pollution can considered as agriculture pollution rather than industrial since goat, cow and bullock skins (agriculture products) are used for the tanning process and the impact of tanning activity is much felt on water bodies and agricultural lands. Several workers have reported higher concentration of chromium in ground water. According to the Food and Agricultural Organisation 230 million metres of hides and skins annually with 24,300,000 head of cattle and 46,700,700 goats. Article 48 of the Constitution of India states, "the state shall endeavour to organize agriculture and animal husbandry on modern and scientific lines and shall, in particular take steps for preserving and improving breeds, and prohibiting the slaughter of cows and calves and other milch and drought cattle".

Under the title, "Economic Valuation of Tannery Pollution Damage to Agriculture", the Tamil Nadu Agricultural University report states that, "in view of the difficulties in measuring the losses in land value, bio-diversity, and human and animal health due to tannery pollution specifically for the purpose of payment of compensation, the present study was limited to the measurement of crop production loss alone. The study was taken up in Palar basin of Vellore district where the tannery effluents pollute the surface and ground water resources thus affecting agricultural production, human and animal health, biodiversity, etc. The total basin area of Palar basin is about 18.30 lakh hectares out of which 10.91 hectares is in Tamil Nadu State. The agricultural land in Palar basin of Tamil Nadu estimated to be 8.75 lakh hectares. Moreover, Vellore district is one of the 17 locations in India identified by the Union Ministry of Forests as CRITICALLY POLLTED. Dr. M.S. Swaminathan, the renowned agricultural scientist and recipient of many national and international awards for his contribution to the advancement of agricultural production and green revolution father has pointed out that method to be found out for preventing damage to agricultural land from tannery effluents.

I am of view the agriculturists, whose lands had become fallow due to the effect of tannery effluents should be given equal extent of fertile lands and the cost of this should be recovered from the tanneries. The Authority and the District Collectors of the five districts should arrange for not only the compensation to the affected parties recovered from polluting units but also order the closure if the amounts are not paid within a month from this date. The compensation for loss of health and ecology should also be recovered from them without any further delay. Action on war footing is the need of the hour to protect not only the interests of affected parties but for assuring a sound Tamil Nadu Economy.

Index

Actual Enrolment in Schools, 93
A Decade of Reforms, 3
Agricultural Commodities, 23
  Price Transmission between Global and Indian Prices, 23
Agriculture Development, 106
  Capital Investment, 106
Alarming Revenue Deficit, 261
All India, 129
  Poverty Estimates, 129
Amarawati, 115
Anderson, J.E., 24
Annadurai, R., 375
Arunachalan, R., 119
Atomic Energy Power Station, 115

Bacteriological Pollution, 379
Balaji, R., 259
Banking and Insurance, 17
  Future, 17
  Sectors, 17
    Convergence, 17
Barathan, A., 355
Bhawani, 115
Bloating Fiscal Deficit, 4
Brahmananda, P.R., 3
Bus Transport Services, 224
  Pricing, 224

Capital Investment in the States, 100
Cethugar, 115
Chand, Ramesh, 24, 41
Chelliah, Rajah, 63-64, 77
Chinnar, 115
Condition of Service of Officers, 21
Constitute a National Socio-econmic Advisory Council, 56
Corruption, 115

Dandekar, V.M., 4
De, Biman Chandra, 79
Decadal Trends of Irrigation, 174
Declining Long-term Fixed Investment, 7
Demographic Changes, 75
  Poverty Levels, 75
  Unemployment, 75
Development Finance Corporations, 142
Development Prospects of Fisheries Sector, 197
Directions of Reform, 144
District Development Indicators, 130, 132
Domestic Investment, 101
Dreze, J., 334
Dynamics of IT Industry, 243

Economic Development, 169
  Role of Irrigation, 169
Economic Growth and Decline of Poverty in the Post-Reform Period, 355
Economic Reforms and Social Sector Development, 333
Effect of Education in the Adoption of Agricultural Technologies, 188
Electricity-Production Capacity, 113
Employment of Women in Industrial Classification, 308
E.N. Murthy Committee, 365
Environmental Assessment of Industrial Effluent in River Cauvery, 375

Enrolment of Children and Dropout, 92
Expenditure Management, 271
Issues, 271
Extent of Contribution of Education to the Adoption of Technologies, 191

Factory Employment, 114
Fare Revisions, 230
Fare Structure and Tariff Concessions, 141
Farmer's Management of Irrigation, 181
Fish and Fish Products, 204
Export, 204
Fisheries Co-operative Societies, 206
Fisheries in Tamil Nadu, 199
Fishermen Population, 200
Fishermen Welfare Programmes, 207
Fishing Industries, 198
Importance, 198
Fish Production, 202
Trends, 202
Food Grains, 187
Production, 187
Foreign Investment, 101

Gandhi, P. Jegadish, 54, 224
Ganesan, P., 23, 215, 235
Ganesh, S., 243
General Agreement on Trade and Tariff, 23
General Insurance Corporation, 20
Govindass, 188
Govindaraj, T., 184
Growth and Poverty, 358
Growth of Social Sector Expenditure, 335
Growth of Software Industries, 245
Growth Rate and Inflation Rate, 127
Growth through Government Capital Expenditure, 296
Guaranteed Employment, 105
Financial Allocation, 105

Haq, Mahbubul, 318
Health Facilities, 350

India, 83, 367
Export of Leather and Leather Products, 367
Trends in Gross Domestic Product, 83
India Vision 2020, 54
Indiresan, P.V., 57
Industrial Development, 105
Capital Investment, 105
Insurance Advertisements Disclosurers, 19
Insurance Agents, 19
Licensing, 19
Insurance Regulatory Authority Act, 1999, 18
Insurers, 20
Assets, Liabilities and Solvency Margin, 20
Irrigation and Hydro-Electric Projects, 115
Irrigation and the Cropping Pattern, 172
Irrigation Pattern and Sources of Water Supply, 177

Jaganathan, Rekha, 346
Janagam, D., 375

Kalam, A.P.J. Abdul, 54
Kaveri, 115
Kenneth, Pomeranz, 24
Kumar, K. Nandha, 119

Lakshmi, S., 318
Leather Exports, 369
World Trends, 369
Levels of Education and Adoption, 190

Macro Forecast Model, 286
Manohar, B. Murali, 243
Marine and Inland Fish Production, 203
Marketing, 18
Innovative Products and Ethics, 18
Masani, Minoo, 63
Mega Missions, 56
Mega Projects, 221
Meyar, 115
Modes of Irrigation, 171

Morisset, Jacques, 24
Muthuraja, A., 305
Naganathan, M., 333
Naidu, Narayanasamy, 68
Naidu, V.N., 375
Naresh, Gautam, 134, 277
National Commission on Education, 188
Nayyar, Deepak, 24
NDP, 122
  Decadal Compound Growth Rate, 122
Noil, 115
Norgaard, R.B., 334

Obligations of Insurers to Rural and Social Sectors, 19
Organised Sector Employment, 360
  Growth Trend, 360

Paddy Technologies, 192
  Levels of Education and Adoption, 192
  Palanidurai, K.V., 72
Palar, 115
Parikh, Kirit S., 333
Parthasarathy, R., 17
Pazhani, K., 197
Period of Economic and Liberalisation, 101
  Industrial Investment, 101
Physical Pollution, 377
  Suspended Organic Substances, 377
  Dissolved Organic Substances, 378
Pollution due to Inorganic Chemicals, 378
Pollution of River Cauvery, 380
  Temperature, 38
  pH (Hydrogen Ion), 383
  Alkalinity, 384
  Chlorides, 384
  Sulphates, 384
  Hardness, 384
  Dissolved Oxygen, 385
  Bio-chemical Oxygen Demand, 385
  Chemical Oxygen Demand, 385
  Mineral Constituents, 385
Ponnar, 115
Poverty, 107
Poverty Trend, 128
Power Reform Process, 12
  Elements, 12
Power Sector Reform Bill, 220
Power Sector, 215
  Reforms, 215
  Regulation of Tariffs, 11
Price Discrimination, 14
Pricing Mechanism, 225
Pricing Policy, 224
Public Expenditure and Social Sector Development, 346
Pursuing Proper Pricing Policies, 9
Pyramiding Financial Transactions, 6

Rajendran, R., 184
Rajalakshmi, N., 375
Rajkrishna, 6
Rangarajan, C., 11
Ravi, P.N., 235
Reform Strategy, 293
Regulatory Commissions, 13
  Role, 13
Rengamani, K.T., 215
Revenue Augmentation, 267
  Issues, 267
Rice Market, 33
  India's Share of World Trade, 33
Rice, 33
  Spread Index, 33
  Production and Export, 32
Road Transport, 139
  Financial Performance, 139
  State Subsidies in lieu of Tariff Concessions, 139
Rudrappan, D., 167

Sacratees, J., 375
Sarma, J.V.M., 134, 277
SCBs, 236-39
  Advances Per Branch, 239
  Credit Deposits, 240
  Credit Deployment, 238
  Deposits Per Branch, 239
  Deposit Mobilisation, 237
  Branch Expansion, 236
Scheduled Commercial Banks, 235
  Asymmetrical Performance, 235

Schultz, T.W., 188
SEBs, 216
  Current Scenario, 216
Sectoral Composition of the Plan Outlay, 339
Sectoral Dynamics, 120
Sector-wise Distribution of NDP, 121
Sen, Abhijit, 24
Sezhiyan, Era, 70
Singh, Manmohan, 69
Sivagnanam, K. Jothi, 333
Social Sector Capital Expenditure, 348
Social Sector Revenue Expenditure, 348
Software Export:
  Performance, 254
  Growth, 245
Software Technology Parks, 247
Spread between:
  Wholesale Price and World Price, 34
  Domestic Consumer and Wholesale Prices, 34
  Domestic Consumer Price and World Price, 31
State Domestic Product, 74
  Growth, 74
State Electricity Regulatory Commissions, 218
State Finances, 76
Storm, Servass, 24
STPI Scheme, 247
  Benefits, 247
Subrahmanian, P.S., 388
Swaminathan, A.M., 70, 395

Tamr, 115
Tamil Nadu Economy, 72
Tamil Nadu IT Policy, 247
Tamil Nadu, 63, 79, 89, 94, 123, 129, 134, 140, 175, 180, 217, 260, 265, 305-06, 310, 318, 320, 365
  Finances, 279
    Power, 281
    Irrigation, 281
    Roads and Bridges, 282
    Education, 283
    Health and Family Welfare, 282
    Transport, 283
    Public Sector Enterprises, 283
  Women Empowerment, 318
  Literacy Rate, 320
  Population and Sex Ratio, 320
  Enrolment of Children in Primary Schools, 321
  Dropout in Primary Schools, 321
  Work Participation Rate, 322
  Role of Leather Industry in the Economy, 365
  Unemployment, 310
  Decadal Compound Growth Rate, 123
  Poverty, 129
  Performance of Public Sector Undertakings, 134
  Performance of Transport Undertakings, 140
  Irrigation Potentials, 175
    Cropping Pattern, 180
  Power Sector, 217
  State Transport, 227
  Profile of Revenue Sources, 265
  Gender and Employment, 305
  Labour Force, 306
  Male-Female Participation Rate, 306
  Mounting Fiscal Deficit, 260
  Economy, 89
  Growth, 79
  Political Economy, 63
Tamil Nadu State Finances, 259
Tannery Pollution, 388
Tariff Fixation, 14
Tariffs and Competition, 15
Tax, 5
  Declining Ratio, 5
Telugu Desam, 69
Thakur, Ram Naresh, 89
Trends in:
  Gross State Domestic Product, 80
  Employment, 360

Unemployment, 107
Utilisation of Irrigation for Sustainble Agricultural Development, 167

Vajpayee, Atal Bihari, 49
Vellar, 115
Venkataraman Committee, 138
Venkatasubramanian, K., 49
Viswanathan, G., 63
Volume of Employment
  Opportunities, 110
  Infrastructure, 110
  Cereal Grains, 114
  Commercial Crops, 114

Waipar, 115
Warr, P.G., 24
Warshali, 115
Water Pollution and Health
  Hazardous, 379
Water Pollution, 377
  Types, 377
Water Quality, 377-78
  Chemical Characteristics, 378
  Standard, 377
Water Related Diseases, 380
Wegai, 115
Well-being of the People, 3
What is Development?, 54
Women Workers, 308, 311
  Participation and Employment Pattern, 311
  Agriculture, Non-agriculture and Industry, 312
  and Unemployment, 314
Working Force, 307
  Cultivators and Agricultural Labourers, 307
World Leather Production *vis-a-vis* India's Production, 366

Yap, Chan Ling, 24
Yousuf, P. Mohammed, 365